CU00750924

# RELIGIONS OF IRAN

*from prehistory to the present*

# RELIGIONS OF IRAN

*from prehistory to the present*

Richard Foltz

ONEWORLD

A Oneworld book

Published by Oneworld Publications 2013

Copyright © Richard Foltz 2013

The right of Richard Foltz to be identified as the
Author of this work has been asserted by him
in accordance with the Copyright,
Designs and Patents Act 1988

All rights reserved
Copyright under Berne Convention
A CIP record for this title is available
from the British Library

Parts of Chapters 15 and 19 previously appeared in
an article entitled "Zoroastrians in Iran: What Future in
the Homeland?", *Middle East Journal* 65/1 (2011): 73-84.

978-1-78074-307-3 (hardback)
978-1-78074-308-0 (paperback)
978-1-78074-309-7 (ebook)

Typeset by Cenveo Publishing Services, India
Printed and bound in the US by Lake Book Manufacturing Inc.

Oneworld Publications
10 Bloomsbury Street
London WC1B 3SR
England

Stay up to date with the latest books,
special offers, and exclusive content from
Oneworld with our monthly newsletter

Sign up on our website
**www.oneworld-publications.com**

*For Manya*

# Contents

# Preface

This book emerged from a desire to build and expand upon my earlier work, *Spirituality in the Land of the Noble: How Iran Shaped the World's Religions*, which appeared in 2004. The primary aim of that book was to spark the interest of the general reader in Iran's contributions to world history; it was therefore deliberately concise in its use of the available data, while aiming for a certain accessibility of style. The present volume, twice the length of that earlier work, seeks to probe more deeply and widely, devoting ten new chapters to various aspects of Iranian religious history while revising and expanding the original nine.

In the years since the publication of *Spirituality*, my interest in exploring Iran's place in the history of religions has not waned. During this time much new research has appeared, fresh questions have been raised, longstanding notions revised. Nevertheless, the importance of Iran remains for the most part sadly underestimated in the history of religions. What I offer here is an attempt to provide an enriched introductory resource for those interested in trying to rectify this imbalance.

Another issue I hope to redress is the oft-seen tendency, shared by those who study Iran and Iranians themselves, to divide Iran's history into two distinct periods, with the Arab invasions of the mid-seventh century serving as the watershed. I believe this division is a somewhat artificial one, obscuring a considerable degree of cultural continuity. The Islamization of Iran surely represents an important transformation, but it was hardly sudden (it took at least three centuries), and over the long term it invigorated Iranian culture more than it damaged it. Iranian history, moreover, is full of transformations, some of which were arguably just as momentous. Many were instigated by similar traumas inflicted by foreign armies— Macedonian, Turkish, Mongol—yet over time became just as productive.[1]

This book is presented first and foremost as a gesture of love and appreciation to the Iranian people and the rich culture they have engendered over the past three thousand years. My own immersion in this culture dates back only a little over a quarter century and was both unplanned and unforeseen. The experience has taught me, among other things, a very Iranian respect for the vagaries of life and the ultimate ineluctability of Fate.

I have learned much during the past twenty-six years from my Iranian teachers, friends, acquaintances, colleagues and students. But for getting a cultural education, it must be said that nothing compares with living in an Iranian family. There is a Persian saying in which a young man is asked where he is from. "I don't know," he replies; "I haven't taken a wife yet." If Iran has come to feel like a second home to me—and even my home in Canada is a distinctly Iranian one, as every visitor instantly perceives—the credit surely goes in large part to Manya, my wife and muse, and to her extended family in Montréal and Tehran, who have made me feel so much one of their own.

In my studies of Iran as in life in general, Manya is my primary and most valued conversation partner. I owe a huge debt to her insights, particularly the idea that much of Iranian religiosity throughout history can be seen as circumventions and subversions of authority. She was also the first to sensitize me to the popularity of "new-age" spirituality in Iran today, alerting me to some of its more fascinating manifestations and explaining their relationship to previous movements throughout Iranian history. I am especially thankful to Manya for contributing a chapter on Iranian Goddesses, which is based on her own doctoral research. The remaining chapters, moreover, contain many ideas and analyses (not all of them credited) that were also provided by her. It is no exaggeration to say that without Manya's constant inspiration and input, this book would simply never have come to exist.

In addition, I have had the benefit of much valuable input from a number of friends, colleagues and students who took the time to read various drafts of the typescript, either whole or in part. They include: Pooriya Alimoradi, Jason BeDuhn, Jorunn Buckley, Houchang Chehabi, Lynda Clarke, Touraj Daryaee, Almut Hintze, Jean Kellens, Philip Kreyenbroek, Sam Lieu, Jim Mallory, Moojan Momen, Reza Pourjavady, Ira Robinson, Nicholas Sims-Williams, and Michael Stausberg. Their suggestions have been immensely helpful to me, but these kind and erudite individuals should not in any way be held to account for the final text, which is my responsibility alone. On the publishing side, Novin Doostdar and the staff at Oneworld have once again shown themselves to be easy and pleasant to work with, to a degree that is well beyond the industry norm.

Finally, I am grateful to my parents, Ruth and Rodger Foltz, and to my children (by birth and by marriage), Shahrzad, Persia and Bijan, for giving me a sense of my place in the world. I hope that my efforts can serve as a tribute to them all.

*R.F.*
28 January 2013
9 Bahman 1391

## TAXONOMY AND HISTORICAL APPROACH

The human mind inevitably circumscribes reality in order to conceptualize it. To process an idea we have to fit it into a framework, although in doing so we necessarily forfeit the big picture. When talking about a historical phenomenon such as religion, there exists a strong temptation to reify reality into a mentally manageable notion of a "core tradition" that remains in place over time and space. In the case of Iranian religion, scholars since Martin Haug in the nineteenth century and Mary Boyce in the twentieth have started from the premise that the available material should be understood in relation to a putative "orthodox" Zoroastrian tradition—whether measured in accordance with a preferred sacred text or with the claims of contemporary practitioners—an approach which led them to relegate any divergence from this contrived standard to the status of "heterodoxy," or worse, heresy.

And yet, the more one explores and contemplates the various information history provides, the harder it becomes to force the data into a coherent and internally consistent whole. One is at times tempted to abandon such a project altogether and simply posit a given religious tradition as a collective of expressions, withholding judgment as to which form is most "authentic." This approach has become popular in the field of religious studies, displacing to some extent the earlier tendency of starting from a body of canonical texts and marking everything else as a deviation (and thereby discounting the validity of most of the available data).

While it is unrealistic for any scholar to claim complete objectivity, I believe that it is both possible and desirable for us to remain mindful of our own cultural lenses and their incumbent biases, and to an extent correct for them in our analysis of the material being studied. One of the most common of these biases is the tendency to project contemporary understandings back into the past, leading to forced interpretations which result in anachronistic readings of history. A more circumspect approach would involve constantly reminding ourselves that the issues and values of the present age—democracy, nationalism, human rights, gender equality, etc.—are not necessarily those of people who lived in other places and times. A society can be best understood in terms of its own basic principles and assumptions, and little is achieved by measuring it against ours.

### Defining Religious Tradition

The same is true for how ideas are defined, including religion. The word "religion" is itself culturally constructed, with a culture-specific etymology and historical development, and translates awkwardly into non-Western contexts. It derives from the Latin verb *religare*, "to bind," perhaps in the double sense of that which "binds [a group together]" and that which one is "bound" to do. Scholarly understandings of "religion" today range from the relatively restrictive definition of Jonathan Z. Smith and William Scott Green, according to which it is seen as "as system of beliefs and practices that are relative to superhuman beings," to the more expansive one of David Chidester, who considers as religious any "ways of being human [that] engage the transcendent— that which rises above and beyond the ordinary."[2]

Both definitions leave considerable scope for variation and pluralism. Yet when referring to a specific religious tradition, there is always the urge to identify a particular strand as normative, which can be used to define the religion in question. This urge ought to be resisted, but then, how is one to conceptualize the religion so that it can be talked about? One solution would be to think not in terms of normative expressions, but rather threads of continuity (over time) and commonality (over space). To take one example, the sacrificial religion of the ancient Israelites described in the book of Leviticus may bear little outward resemblance to the Judaism of the Talmud, but they are connected by a continuous cultural stream. The question remains, however, of what exactly to name this continuous stream, since simply to call the whole thing "Judaism" would be highly misleading. Even today, Judaism, like all living religions, plays out in a wide range of forms, possessing a fluid range of commonalities and differences.

This is even more the case with the national pre-Islamic religion(s) of the Iranians. In my opinion, to refer to its best-known strand as "Zoroastrianism" (even if its current practitioners mostly don't seem to mind) is as inappropriate as referring to Islam as "Muhammadanism," and reinforces a parallel early modern European mindset. Moreover, notwithstanding the undeniable antiquity of the Avestan liturgy, the evidence for a specifically "Zoroastrian" religion prior to the Sasanian period is not very widespread, and it clearly existed alongside a number of parallel traditions, some of which it rejected and some of which it consciously tried to incorporate as the Younger Avesta shows.[3]

Thus, it is one thing to acknowledge the continuity of the Avestan oral tradition over a very long period of time within a particular priestly community, but quite another to imply, as many scholars continue to do, that it somehow served as a basis for the religious life of an entire society. More likely, as Bausani noted half a century ago, "we are not dealing—as some believed when these studies started in Europe—with one Iranian religion, but with various 'religions' or types of religiosity characteristic of one or another branch of the Iranian family."[4]

### The "Pool Theory": Possibilities, not Essence

My own approach to the notion of "religion," which sees the term as being, for practical purposes, nearly synonymous with "culture" and not a separate category, places less of an emphasis on providing a description as such, than on identifying a pool of ideas and behaviours from which communities and individuals may draw in constituting their particular worldviews. I shall call this approach the Pool Theory: it posits that religion/culture is best understood not in terms of essential features, but as a set of possibilities within a recognizable framework, or "pool."[5] Some of these possibilities will be seen as so widely occurring as to be nearly universal, others as exceedingly rare. The Pool Theory resists, however, the assumption that near universality is proof of essentiality, since such an assumption will falsely exclude some elements from the data set.

This book devotes separate chapters to what appear to be the three most visible religious tendencies in pre-Islamic Iran: the worship of Mithra, of Mazda, and of the Goddess (who is most recognizable as Anahita). In accordance with the Pool Theory, they are not mutually exclusive. Zoroastrianism, in my view, is most properly viewed as a relatively late-developing sub-expression of the second of these three broad tendencies, which we can call Mazdaism—a more precise term, which also happens to reflect the actual self-identification of its pre-modern adherents. As to the contemporary forms of Zoroastrianism, once again, alongside the many obvious commonalities one also finds considerable differences, not just between its Indian and Iranian practitioners but also in terms of such basic questions as who can claim membership in the community and whether ancient rituals can be altered to better suit the present age.

## What is "Monotheism"?

The very nature of monotheism tends toward another kind of back-projection. Monotheisms are notoriously exclusivist and intolerant. Yahweh is said to be a jealous god, but apparently so are Jesus, Allah, and—perhaps by contagion, since he is neither Semitic nor Near Eastern—Ahura Mazda. Since the followers of these singular deities now collectively represent most of the world's population, it is easy to take religious exclusiveness and intolerance to be universal historical norms. There is danger, however, in allowing ourselves to assume that monotheism represents "a more advanced stage in the development" of religion, not least because a progressive notion of history is itself a cultural construct not universally shared among human societies, many of whom even today see history as cyclical or even degenerative.

If we attempt to suspend our own culturally-generated preconceptions about religion, a number of current interpretations begin to seem less certain. The oft-held notion of a global trend toward monotheism emerging during an "axial age"[6] of "monotheistic" figures called "prophets" is riddled with problems, and only really makes sense if one has decided in advance that the facts should fit into this particular historical paradigm. Even then, Zoroaster can be cast as a prophet and a monotheist only by applying extraordinarily broad definitions of those terms. Similarly, the "monotheism" of Moses ("Thou shalt have no other gods before me") is relative, not absolute as one finds in later "monotheisms."

In fact, a comprehensive view of human history would suggest that the default religious norm is in fact polytheistic and non-exclusive. Throughout the world, prior to and alongside the various monotheisms—which, by the way, historically speaking were mostly imposed by force—we find a much less restricted religiosity, where on a local level people may have their own particular favorite deity but not exclude the existence or at times even the worship of others. (The nineteenth-century German scholar Friedrich von Schelling coined the term "henotheism" to describe this phenomenon.) One can still see this approach today in South and East Asian religions, and the ancient Iranians held to it as well. Thus, the history of Mazda-worship is intertwined with that of Mithra, Anahita, and numerous other divine figures, even into the Sasanian period, when Mazdaism became the officially-approved religion for Iranians.

## Orthodoxy and Power

Against this pluralistic backdrop, the emergence—or, as is more often the case, the imposition—of monotheism appears closely connected with the consolidation of power by a particular group. Accordingly, the ancient Mesopotamian god Marduk's rise to supremacy is tied to that of the centralizing efforts of his devotees among the Babylonian elite. Cyrus the Great, living at a time when the Iranians were a newly arrived presence in the region, accommodated his religious policy to the existing situation, whereas a few decades later, Darius I felt sufficiently emboldened to assert the superiority of his preferred deity, Mazda, over the "other gods who are ..." But that was Darius' preference, and not necessarily that of the Achæmenids as a whole. The partisans of Mazda would have to wait another six centuries before they could suppress their rivals with full government support, and even then their success would not be complete.

Mazdaean orthodoxy, moreover, like all suppressive projects, could not eliminate unauthorized views and practices, though history has long accepted its claims to have done so. While scholarship has at last begun to take seriously the multifarious religio-cultural expressions long obscured by a singular reliance on "authoritative" sacred texts for describing the world's religious traditions, it remains difficult to form a clear picture of these alternate realities, mostly because their principal custodians have been the illiterate rural masses. Rustic societies are prized by anthropologists for the wealth of ancient rituals and beliefs they often preserve, but these are not always easy to isolate and identify.

It is a universal and ever-recurring historical pattern that when urban elites attempt to impose their religious norms upon the non-urban majority, the latter find subversive ways of stubbornly maintaining their own traditions by reshaping and redescribing them according to the models of the former. The Kurdish Yezidi and Yaresan communities, who preserve traces of ancient Iranian beliefs and practices up to the present day, offer interesting case studies in this regard. It is worth remembering that for rural peoples the preservation of ancient rituals, especially those connected to the cycles of nature, was often considered by them to be a matter of life and death, since failure to properly observe a ritual could result in drought, famine, infertility, and other catastrophes.

### What is "Iranian Religion"?

The question remains whether such a thing as "Iranian religion" can be said to exist in its own right. The non-sectarian tradition of the Iranian new year, Nō rūz, along with its attendant ceremonies, provides perhaps the most visible example that it does. Also, since the Sasanian period at least, large numbers of Iranians have resisted the imposition from above of any kind of state religion, whether Zoroastrian, Sunni, or Shi'i, outwardly following the prescribed motions but privately favoring the esoteric teachings of heterodox spiritual masters. Generally speaking, an affinity for hidden interpretations ('erfān) and a usually passive resistance to imposed religious authority can be considered characteristic of Iranian spirituality.

Alessandro Bausani and Henry Corbin are two well-known Iran scholars of the twentieth century who sought to identify an unbroken strand of specifically "Iranian" religiosity throughout history, though their efforts focused mainly on demonstrating continuities from Zoroastrianism to Iranian Islam.[7] A roundtable of Iranists held in Bamberg, Germany in 1991 likewise took the continuity of Iranian religious ideas as its theme.[8] More recently, in discussing the range of local resistance movements that emerged in Iran during the period following the Arab conquests, Patricia Crone has claimed to describe "a complex of religious ideas that, however varied in space and unstable over time, has shown a remarkable persistence in Iran over a period of two millennia." Crone's thesis is somewhat circumscribed, however, since she largely limits it to "the mountain population of Iran."[9]

Numerous examples taken from the Iranian religious "pool," including notions and customs connected with water, fire, and light, as well as marriage ceremonies and other life-cycle rituals, are often dressed up in new garb or considered simply as "old superstitions" that nobody understands or questions. Nowhere is this more evident than in popular customs associated with the countless sacred sites that dot the Iranian landscape, including transformed goddess temples such as the

Bibi Shahrbanu shrine in Rayy, south of Tehran, as well as the country's ubiquitous *emāmzādehs*—ostensibly shrines to the numerous offspring of the various Shi'ite Imams but which in former times were probably in most cases Zoroastrian fire temples or other holy sites.

One striking example of this phenomenon of unwitting preservation could be seen in a report broadcast by Iranian state television on 19 March 2012, on the eve of Nō rūz, from the shrine of Halimeh and Hakimeh Khatoon in Shahr-e Kord, in the Zagros Mountains of Western Iran. The report showed women bringing lamps to be lit at the shrine, which they would then take home again. Unbeknown to themselves, these women were most likely preserving an ancient ritual by which Iranians carried back to their individual houses a portion of the sacred fire kept at their local temple. The televised report made no such connection, but as will be obvious to the reader of the pages that follow, the belief that Iran's deep cultural continuity is both real and important underlies the writing of this book.

# A Note on Transliteration

The Avestan alphabet is phonetic, making transliterations fairly straight-forward. Renderings of Middle Persian are more difficult, given the notorious ambiguities of the Pahlavi alphabet. For the Arabo-Persian alphabet, an attempt has been made here to strike a compromise between adherence to a regular system of representing the various letters and representation of how words and names are actually pronounced in modern standard Persian, along with a third variable which is that some of them have established English forms. In Chapter 16, acknowledgment is made to Bahá'í usage. In sum, the transliteration choices made in this book are somewhat irregular, but hopefully not illogical.

# Historical Timeline

| | |
|---|---|
| ca. 4000 BCE | Proto-Indo-European speakers in Central Eurasia |
| ca. 2000–1000 BCE | Aryans migrate onto Iranian plateau |
| ca. 1750 BCE | Life of Abraham |
| ca. 1200–1000 BCE (?) | Life of Zoroaster (Zaraθuštra) |
| 549–330 BCE | Achæmenid Empire |
| 539 BCE | Conquest of Babylonia by Cyrus the Great, liberation of Israelites and other subject peoples |
| ca. 500 BCE | Life of Siddhartha Gautama, the "Buddha" |
| 247 BCE–224 CE | Parthian Empire |
| 3 BCE–30 CE | Life of Jesus of Nazareth |
| 1st–4th CE | Spread of Roman Mithraism |
| ca. 100–300 CE | Mandaeans relocate from Palestine to Southern Mesopotamia |
| 216–276 CE | Life of Mani |
| 224–651 CE | Sasanian Empire, codification of Zoroastrianism |
| 520s CE | Mazdakite movement |
| ca. 570–632 CE | Life of Muhammad |
| 641 CE | Arabs defeat Sasanian army at battle of Nahāvand, begin conquest of Iran |
| 680 CE | Massacre of third Shi'ite Imam, Husayn, along with his followers, by forces of the Umayyad Caliph Yazid at Karbala in southern Iraq |
| 749–751 CE | Iran-based Abbasid revolution overthrows Umayyad dynasty |
| 816–837 CE | Rebellion of Babak |
| ca. 980–1010 CE | The Book of Kings (Shāh-nāmeh) redacted into verse by Abo'l-Qasem Ferdowsi from various Iranian heroic epics |

| | |
|---|---|
| ca. 1070–1162 | Life of Shaykh 'Adi |
| 1090–1256 CE | Assassins wage campaigns from base at Alamut castle |
| 1207–1273 CE | Life of mystic poet Jalal al-din Rumi |
| 1256–1336 CE | Mongol Il-Khan dynasty rules Iran |
| 1258 CE | Mongol conquest of Baghdad, end of Abbasid Caliphate |
| 1370–1405 CE | Central Asian Turkic empire of Timur Barlas (Tamerlane) |
| 14th–15th CE | Life of Soltan Sohak |
| 1501 CE | Foundation of Safavid Empire; formerly Sunni Iran becomes Twelver Shi'ite state |
| 1785–1925 CE | Qajar dynasty |
| 1819–1852 CE | Life of the Báb |
| 1817–1892 CE | Life of Bahá'u'lláh |
| 1925–1979 CE | Pahlavi dynasty |
| 1978–1980 CE | Iranian revolution; Iran becomes Islamic Republic |

# List of Illustrations

# Part 1

# ANCIENT IRANIAN RELIGIONS

# 1

# The Origins of Iranian Religion

Iranian cultural identity has been strong for over twenty-five centuries, yet it remains hard to define. The notion of "Iranian" as contrasted with "non-Iranian" (*anērān*) dates at least back to Achæmenid times (ca. 550–330 BCE), but even then the Iranian lands were considered to include non-Iranians, and the relationship between "Iranian" (*aryān*) and "Persian" (*pārsa*) was, as it remains today, somewhat confused. In the famous inscriptions at Naqš-e Rostam, Darius I describes himself as "an Achæmenid, a Persian, son of a Persian, an Aryan, having Aryan lineage" (*haxāmanišiya pārsa pārsahayā puça ariya ariya ciça*).[1]

It is possible, however, to point out at least two features that have been strongly associated with Iranian identity throughout history. One is land—broadly speaking, the so-called Iranian plateau, which occupies the nexus between the Caucasus Mountains, the Mesopotamian plain, and the high mountain ranges of Central Asia (Middle Persian (MP.) *Ērānšahr*, New Persian (NP.) *Īrānzamīn*). The other is language—broadly, again, the Iranian branch of the so-called Indo-European family of languages, but often more specifically the language known as Persian, which is the official language of the Islamic Republic of Iran, as well as being one of the official languages of Afghanistan (where it is called *darī*) and Tajikistan (where it is called *tojīkī*).[2] "Farsi" (*fārsī*) is the Persian term for Persian, like *deutsch* for German or *russkii* for Russian. The English word for Persian is "Persian."

In past times Persian was also the administrative and literary language of non-Iranian regions such as the Indian subcontinent and Anatolia. It is important to note that Iranian identity merely requires a strong *affinity* for the land and language, since many Iranians do not live in Iran, and many others even in Iran speak (or write) Persian only as a second language.

## INDO-EUROPEANS AND THE SEARCH FOR ORIGINS

In Iran's case, land and language came together during a period some three thousand years ago, following several centuries of southerly migration by nomadic bands of Proto-Iranian speakers from their previous home in western Siberia.[3] These ancient Iranians, including the ancestors of the Medes, the Parthians, and the Persians, came into contact with the existing inhabitants of the regions south of the Caspian Sea, such as Hurrians, Kassites, Elamites and others, with whom they mixed and who eventually became Iranicized. Further east, some of their Indo-Iranian cousins became integrated into the more advanced Central Asian society, as attested by remains found within the Bactriana-Margiana Archaeological Complex (BMAC), while others continued their south-eastward migration into the heavily populated Indian subcontinent.

These migrations highlight why it is a mistake to equate language with ethnicity, since when different human groups come into contact they typically blend their traditions over time, but with some cultural artefacts—for example, the language of one group—eventually taking over at the expense of the other. We should therefore understand that Etruscans, Aztecs, and others did not "die out" or become exterminated, so much as adopt the language (Latin, Spanish) and many of the customs and beliefs of their conquerors. The same is true for the ancient inhabitants of the Iranian plateau. What is less apparent are the influences that went the other way, from conquered peoples to their conquerors, but in many cases these can, at least to some extent, be surmised.

Since historically speaking this process of encounter and mutual influence ultimately takes the form of infinite regression, the same remarks could be made about the constitution of prehistoric peoples of the Central Eurasian steppes, whose ethnic or racial homogeneity cannot be presumed. Their culture must already have been a composite of previous encounters between distinct groups of people, including the inhabitants of the so-called BMAC.[4] But beyond a certain point, the details disappear over the horizon of history like a ship sailing into the sunset.

Thus, in attempting to reconstruct the cultural and belief system of the Iranians' prehistoric ancestors, we must be content to abandon our quest for "ultimate" origins and focus our attention on the period about six thousand years ago (give or take a millennium or so), long before these peoples began their migration into what is now Iran. By applying the methodologies of historical linguistics to literary vestiges which survive in various languages of the so-called Indo-European family (which includes the Germanic, Celtic, Romance, Greek, Slavic, Iranian, Indic, and many other branches), and combining this understanding with archaeological evidence from areas where these languages came to be spoken, scholars have begun to form a picture of the culture of the prehistoric steppe peoples who spoke the ancestor language now referred to as "Proto-Indo-European," or PIE.

For example, common derivations of the name for the sky god worshiped as "Father" (*$ph_2t\acute{e}r$*) by the PIEs, *$deiw\acute{o}s$*,[5] can be found in many Indo-European languages: *Ju(piter)* in Latin, *Zeus* in Greek, and *Tiw* in Old English—Tuesday (Tiw's day) being originally devoted to him. The Iranian and Indian variants, *Dyaoš* and *Dyáus(-pitar)*, respectively, refer to a deity who had become remote and was no longer worshiped by the time the Avestan and Vedic texts were composed. Other common roots suggest elements of the PIEs' technology (*$k^wek^wl\acute{o}m$* → "cycle", "wheel"), economy (*$g^w\bar{o}us$* → "cow"), environment (*$bherh_{\!x}\hat{g}os$* → "birch [tree]"), and so on.

## The Aryans

Efforts have been made to reconstruct the PIE language itself; its grammar as well as its vocabulary, through comparisons of later languages which are genetically related, and projecting back in time transformations that are known from the laws of linguistics. However, since the PIE language was never written, such attempts are ultimately speculative.

Among the hundreds of Indo-European roots reconstructed by modern scholars, one finds the word *$h_4eryos$*, likely meaning "member of our own group."[6] A later Indo-Iranian form, *arya*, seems to have acquired the meaning "noble," and became the principal self-designation (that is, Aryan) used by the ancestors of Iranian-speakers, who also applied the term to the lands where they eventually settled, which they referred to as *Airyanəm vaējah*. (The Vedic term *Āryavarta* has the same meaning, and the Irish name for Ireland, Eire, from the Old Irish *aire*, "freeman," may reflect a similar notion.) In Middle Persian the term became *Ērān-vēj*, which is today's Iran. Thus, etymologically, "Iran" means "Land of the Noble."

Attempts during the nineteenth and twentieth centuries to construct a theory of racial superiority on the basis of a purported "Aryan" heritage constitute one of the most egregious examples of how history can be abused through inappropriate back-projection. Ironically, during the earlier part of the nineteenth century, European scholars searching for an "original" Indo-European homeland tended to favor the Indian subcontinent, based on their assumption, now regarded as inaccurate, that Sanskrit represented an older form than other ancient Indo-European languages. By the end of that century the pendulum had swung the other way, with racialist theories resisting the notion that European civilization might owe anything to the non-white peoples they had colonized. Still later, with the reassertion of Indian (and specifically Hindu) identity in the wake of independence, within India an "indigenous Aryan" theory was championed once again, though it has not gained credence outside the subcontinent.[7]

Although the controversy over Indo-European origins remains a live one, continuing to treat it as a competition is surely a misplaced endeavour. Despite nineteenth-century European romanticism on the subject of Aryans and apart from the obvious perversions of the term perpetrated by the Nazis, PIE society seems a peculiar choice as an example of early "civilization," since by the standards of their own time they were far less "civilized" than the various societies—Old European, Minoan, Mesopotamian, Indus—they appear in many cases to have subdued. (One should note that "civilizations" are almost always brought down by "barbarians.") Moreover, from a twenty-first century perspective the most distinguishing characteristics of this society, which include patriarchy, aggressiveness, social stratification, and illiteracy, would hardly offer an inspiring model, although Christopher Beckwith has recently made a grand attempt to rehabilitate them.[8]

### Probable Homeland and Cultural Features

Based on the available linguistic and archaeological evidence, it seems most likely that the PIE-speaking peoples lived in the area of the southern Russian steppe, ranging from what is now Ukraine to western Kazakhstan.[9] Recent research has supported an alternate theory previously advanced by Colin Renfrew, placing the PIE homeland in Anatolia several millennia earlier, but even if true this could represent merely an earlier stage in their migration history.[10]

Their mixed agricultural and pastoral nomadic existence was precarious even by prehistoric standards, since they occupied lands subject to an extreme continental climate of very cold winters and very hot summers, along with very little rainfall. They were a people living on the margins, both literally and metaphorically. To the great civilizations with which they were contemporary—those of Mesopotamia, Egypt, the Indus valley, and eventually China—they were entirely peripheral, though there must have been some occasional contact with Mesopotamia across the Caucasus Mountains. And in terms of their subsistence lifestyle, the harsh ecology of their environment must have kept them more or less constantly on the edge of survival.

It may be assumed that the particular life circumstances of the PIE-speakers significantly influenced their culture and belief system. This hypothesis is consistent with much of what survives as distinctively Indo-European elements in the worldviews of historical cultures (especially where these survivals seem more compatible with the realities of steppe pastoralism than, say, those of agrarian India or even worse, industrial Germany!). Indeed, part of the enterprise of reconstructing this ancient culture, in the absence of any documents of its own, entails resituating what appear in their later forms to be anomalies—as with the Hindu *soma* and Zoroastrian *haoma* rituals, which must be performed without access to the original sacred substance, or the horse sacrifice, which was abandoned for scarcity of horses—into a putative "original" context.

According to the views of most contemporary anthropologists, pastoralism is said to have developed after agriculture, and not before it.[11] Presumably the ancestors of the PIEs practiced agriculture, but having experienced the ecological constraints of their steppe environment, many of their descendants largely abandoned tilling the soil in favor of a pastoral nomadic economy augmented by raiding. They did keep domestic animals, especially cattle and sheep. Indeed, wealth and social status were apparently measured mainly in terms of cattle ownership. (Even much later in Ireland, *bo airig*, "cattle-owning," was the Celtic term for a freeman.) The PIEs endowed the act of cattle raiding with a sacred importance, and raids were accompanied by a variety of rituals which included the drinking of intoxicating beverages. The oldest such drink was apparently mead; later they discovered wine and the mysteriously hallucinogenic *soma*.

Sharing their grassy landscape with grazing animals also provided another boon to the PIE peoples: at some point, perhaps five and a half thousand years ago or even earlier, it occurred to someone that horses could be ridden.[12] The oldest evidence for horse domestication, in the form of bit-worn jawbones, comes from northern Kazakhstan and has been dated to approximately 3,500 BCE.[13] To the PIEs would seem to go the credit for initiating the world's first great revolution in transportation technology, an innovation that would be central to their eventual success in spreading out and conquering much of the world. No wonder that the horse would become, alongside the bull, one of the most significant symbols in PIE religion, attested in copious examples of later Saka gold-work, the Greek myth of Apollo, the Vedic horse sacrifice, and elsewhere.

If the domestication of horses made PIEs the ancient world's most mobile people, their eventual mastery of metallurgy gave them the edge—a sword's edge, more often than not—over those with whom they came in contact, even when their opponents were more culturally "advanced" by almost any other measure. Again, ecological factors, so cruel in some respects, favored the PIEs in others. More so than any other human group of their time, PIEs were blessed by their proximity to horses—which enabled them to extend their range and speed beyond what any prior human group had known—and, in the Ural and Altai mountains, to copper, tin, and eventually iron ore which could be smelted into durable weapons. A climate that offered only limited agricultural potential ensured that a constant need to attack and steal from others would be a permanent feature of the PIE economy.

Here again, it comes as no surprise to find martial, and correspondingly, patriarchal, values as being highly esteemed in PIE society. The PIE class structure, echoes of which can be seen in the caste system of India, placed priests and chieftains at the top of the social pyramid, followed by a larger class of warriors (Sanskrit (Skt.) *kṣatriya*), then herdsmen or other "producers" (Skt. *vaiśya*, Avestan (Av.) *vāstrya*).[14] When Aryan groups arrived in India beginning some thirty-five centuries ago, they came to view the vast population of indigenous South Asians as a massive, fourth underclass (Skt. *dāsa*, "slaves").

In other words, PIE society was both highly authoritarian and distinctly stratified. The attribution of absolute authority to the leader survives in such notions as the English "divine right of kings" and the Iranian–Islamic concept of the king as "shadow of God on Earth." In PIE times and after, the priests (think of the Druids of old Britain or the Brahmins of India) were the ones who knew the sacred formulas (Av. *manθra*, Skt. *mantra*) and rituals (Av. *yasna*, Skt. *yajna*) that could appease and maintain balance with the capricious supernatural forces such as storms, the alternately life-giving and scorching sun, and the various animal and other spirits whose goodwill or malice meant life or death for the community. Needless to say, in this warlike society martial deities such as the thunder god (the later Scandinavian Thor, Slavic Perun) received special attention and tribute.

### Worldview and Rituals

As mentioned above, the major sources for reconstructing PIE culture are archaeological evidence and later texts. Artefacts from the ground are hard to interpret in the absence of supplementary data—imagine trying to reconstruct the beliefs and practices of Christianity on the basis of nothing more than a dug-up old crucifix and a chalice!—but extrapolation from later written sources can help one at least to make thoughtful guesses.

One technique is to comb through available literature, such as myths, in various Indo-European languages, and look for apparent commonalities. After centuries of oral transmission in diverse locales one would hardly expect the stories to remain the same, but if similarities exist, they may indicate a common origin. If this process of collation and comparison turns up identifiable characters, plots and themes in stories from ancient Greece and India, medieval Germany and Iceland, and perhaps elsewhere, as it turns out is often the case, then the common elements may have been present as far back as the period of the original PIE language, and may even be older than that. Obviously any differences between the stories can be attributed to later variations in storytelling that were adapted to local contexts.

Once a core "original" version of a myth or idea is distilled in this way, it can be applied to the interpretation of archaeological data. Thus, if an archaeological dig turns up a small winged horse figure which is determined to date from prehistoric times, one can attempt to infer its original use and significance by reconstructing a proto-myth about winged horses, based on what we know from comparing versions that are attested later. Frustratingly, we can never know for sure if the conclusions we are drawing are accurate, and the best guesses of the most erudite scholars are forever being questioned and re-evaluated.

The common Indo-European creation myth has strong resonances in later Iranian mythology. In the proto-myth, the world is created through the sacrifice and dismemberment of a giant (either a cow or a man) by his twin (Av. *Yima*, Skt. *Yama*, ON *Ymir*; the name itself means "twin"). The victim's bodily components become the seeds germinating the various natural phenomena. Many ancient rituals reflect aspects of this primordial sacrifice, along with its attendant homologies with the body as a microcosm of the natural world. Rituals, as Mircea Eliade and a host of subsequent historians of religion have noted, are often intended as a re-enactment of some primordial event, the performance of which is vital to the constant regeneration of the cosmos and all it contains.

Another widespread myth among Indo-European cultures, and therefore certainly very old, is that of the hero who slays (or binds) the dragon (see Figure 1), St. George in Christianity and Fereydun in the Persian *Book of Kings* being but two of many examples.[15] Many hero myths may represent distant memories of actual events from a culture's remote past, expanded and glorified over time and thus constituting a kind of ancestor-worship. Perhaps some long-lost moment in the prehistory of the PIEs is preserved in the dragon-slaying story. While in a metaphorical sense the dragon can be interpreted to represent chaos, with its destruction by the hero symbolizing the victory of cosmic order, it is interesting to speculate on the possibility that some actual event originally served as the source for the story. A dragon is really just an exaggerated snake—in fact, in many traditions the hero kills a snake, not a dragon—and the myth usually has it guarding a body of water. Did the dragon-slaying tradition begin with a band of nomadic PIEs unable to access a water source due to the deterring presence of a snake (or snakes), until someone among them found the courage to step forward and clear the way?

A number of Indo-European mythologies also possess a common eschatology, in which the world is brought to an end in an all-encompassing cosmic battle. Echoes of this can be seen in the Iranian *Frašo-kərəti*, the Norse *Ragnarök*, and the battles of Lake Regillus (Roman), Mag Tured (Irish), Ervandavan (Armenian), and Kurukśetra (Indian). Given the great antiquity suggested by the prevalence of the eschatological myth among widely dispersed Indo-European peoples, it was most likely the source, in its Iranian form, for the Apocalypse tradition in Judaism, Christianity and Islam which finds its first textual expressions in post-exilic Babylonia.

The literary heritage of Indo-European myth reflects the view of the PIE elite, the class of priests and chieftains, who were the ones who preserved cultural knowledge (history as well as ritual) through the composition and recitation of poems (hero stories and hymns). Their poetic culture, in which the power of the word reigned supreme, emphasized values or truth, order, and reciprocity. Thus, the divine protection and enforcement expected to come as a result of propitiatory sacrifices to the gods was mirrored in the obligations accruing to guests and their hosts.

The same kind of reciprocal obligations bound wealthy patrons to the poets who sang their praises, ensuring the patron "imperishable fame"—a central notion found across the range of Indo-European literatures—in exchange for rewarding the poet (usually with livestock). Any violation of these reciprocal expectations was seen as a threat to the cosmic order, and in turn would be punished not only by the vengeance of gods and warriors, but by the condemnation of the poets and their everlasting words as well. Their custodianship of the spoken word guaranteed the supreme social status of the poet-priest who, according to Calvert Watkins, "was the highest-paid professional in his society."[16]

## THE INDO-IRANIANS

Taking advantage of their unique, horse-assisted mobility, and perhaps spurred on by unfavorable climatic events, the ancient Proto-Indo-European-speaking tribes split over time, as smaller groups branched off and went their separate ways. Among the first to strike off on their own must have been the ancestors of the Celts, who went West, and the Tokharians (partial ancestors of the modern Uyghurs in western China), who went East; since their descendant languages differ most dramatically from the other Indo-European tongues, one assumes they were the earliest to begin the process of differentiation. Because Anatolian languages such as Hittite appear to have split off even earlier than that, they may be more properly considered "sister" languages to Proto-Indo-European than "daughters."

Among the various descendants of the proto-Indo-European speakers, the most direct ancestors of the Iranians are the so-called "Indo-Iranians," a people who occupied the region surrounding the southern Ural Mountains during the centuries around 2,000 BCE. Archaeological remains associated with the so-called Andronovo culture have been identified with them. In an unusually fortunate convergence of archaeology and historical linguistics, a site known as Sintashta, just east of the Urals, has revealed tombs which closely follow the burial and horse sacrifice (*aśvamedha*) rituals described in the Sanskrit Rig Veda.[17]

Considered by many Hindus today as a holy text, the Rig Veda is one of the oldest extant Indo-European literary sources. (Others, all dating from the second millennium BCE, include Hittite tablets from Anatolia, the Gathas and Seven-part Worship sections of the Iranian Avesta, and Mycenaean Greek inscriptions in the alphabet known as Linear B.) The Rig Veda in its present form dates probably to around the eighth century BCE, but its content is much older. And while certain passages— particularly references to "seven rivers" including the long-extinct Sarasvati—might seem to place its composition in north-western India, the world and culture evoked in the Rig Veda are more compatible with the lonely steppes of Central Eurasia. The recently discovered Sintashta remains corroborate this interpretation.

On the other hand the highly advanced Indus Valley civilization, attested by remains at Mohenjo-Daro and Harappa, is almost certainly pre-Aryan, since as one Indian scholar has pointed out, ". . . the Rig Vedic culture was pastoral and horse-centered, while the Harappan culture was neither horse-centered nor pastoral."[18] It is worth noting that the "Seven Rivers" designation, which also occurs in the Avesta, has been used in historical times to refer to a region of southern Kazakhstan (Russian *Semirechye*; Kazakh *Žety su*). Moreover, the Russian archaeologist Elena Kuz'mina has argued that a number of petroglyphs from that area represent recognizably Indo-Iranian scenes of battles and ritual dances.[19] In any case, as is known from a range of examples, migrant peoples often transpose their sacred geography on to new locations.

A comparison of the Old Avestan texts with the Rig Veda is particularly helpful for the reconstruction of the common Indo-Iranian religion and culture from which they are both descended. Indeed, these texts are so similar linguistically that their composition probably dates from a time very soon after the Indo-Iranian split around thirty-five centuries ago. Since Zoroaster's hymns, the Gathas, are usually interpreted as a "reform" of the original Indo-Iranian religion, the Rig Veda probably more closely reflects the earlier reality.

Given their shared languages and basic worldview, the Rig Veda and the Avesta can be used to complement each other in forming a picture of the prior Indo-Iranian society. Ironically, because the Rig Veda preserves the common pantheon, and perhaps the rituals, which become inverted in the Avesta, the former text can actually be more helpful in re-imagining the pre-Zoroastrian religion of the Iranians than the Iranian text itself.[20]

The Vedas (the term is derived from the idea of "knowledge," cognate with the English words "wisdom" and "wit") are often described as "hymns," though to contemporary ears this might give a misleading impression.

They are formulaic incantations, known only to the privileged priestly class and memorized so as to be performed under specific circumstances in a strictly defined way. Even by the time the first Brahmin priests transcribed them twenty-seven centuries ago these verses were no longer completely understood, but that surely bothers us more than it would have concerned them. As with any magical undertaking, the important thing was to "do it exactly right," not necessarily to comprehend what was being done, as long as the desired result was obtained.

The following excerpt from the Rig Veda is dedicated to Soma, which is at once a substance and a deity. The substance itself, which was ritually processed into a drink, has been the subject of much speculation, since it has apparently not been available as such since very ancient times. What is clear is that it was a powerful hallucinogen. Some scholars have guessed at a beverage concocted from hallucinogenic mushrooms, others from a plant, such as ephedra. (Considerable scientific effort has been expended trying to replicate this marvellous drug!) Presumably we are dealing with a source plant endemic to western Eurasia, since in ancient India and Iran alike priests had no access to it and had to use innocuous substitutes.

It may be helpful to prepare for reading the following example, a Vedic hymn to Soma, by taking a moment to close one's eyes and mentally picture oneself as a part of the ancient steppe world. Sitting around a campfire with family and friends beneath a crisp Montana sky might inspire the appropriate sort of image (think Hollywood westerns if you haven't been there yourself). Earth and the heavens recede in all directions, meeting each other beyond the horizon. The sun sets; nearby cows low and horses whinny. Add the tension of some imminent threat—a looming storm, a band of strangers in the distance—and look to those among you most gifted with insight to guide the course your group will take. They know the techniques for transcending mundane reality, for bridging the seen and the unseen. The proper preparation and consumption of Soma is one such technique.

Slowly, carefully, methodically, your priests bring out the Soma bowl and implements. Using means known only to themselves, they mix the sacred nectar that will enable them to collapse the boundaries between heaven and earth, human and divine. They finish their preparations and drink the Soma.

> This, yes this is my thought: I will win a cow and a horse. Have I not drunk Soma?
> Like impetuous winds, the drinks have lifted me up. Have I not drunk Soma?
> The drinks have lifted me up, like swift horses bolting with a chariot. Have I not drunk Soma?

The prayer has come to me as a lowing cow comes to her beloved
son. Have I not drunk Soma?
I turn the prayer around in my heart, as a wheelwright turns a
chariot seat. Have I not drunk Soma?
The five tribes are no more to me than a mote in the eye. Have I
not drunk Soma?
The two world halves cannot be set against a single wing of mine.
Have I not drunk Soma?
In my vastness, I surpassed the sky and this vast earth. Have I
not drunk Soma?
Yes! I will place the earth here, or perhaps there. Have I not
drunk Soma?
I will thrash the earth soundly, here, or perhaps there. Have I not
drunk Soma? One of my wings is in the sky; I have trailed the
other below. Have I not drunk Soma?
I am huge, huge! flying to the cloud. Have I not drunk Soma?
I am going to a well-stocked house, carrying the oblation to the
gods. Have I not drunk Soma?[21]

One student who read this passage explained to the class that the
popular party drug Ecstasy provides much the sensation described in
this ancient text. Interestingly, a pharmacy student in the same class
added that the chemical properties of Ecstasy are similar to those in
ephedrine—ephedra, remember, being one of the candidates for the
original Soma plant. In any event it is easy to imagine Indian and Iranian
priests of historical times bemoaning the fact that the substance could
no longer be found in their adopted lands.

The Soma drinker not only collapses the boundaries between heaven
and earth—that is, earth and sky, the "two worlds"—he also effaces
any distinction between himself and the divine. The Soma, being at once
substance and divinity, courses through his veins, metabolizes within
him. Space and time no longer confine him; he can fly anywhere, see
anything. The resonance of this tradition spans the human experience,
since it is surely very old and because the shamanic experience of
"flying," breaking all barriers of time and space, is so widespread in
human cultures.[22]

## FEATURES OF OLD IRANIAN RELIGION

As noted above, the Rig Veda and the Avesta, as the oldest literary vestiges
of the Indo-Aryans and their ancient Iranian cousins, are similar enough
in both language and content that, when compared with each other and
with later Hindu and Zoroastrian writings, they suggest a fairly detailed
picture of what the Indo-Iranians did and believed. Archaeological finds
can be weighed against what is understood from these texts.

### Creation and the Nature of the Universe

Ancient Iranians believed that the universe was created in seven stages—
the number "seven" having a lasting mystical significance and widespread
influence in later cultures. First was created the sky, then water, earth,
plants, animals, humans, and finally, fire. Exactly what force, or forces,
they believed set the process of creation in motion is not clear, though for
many of the world's ancient peoples, the problem of original agency is of
far less concern than it is in later philosophical traditions. Originally the
universe was static; then the first plant, the first animal (a bull), and the
first human were all sacrificed and their seeds dispersed, setting the cycle of
death and rebirth in motion.

The sky was imagined as a vast sphere encompassing the earth, but
viewed from a human perspective as an inverted bowl of brilliant stone.
Water was thought to flow beneath the earth, which floated upon it like
a plate. The tallest mountain, *Harā Bərəzaitī* (Harburz, Hara), reached
so high that it pierced heaven, and the sun, moon and stars all revolved
around it. A distant memory of this belief is echoed in the name of Iran's
northern mountain range, the Alborz, which includes the country's
highest peak, Mount Damavand.

Indo-Iranians divided the world into seven climes,[23] of which they
believed theirs, *Xᵛaniraθa*, to be the largest, central, and most pleasant.
The various rivers, mountains, and other natural features that appear in
the myths are difficult to associate with actual places, since the ancient
Iranians were mobile and probably shifted their identifications in
keeping with their changing locales. Migrants typically give old names
to new places, as a map of any North or South American country
will amply illustrate. Ancient Iranians called their immediate territory
*Airyanəm vaējah*—meaning, like the Vedic *Āryavarta*, "Land of the
Noble"—but, bearing in mind the mobility of sacred geography, this
would have referred to different actual locations at different periods in
their prehistory.

### Cosmic Principles and Supernatural Beings

Like most ancient (and some modern) peoples, the Indo-Iranians saw an
association between supernatural beings—which they called *mainyus*
(Vedic *manyu*)—and natural phenomena. Meteorological forces and
animate and inanimate objects were each identified with their own spirit
dimension, as were abstract notions like fate and moral qualities. Nature
deities included the sun, the moon, the sky, fire, water, and wind, as
well as specific items like the soma plant mentioned above. The most
important cosmological principle was the concept of a universal order
of Truth—the Sanskrit word *ṛta*, the Old Persian *arta*, and the Avestan
*aša* all being likely cognates with English "right." Different deities were

seen each as playing their own role in upholding this cosmic order. An opposing principle, *drūj*, accounted for disorder and calamity. Iranians would eventually come to see the world in terms of an ongoing struggle between these two opposing forces.

Another abstract idea which would become a central feature in the Iranian worldview was that of heavenly blessing, called *x$^v$arənah* (*farr*, in modern Persian). Those thus favored by the gods would enjoy success and prosperity, while its withdrawal led to all manner of misfortune and disaster. Heroes, kings, and prophets owed their glory to this divine investiture, which is symbolized in later Persian painting as golden flames leaping up from around the figure's head. (Even the Buddha and the prophet Muhammad are portrayed in this way.)

Among the other divine beings, one major class was a group of benevolent deities known in India as *asuras* and in Iran as *ahuras*. (The word, which means "lord," may first have been applied to tribal elders and only later to deities.) Another grouping, more morally ambiguous, was called *devas* in India and *daēvas* in Iran. The *ahuras* employed magical powers to intervene in world events, while the *daēvas*, characterized mainly by their strength, were particularly favoured by warriors.[24] According to Georges Dumézil, the Proto-Indo-Europeans classified their deities into three broad groupings that mirrored the tripartite structure of their own society comprising priests/rulers, warriors, and commoners. Reflections of this paradigm can be found in the mythologies of all Indo-European peoples, Indo-Iranians included. Thus the gods Mitra and Varuna are associated with the priestly group, Indra with the warriors, and fertility deities with the more numerous "producers."[25]

Certainly one of the oldest forms of human religiosity is the worship of ancestors and departed heroes, an impulse that survived among the Indo-Iranians. *Fravaši*s, as ancestor spirits were known to the ancient Iranians, could help and protect their living relatives, providing of course that they were properly remembered and propitiated. The afterlife was originally thought of as a dreary existence in a dark underworld, although passages in the Rig Veda together with archaeological evidence indicate an emerging belief in bodily resurrection by around thirty-five hundred years ago.

### Rites and Practices

Based mainly on archaeological evidence dating as far back as seven thousand years, scholars have supposed that the oldest Indo-European ritual traditions included the veneration of sky and earth deities, ancestor worship, and cults of fire and water. Traces of all of these are detectable in the various later Indo-European cultures. Among the oldest rituals, attested by excavated objects and surviving rituals in later cultures, appear to have been the regular pouring of libation offerings to bodies of water and the burning of offerings, such as animal fat, to the hearth fire, which was kept going (in the form of embers) even when travelling. Ritual vessels were "purified" using cow urine, rich in ammonia.

In the Indo-Iranian society of the third millennium BCE there were apparently several basic categories of priestly functions. The most important were the libation-pourers, called *zaotars*. (Zoroaster was a member of this group.) Another was the *aθravan*, charged with keeping the sacred fire. A third category, the *kavis*, had the knowledge of magic and immortality. Finally there were the *usigs*, who accompanied the warriors on cattle raids.

Ancient Indo-European societies did not have governments or police forces to maintain order. Social cohesion and stability were ensured through mutually agreed-upon codes and conventions. Preliterate peoples tend to place a great importance on orality, and Indo-Iranians in particular developed a strong affinity for spoken pacts, which essentially served as the society's legal system. Pacts had more than a merely temporal legal importance, however, since their proper observance was the means for upholding the cosmic order (*arta/aša*) while failure to do so would lead to chaos (*drūj*).

One type of pact performed by the PIEs was the *miθra*, a covenant between two parties, the other being a *varuna* or individual oath. In keeping with their belief about the supernatural inhering in abstract notions as well as in material things, Indo-Iranians personified the spiritual qualities (*mainyus*) of these verbal pacts as powerful and important deities. The veracity of one's oral proclamations could be put to the test, through fire ordeal in the case of *miθra*s and water in the case of *varuna*s, which may explain why Mithra and Varuna, who were responsible for sparing the truthful and punishing the unworthy, became such important gods. Among the Iranians Mithra retained his central importance, whereas oversight of the *varuna* oath came to be assumed by other deities.

Our most abundant evidence for the particular behaviours of Indo-Iranians pertains mainly to the priestly class, since priests were the ones who memorized and passed on to future generations the sacred formulas (*manθra*; Skt. *mantra*) which eventually came to be written down in religious texts such as the Rig Veda and the Avesta. Thus, much of the written material available to us is associated with forms of sacrifice, called *yajna* in the former text and *yasna* in the latter.

The word "sacrifice" should be understood here not according to the contemporary definition of "giving up something valued," but more the original literal sense of "making [something] sacred." In general the purpose of this is to create a situation of sharing—a communion—between humans and the divine. Often this takes the form of a shared meal, which is why the food offering must be "made sacred" (that is, "sacrificed") so that it is acceptable to the divine co-participant. Usually the bulk of the ritual consists of performing the appropriate preparations, incantations, and the like for bringing about the required transformation of the object to be sacrificed.

The most basic form of sacrifice entails a ritual re-enactment of some pivotal primordial event, collapsing time, as it were, to bring the present together with the distant past (what Mircea Eliade calls *in illo tempore*, "in that time"). Thus to some extent at least, the enduring popularity of bull sacrifice, the crushing and consuming of soma, and perhaps occasionally human sacrifice, would seem to re-enact aspects of the original creation myth. Sacrificial instructions from an ancient Indian text, the *Aitareya Brahmana*, show how the dismemberment of the victim was intended to nourish and regenerate all the vital elements of the living world:

> Lay his feet down to the north. Cause his eye to go to the sun. Send forth his breath to the wind, his life-force to the atmosphere, his ears to the cardinal points, his flesh to the earth. Thus, the priest places the victim in these worlds.[26]

Before performing this sacrifice the Indo-Iranians would lay out a bed of sacred grass (Sanskrit *barhis*, Avestan *baresman*) as a "throne" for the deity being invited; the sacrificial victim would then be laid upon it. In later Iranian religion the sacred grass became the bundle of "twigs" (*barsom*— now metal rods, held fanned out in the left hand rather than spread out on the ground) used by Zoroastrian priests during certain rituals.

Many different types of sacrifices are described in the ancient texts, however. As might be expected in a military society, much of the Rig Veda involves sacrifices to the war god, Indra, whose martial qualities are lauded in a way that suggest a sort of warrior ideal or role model. Sacrifices to Soma are also very prominent. The latter substance/deity figures in the Avesta as well, under the variant *haoma*, although somewhat more ambivalently.

Other rituals were connected with lesser deities, and with life-cycle events such as birth, puberty, marriage, and death. For non-priests, apparently the primary religious duties were to pray to the gods three times a day (at sunrise, midday, and sunset), to keep their hearth fires burning and maintain the purity of their vital water sources, and finally, to materially support their priests, who performed the ritual sacrifices (*yasna*) on behalf of the entire community.

Unfortunately the extent of our knowledge—or more accurately, our best guesses—about the nature and details of Indo-Iranian religious beliefs and practices does not extend very far beyond what has been briefly sketched out here. We know far more about those that existed later in India, by which time the Aryans had mingled their culture with that of the original South Asians, and in the Iranian world following the "reforms" commonly attributed to Zaraθuštra (Zoroaster), which will be discussed in Chapter 3.

# 2

# Mithra and Mithraism

As noted in Chapter 1, Mithra (Skt. Mitra) is one of the principal deities of the early Indo-Iranian pantheon. Originally the god of contracts[1]—his name means "that which causes to bind"—his enforcement of verbal commitments was central in a pastoral–nomadic society that lacked any formal policing agency. Spoken agreements were the very foundation of social stability; failure to uphold them could lead to anarchy.

Mithra was (and to some extent remains) an object of veneration in Zoroastrianism and Hinduism, with both Avestan and Vedic rituals devoted to him. Also, for several centuries his cult enjoyed unparalleled popularity within the army of the Roman Empire, leaving hundreds of archaeological traces across Europe. Yet only in the Roman context—where the actual connections with Iranian religion are unclear—does one typically speak of "Mithraism" as a distinct religion.

It may be that the proper status of Mithra-worship in the ancient Iranian world has been underestimated. Most often subsumed under Mazda-worship, as in Sasanian Zoroastrianism, Iranian Mithraism may deserve to be considered a religion in its own right. As has been argued in the Preface, too much of Iranian religious history is read as backward projection. This tendency has led even respectable scholars to categorize all manner of pre-Islamic Iranian religiosity as "Zoroastrian," an overgeneralization not warranted by the available data. In fact pre-Sasanian Iranian societies were highly diverse, in religion as in other domains, and there is little justification for assuming that most of their rituals and beliefs were specifically Zoroastrian.

The codified form of Mazda-worship now referred to as Zoroastrianism took shape rather late, during the Sasanian period (224–651 CE). Prior to the political efforts of the early Sasanians (backed by fanatical and ambitious Mazdaean priests such as Kerdir) to articulate and forcibly impose a particular Zoroastrian orthodoxy upon a very religiously heterogeneous Iranian society, it seems more likely that across the Iranian lands there were at least three major religious tendencies (alongside many minor ones). Of these, Mazdaism is the best known, but its establishment by a favored priestly caste does not in and of itself prove that it was the preferred religion of most Iranians. Among the general population there is much evidence of Mithraism, which may actually be the older tendency.

The survival of Mithraic elements in the Iranian world was largely a rural phenomenon, consistent with the observation made earlier about the importance for rural peoples of preserving their rituals. Mehrdad Bahar has emphasized the role of the bull sacrifice in rural areas of Western Iran, even arguing that it predates the migration of the Iranian tribes into the region. Pointing out that the sacrifice and consumption of cattle was abhorred in both the Vedic and Zoroastrian traditions, Bahar suggests that the bull sacrifice was a pre-existing tradition that was preserved by the Mesopotamian and Elamite peoples who came under Iranian subjugation. According to Bahar's analysis, as rural populations became Iranicized they adopted Mithra as the most sympathetic Iranian deity—being associated with justice, something of which they, as an underclass, were so often deprived—and came to associate their most important ritual with him.[2]

Beginning in the Achæmenid period (ca. 550–330 BCE), evidence of Mazda-worship is strongest in the western parts of Iran; further east, Mithra appears to have been the more prominent god. Even in the west Mithra was worshipped, however, while in later Achæmenid times the most popular divine figure seems to have been the goddess Anahita. Similarly, her Central Asian counterpart Nanai was apparently the principal deity of the Sogdians up to the Islamic conquest. The Mazdaean magi sought to co-opt rival religious tendencies by incorporating them into their own religious framework. Thus, Mithra- and Anahita-focused religiosities are subsumed under Mazda-worship in the Zoroastrian texts.

## INDO-IRANIAN ORIGINS

Mithra first appears in recorded history as one of four Indo-Iranian deities invoked in a contract between the north Mesopotamian Mitanni ruler Kurtiwaza and the Hatti king Shuppiluliuma I, dated to between 1375–1350 BCE.[3] The other deities mentioned are the easily recognizable Varuna, Indra, and Nasatya. Some of the material pertaining to these four deities that appears in the Avesta and the Rig Veda may be older than the Mitanni contract, but the written forms of these texts do not appear until many centuries later. An even earlier piece of evidence, a Mitanni royal seal from ca. 1450 BCE, depicts a bull-slaying scene in which the bull-slayer may be Mithra.[4]

The Mitanni rulers, who were from the Indic branch of the recently divided Indo-Iranians, entered Mesopotamian society as a military elite, so their attachment to Mithra is consistent with his role in later Iranian and Roman (but not so much Vedic) traditions. One of Mithra's recurring features is as an enforcer: when people don't abide by their contracts, he punishes them without mercy.[5] It is not difficult to see how the warrior class might identify with such a deity, notwithstanding the greater importance given to Indra in the Rig Veda.

In its visible traces—which are mostly but not exclusively Roman—Mithra-worship is associated foremost with the tauroctony, the bull sacrifice illustrated on the walls of Mithraic temples across Europe and the Near East. The cosmic significance of this ritual can be seen in the association of Mithra with the "unconquered" sun and its relationship to the moon, symbolized by a bull, which is "killed"—indeed *must* be killed—every month so that life may be regenerated. The cosmogonic myth found in the Zoroastrian *Bondahešn* is but one version portraying this belief.

In later Roman times the Mithra cult appears to have been exclusively male, and this may also have been the case among the ancient Iranians. Paul Thieme has suggested that this is because in ancient Indo-Iranian culture the concluding of contracts was done between men; Frantz Grenet has observed that in the Kushan Empire the Mithra cult seems to have been paired with that of the goddess Aši, which would indicate the existence of parallel male-female cults.[6]

## MITHRA-WORSHIP IN ACHÆMENID TIMES

While the early Achæmenids are usually claimed to have been Mazdaists, the picture is actually more complicated than that, and evidence for Mithra-worship is abundant. Cyrus the Great, known for his accommodation of religious diversity, may even have considered Mithra the supreme deity: the entrance to his tomb features a Mithraic-looking solar disc.[7] Mithra holds an important place in Cyrus' royal procession, as described by Xenophon; Philippe Swennen goes so far as to suggest that the ceremony was originally Mithraic, and that Mazda's introduction into it was an innovation.[8] The head of Cyrus' treasury in Babylon was an individual named Mithradata; in fact this name ("given by Mithra"), along with its variants, is one of the most commonly occurring names in documents from ancient Iran up through the Parthian period. The name Mithrayazna ("Mithra-worshiper") is also frequently found. Such names also regularly appear in mentions of Persian settlers in Achæmenid Mesopotamia and Egypt. A Mithra temple in Memphis, Egypt has been dated to the fifth century BCE.[9] According to Alexander the Great's chronicler, Arrian, a white horse was sacrificed at Cyrus' tomb every month, which may also indicate a Mithraic connection.[10]

Darius I (550–486 BCE) is considered on the basis of his inscriptions to have been a Mazda-worshiper, but these same inscriptions acknowledge the help of other, unnamed gods. Moreover, Aramaic tablet records at Persepolis during the time of his reign actually indicate a higher number of donations for rituals in honour of Mithra than for Mazda.[11] The Achæmenid kings Artaxerxes I (465–424 BCE) and Darius III (ca. 380–330 BCE) were devotees of Mithra, as was the prince known as Cyrus the Younger (died 401 BCE; he was killed accidentally by one of his own soldiers, ironically enough named Mithradata).

The Greek writer Xenophon (ca. 430–354 BCE) observes that Persian rulers "swore by Mithra,"[12] which is consistent with the deity's role as guardian of contracts. Inscriptions of Artaxerxes II (404–358 BCE) and Artaxerxes III (ca. 425–338 BCE) name Mithra and Anahita together with Mazda; this fact is generally taken to indicate the sovereigns' recognition of the three deities who held the greatest followings in Iranian society at the time.

Richard Frye believes that in Achæmenid times the Mithra cult was restricted to the military, noting that it could have existed "within the Mazdayasnian religion."[13] But he provides no reason why we should assume that Mithra-worship was restricted to the military, or that it was subsumed within a broader Mazdaist tradition; these impulses seem rather to be the result of reading later conceptions backward.

## MITHRAISM UNDER THE PARTHIANS

The northeast Iranian Parthian (*Aškānī*) dynasty (247 BCE–224 CE) is generally described as being "religiously tolerant," having no official state religion. However, there is some evidence that the ruling elites and perhaps much of their subject population in eastern Iran were primarily Mithraists. No fewer than four Parthian kings were named in Mithra's honour (Mithradata, "given by Mithra"), and the easternmost of the three sacred fires known from Sasanian times, Burzin-Mehr ("exalted is Mithra"), was likely established in Parthian times.

Parvaneh Pourshariati has recently advanced an intriguing (though hotly contested) argument according to which the Mithraist tendencies of elite Parthian families such as the Karens and the Mehrans (whose name itself means "Mithraists") remained a source of tension throughout the Sasanian period. She points out that the late sixth-century rebel Bahram Čubin was known in Armenian sources as Mehrvandak, "servant of Mithra," and that his movement centered on the Burzin-Mehr fire in opposition to the two Sasanian fires further west. Pourshariati concludes that the religiously expressed tensions between the Sasanian and Parthian elites ultimately led to the breakdown of Sasanian imperial power during the mid-seventh century, when the Parthians, ever resentful of their Mazdaist rivals in the west, chose to ally themselves with the invading Arabs.[14]

The earliest documented association of Mithra with the sun is found in Strabo (63 BCE–24 CE).[15] It is in the Parthian language that Mithra's name first comes to be used as the word for "sun" (*mehr*); this equivalence is maintained in New Persian, where it acquires the additional meaning of friendship or love. Ilya Gershevitch has argued that the association of Mithra with the sun from Parthian times onwards derives from Manichaeism, which identified Mithra with the third divine emanation, called the Third Messenger, and referred to the sun as Mihryazd ("God Mithra"). The Manichaean Third Messenger "dwells within the sun," whereas in the Avesta Mithra is said to *rise before* the sun, representing for Gershevitch a fundamental change transforming Mithra into a solar deity.[16]

It is significant that in his own writings Mani referred to the Third Messenger as "Naryosangha," who in the Avesta is Mazda's messenger, not Mithra's. The shift in association to Mithra among the Parthians and Sogdians as Manichaeism spread east may constitute evidence that these peoples preferred Mithra to Mazda. In addressing his Persian audience Mani assigned Mithra the identity of the demiurgic Living Spirit, which led Porphyry to identify him as a creator god, displacing Mazda.

In Bactria, at the time of the Kushans (first to third century CE), who were eastern contemporaries of the Parthians, numismatic evidence from Kapisene and elsewhere suggests that Mithra (Bactrian: Miiro or Mioro) was the most popular male deity.[17] Oddly, this has been taken by scholars including Mary Boyce, Nicholas Sims-Williams, and Frantz Grenet as evidence of "Bactrian Zoroastrianism." A more elegant treatment of the facts would conclude that, just as in much of eastern Iran, a preponderance of Bactrians at that time were Mithraists, not Mazdaists. Indeed, in this and other contexts where the evidence for Mithra-worship outweighs that of that for Mazdaism, describing the former as merely a component within a generalized Zoroastrian culture seems a nonsensical proposition, rather like stating that "worship of Ba'al was prominent within the Judaism of the Canaanites."

Reflecting a Greek presence dating back to the time of Alexander's conquest, Kushan coins visually depict Mithra with the iconography of the Greek sun god, Helios, with whom he is identified. In other cases Mithra takes the place of Zeus, lending weight to the hypothesis that for at least some eastern Iranians he was the principal deity.[18] As one moves further eastwards into Gandhara and Kashmir, Mithra is still represented, but as one among a number of popular deities. This may indicate a diluted presence of east Iranians in northwestern India at that time.[19]

## MITHRAISM IN THE ROMAN WORLD

Communities of Iranians existed throughout the eastern Mediterranean from ancient times. Presumably most had established themselves there for purposes of trade; others likely came as soldiers or slaves. At times Egypt, Syria and Anatolia had been under Achæmenid rule, which facilitated the settlement and flourishing of groups of Iranians. As these territories came under first Greek, then Roman control, Iranian expatriates continued to live there. Despite their minority status, many seem to have thrived, since Iranians are mentioned as underwriting the building of public structures and sponsoring athletes. The influence of Iranians was also felt in what would become a major movement in Roman society, particularly the army: namely, the cult of Mithra.

This cult appears to have taken shape in the culturally mixed environment of northwestern Mesopotamia and Asia Minor during the first century BCE, and by the late first century CE it had spread throughout the Roman Empire. Plutarch, in his *Vita Pompei*, mentions a group of pirates from Cilicia, defeated in 67 BCE, who practiced a Mithraic cult. The famous site at Nimrut Dagh (now in eastern Turkey) erected by Antiochus of Commagene (69–34 BCE) contains a sculpture and tomb inscription dedicated to Mithra. Franz Cumont observes that the crude workmanship of a bas-relief near Antioch depicting a Mithraic bull-sacrifice "implies that it was dedicated by humble people."[20]

In its Roman form, Mithraism was a secretive, exclusively male cult. If, as it appears, this movement first took shape among bands of thieves or soldiers, the notion of basing membership on an inviolable pact, enforced by a ruthless deity, would have been appealing. Its central ritual was a re-enactment of the primordial myth, the tauroctony, according to which Mithra slays a bull. Apart from some inscriptions in the ruins of Mithraic temples, no texts have survived which can shed light on the details of their rituals, apart from a few mentions in outside sources.

Scholars have therefore been divided on how to fill the void of knowledge regarding the specifics of belief and practice when discussing Roman Mithraism. Some (for example Franz Cumont) assume a basic continuity from Iranian Mithraism and seek to explain the evidence from Mithraic temples and references in Greek and Latin sources by supplying Iranian models. Others (for example Stig Wikander) reject any such continuity, believing that in Roman Mithraism little more than the name of the god himself is Iranian, the rest having Mediterranean origins. Still others simply throw up their hands in despair, and insist that such questions cannot be answered from the available evidence.

John Hinnells comes down tentatively on the side of continuity, noting a number of similarities between elements in the artistic scenes found in Roman Mithraic temples and attested Iranian rituals. Bread, fruit, wine and water offerings figure in both, as does the presence of a dog (who in Zoroastrian rituals is the first to be offered the sacrificial food). In a particularly interesting parallel, Mithraic worshipers wore animal masks, a practice that continued among Iranians celebrating *Mehragān*. In light of this evidence, Hinnells considers it "plausible that some of these details on Roman monuments represent archaic survivals of ancient Iranian ideas whose significance may no longer have been appreciated." Thus, ". . . the Roman Mithraic reliefs depict the divine sacrifice which gives life to men, a concept which ultimately derived from Iran but which was expressed in terms meaningful to people living in the Graeco-Roman world."[21]

Bruce Lincoln likewise sees Iranian survivals in Roman Mithraism, not just the tauroctony ritual but also in the association of Mithra with the sun and "his role as savior or conductor of the soul."[22] It is interesting that in at least two Zoroastrian texts, the *Mehr Yašt* (10.93) and a passage from the *Vīdēvdāt* which seems to be based on it (19.28–9), Mithra is depicted as saving the devotee from death's bonds and assisting the ascension of his soul just as he assists the rising of the sun.

Roman Mithraism centered on the notion of the soul's journey upward through seven spheres, symbolized by the devotee's passage through the seven stages of secret initiation: the Raven, the Bridegroom, the Soldier, the Lion, the Persian, the Sun-Runner, and the Father. Each stage was associated with a planet and had its own set of symbols. Mithra was held to be the god of salvation, associated with the sun. Not insignificantly, his birthday was celebrated on 25 December, and his depiction in popular stories celebrating "the infant Mithra" is remarkably Jesus-like.

The Mithraea, where devotees of Mithra congregated to perform their ceremonies, were underground temples meant to evoke the cave where, according to myth, Mithra had captured and killed the primordial bull— an echo of the bull sacrifice in ancient Iranian religion, but which the Zoroastrian tradition attributes to the evil deity Ahriman. The Roman Mithra cult, which was exclusively male, fostered camaraderie among its adherents, particularly soldiers who were frequently relocated from one post to another and thus lacked social roots.

The rituals of Roman Mithraists can be guessed at only through analysis of the panel reliefs and paintings which adorn the walls of Mithraeum temples. From these it would appear that some kind of animal sacrifice, mimicking the original tauroctony, was the central ritual. Another important ritual, evoked by initiation and banquet scenes, seems to have entailed the consumption of the sacrificed animal's flesh and may, according to Franz Cumont and some others, have preserved elements of the ancient Indo-Iranian *haoma* sacrifice. Parallels for these scenes can be found in the Christian Eucharist and in the Manichaean Bema feast, in which the actual killing and consumption of flesh have been sublimated.

Mithra is depicted in these temple panels in the company of the Invincible Sun, *sol invictus*, inherited from the Romans and the Syrians. Another recurring image is of a winged, lion-headed figure entwined with a snake, which inscriptions identify as Arimanius. Presumably this is a Romanization of Ahriman, but his function and role in the Mithraic mysteries are unclear. It is interesting that the tenth-century catalog of Ibn Nadim quotes Mani, the founder of Manichaeism, as describing the devil as having the head of a lion and the body of a dragon.[23] David Bivar has proposed that the iconography of the lion-headed figure seen in Mithraea derives from that of Nergal, the Babylonian god of the underworld.[24] Thus, Mithraic rituals devoted to Arimanius may have aimed at appeasing the god of death. A related interpretation holds Arimanius to be the god of Time (bringer of death), which would connect him with the Iranian Zurvan.

Roman sources marvel at the rapid spread of Mithraism throughout the empire during the early centuries of the Common Era. To date some four hundred and twenty Mithraea have been identified across Europe and the Near East, from northern England (Carrawburgh) to upper Mesopotamia (Dura-Europos). But with the adoption of Christianity as state religion of the Roman Empire in the early fourth century CE, Mithraism along with other pagan cults and heterodox Christian groups was increasingly persecuted and soon disappeared.

## MITHRA-WORSHIP IN ZOROASTRIANISM

Mithra is not mentioned in the Gathas, so in the strictest sense he is not a "Zoroastrian" god. However, as noted above, the Mazdaean magi attempted to incorporate his cult (possibly as early as the Achæmenid period), and included a liturgy devoted to him, the *Mehr Yašt*, in the Avesta (Yašt 10). The *Mehr Yašt*, while reflecting a Mazdaist vision, likely preserves some pre-Mazdaean ideas. It is thus our principal source of information for Iranian conceptions of Mithra. Other Avestan sources include Yašts 1 and 3, *Vīdēvdād* 4, and the *Khcoršīd Niyāyeš* ("Liturgy of the Sun") in the Zoroastrian prayer-book, the Khorda Avesta. The Young Avesta places Mithra within a so-called "ahuric triad" along with Mazda and Apam Napat, god of the waters (a male deity whose features are later taken over by the goddess Anahita).

The *Mehr Yašt* begins with the statement that Ahura Mazda created Mithra, and made him "as worthy of sacrifice, as worthy of prayer as myself" (10.1.1). Later, it is said that Mithra is "master of the world," but with the qualification that this position has been granted him by Ahura Mazda (10.23.92). These would seem to be fairly transparent attempts on the part of the Mazdaist clergy to accommodate the huge importance of the Mithra cult among Iranians while subordinating him to Mazda by making the latter the original creator figure.

In the *Mehr Yašt* and elsewhere, Mithra is frequently described as overseeing the pastures where livestock graze. One assumes this to be a reflection of the fact that in the pastoral–nomadic society of the proto-Indo-Iranians livestock were the major form of wealth, and that covenants among tribes were the only restraint on indiscriminate raiding which was the primary source of social instability. When such covenants were transgressed, it was incumbent upon the warrior class to go out and set things right.

Watching over these societies, Mithra is described as having a thousand (or ten thousand) eyes and ears, and as always being awake. In other words, no misdeeds can escape his notice. Contract-breakers may flee, but cannot outrun him. Spears thrown by his enemies will fly backwards towards those who fling them. He "breaks the skulls of *daēva*s," and saps the strength of havoc-wreakers, taking away their glory and beating them with "ten thousand strokes." He provides homes to the truthful, and destroys those of liars. In sacrificing to him, devotees hope that he will:

(33) Give us the following boon(s) for which we ask you, O strong one, by virtue of the stipulation of the given promises: riches, strength, and victoriousness (*vərəθraɣna*), comfortable existence and ownership of Truth (*aša*), good reputation and peace of soul, learning, increment, and knowledge, Ahura-created victoriousness, the conquering superiority [deriving from] Truth which is what is best, and the interpretation of the incremental divine word (*manθra*), (34) so that we, being good in spirit, cheerful, joyful and optimistic, may overcome all opponents, so that we, being good in spirit, cheerful joyful, and optimistic, may overcome all enemies, so that we, being good in spirit, cheerful, joyful, and optimistic, may overcome all hostilities of evil gods and men, sorcerers and witches, tyrants, hymn-mongers, and mumblers . . .

(93) Now then, in both lives, O grass-land magnate Mithra, in both—this material existence, and the one which is spiritual— do protect us from Death and Wrath (*aēšma*), the two owners of Falsehood (*drvatat*), from the evil armies of the owners of Falsehood who raise a gruesome banner, from the onslaughts of Wrath, which are run by Wrath the malignant with [the cooperation of] the Disintegrator [of the body] with whom the evil gods created! (94) Now then, grass-land magnate Mithra,

give strength to our teams, health to ourselves, much watchfulness
against antagonists, ability to strike back at enemies, ability to
rout lawless, hostile, opponents![25]

Mithra the Enforcer is assisted by some well-known figures in Iranian
mythology, including the dragon-slayer Vərəθraγna (Bahrām) and the
spirit of wakefulness and obedience, Sraoša (Sorūsh), symbolized in later
art as a rooster. He is also accompanied by Rašnu (the Judge) and the
goddess Aši ("Reward"). Mithra appears alongside Sraoša and Rašnu
in the myth of the Činvat Bridge, over which the dead must pass, though
it is Sraoša who actually conducts souls across the bridge. Mithra is the
bestower of divine glory, $x^v$arənah (farr), symbolized in art as a halo,
flames, or ribbons encircling the head of the figure who possesses it.

Zoroastrian fire temples are called *Darb-e mehr*, "Gate of Mithra."
The reason for this is obscure, and may go back to a very ancient period.
In any case, as John Hinnells observes, "Such a nomenclature could
have developed only if Mithra was traditionally a god of outstanding
ritual significance."[26] Zoroastrian priests receive a bull-headed "mace
of Mithra," called a *gurz*, when they are initiated, and their power in
performing important ceremonies is believed to derive from Mithra.

Another mark of Mithra's importance in Zoroastrianism is found
in the calendar, which dedicates the sixteenth day of each month, and
the seventh month of the year, to Mithra (Mehr). The great fall harvest
festival, moreover, is devoted to him.

### Mehragān: the Festival of Mithra

Mehragān (Old Persian Mithrakāna) is historically one of the most
important Iranian celebrations, mirroring the New Year festival, Nō
rūz, which is held at the spring equinox. Originally the Iranian peoples,
like the Indo-Aryans, may have considered the new year to begin in the
fall; thus, the annual festival of Mithra was likely the most important
occasion of the year. The spring celebration of Nō rūz, on the other
hand, most probably originated in Mesopotamia, and was adopted by
the Iranians after they migrated into the region.

In Achæmenid times both Mithrakāna and Nō rūz were major official
occasions presided over by the state. The Achæmenid Mehragān ceremony
culminated in the ritual killing of a bull. Until recent decades, Iranian
Zoroastrians celebrated Mehragān by conducting an animal sacrifice,
usually a sheep or a goat. Significantly, Mehragān is the only Zoroastrian
festival in which (some) priests omit a formal dedication to Ahura Mazda,
dedicating the ceremony instead to Mithra.[27] According to Mary Boyce:

It seems very possible that the intention of the ancient Iranian
blood sacrifice to Mithra was the same as the Athenian sacrifice

of a bull to Apollo at the autumn festival of the Bouphonia, and of similar harvest rites among other peoples, namely to fertilize the fields with life-blood and so ensure that the corn and other crops would sprout afresh in the coming year.[28]

Iranian myth reflects the pairing of the fall and spring equinox festivals, with Mehragān being the occasion where the hero Θraētaona (Fereydūn) kills (or imprisons) the evil serpent-king Aži Dahhāka (Zahāk) in revenge for the latter's slaying of Yima-xšaēta (Jamshīd), the primordial ruler who first established Nō rūz; the cosmic balance is thereby restored. The eleventh-century scholar Abu Rayhan Biruni noted that the Iranians "consider Mehragān as a sign of resurrection and the end of the world, because at Mehragān that which grows reaches its perfection . . ."[29]

### Yaldā

The Iranian imagination saw the winter solstice—the shortest day of the year—as the culmination of the sun's annual "dying" trajectory. Iranians therefore believed they should stay awake throughout longest night, seen as inauspicious, and collectively work to regenerate the sun by eating red (therefore "solar") fruits, such as pomegranates and watermelons, to help it get stronger so that the days would start to grow longer again. This ritual was likely associated with Mithra, since he was the principal solar deity. Moreover, myths about Mithra's birth (which mirror those of the Christian Nativity) have him born the following day.

The all-night winter vigil known as *shab-e yaldā*, which is still practiced by Iranians, has its roots in this ritual. The term *yaldā* is borrowed from Syriac, and means "birth," perhaps conflating the annual rebirth of the sun with legends about the birth of Mithra. Yaldā is the first day of the forty-day period known as *chelleh*, which culminates in the winter fire festival of Saddeh. The end of winter at the vernal equinox is also marked by a fire ritual on Chahār shanbe sūrī, the Wednesday before Nō rūz. Since fire is associated with the sun, the three winter celebrations would seem to have ancient connections.

## MITHRA AND THE PRIMORDIAL BULL SACRIFICE

As mentioned in Chapter 1, bull sacrifice was apparently one of the main rituals of the ancient Indo-Iranians, seen by them as a re-enactment of a primordial event by which life, symbolized by the bull, had to be killed (at the beginning of winter) so that it could be resurrected (in the spring). This paradigm is present in ancient Mesopotamia as well, as evidenced in the myth of Dammuzi and other stories. (Note that in Mesopotamian mythology a primordial bull sacrifice is carried out by Gilgamesh.) Scenes from the stone reliefs at Persepolis of a lion attacking a bull may be representations of the Iranian version of this regeneration myth.

In Iranian mythology, the seasonal cycle of death and rebirth is replicated at the daily level by the "death" of the sun at nightfall and its "resurrection" every morning. Thus, the mythological association of Mithra with the sun/lion and the bull with the moon suggests a connection with the bull sacrifice ritual which may date to a very early, pre-Zoroastrian period. For this reason, some scholars see the version of the myth in which Mithra kills the bull as being the original form, with the Zoroastrian version where Ahriman plays this role being a later innovation.[30] The reason for the substitution, according to Bahar, is that since the Zoroastrians saw death as evil and polluting, it could not be associated with a beneficent deity.[31]

An echo of the Mithraic tauroctony from the Muslim period may be seen in the story from the *Kalila and Dimna* animal fables in which the lion-king is persuaded by a duplicitous jackal advisor to kill his own best friend, a bull by the name of Shanzabeh. The scene is illustrated in miniature paintings from several well-known *Kalila and Dimna* manuscripts (see Figure 2).

## SURVIVALS OF MITHRAIC IDEAS IN OTHER RELIGIONS

Some of the most evident survivals of Mithraic elements are found in Christianity, notably the custom of celebrating Jesus' birthday on 25 December. This arbitrary choice of date, decided upon by the Church Fathers in the fifth century, was deliberately calculated to re-brand celebrations of Mithra's birthday which Roman Mithraists had held on that date. (In modern times the government of Pakistan has attempted a similar transference by declaring 25 December "Muhammad Ali Jinnah Day.") Moreover, Mohammad Moghaddam has argued that the virgin birth story was appropriated from a myth in which the baby Mithra, a future Saošyant, is born of a virgin, Anahita.[32] The sign of the cross, formed by the elliptic and the celestial equator, was one of the symbols associated with Mithra. And finally, the mitre (Latin *mitra*) worn by many Christian bishops and abbots, may be derived from the Phrygian cap in which Mithra is represented in countless friezes.

Aspects of the Mithraic cult survived in heterodox sects of the Islamic period, notably in Kurdistan among the Yazidis and the Yaresan (Ahl-e Haqq). Both groups preserve the myth of a primordial contract, sealed by the sacrifice of a bull. This sacrifice, moreover, involves first setting the bull to run free and be chased by its designated slaughterer, just as in the Mithra myth.

The actual extent of Mithraic influence during the Islamic period is unclear, however. Hassan Pirouzdjou goes so far as to argue that "within the resurgence of ancient cults, it is first and foremost Mithraism that occupies the center stage."[33] Pirouzdjou sees Mithraism as the inspiration for radical movements from the Mazdakites to the Sarbedars to the Horūfīs to the Qizilbāš, and while his argument may be somewhat overextended, he does draw some interesting parallels between the Mithraic tauroctony and a sacrificial ritual attributed to the followers of the rebel Bābak *"khurram-dīn"* in the ninth century.[34] He also points out that the *khurram-dīniyya* and other related groups were referred to as "those who wear red" (*sorkh-jāmegān*), the colour of clothing in which Mithra is generally depicted.

The art historian, Abolala Soudavar, goes so far as to argue the presence of Mithraic symbols in the royal iconography of every period of Iranian history from the Achæmenids onwards. The halo of divine glory (*farr īzadī*) in particular, which is a constant in Iranian art, he sees as an ever-present evocation of Mithra's power. This solar symbol reaches its highest form of expression in the art of Mughal India beginning with the reign of Akbar the Great (1555–1605), in the shape of a starburst (*šamseh*) seen in many royal Mughal illustrated manuscripts.[35]

Similar to Pirouzdjou but relying less on forced interpretations, Mehrdad Bahar has detected Mithraic survivals in the rituals of various kinds of fraternities that have survived up to the present day in Iran, notably the *pahlavān* ("heroes") associated with the traditional gymnasia known as "Houses of Strength" (*zūrkhāneh*), which are underground and cave-like.[36] Bahar also sees echoes of Mithraic ethics in the codes of behaviour (*ādāb*) adhered to by contemporary *pahlavān*.

# 3

# In Search of Zoroaster

Among the founders of the world's major religious faiths, none is more shrouded in mystery than Zoroaster. Basic questions, such as where and when he lived, remain unresolved. Although the dates, places, and personal biographies associated with Abraham, Moses, Buddha, Jesus, and Muhammad are still open to varying degrees of discussion, the range of uncertainty nowhere approaches that facing students of Zoroastrianism.

For example, it has been proposed that Zoroaster lived as early as the time of Abraham (ca. eighteenth century BCE), or as late as the Buddha (sixth to fifth centuries BCE). Some ancient Greek sources even place him as far back as six thousand years before their own time! Scholars today debate whether he lived in the Kazakh steppes or the Tajik Pamirs, beyond the northeastern fringe of the Iranian world, whereas Zoroastrian texts place him far to the west in Azerbaijan. A few contemporary Kurdish nationalists, claiming their nation to be descended from the Medes, consider Zoroaster to be a "Kurdish" prophet.

Much of the confusion arises from the fact that once a kind of Zoroastrianism had spread throughout the Iranian world, priests in various parts of Iran concocted legends (or distorted existing ones) connecting the prophet with their own regions. Scholars such as Jean Kellens and P.O. Skjærvø have suggested that Zoroaster may be a composite character rather than a historical individual as such.[1] Others, notably Martin Schwartz, have attempted to prove Zoroaster's singular authorship through compositional analysis of the Gathic texts, arguing that their incredibly complex structure bears the mark of a unique personality.[2]

The heroic epic tradition, which arose as a sort of semi-mythological genealogy for local rulers in eastern Iran, wove in various strands of Zoroaster stories taken from diverse traditions. This process culminated in the tenth century with the poet Abo'l-Qasem Ferdowsi's version of the *Shāh-nāmeh* or "Book of Kings," often referred to as the Persian national epic. Priests who compiled or composed the Zoroastrian religious books during and after the Sasanian period (224–651 CE) selectively redacted their version of Iranian pre-history from the vast body of existing oral tradition—and possibly some lost texts as well—in accordance with their own particular agendas.

Most of what is reliably known about Zoroaster derives from philological analysis of the Zoroastrian sacred text, the Avesta. But while certain passages of this scripture are surely very archaic, the version available to us dates only as far back as the Sasanian period, many centuries after Zoroaster himself must have lived. Even more perplexing is the fact that the written sources of the great Persian Empires, Achæmenid (549–330 BCE) and Sasanian (224–651 CE) fail to mention him at all, whereas a number of Greek and other sources do.

For these, and other reasons, it is probably preferable to reserve the term "Zoroastrianism" for the religion adopted and codified by the Sasanian Iranian state from the third century CE. Iranian religiosity prior to that time must have differed considerably from one locality to another, with each local culture playing its own variations upon ancient Iranian themes and variously drawing in non-Iranian influences from neighboring peoples.

Certain developing notions, like the rising pre-eminence of Ahura Mazda and an increasingly sophisticated eschatology and soteriology, among other things, became widely present among dispersed Iranian societies throughout the first millennium BCE. Other beliefs and practices, such as particular hero cults, were more strictly local in nature, the hero-cult of Sīyāvaš in Bukhara being one example. The codification and state-enforced adoption of a specifically "Zoroastrian" faith in Sasanian times would appear to be a case of one form of Iranian devotion surging to prominence, mainly for political reasons, and using its powerful resources to push competing versions of Iranian religion into the margins. Since many Iranian groups, including not only the imperial Achæmenids but also the nomadic Sakas (Scythians), seem to have worshiped Ahura Mazda but not necessarily known of Zoroaster, some scholars have proposed referring to pre-Sasanian Iranian religion as "Mazdaism." After all, just because within a range of societies Mazda was venerated it need not be assumed that his worship was everywhere conducted in the way Zoroaster prescribed.

The oldest evidence for Zoroaster is found in the portions of the Avesta known as the Gathas, which modern Zoroastrians (as well as many scholars) consider to be the preserved words of Zoroaster himself. The language of these verses is archaic in the extreme, and very close to that of the Rig Veda. Like most ancient works of literature, including the epics of Homer and the Hebrew Bible, both of these texts were transmitted orally from one generation to the next over the course of many centuries before eventually being written down.

The language of sacred oral literature tends to change far more slowly than regular spoken dialects, if at all, and even in its original context may have represented a special, lofty form of speech rather than an idiom in which people ordinarily spoke. In the case of the Gathas, the absence of any other examples of the language in which they are preserved (except for the *Yasna Haptaŋhāiti*, discussed below) makes for very difficult comprehension, even after a lifetime of study. As a source for information about the life and times of Zoroaster, the Gathas leave much that is unclear or untold. Nevertheless, they do provide a kind of rough portrait that can be compared with other evidence such as the rest of the Avesta, Greek sources, and the later Zoroastrian books of Sasanian times.

The name Zaraθuštra—"Zoroaster" being derived from a form used by the ancient Greeks, Ζωροάστρης—probably meant something like "camel-manager," which gives some clue about the man and the kind of society he lived in. The Gathas depict a pastoral but settled form of society and a geography compatible with the steppes of Inner Asia. The dialects of the Avesta, both that of the Gatha verses and of most of the remainder, called the *Younger Avesta*, are very closely related, but distinct from those of the Median, Achæmenid, and Parthian languages of western Iran. The Younger Avesta contains a number of identifiable place names which have been located within the general area of eastern Iran, but the Gathas seem to be set further north. This may be due to the southward movement of the proto-Iranians throughout the second millennium BCE.

Early Greek accounts describe Zoroaster as having lived more than six thousand years before their own time, but this is unlikely. On the basis of linguistic evidence, for the most part, Mary Boyce posited a range of dates for Zoroaster during the second millennium BCE. Gherardo Gnoli, meanwhile, having reviewed Boyce's and other arguments, concluded that the Zoroastrians' traditional reference point, situating him "258 years prior to Alexander" is basically valid.[3] Gnoli argued for a set of dates earlier posited by Boyce's teacher, W.B. Henning, placing Zoroaster's lifetime from 618–541 BCE, but most other scholars consider this too late. The archaic nature of the Avestan language and its similarities to that of the Rig Veda, as well as the social and ecological environment it describes, would suggest a date somewhere between these two extremes, but not much later than 1000 BCE.

At present, it must be conceded that questions about Zoroaster's time and homeland have still not been definitively resolved. Nor is there any evidence that can suggest when and by what means Zoroaster's teaching was transmitted from the eastern Iranian world to the western regions which gave rise to the great Iranian empires; all we can say with certainty is that, somehow, sometime, it was.

Zoroaster was a member of the priestly class of *zaotar*s, living at a time when his society was undergoing internal tension and change. Apparently certain elements among the Aryans were inclining more toward the raiding aspect of their mixed pastoral economy, living by theft in preference to pasturing. (This may have been fostered by the development of the war chariot and bronze weapons; in Inner Asia both these technologies arose during the first part of the second millennium BCE.) The resulting violence and chaos would have seemed to some, Zoroaster included, as an indication that *aša* (order) was giving way to *drūj* (chaos). Yet in the minds of others, no doubt, taking livestock from undeserving inferiors was a moral imperative. In the Rig Veda, for example, brave Aryan warriors, supported by Indra, take great pride in their ability to steal from the hapless natives of South Asia, to whom they refer by the derisive term *dāsa*s ("servants," or "slaves").

## ZOROASTER'S "REFORM"

Beginning with the German Sanskritist and theologian Martin Haug in the mid-nineteenth century, some European scholars of the Avesta sought to characterize Zoroaster as a monotheistic reformer of the pre-existing polytheistic Iranian religion. They invite us to imagine the moral indignation and outrage of a conscientious priest surrounded by soma-intoxicated partiers revelling in the bloodbath of a cow sacrifice. Yasna 29 in the Avesta, they suggest, evokes a situation in which the champions of injustice had thrown the cosmic balance into a hopeless state of disorder, causing unwarranted suffering to man and beast alike:

> The Soul of the Cow lamented to you: For whom have you determined me? Who fashioned me? Wrath and Violence, Harm, Daring, and Brutality [each] have bound me! I have no other pastor than you—so appear to me with good husbandry!

> Then the Fashioner of the Cow asked Aša: Hast thou a *ratu* (priest) for the Cow such that you are able to give him, together with a herdsman, zeal for fostering the Cow? Whom do you want as a lord for her, who, hostile toward Liars, may repel Wrath?

> Mazda is most mindful of the declarations (*varuna*s) which have been made previously by *daēva*s and men and those which shall be made afterward, [for] he is the decisive Lord. Thus may it be for us as he may will!

> Thus we are both calling out to the Lord with outstretched hands, my [soul] and the Soul of the pregnant Cow, in order that we may address Mazda with questions. [For as matters now

stand] there is no possibility of continuing life for the righteously living husbandman [residing] among Liars.

Then Ahura Mazda, knowing, spoke [these] words through his life-breath: Not one [of us] has found an *ahu* (powerful man), not even a *ratu* in accordance with Truth. So, indeed, the Artificer fashioned thee for the husbandman and the herdsman.

Ahura Mazda, in agreement with Aša, fashioned the *manθra* of [something from] butter and [also] milk for the Cow, he [who] through [his] commandment is beneficial for those who are undernourished. Whom dost thou have [for us] through Good Mind (Vohu Manah), who will give us two to men?

Here I have found this one who alone listens to our commandments, Zarathushtra the Spitamid. He wants, O Mazda, to recite hymns of praise for us and Aša, if I should bestow on him sweetness of speech.

The Soul of the Cow lamented: Must I suffer a powerless caretaker—the speech of a man without strength—whom I wish to be a powerful ruler? When ever shall he come to exist who can give him a helping hand?

O Lord, may you [*ahura*s] give power and dominion (*xšaθra*) to them, that [dominion] through Vohu Manah by which he might grant good living and peace. I, in any case, consider Thee, O Mazda, to be the original possessor of this.

Where are Aša and Vohu Manah and Khšathra? Now you should accept me, through Aša, O Mazda, for [giving] instruction to the great community. O Lord, [come] now to us [here] below on account of our liberality to such as you.[4]

In terms of the ancient Iranian religion outlined in Chapter 1, one can detect much in this passage that appears revolutionary. Most significant is that the *ahura* called "Mazda" is elevated here above all other deities. He is "the decisive Lord," whose judgments are binding upon gods and humans alike. *Daēva*s and men are to be mindful that he (and not, for example, Mithra or Varuna) is the force which will hold them accountable for their oaths and covenants. It is through his commandment that the undernourished receive their sustenance. He is "the original possessor" of "power and dominion (*xšaθra*)," which are to be used not for oppression but for the maintenance of "good living and peace." All other divine forces and qualities, including "Good Mind" and even Truth itself, are only instruments of his will.

Whereas in prior Iranian cosmology creative agency was dispersed or unattributed, this role is said now to belong to Ahura Mazda. The all-powerful Creator, he is the proper focus of devotion and supplication.

Avesta scholars who consider monotheism to be one of the major innovations in the history of religious thought therefore insist that the Israelites and the Iranians must share the credit (or the blame?) for its conceptualization three thousand years or more ago.

The passage above is also remarkable in that it establishes a unique role for a single individual, Zoroaster. In a world given over to violent champions of the Lie, he is the only one who listens to Ahura Mazda's commandments; it is he who has been appointed to "give instruction to the great community," even though his power is that of words alone, since he is "a powerless caretaker . . . a man without strength." There is also a foreshadowing here of Zoroaster's fate, that of a prophet ignored in his own country, since the one "who can give him a helping hand" will be the distant chieftain Vištaspa, and not one of Zoroaster's own tribe.

In perceiving Ahura Mazda as the Creator force, Zoroaster also attributed a purposefulness to Creation which was apparently not present in earlier Iranian thought. Zoroaster's ethics emphasized human choice: both good and bad (conceptualized as *aša* and *drūj*) existed in the world, and it was up to the individual to take a position and actively embrace one or the other. The world then was properly understood as a stage on which this human drama would be played out.

This thinking in turn implied a much stronger eschatology than that of the then-existing worldview inherited from the Proto-Indo-Europeans. While the usual conception of time in ancient human societies was cyclical, Zoroastrianism sees it as a linear progression heading toward a great culminating event. The universe is conceived as a battleground for an ongoing struggle between the forces of good and evil, a struggle in which each individual human being must take a side. The final resolution will come at the end of time in a great battle, called *Frašō-kərəti* (literally, the "making glorious"), in which good will ultimately prevail. This eschatology is unclear in the Gathas, and likely took shape during the period between the composition of the older and younger parts of the Avesta between 1000 and 600 BCE.

Against this backdrop of cosmic conflict Zoroaster is said to have refined his society's conception of supernatural beings in terms of which side they were on. The *daēva*s, popular among the warrior class, came to be seen as being on the side of evil, giving rise to the notion of demons. Beneficent spirits, which the Avesta refers to as *yazata*s, literally "beings worthy of sacrifice," became the model for what later societies would identify as angels. Zoroaster seems to have been the first of the world's major religious thinkers to posit a self-existent evil deity. Called Aŋra Mainyu—"the hostile spirit"—in the Gathas (Y 45.2), and Ahriman in later sources, this evil god is the basis for the figure Semitic peoples would later call Satan.

Another significant innovation attributed to Zoroaster is an elaboration on the ultimate fate of individuals as a result of the choices they make during their lives. Zoroaster is claimed to have been the first to fully articulate the notion of a posthumous judgment, where each person's good deeds would be weighed against their evil ones,[5] following which the good people (*ašavān*) would ascend to the heavenly realm presided over by Ahura Mazda while the evildoers (*drūgvant*) would descend to a hell of suffering ruled by Aŋra Mainyu. This judgment occurred at Mount Hara on the fourth day after death; the deceased would then cross a bridge, called Činvat. For the *ašavān*, the bridge would grow wide and easy to cross, whereas for the *drūgvant* it would become as narrow as a blade. The good would be met along the way by a beautiful female spirit, Daēnā, a reflection of their own inner goodness, who would accompany them to heaven. (Daēnā, originally a personification of individual character, much later evolves into the simple abstract notion of religion itself, MP. *dēn*, Ar. *dīn*). Wrongdoers, on the other hand, would find a horrible, smelly hag, in whose embrace they would plunge over the edge into the gaping mouth of hell.

The belief in an ultimate bodily resurrection (*rastaxīz*) has also been attributed to Zoroastrianism. This would occur after the final defeat of the forces of evil by those of good at the end of time. All beings, good and bad, will have to pass through a river of fire; the good will be saved by the *yazata*s, while the bad will be utterly destroyed, and thus will evil be banished from the world once and for all. The earth will blossom and the good will live forever in Mazda's divine kingdom. It is not clear whether the belief in an eschatological saviour figure, known in Zoroastrian texts as the Saošyant, dates from Zoroaster's time or later.[6] Eventually the belief emerged that the Saošyant would be born of Zoroaster's own seed, miraculously preserved in a lake in which a future virgin would bathe and become impregnated.

The Gathas indicate that Zoroaster was rejected by his original community. He is said to have found a home among another group of Iranians some distance away, where he converted a chieftain by the name of Vištaspa after first winning over the ruler's wife to his new teaching. (It is an interesting pattern in the spread of religions that religious teachers often have their greatest successes with royal womenfolk. Perhaps aristocratic women had more time on their hands to devote to their intellectual and spiritual curiosity? It is impossible to say.)

With Vištaspa's support and patronage Zoroaster spent the rest of his reportedly long life training followers in "the Mazda-worshiping religion" and sent missionaries to preach his message far and wide. Presumably this activity was carried out mainly among neighboring Iranian groups, although one sees later echoes of Zoroastrian concepts among non-Iranians as far afield as Asia Minor and even China.

Apparently Zoroaster's ideas were often seen as a threat, since there are hints, in the Avesta and elsewhere, of his missionaries being persecuted and even killed. The same sources state that such persecutions only strengthened the resolve of Zoroaster's followers, and that their steadfast example inspired many others to join the faith. Though there may be an element of propaganda in this, the fact that eventually many Iranian tribes came to adopt at least some forms of Zoroaster's teaching shows that his ideas were ultimately spread successfully.

It should be noted that in the context of the ancient world the very notion of religious proselytizing was uncommon or even absent altogether, and to most people would probably have seemed highly unnatural. What we think of today as "religion" was not perceived as something apart from the general culture of a community. People likely would not have thought in terms of one religion (or culture) being "truer" or less so than another, but simply *different*, and one's adherence would be unquestioningly to the norms of one's own group. What one "believed" was of far less importance than what one *did*. Against this backdrop, the emphasis on "correct" belief and on personal choice and responsibility attributed to Zoroaster would have been quite revolutionary.

## THE AVESTA AND ITS TRANSMISSION[7]

The conclusions reflected in the preceding overview are not without their problems. Indeed, the portrayal of Zoroaster and his teaching provided in the summary above largely took shape in the nineteenth century under the influence of European scholars, and reflect a rather "Protestant" approach to sacred texts. Zoroastrians themselves—specifically the priests who were the Avesta's custodians—apparently understood the text poorly or not at all, a situation which demonstrably goes back at least to Sasanian times.

The Avesta is not, properly speaking, a text but rather an assemblage of texts, selected and preserved according to organizing principles we cannot hope to understand. As noted above, its various components clearly originate from different places and times, as proven by linguistic analysis. In the mid-nineteenth century, Haug noted that the Avestan texts were composed in two related but distinct languages, one several centuries older than the other. This older portion, which consists of the verse Gathas and the prose *Yasna Haptaŋhāiti* (the "Seven-part Sacrifice"), Haug attributed to Zoroaster. The older texts he construed as monotheistic, whereas the portions known as the Younger Avesta are devoted to a range of deities, thus posing a problem for those who see Zoroaster's monotheism as an "advancement" over a pre-existing polytheism. Did later generations of Zoroastrians "backslide" into polytheism, or do the liturgies of the Younger Avesta represent a stubborn refusal to abandon the ancient gods they held dear? A third possibility, of course, is that the two sets of texts actually represent parallel traditions which were brought together later.

In fact, the field of historical linguistics has made such strides over the past century that the interpretations of earlier scholars have now been dismissed almost in their entirety. Moreover, the first translations of the Avesta into European languages were made by scholars who began with assumptions that are for the most part no longer held. For example, Christian Bartholomae titled his 1905 translation of the Gathas *Sermons of Zoroaster*, suggesting that they were intended for a human audience, whereas subsequent translators have considered them to be hymns, meant for divine rather than human ears.

The implications for such highly divergent interpretations of the Gathas' content are obvious. A century ago scholars assumed that they contained at least the following elements: 1) A radical monotheism in which a whole class of Indo-Iranian deities, the *daēvas*, was demoted to demonic status, 2) a condemnation of the *haoma* ritual, 3) a prohibition of animal sacrifice, and 4) a description of the afterlife. Of these four essential principles, the first and the fourth have been considerably nuanced by recent scholarship, and the second and third argued to be almost without basis.

Historical linguistics has also demonstrated (through the identification of grammatical mistakes and confused commentaries) that the Avestan corpus was preserved, transmitted, and eventually written down by people who did not fully understand it. But we should remember that an emphasis on literal comprehension is a distinctly modernist preoccupation. The historical custodians of the Avesta were more concerned with function—specifically, the performance of rituals—than with meaning.

As with any liturgical text, the important thing in reciting the Avesta was to recite it *correctly*, so as to ensure that the ritual would have the desired result. Any mistake in recitation would jeopardize this outcome. Thus, when the decision was eventually made by a group of priests to finally write down this body of material that had been passed on orally for centuries, they devised one of the most phonetically exact alphabets ever known to humankind, consisting of no fewer than fifty-two letters! This occurred very late in the history of the Avesta's transmission, however, no earlier than the sixth century CE.[8]

The Avesta we possess today was first edited during the mid- and late nineteenth century by N. L. Westergaard and then Karl Friedrich Geldner, based on manuscripts collected from Zoroastrian priests in India and Iran. The oldest of these manuscripts is not in fact very old, dating to 1323. That manuscript was copied from an earlier one dating to the year 1020. The oldest existing written fragment of the Avesta—a Sogdian translation of the *Ašəm Vohu* prayer—dates to the century before that.[9] In other words, something like two millennia separate the oldest physical sample of the Avesta we have from the time it was originally composed. Moreover, the sum total of surviving Avestan texts consists of five books, whereas a Zoroastrian compendium known as the *Dēnkard*, completed in the year 870, describes twenty-one volumes (called *nasks*) which are claimed to have constituted the Avesta in Sasanian times.[10] The "lost" *nasks* are assumed to have vanished during the intervening 150 years, possibly in connection with the migration of significant numbers of Zoroastrians from Iran to India.

On the other hand, Jean Kellens believes that even the Avestan fragments we now possess are not after all "survivals" of the complete Sasanian version, as most scholars have long assumed. Rather, he believes that the Sasanian Avesta has been *completely* lost, and that the existing version is descended from a parallel tradition dating back to Achæmenid times. For Kellens, the Avesta we have is not the fragmented remains of a lost whole, but a complete and coherent collection of its own, which survived intact precisely because it was constantly in use as the liturgy performed by the priests.[11]

## ZOROASTRIAN PRACTICE

The main ritual practice enjoined of Zoroastrians is to pray five times a day. To the traditional three daily devotions of the Aryans, Zoroastrianism added prayers at dawn and at midnight. The devotee of Ahura Mazda was always to pray standing in the presence of fire, either the sun or the sacred hearth. The ancient Aryan sacred cord, which boys received at puberty (a tradition found also in the Vedas), was to be tied and untied around the waist at every prayer. Zoroastrianism extended this formerly male-only custom to women as well.

Within each Zoroastrian household one member was responsible for maintaining the sacred fire, which must never be allowed to go out. This became the most visible identification of Zoroastrians to outside observers such as the ancient Greeks. After the Arab conquests of the seventh century CE, Muslim writers derisively—and inaccurately—referred to Zoroastrians as "fire-worshipers."

Zoroastrians were to show reverence and gratitude to all of natural creation, and strive always to maintain its purity, since everything in nature is indwelt with its own *mainyu*. Water sources especially were to be scrupulously protected, as was the sanctity of the soil. Since dead bodies were seen as polluting, Zoroastrians eventually abandoned the practice of burial in favor of exposure in *dakhme*s (known in India as "towers of silence"), leaving corpses to be picked clean by vultures and the bones bleached pure by the sun.

For priests the daily rituals were elaborate and time-consuming. They were to recite all five Gathas every morning, along with a modified version of the ancient *yasna* sacrifice, using both animals and the plant-based substance known as *haoma*. Whereas formerly priests had extemporized the sacrificial formulas within certain patterns, Zoroaster, or priests roughly contemporary with him, set down the seven-part liturgy known as the *Yasna haptaŋhāiti*. (The hymns of the Younger Avesta may represent survivals of the older improvisatory tradition.)

The formal liturgy begins with the intention to practice "good thoughts, good words, and good deeds"—the threefold essence of Zoroastrian ethics. Mazda is then worshiped, along with four of the six other "good" *mainyu*s (called the *Aməša spənta*s, "Bounteous Immortals") which in the Zoroastrian reform were believed to emanate from him: Aša Vahišta (best truth), Vohu Manah (good mind), Xšaθra (power), and Armaiti (conformity to proper thought). The two others included in the divine heptad, Haurvatat (health, wholeness) and Aməretat (immortality), for some reason do not figure in the Seven-part Sacrifice. Scholars continue to debate whether the *Aməša spənta*s represent deities that came to be subordinated to Ahura Mazda, or should be interpreted as mere aspects of his divine character, or are deifications of previously existing abstract notions.

The most important feast day of the Zoroastrian calendar was held at the spring equinox, which marked the New Year. This occasion, called Nō rūz ("New Day"), is still celebrated by Iranians and by many neighboring peoples as well. It is a very old festival indeed, probably dating back into remote prehistory, but most likely originated in Babylonia rather than among Iranian peoples. (It is not mentioned in the Avesta.) In Zoroastrianism its symbolism of renewal was extended to include not only the resurgence of life every spring, but also to foreshadow the glorious future renewal of *Frašō-kərəti* when evil would be forever overthrown. The annual festival has long been one of the most joyous occasions of the year for Iranians and remains so today.

The Young Avesta further identifies six more festivals connected with the agricultural year—combined with Nō rūz, making seven altogether— which were celebrated by Zoroastrians from the earliest times. These seven holy days mirrored the seven aspects of the godhead expressed through Ahura Mazda and the *Aməša spənta*s, as well as the seven stages of original creation. Zoroastrians considered failure to observe each of these seven feast days to be a sin.

Along with Nō rūz, Zoroastrianism absorbed and redefined a number of other ancient festivals, just as other religions such as Christianity would do later. The result was sometimes slightly awkward, as in the case of an annual "all souls" ritual on the last night of the year. This appears to be of Indo-European origin, sharing its genealogy with Halloween in Anglo-American tradition. There may have been some tensions connected with continuing to observe this ritual, and at the very least Zoroastrians were reminded to make offerings only to the departed souls (*fravašis*) of those who had been good (*ašavān*). Over time the old ancestor cult seems to have crept back in, since the worship of *fravašis* reappears in the later tradition.

Further persistence of religious rites "by popular demand" is evidenced in the Yašts of the Young Avesta. The Yašts, which are devotions directed toward a wide range of deities, were composed by priests. Since priests earned their living by performing specific rites at the request of lay patrons—for success, for children, for a good harvest, or whatever—it can be imagined that the content and focus of the Yašts mainly represents an accommodation to the desires of the patrons and not necessarily those of the priests. As a result, the divine landscape of "beings worthy of worship" (*yazatas*) portrayed by the Yašts is considerably more "polytheistic" than that of the Mazda-focused Gathas.

Zoroastrian priests also composed a set of purity regulations, called the *Vīdēvdāt*, literally, "Laws Keeping Away the Demons (*daēvas*)." Best known by its later name, the Vendidād, this compilation contains extensive instructions on maintaining the purity of earth, fire and water. It prescribes capital punishment for anyone polluting a sacred fire, and advocates the killing of creatures believed to be "demonic," including insects, scorpions, and snakes, collectively known as *xrafstra*, which were seen as doing the evil work of Aŋra Mainyu.

The practice of consanguineous marriage, noted by the ancient Greeks and later ridiculed by the Jews, Christians, and Muslims, is held up as a virtuous deed in the Zoroastrian texts. Consanguineous marriages are no longer practiced today, but among Iranians of all religions there remains a preference for unions between first cousins.

# 4

# Mazda and His Rivals

The oldest concrete evidence for the worship of Ahura Mazda (lit., "the god who puts [everything] into the mind") dates back to the Achæmenid period, where mention of the deity first appears in the Behistun inscriptions ordered by Darius I (reigned 522–486 BCE).[1] The cult of Mazda must have existed much earlier, however; the existence of a cognate term in Vedic Sanskrit, *medhā*, suggests a proto-Indo-Iranian origin.

The worship of Mazda as a deity superior to all others is characteristic of the ancient texts known as the Gathas, attributed to Zoroaster. As noted in the preceding chapter, while linguistic analysis would date the Gathas to as early as the second millennium BCE, surviving written copies are much later, and the text itself presents so many problems of interpretation that drawing any clear picture of how Mazda was understood and worshiped (and how widely) prior to the Sasanian period (224–651 CE) is all but impossible. Moreover, the abundance of evidence for worship of other deities throughout the ancient Iranian world shows that the Mazda cult was one of many. It is not until Sasanian times that the dominance of a uniquely Mazda-centered religion becomes convincingly demonstrable, and even then the story is that of an ongoing struggle between its official custodians, the *mobed*s or Magi, and the partisans of rival religious expressions.

In their own writings the magi referred to their faith as *daēnā māzdayasniš*, the "religion of those who sacrifice to Mazda,"[2] or alternately as *veh-dīn*, the "Good Religion." They sometimes described themselves as *zaraθuštri*—as in the well-known "profession of faith" referred to as the *fravarānē* (Y 12.1)—but this should perhaps best be understood in the sense of claiming to follow Zoroaster's prescriptions in sacrificing to this particular god. The habit of calling the Mazda-sacrificers' religion "Zoroastrianism" comes much later, following its discovery by European scholars of the eighteenth century and after. Set against the backdrop of European colonialism and the Christian missionary effort, this designation appears misleading, perhaps deliberately so. The Mazda-worshiping Parsis of India, in particular, were put on the defensive in debates with the missionaries, and both welcomed and fostered conceptualizations of their religion which mirrored the schema laid down by Christianity.

Such pressures resulted in a similar degree of reconfiguration among proponents of indigenous Indian traditions, resulting in the creation of a composite tradition called "Hinduism." In both cases the religions of India's natives became reified, with their respective histories being reinterpreted according to the Christian model. For the Parsis, this project offered the benefit of being able to claim a prophet as old as Moses, as well as the more dubious claim to have invented monotheism. However, if one abandons the assumption that latter-day expressions of a religion are necessarily reflections of its earlier forms, a very different picture often emerges.

## RELIGION UNDER THE ACHÆMENIDS

The first group of western Iranians to win mention in written sources of the Near East is the Medes, who were based in what is now north-central Iran south of the Alborz Mountains. By the eighth century BCE it is likely that a group of Median priests (but not necessarily all of them) had been won over to some form of Zoroastrian practice absorbed from the east, albeit one incorporating many local variations. During the mid-sixth century BCE, Median power was overthrown by an army led by Cyrus II, ruler of the kingdom of Anshan to the south. The ethnic mix of this region included Iranians, Elamites, and others, and while it is debated today whether Cyrus "the Great" was himself Iranian or Elamite,[3] by the time of Darius I's accession in 522 the new imperial house, claiming descent from an ancestor named Achæmenes (Haxāmaniš) clearly defined itself as "Persian" (*pārsa*).

The Achæmenid sources are cuneiform inscriptions, usually in a western Iranian dialect known as Old Persian—the direct ancestor of the modern Persian language. They are mainly in the form of royal decrees, declarations, and memorials, so the information they provide is somewhat limited. Although they nowhere mention Zoroaster, they do make frequent reference to Ahura Mazda and the "Mazda-sacrificing religion," which at least some of the Achæmenid rulers, beginning with Darius I, used as an ideological tool to underpin the legitimacy of their conquests. Enemies, especially other Iranian tribes, are disparaged for not sacrificing to Mazda, and occasionally the Achæmenids boast of having destroyed temples devoted to "*daēva*s." Although the Old Persian texts are political rather than religious in nature, Skjærvø sees certain aspects of Darius' proclamations as mirroring Avestan notions.[4]

It should be noted that references to Mazda in royal inscriptions should be taken primarily in a political sense as referring to the patron deity of the ruling class, since throughout the Achæmenid period the Persian government subsidized the cults of a wide range of deities, mainly Iranian and Elamite. Records of expenditures on religious rituals from the Persepolis fortification tablets (509–494 BCE) mention offerings to the Iranian deities Visai Baga, Drva, Haurira, Naryasanga, Ardanafravartiš, Spentaragardya, Mizhdušiš, and Bartakamya, as well as to the spirits of mountains and rivers and to the Elamite deities Humban and Napiriša. Among all the ceremonies thus recorded, only ten are stated to have been in honour of Ahura Mazda.[5] This curious hodgepodge has inspired the Dutch scholar Wouter Henkelman to observe that the religion of the Achæmenids was, as elsewhere in the ancient world, a hybrid of the cults of the conquerors and the conquered: in the Persian case, " . . . the heterogeneous unity of religious beliefs and cultic practices that emerged from a long Elamite–Iranian co-existence and that were considered as native by the inhabitants of Achæmenid Fars and its rulers."[6]

Around the time of Artaxerxes II (404–359 BCE) the royal inscriptions begin to mention Anahita, goddess of the waters (who had become conflated with the Babylonian Ištar, identified with Aphrodite of the Greeks and later Nanai among the Sogdians of Central Asia), alongside Ahura Mazda and Mithra. Indicative perhaps of Greek influence, Anahita is the first deity whom the Persians represented in statues.

The Greek sources give the most detailed information about religion in Achæmenid times. Since the Persians were the main rivals to Greek power in the eastern Mediterranean region, the Greeks were very interested in learning about the culture of their opponents. Greek travelers to the Iranian world, such as Herodotus, were at least on some level acting as spies, gone to report on the enemy. Interestingly, unlike the royal Achæmenid inscriptions, the Greek sources do mention Zoroaster as the most important Persian religious teacher-philosopher; one explanation for this discrepancy could be that Greek writers received their information from ordinary human informants rather than from royal inscriptions.

Cosmic dualism may have made its way into Greek thought via Iranian influence during the Achæmenid period, perhaps later appearing in Gnosticism. According to Aristoxenos (lived around 335 BCE), Pythagoras was a student of a Persian sage named "Zaratos."[7] The latter name is presumably a Hellenification of Zaraθuštra; however, given the unlikelihood of the well-known Greek and Persian thinkers actually meeting, the story is probably either apocryphal or refers to another Persian bearing Zoroaster's name. The latter scenario is not at all implausible, but one should also consider that it was popular among the Greeks (as later among the Jews) to attribute "ancient wisdom" to the Persians, thereby giving their ideas an exotic flair.

Herodotus states that in his time the Persians did not build temples to their gods, but performed their sacrifices "on every mountaintop" throughout the land. Eventually, around the middle of the fourth century BCE, the Persians adopted the habit of building sacred shrines, presumably through the influence of their Babylonian and other Near Eastern neighbors. Most were in the form of mountaintop "fire temples" (*ātaš-gāh*), though some were lavish buildings endowed and supported by the elites. Even today when travelling through Iran, it is possible to see the remains of these structures all over the country, if one knows what to look for.

## THE GREEK INTERLUDE

After two centuries of struggle against their Persian rivals it was the turn of the Greeks to prevail in their long contest for control over western Asia. In 332 BCE Alexander of Macedon led his army into Persepolis, the ceremonial capital of the Achæmenids near modern Shiraz, and burned it almost to the ground. For the next two centuries the bulk of Iranian territory, from the Mesopotamian plain to the borders of northwestern India, was under a Greek administration—known as the "Seleucid" dynasty, after one of Alexander's generals—which fostered the spread of Hellenistic culture throughout the Semitic and Iranian lands.

Wherever they went, Greek armies built cities on the pattern of the Greek *polis*, complete with theatres, *agora*s (marketplaces), and temples to the Greek gods. These garrison towns were usually constructed adjacent to existing ones, so that the Iranian world became a mosaic of twin cities. (The Russians and British did the same when they moved, respectively, into Central Asia and India during the nineteenth century.) Excavations in the Oxus River region have turned up evidence of a curious Greek–Iranian religious and cultural synthesis. Greek deities were identified with Iranian ones (Zeus with Ahura Mazda, Aphrodite with Anahita, and Apollo with Mithra, for example), and in some cases, such as at Taxt-e Sangīn in southern Tajikistan, Greeks and Iranians both worshiped their own gods in separate sections of the same temple. The practice evolved of representing Iranian deities in the Greek style, for example on coins. Greek–Iranian sites in western Iran include a shrine to Heracles/Vərəθraγna at Behistun, dated to 147 BCE, and a temple in Kurdistan at which both Artemis and Anahita were worshiped.

## THE PARTHIANS

Eventually Iran's Greek rulers were overthrown by an indigenous tribe, the Parni, who established a power base in northeastern Iran (including what is now southern Turkmenistan). The *Aškānī* or Arsacid dynasty, known in the West as the Parthians, would hold sway for almost four centuries, through the peak period of Roman empire-building. Indeed, it was the Parthians who halted that expansion to the East, blinding the Roman legions with their huge silk banners shimmering in the sunlight and antagonizing them with feigned cavalry retreats followed by volleys of over-the-shoulder arrows—the famed "Parthian shot."

Parthian rule was less centralized than that of either the Achæmenids before them or the Sasanians who came after. And unlike the other two empires that were based in Persia—that is, the southwestern part of the Iranian world, on the fringes of Mesopotamia—the Parthians were centered in the northeast and thus more remote from the Semitic world. The Parthians left almost no records of their own apart from coins, so it is difficult to know much about their religious beliefs and practices. From onomastic and other evidence it would appear that Mithra was the principal deity among the important ruling families, but a wide range of cults existed throughout their empire. In matters of religion the Parthians seem to have been largely indifferent, allowing their various subject peoples to carry on as they like, provided of course that they paid their taxes.

The decentralized policy of the Parthians meant that no one priestly group could exercise any kind of widespread authority. Even among followers of the Avestan tradition there were different schools, each with their own approach and variants of the sacred oral liturgy. The later Zoroastrian tradition implicitly confirms this through its historical narrative of the foundation of the Sasanian Empire, in which the Mazdaean priests apparently played an important role.

## THE SASANIAN STATE RELIGION

Five hundred years after the fall of the Achæmenids, the Persians of the southwest once again rose to prominence under the leadership of Artaxšaθra Pāpakān (died 242 CE), known as Ardeshir I, whose family's status as caretakers of an important shrine to the goddess Anahita enabled him to raise an army against the Parthians. After years of resistance to Parthian overlordship, Ardeshir defeated his former masters once and for all in 226, establishing a new dynasty that would be known as the Sasanids (after a purported ancestor, Sāsān). Anahita would remain the patron deity of the Sasanians throughout their four hundred year reign.

At first the Sasanian administration maintained the cultural policy of their Parthian predecessors, allowing their diverse subjects freedom in religious matters. Shortly, however, egged on perhaps by the Mazdaean priests seeking to centralize their own power, the Sasanian emperor began authorizing the destruction of cult statues all over Iran and their replacement with sacred fires. The three greatest fires—Adur Burzīn-Mehr in Parthia, Adur Gušnasp in Media, and Adur Farnbag in Pars—had probably been burning since Achæmenid times, but their shrines were greatly built up during the early Sasanian period. Purportedly at the instigation of his court priests, led by Tansar, Ardeshir is also said to have called for the collection of religious teachings from throughout the empire, in an attempt to codify a state religion by allowing his priestly entourage to decide which versions would be allowed and which suppressed.

Thus, from its very origins the consolidation of political power by the Sasanian state was intertwined with that of religious authority by the Mazdaean priests. Under Ardeshir the earlier Parthian policies of separating church and state appear to have been formally rejected. The Muslim historian Mas'udi, writing several centuries later, attributes to Ardeshir the following statement:

> Religion is the foundation of kingship, and kingship is the protector [of religion]. For whatever lacks a foundation must perish, and whatever lacks a protector disappears.[8]

This privileging of a particular class of religious leaders foreshadowed what would occur with Christianity in the Byzantine Empire during the following century. In Iran, however, the rise to power of the Mazdean clergy suffered a setback under Ardeshir's successor Shapur I (reigned 242–272 CE). Early in his reign Shapur received at court a religious figure of Parthian origin by the name of Mani, whose eclectic teaching allowed him to present himself as a Zoroastrian, a Christian, or a Buddhist, depending on his target audience. Mani won the sympathy and support of the emperor and several of his close relatives, and reciprocated by composing a religious text, the *Šābūragān*, in honour of the Sasanian ruler.

Mani's influence at court alarmed the Mazdaean priests. Their leader, Kerdir, spent years intriguing against his rival, but to no avail. Finally Kerdir and his contingent were able to engineer a palace coup following Shapur's death in 272, eliminating his pro-Mani successor, Hormizd I (possibly by having him poisoned) and replacing him with Vahram I. The new king promptly obliged his priestly patrons by having Mani thrown in prison and tortured to death.

Thus, the beginnings of the Mazdaean priesthood's iron grip on religious authority in the Sasanian period really began in the last quarter of the third century, under Vahram's patronage. But there were other threats as well: Christianity had won many converts in Iranian territory, fueled by the immigration of Christians fleeing persecution in the Roman lands and the forced transfer of Christian populations from conquered Roman territories. Kerdir campaigned vigorously against these and other foreign religions being practiced in Iranian lands, including Judaism, Mandaeism, Buddhism, and Brahmanism.

In the end the Mazdaean priesthood, under Kerdir's leadership, managed to win for their faith the status of official religion of the Sasanian state. Thus empowered, they sent their representatives throughout the realm to enforce their own religious policies. At first these seem to have centered mainly on rituals associated with fire, water, the sun and moon, and cattle.

Later, probably under Shapur II, the magi began writing down the sacred prayers and formulas that had been passed down orally since Zoroaster's time. The written form of the Avesta, including its Middle Persian translation and commentary called the *Zand*, dates from around the sixth century CE. This was the formal beginning of the Zoroastrian textual tradition. While some of these previously oral texts, such as the Gathas, were surely very old, there was no real way to know the true origins of most of what would become a vast body of sacred literature.

Among the rituals practiced during the Sasanian period, A. S. Melikian-Chirvani has cited wine libations, which at some earlier point had become a sublimation (as in the Christian Eucharist) of sacrifices originally performed with blood. "From the earliest times," he speculates:

> Persian literature echoes the ceremonial in which the wine would be poured out of animal-shaped vessels into crescent-shaped wine cups. Just as the wine was seen as liquid sunlight, red like sunset light, or liquid fire standing for sunlight, the crescent wine cups symbolized the moon. When filled with the "body" of the sun, they signified the conjunction of the sun and the moon.[9]

Although the significance in this regard of bull-shaped vessels is fairly obvious, far more preponderant is the occurrence of wine jugs shaped as ducks and other birds. The association of ducks with wine recurs later in Persian Sufi poetry.

With the establishment of Mazdaism as state church of the Sasanian regime, the mutual reliance of politicians and priests was likewise institutionalized. Nevertheless, over the subsequent three and a half centuries of Sasanian rule, official attitudes toward religious orthodoxy varied depending on the moods of the emperor and changing political conditions. Perhaps the least tolerant of all the Sasanian emperors was Shapur II (reigned 309–377). According to a later Zoroastrian text, the *Dēnkard*, early in his reign Shapur called together a consultation of representatives from the various religions present in his realm. At this event the primacy of the Mazdaean priests was confirmed. Shapur is reported to have declared, "Now that we have seen the faith as it truly is, we shall not tolerate anyone of false religion, and we shall be exceedingly zealous."[10] As indeed the record shows that he was.

Nevertheless, evidence from various Pahlavi sources suggests that non-orthodox forms of Iranian religion—referred to dismissively as *dēvāsnīh*, or "demon worship"—continued to be practiced throughout the Sasanian period. The following passage from the *Dēnkard* purports to describe the devotions of one such sect:

> The perverted, devilish, unrighteous rite of the "mystery of the sorcerers (*yātūkān*)" consists in praising Ahriman, the destroyer, in prowling around in great secrecy, in keeping home, body, and clothes in a state of filthiness and stench, in smearing the body with dead matter and excrement, in causing discomfort to the gods and joy to the demons, in chanting services to the demons and calling on them by name as befits their activity, in the worship of the demons and false religion, in thinking in accordance with the Evil Mind, in false speech and unrighteous action—the disreputable sorcerers and villains—and in all else that befits the devilish and is far from the godly.[11]

R. C. Zaehner points out the "remarkable fact that the doctrine of the 'sorcerers' of the Avesta and Pahlavi books agrees in many respects with that ascribed to the Magians by many Greek and Latin writers."[12] In other words, the version of Iranian religion best known to Iran's western neighbors was apparently not the form canonized in Zoroastrian texts. Zaehner also notes that Pahlavi polemics use the word *dēn* when referring to the cultic practices of "sorcerers" and "demon-worshipers," but other terms when referring to religions such as Judaism or Manichaeism.[13] These observations bear witness to the contestation over religious authority that persisted even after the establishment of state-supported Zoroastrianism under the early Sasanians.

### Zurvanism

Questions have been raised concerning the actual beliefs of the Sasanian priestly elites in comparison with those found in the extant Zoroastrian texts, most of which date to the post-Sasanian period after the Arab conquest. In particular, evidence from contemporary Armenian polemical sources, as well as some elements surviving in later Zoroastrian works, suggest the predominance of Zurvanism, whose cosmology and worldview are at some variance with the form of Zoroastrianism preserved in the textual tradition.

Zurvan is the god of Time (*zamān*) and Fate (*baxt*). In the mythical tradition referred to as Zurvanite it is he, not Mazda, who is considered to be the primordial deity, from whom Mazda and Ahriman emerge as twin sons. Interestingly, in what may be a relic element surviving in the Avesta, the Gathas describe the good and evil spirits as twins (30.3).

According to the Zurvanite cosmology, as reported in Christian and Zoroastrian sources, Zurvan wished for a son and for one thousand years he performed sacrifices in the hope of obtaining one. Eventually he conceived Ohrmazd within himself, but before Zurvan could give birth he experienced doubt (presumably about whether he had truly conceived; that is, about the efficacy of his sacrifices). From this doubt— the first "sin"—Ahriman was conceived. Since Zurvan had promised dominion to his firstborn, the ambitious Ahriman fought his way out through his father's navel, upon which Zurvan (being just) was forced to accord him a nine thousand year reign. When Ohrmazd emerged, Zurvan, having revealed his imperfect faith in the performance of sacrifice, duly handed over the *barsom* of priesthood to Ohrmazd.[14]

In Zurvanite mythology the final outcome of the ongoing cosmic battle between good and evil is less optimistically certain than in the Zoroastrian eschatological texts. The role of human choice, likewise, is diminished, with fate playing a more determining role. Some scholars have argued that Zurvan, who is equated to Kronos in Greek mythology, reflects the intrusion of non-Iranian influences from Greece and Mesopotamia.

The earliest reference to Zurvan—reflecting his possible Semitic origin—may date back as far as the twelfth century BCE, where a deity called Zaarwaan appears in Akkadian tablets from Nuzi in northern Mesopotamia. He is mentioned again in a Greek source of the fourth century BCE, but it is not until the Sasanian period that Zurvan begins to emerge with any clarity.

Of particular interest is the fact that Mani, who founded a new religion during the mid-third century CE, chose to refer to the Supreme Being as Zurvan, and not as Ohrmazd. Following Arthur Christensen, Zaehner concludes from this that at least during the early Sasanian period, Zurvanism was the dominant form of Iranian religion.[15] This hypothesis is supported by the fact that "when the Christian polemicists attack the Magian religion, they attack not Mazdean dualism, but Zervanite polytheism."[16] An inscription left by the Zoroastrian zealot priest Kerdir at Naqš-e Rajab reminds its readers that the virtuous will go to heaven and the sinful to hell, implying that many people at the time questioned these doctrines. Possibly such people were Zurvanites, with their emphasis on the overriding power of fate.

Christian polemicists of the Sasanian period, such as Eznik of Kołb and Paul the Persian, emphasize the diversity of doctrines existing among the Iranians, treating it as a defect. Among the major tendencies they note are those who speak of "two principles"—presumably the Mazdaeans—and those who admit three. The latter would seem to indicate Zurvanists, who associated good with Ohrmazd, evil with Ahriman, and justice with Zurvan.

If Zurvanism was indeed so prevalent among the Iranian population, then the Pahlavi Zoroastrian texts, which in their existing form date to the post-Sasanian period, could reflect an editorial reform which belies the true nature of Sasanian religion. Zurvanism may be connected as well with the materialist sect of fatalists known as the *dahriyya* in early Islamic times. Extending into an even later period, a thirteenth-century text misleadingly titled as the *'Ulemā'-e islām* is deemed to be a Zurvanite work.[17] (The title derives from the text's claim to relate the Zoroastrian high priest's answers to questions posed by Muslim scholars.) The following passage makes this clear:

> Except Time (*zamān*) all things are created. Time is the creator; Time has no limit, neither top nor bottom. It has always been and shall be for evermore . . .
>
> . . . it created fire and water; and when it had brought them together, Ohrmazd came into existence, and simultaneously Time became Creator and Lord with regard to the creation it had brought forth.
>
> Ohrmazd was bright, pure, sweet-smelling, and beneficent, and had power over good things. Then, when he looked down, he saw Ahriman ninety-six thousand *parasang*s away, black, foul, stinking, and maleficent . . .
>
> Whatever Ohrmazd did, he did with the aid of Time; for all the excellence that Ohrmazd needed, had (already) been created.[18]

Apart from the somewhat anomalous *'Ulemā'-e islām*, no known Zurvanite texts exist, and the religion is known only from its description in the polemics of its Mazdaean and Christian adversaries. Details regarding the beliefs and practices of actual Zurvanists, therefore, are difficult to establish. However, many disparate references from a range of sources from different periods suggest a religious practice that alternated daytime and night-time religious ceremonies, which were devoted in turn to the deity associated with each.

For example, certain groups of Iranians may have sacrificed to Mithra during the daytime—Mithra being associated with the sun (fire)—and to Anahita at night, she being associated with the moon (water). A Zurvanist version of this practice might have involved daytime sacrifices to Ohrmazd and nocturnal ones to Ahriman. This would explain references in the Zoroastrian literature to "false Mazdaeans" who worship Ahriman in secret. The Zurvanite view, in a sense more holistic than the radically divided dualism found in Zoroastrianism, may reflect a system of alternating rituals tied to the constantly recurring day–night/light–dark/fire–water cycle. Interesting echoes of this possibility can be detected in later Iranian heterodoxies such as those of the Yezidis and Yaresan, which are discussed in Chapter 16.

## RELIGION IN THE *SHĀH-NĀMEH*

Many of the characters in the Iranian national epic are familiar from the Avesta, albeit under differing forms. Early in the narrative Ferdowsi states that the original religion of the Iranians was ancestor-worship, which is consistent with the theory found in comparative mythology that heroes, generally speaking, derive from glorified ancestors. Fire-worship, and the Saddeh festival related to it, are said to date all the way back to the reign of Hūšang, grandson of the first king, Kiyūmars (Av. Gayō Marətan). A little less than halfway into the story Zoroastrianism is said to have been introduced during the reign of Goštasp (Vištaspa). Henceforth Rostam swears "by the Zend Avesta," but beyond that there is little reference to specifically Zoroastrian beliefs and practice. In an overall sense the religion of the Iranian peoples described in Ferdowsi's work does not conform to orthodox Zoroastrianism as described in the Sasanian texts.

Religion is everywhere present in the *Shāh-nāmeh*, but it is never explicitly spelled out. Rather, it appears in the form of heroes constantly praying to God—usually referred to as *Yazdān* ("the deities") and only occasionally by the proper name Hormoz—for victory, the presence of Sorūsh as a kind of analogue to the Islamic angel Gabriel, and most prominently, through constant references to the inevitability of Fate.

Indeed, the dominance of Fate throughout the *Shāh-nāmeh* would suggest a Zurvanist influence. This speculation is reinforced by the fact that God is frequently described as being the creator of both good and evil—a thoroughly un-Zoroastrian notion—as in the following quote, attributed to the hero Esfandiyār:

> A noble warrior whose audacity
> Lights up the world and brings him victory
> Laughs at both good and evil, since he knows
> Both come from God, whom no one can oppose.[19]

Despite this fatalism, Esfandiyār is presented as an early champion of Zoroastrianism. He makes the anachronistically Islamic-sounding boast of having destroyed idols and "lit the sacred flame of Zoroaster in their place." He also attributes to Zoroaster the teaching that "hell will be the home of whoever turns aside from his king's command,"[20] a notion not found in the Gathas. In the same passage he refers to the devil by one of his Islamic names, Eblīs, which appears throughout the *Shāh-nāmeh* interchangeably with Ahriman.

The generally confused picture of pre-Islamic religion provided by Ferdowsi can be attributed to three things: 1) his own imperfect knowledge of the subject, 2) anachronistic projections of Islamic norms and ideas onto a pre-Islamic past, and 3) the fact that religion throughout the pre-Islamic lands of Iran was not monolithic even by late Sasanian times.

# 5

# Iranian Goddesses
## *Manya Saadi-nejad*

T he religion of the early agricultural societies that predated the
migration of the Iranians into southwest Asia was mainly goddess-
centered. The importance of fertility, both among domesticated
animals and within the tribe itself, was of paramount importance to the
survival of these peoples. The female life-giving principle was considered
divine.

The best-known visual representations of goddesses from this ancient
period are figurines, generically referred to as "Venuses," which have
been found over a wide territory across western Eurasia. They are usually
nude, with prominent breasts, hips, and vulva, leading archaeologists
to assume that they represent fertility. The presence of such figurines
throughout the territory of the Iranian plateau, from Geyan Teppe near
Nahavand in the west to Teppe Sialk near Kashan in central Iran, and as
far as Turang Teppe near Gorgan to the northeast, attests to the existence
of goddess worship across the region prior to the arrival of the Indo-
European-speaking Iranians during the late second millennium BCE.

Slightly further west, the ancient Mesopotamian peoples had a number
of important goddesses, whose roles and functions were slowly taken
over by male deities. Yet the importance of these goddesses survived
for many centuries. The Sumerian goddess Inana and the Babylonian
Ištar, with many similarities in their functions and associated rituals,
are two examples of goddesses who were of central importance in their
respective societies.

When the first Iranians entered Mesopotamia, beginning in the eighth
century BCE, the culture they brought with them included a heavy
reliance on the horse and a strong attachment to male gods, divided
into three castes, associated with rituals and governance, war, and
fertility. The goddess worship of the peoples conquered or otherwise
encountered by the Iranians was gradually combined with worship of

their male gods. The survival of goddesses within the religious context of ancient Iran raises important questions about the role of female deities in a male-dominated society. Within this developing context, Inana, Ištar and other goddesses come to appear as the same goddess in different cultural guises. The Iranian goddess Anāhitā is central to this discussion, because of her unique power and importance in ancient Iran. Spəntā Ārmaiti, Haurvatāt and Amərətāt, who are the three female *Aməša Spəntas* ("Bounteous Immortals") mentioned in the Avesta, and the other Avestan goddesses, Aši and Daēnā, are additional examples.

## ANĀHITĀ

According to both the Avesta and the royal inscriptions of three successive Iranian empires, Anāhitā and Mithra were the two most powerful deities created by the supreme being, Ahura Mazdā. Anāhitā was primarily a water goddess, and as such she probably incorporated aspects of pre-existing water deities in the areas where she was worshiped. She was specifically the goddess of rivers and lakes. Temples devoted to her have been identified at Sardis, Babylon, Damascus, Persepolis, Bishapur, and Hamadan, as well as in Afghanistan and Armenia, usually alongside rivers. More sites continue to be identified, and numerous place-names throughout Iran (such as Pol-e doxtar, Qal'e-ye doxtar, and so on) may reflect her memory. Many holy sites across the Middle East are thought to have originally been temples devoted to Anāhitā.

Anāhitā was worshiped in different periods during the Persian and Iranian empires. By the late Achæmenid period she had become one of the most important and popular deities, alongside Ahura Mazdā and Mithra. Her name first appears in Artaxerxes II's inscriptions in Hamedan and Susa (ca. 400 BCE). Berossus, a Hellenistic-era Babylonian writer, mentioned many statues of Anāhitā that Artaxerxes had erected in different cities throughout the empire. Incorporating influences from Greek goddesses such as Aphrodite and Artemis and their associated rituals, Anāhitā became even more popular during the Seleucid and the Parthian periods. During the subsequent Sasanid Empire she appears alongside Ahura Mazdā in stone reliefs commemorating Shapur I (242–272 CE), and in the case of the coronation of Narseh (293–302) depicted at Naqš-e Rostam, it is she that crowns him—the only instance of a goddess bestowing kingship in Iranian history. Throughout the Sasanian period there were many temples devoted to Anāhitā, who was the patron deity of the ruling dynasty, and she was venerated in a number of rituals and celebrations.

Anāhitā is connected both functionally and linguistically with water goddesses found in many Indo-European societies. It may therefore be assumed that certain basic elements of her role and personality date as far back as the common Indo-European period. It seems possible to detect in Anāhitā an original Indo-European river goddess, traces of whom are found in the myths of a broad range of Indo-European peoples. Based upon mythological research including iconographic evidence, there appear to have been numerous river goddesses in ancient Europe, who gave their names to rivers (or themselves received the river's names). These goddesses had a variety of functions, among them fertility and healing. There is evidence for this in non-Mediterranean Europe from at least around 1300 BCE, where water was emphasized in the rituals.

European water goddesses were widely distributed, from Ireland and England to France, Germany, and into Russia. These goddesses were usually associated with rivers, springs, and lakes, and possessed some similar functions and water-based rituals. Healing was one of these functions, and some springs, which were considered to be sacred, were believed to have healing properties. Since water was symbolic of health and healing, the goddesses who were related to water usually also had a healing function. Anāhitā possessed all these functions.

## Anāhitā in the Avesta

Anāhitā, or as she appears in Avesta, *Arəduuī Sūrā Anāhitā*, was the goddess of the waters, specifically rivers and lakes. Her name is probably composed of three adjectives. P. O. Skjaervø somewhat expansively translates the series of terms by giving Anāhitā the epithet "[the] lofty, rich in life-giving strength, unattached (or "unsullied") [water]."[1] In fact, a daunting range of meanings has been proposed by scholars for each of these three Avestan terms, highlighting the linguistic difficulties associated with studies of the Avesta.

The first component of this compound name, *arəduuī*, has been taken by many scholars, from Bartholomae onwards, to refer to wetness; the epithet, accordingly, would literally mean "the moist one." It may be that at some remote time it was the name of a specific river, which gradually came to be deified.[2] Emile Benveniste has even suggested that *Arəduuī* was the goddess's original name.[3] It also has said that the adjective *arəduuī* was originally applied to Sarasvati, the sacred river in Vedic mythology, which is related to Anāhitā.[4] There is a direct Iranian parallel in the term Haraxvati (Gk. Arachosia), which, however, referred to a place that had many rivers. According to this model of transition, Sarasvati as the sacred river was forgotten but her epithet, *arəduuī*, remained.[5] As Antonio Panaino notes in this regard:

> . . . we may recall that both the warlike and fertility functions of Ištar are present in the Avestan goddess, who, in her turn, *possibly* had assumed the characteristics of an old Iranian

divinity (the Heavenly River, that is, Ir. *\*Harahvatī*), but appears also as a syncretic figure, which perhaps was under the influence of Mesopotamian cults.[6]

The translation of *arəduuī* as "moist," while popular, has not been universally accepted. Jean Kellens suggests that the term should be translated as "the Competent One," or "She Who Succeeds."[7]

The second component of the goddess's name, *sūrā*, is less problematic. Scholars generally agree that it means "mighty" or "powerful" in Avestan. The third component, *anāhitā*, bears some scrutiny. Mary Boyce believes that *sūrā* and *anāhitā* are generic Avestan adjectives. She defines *anāhitā* as "undefiled" or "immaculate."[8] Kellens, however, argues that this cannot have been the original meaning.[9] In Avestan, as in several other Indo-European languages, the prefix "a-" or "an-" creates a negation. It is followed here by a directional marker, "ā-". "Hi-" is a weak root derived from √hāii, "to bind." To this is appended the suffix "-ta," creating a verbal adjective. Thus, "*hita*" is a past perfect participle meaning "bound." "*Anāhitā*," therefore, means "not bound [to anything]."[10]

Since the three terms discussed above are clearly epithets, the question remains, what was the goddess's actual name? Boyce contends that her name is taken from a parallel, unattested goddess, *\*Anāhiti* (based on the Greek form Αναϊτις),[11] but this suggestion is neither supported nor particularly enlightening. Eric Pirart, based on a recurring strophe in the *Ābān Yašt*, proposes that her name is Hī.[12] The most likely possibility, however, as Kellens indicates, is that her name is simply Āp, "The Water," attested by Yasna 65.1, which reads, *yazāi āpəm arəduuīm sūrąm anāhitąm*, "I sacrifice to the Water, *arəduuī sūrā anāhitā*."[13]

An interesting parallel can be found in Herodotus' reference to the Scythian goddess Api, whom he equates (perhaps wrongly?) with Ge, a wife of Zeus who was originally called Papaios.[14] Herodotus describes Tabiti, whom he equates with the Greek Hestia, as the most important Saka goddess. An indication of a deity named Āp can also be found in the Elamite tablets from Persepolis, which mention personal names composed with OP *ap-* "water", such as *\*Apiyazna-* "Who sacrifices to the water." Thus, one must concur with Kellens that the actual name of the water goddess known as *arəduuī sūrā anāhitā* was in fact Āp.

Yasna 38 in the *Yasna Haptaŋhāiti*, which is linguistically as archaic as the *Gāthā*s, provides the Avesta's earliest mention of "sacred waters," though the connection to Anāhitā is not yet clear. However, Nyberg has suggested that some parts of the *Ābān Yašt*, the section of the so-called *Younger Avesta* dedicated to Anāhitā, may be almost as old as the *Gāthā*s.[15] Subsequent scholars, from Widengren to Boyce, have agreed with this assessment. The Yašts, a section of the Avesta consisting of devotional hymns, are full of ancient Iranian deities who were ignored by Zoroaster and are almost never mentioned in the *Gāthā*s. Their survival in the Yašts attests to their enduring popularity in Iranian societies, despite Zoroaster's apparent attempt to make of Ahura Mazdā a singular focus of worship.

The *Ābān Yašt*, which is part of the Avestan sacrificial liturgy, is devoted to Anāhitā, who is the ultimate source of all watercourses created by Ahura Mazdā. She is thus first and foremost a river, possibly originally a heavenly river, symbolized by the Milky Way.[16] However, she has many functions: she increases power and wealth (specifically land and cattle), she creates abundance, ensures fertility by purifying men's sperm and the woman's womb, eases childbirth, and assures timely lactation (Yašt 5.1).

The *Ābān Yašt* speaks of all the waters that Ahura Mazdā created, specifically mentioning seven rivers flowing to seven countries. Although Anāhitā might have originally been the goddess of a particular river, it seems that she became the goddess of all rivers, and not just a local one (Yašt 5.5). According to the *Ābān Yašt*, different people in different locations, usually around rivers, lakes and mountains, worshiped her.

## Visualizations of Anāhitā in the *Ābān Yašt*

The Yašts contain many descriptions of various deities, but for the most part they do not evoke any specific visual image. Thus, while Tištrya and Vereθraγna occasionally take on human or animal form (Yt. 8. and Yt.14), it is their traits and functions that are emphasized rather than their actual appearance. Vayu, the deity of wind and weather, is merely described as being a warrior (Yt. 15). Daēnā, the goddess of the conscience whom every person encounters on the Činvat (*činuuatō*) bridge after death, appears either as a beautiful maiden in the case of a good person, or as a smelly, disgusting hag in the case of sinners (Yt. 16). There exist other goddesses, Spentā-Armaiti for example, who are worshiped but whose visual aspect in Avesta is never described.

It is noticeable that, in contrast to the Greek and Mesopotamian cases, Iranian texts mostly do not portray their deities as human-like, either in form or lifestyle. It would therefore seem that Iranians, for the most part, did not conceptualize their deities in human terms to the extent that the Greeks and Mesopotamians did. The deities in the Avesta are sometimes described in visual terms. However, these visualizations do not typically describe the deities in human terms, either resembling humans physically or having similar lifestyles. Thus, it can be said in general terms that Iranians either did not visualize their deities as human beings, or did so only very rarely. It seems that for the most part Iranians did not communicate with their deities on any kind of human level.

In cases where visual descriptions do exist, they tend more to reflect the conceptual meaning of the deity's function and duty rather than any actual physical reality. For example when Mithra is described as having ten thousand hands or ears, it is to emphasize his function and ability to see and hear everything going on in the world, to help human beings when they ask him, or to catch anyone committing any sin. These visualizations are therefore primarily symbolic.

Thus, one of the most interesting aspects of Anāhitā is the way she is described in the *Ābān Yašt*, which differs from that in any other source. Her description there is uniquely rich and specific, enabling one to visualize the goddess almost as much as through visual art. Her clothes, her body, her palaces, her horse-drawn vehicle, and many other things about her are described in detail. It was said that one almost suspects the author had a clear image of her in his mind, as if he were observing one of her statues.

In fact, a number of scholars have speculated that this was precisely the case, suggesting that the author of the *Ābān Yašt* may have based his description on an actual statue or statues which are known to have existed by the mid-Achæmenid period at the latest.[17] Antonio Panaino is among those who believe that the *Ābān Yašt* "Presents a description of the goddess (in particular of her dress), which seems to be based on a statue or something similar."[18]

Kellens dismisses the theory that the text is based on an existing statue, saying it could just as well be based on an apparition. Moreover, he points out that her physical description, which is "brief and concise," resembles that of Daēnā, whereas the far more detailed description of her clothing is without parallel in the Avesta and may be a literary trope, like the description of Mithra's armor.[19] Indeed, in certain respects, the descriptions of Anāhitā in the *Ābān Yašt* seem more likely to be based on a vision than on observation, for example 5.129, which states that her coat is made from the skins "of thirty beavers of those that bear four young ones"—how would such a detail be discernible from a statue? These passages, therefore, could simply be the product of an existing tradition or a strong imagination, that of someone who genuinely believed in a goddess who was very popular in his society.

The *Ābān Yašt*'s combination of female beauty and splendor on the one hand with strength and power on the other associates Anāhitā with the attributes and characteristics of fertility, life and water's overwhelming force. She is a shape-shifter, repeatedly transforming herself from a river into a beautiful woman and back into a river.

The *Ābān Yašt* describes Anāhitā as an awe-inspiring deity, super-human in size, and strong enough that even Ahura Mazdā occasionally seeks her assistance. It depicts Anāhitā as a powerful spirit helping Ahura Mazdā and some other positive figures, changing into a beautiful woman of superhuman size. Although in this Yašt she is described by emphasizing her femininity, but she also has an adjective, *bāzu.staoiiehi* ("strong arms") showing her strength. Her arms are said to be the size of a horse's thigh! The goddess's clothes and shoes, and her crown, are all described with precision and detail.

The image of Anāhitā in Yt. 5.128, wearing "above (the head) a diadem (studded) with one hundred stars, golden, having eight towers, made like a chariot body, adorned with ribbons, beautiful (and) well-made," immediately recalls that of Ištar, with her high hat and the eight-pointed star behind.[20]

An interesting point arises from the fact that she is described as wearing a beaver skin. Although there is some geographical evidence for the existence of beavers in Iran in the past, this particular aspect of Anāhitā's imagery could date back to at least around four thousand years ago, prior to the Indo-Iranian split, when proto-Indo-Iranians occupied the southern Ural region, as evidenced by remains at Sintashta and elsewhere.[21] In any case, whether beaver fur existed in the Avestan lands or harks back to an earlier era, references to beaver skins in the *Ābān Yašt* suggest that its author is quoting a very old oral tradition which cannot be, for example, from Mesopotamia. Rather, it shows that at least initially, Anāhitā was worshiped in lands with a cold climate.

The description of a goddess clothed in animal skins, like the snow-queen who appears in many legends, allows us to imagine some things about the climate and natural environment in which she was first conceived. Most of all, it suggests somewhere cold. This is consistent with the Avesta's description of the original homeland of the Iranians, *Airyanəm vaējō* (\**aryānām waiǰah*). In the Yašts, this cold country is the place where Zoroaster (Y. 9.14), sacrificed to *Arəduuī Sūrā* and the other deities (Yt. 5.104; 9.25; 17.45). Likewise, in the *Vīdēvdāt* this land is described:

> There are ten months of winter there and two of summer and (even) those are (too) cold for water, for earth, for plants. It is the middle and the heart of winter, and (when) the winter ends there are many floods.[22]

Thus, it may be possible to link the climate of the Iranians' former homeland with the clothing style of their water goddess.

Alongside the many passages which depict Anāhitā as a beautiful, powerful goddess, she is poetically and artistically transformed into a waterfall-river which flows down from high mountains: Hara, with its highest peak *hukairiia*—the mountain, which in the Avestan world, established a physical link between the earth and the sky.[23]

In summary, images of Anāhitā are described with such precision and detail that one could conclude that they were connected with very old traditions, her statues and her worship rituals. These images are highly specific; with a nice turnaround this goddess is transformed into the mighty flowing waters. According to these various descriptions, some more realistic and others abstract, she mainly appears as a mythological queen. Her strength and power, her beauty and glory, and her fertility and warrior functions and capabilities, all combined to make for a very real image. Such an image would be a natural and inviting focus for wishes and requests, which perhaps helps explain why she was so popular in ancient Iranian society.

## OTHER IRANIAN GODDESSES

Anāhitā is not the only goddess to appear in Iranian texts. In fact there are many goddesses in the Iranian pantheon, some of whom are also very important. Anāhitā is unique for her multi-potential characteristics. Other goddesses worshiped by the ancient Iranians included Spəntā Ārmaiti, Haurvatāt and Amərətāt, who are the three female *Aməša Spənta*s ("Bounteous Immortals") mentioned in the Avesta, along with two other Avestan goddesses, Aši and Daēnā. Among these, Spəntā Ārmaiti, Aši and Daēnā are the most important ones appearing in the Avesta. All three are related to the sky, passing across it with or without a chariot. Also, in each case, their beauty is emphasized.

### Spəntā Ārmaiti

Spəntā Ārmaiti (Phl. Spandārmad) is the spirit of the earth. Alongside Haurvatāt and Amərətāt, she is one of three female *Aməša Spənta*s mentioned in the Avesta, being a symbol of femininity and motherhood. An Indo-Iranian deity, she appears in the Vedas as Aramati. Thus, Ārmaiti (literally, "holy devotion") is her actual name, with Spəntā being an adjective meaning "bounteous." Among the *Aməša Spənta*s, who are said in the Avesta to have been created by Ahura Mazdā from his own aura to represent his different aspects, she is fourth, but first among the female ones. While she represents the earth, she also is considered to represent the luminous cover of the sky.[24]

Spəntā Ārmaiti represents the qualities of kindness, wisdom, patience, faith and devotion. She is the spirit of the earth, who sits in the left side of Ahura Mazdā in the sky. Zoroaster considers Spəntā Ārmaiti as a manifestation of Ahura Mazdā, and as a source of achieving goodness, the correct path and cosmic order (*aša*).

In the *Younger Avesta* Spəntā Ārmaiti is the symbol and guardian of the earth. As a female symbol, Spəntā Ārmaiti is an object of worship by women.

Righteous (*ašavān*) women worship her first when they worship the *Aməša Spəntas*. She empowers those warriors who fight against demons, instilling them with intense ferocity. Alongside her identification with the earth, Spəntā Ārmaiti is associated with obedient, enduring, tolerant and patient femininity, putting her in contrast with Anāhitā, whose divine femininity emphasizes her strength. Moreover, unlike Anāhitā she does not have any visualized image in the Avesta. There are, however, some images of her in the Pahlavi texts. In the *Wizīdagīhā ī Zādspram* ("The Selections of Zādspram"), for example, she is embodied and personified as a beautiful young maid. The *Bondahešn* (Primal Creation) also describes Spəntā Ārmaiti as patient and enduring, like the earth, which is her symbol. She is presented as friendly and softly maternal. Like the earth, Spəntā Ārmaiti receives with tolerance and forbearance any harm humans do to her.

### Daēnā

Daēnā (Phl. *dēn*) is the hypostasis of one's own moral qualities. According to Zoroastrian beliefs, on the fourth day after death the soul of the deceased finds itself in the presence of either a beautiful maiden who leads it to heaven, or an ugly disgusting hag who takes it to hell, depending on whether the person has led a righteous or sinful life. Thus, as a divine power Daēnā takes shape according to an individual human's behaviors and deeds while alive in the world.

With the function and capacity of distinguishing good actions from bad ones, Daēnā is an embodiment of moral conscience, given to humans as a gift from Ahura Mazdā. In the *Gāthās*, this capacity is presented as mostly conceptual, rather than having an actual divine form. In the *Younger Avesta*, however, this capacity for moral discernment is hypostatized, as a beautiful maiden in the case of a good person's soul after death:

> ... the shape of a maiden fair, bright, white-armed, strong, tall-formed, high-standing, thick-breasted, beautiful of body, noble, of a glorious seed, of the size of a maid in her fifteenth year, as fair as the fairest things in the world. (*Hāδōxt Nask* 2.9)

This description of Daēnā is strikingly exact, emphasizing her beauty. Interestingly, many of the adjectives applied to Daēnā are elsewhere applied to Anāhitā. Also, Daēnā, or the capacity for moral discernment as a beautiful maiden, is said to have a precise age: she is a fifteen-year-old girl! This detail clearly represents an aspect of ideal beauty in the mind of ancient Iranians, and it is surely not coincidental that in Persian poetry of the Islamic period the *sāqī*, or wine-bearer, with whom the poet falls in love, is said to be this age as well. The scene where the soul meets Daēnā also occurs in the *Vīdēvdāt*: "Then comes the beautiful, well-shaped, strong and well-formed maid . . ." (*Vīdēvdāt* 19: 30). Daēnā is accompanied by the goddess Aši, who is said to be her sister. Together, they are guardians of women in the Yasna. Daēnā's depictions in Pahlavi texts are very similar to those cited above. In three Pahlavi books, the *Bondahešn*, the *Ardā Wīrāz nāmag* and the *Dādestān ī Mēnog ī Xrad*, she is mentioned as a beautiful young maiden who meets the souls of the deceased as they cross over the Činvat Bridge.

## *Aši*

Aši is the goddess of fortune and abundance. Her name, an abstract feminine noun in Avestan, derived from the root *ar-* meaning "to grant" followed by the suffix *–ti*, is an Avestan feminine noun meaning "thing attained, reward, share, portion, recompense," and, as a personification, the goddess "Reward, Fortune." The term is one of a group of Young Avestan personified abstracts including Rāman ("joy," "peace") and Daēnā ("conscience," "religion"). In the Younger Avesta she is one of the deities who receive the epithet Vaŋuhī, meaning "the good one," giving the later Pahlavi form Ahrišwang (from *Aši Vaŋuhī*).[25] According to Boyce, Aši also possesses a fertility function.[26]

Aši was worshiped widely in Iran, is mentioned in the *Gāthā*s, and has a specific Yašt (Yašt 17 of the Avesta, the *Ard Yašt* or *Aši Yašt*) devoted to her. If one accepts that the *Gāthā*s are the oldest preserved expression of Zoroastrian thought, it would seem highly significant to note that apart from Ahura Mazdā and the *Aməša Spənta*s, the only other deities they mention (although not clearly as deities) are Sraoša, Fire, and Aši.

Looking at a later period, Frantz Grenet has observed that in the Kushan Empire the Mithra cult seems to have been paired with that of the goddess Aši; this would suggest that parallel male–female cults existed at that time.[27] On Kushan coins, Aši appears as Ardoxšo, with a cornucopia in hand. She was also worshiped in Manichaeism.

In the *Gāthā*s Aši is represented as an abstract concept, actually identified with *aša* ("truth"). Schlerath allows that she may have been a fertility goddess in pre-Zoroastrian times, though she does not appear in the Vedas.[28] It is in the Young Avesta that Aši emerges clearly as a divinity, the subject of her own Yašt. In the Zoroastrian calendar the twenty-fifth day of the month is dedicated to her.

Aši is an important goddess, providing wealth, happiness and rest. She is said in the *Aši Yašt* to be the daughter of Ahura Mazdā and Spənta Ārmaiti, the sister of the *Aməša Spənta*s and of Sraoša, Rašnu, Mithra, and Daēnā. Like other important deities she has a chariot, and also appears driving Mithra's.

Aši has some strong similarities to Anāhitā. Indeed, many of the hymns contained in the *Ābān Yašt* are repeated in the *Aši Yašt*. Like Anāhitā, Aši is mostly concerned with women, although Aši's "support" mostly is emphasized in their abundance. In other words, when Aši is described as giving her assistance, it is not given to women in their own right but rather as women who want to please their men. Both Anāhitā and Aši are fertility goddesses. Also like Anāhitā, Aši is closely connected to Mithra, appearing in the *Mehr Yašt* as his charioteer (Yašt 10.17.68).

As in Anāhitā's, Aši's Yašt contains a list of heroes and kings who sacrifice to her asking for her support and are rewarded for it, although unlike Anāhitā's, this list is made up uniquely of "good people." Also in contrast to Anāhitā, whose aristocratic female devotees in Anatolia are said by Strabo to have engaged in sacred prostitution prior to marriage, Aši is free of any association with such "immoral" rituals. On the contrary, Aši is portrayed as a strong advocate of female morality. She laments about women who abort their children, who cheat on their husbands, and who lie to their husbands about their children's paternity (Yašt 17.10.58).

Thus, as a major Iranian goddess, Aši differs from Anāhitā in important respects. These differences are likely connected to socio-economic transformations in ancient Iranian society. As noted previously, agricultural societies such as those of the pre-Iranian peoples of the Iranian plateau and adjacent regions were mostly goddess worshipers. Accordingly, they gave many roles to their powerful goddesses, who over time merged into a single specific goddess under different names; these roles were mostly related to fertility.

While certain rituals, ceremonies, and myths associated with the goddess came to be seen as "immoral" by later patriarchal societies, to the people concerned they were very important and necessary. As the more patriarchal society of the Iranian immigrants imposed itself, the earlier inhabitants nevertheless clung to their goddess and her rituals, which were gradually absorbed and appropriated into Iranian culture.

Anāhitā, who was originally an Indo-Iranian river goddess related to fertility, replaced the pre-Iranian goddess(es) and acquired some of her (their) functions. It is doubtful that the male-centered Iranians—including Zoroaster himself—would have been pleased by the importance of the goddess and her rituals among the inhabitants of the lands brought under Iranian control. Aši, promoting values of female subservience, seems to have emerged as a preferred alternative, although it is unclear whether she ever achieved an importance in Iranian society comparable to Anāhitā's.

Nevertheless, Aši can be seen as the guardian of a "new morality" for women living in a world dominated by Iranian men. Her complaints regarding "immoral" behaviors of women demonstrate that such behaviors existed and were perhaps even prevalent, and that her role was to remove them. She embodies the female characteristics desired by those in control of this society-in-transformation. In short, Aši fulfills a patriarchal dream as the goddess of "stay-at-home women" who wait for their husbands.

### Haurvatāt and Amərətāt

Haurvatāt (Phl. Hordād, NP. Khordād) means "integrity (of body)," "wholeness." Amərətāt (Phl. Amurdād, NP. Mordād) literally means "immortality." These two goddesses mostly act in tandem. According to the the *Bondahešn* (26.8) they stand on Ahura Mazdā's left, together with Spəntā Ārmaiti.

Haurvatāt, who is the subject of Yašt 4, is devoted to water. She also ensures the healthy growth of plant life (*Bondahešn* 16:103–4). Humans can either please or offend her, depending on how they treat water: "He who will please or distress the water shall have pleased or distressed Hordad" (*Bondahešn* 16:106).

Amərətāt is devoted to plants. In the Iranian creation story, as related in the ninth-century *Selections of Zādspram*, after the first plant is destroyed by demons during the primordial battle Amərətāt regenerates plant life all across the earth. According to the version in the *Bondahešn*, Amərətāt is either pleased or angered by humans, depending on how they treat plants (*Bondahešn* 113). Haurvatāt and Amərətāt are said to be offended by chatter (*Mēnōg ī xrad* 2.33), and harmed by women who do not observe the stipulated procedures when menstruating (*Ardā Wīrāz-nāmag* 72.5).

Some scholars have sought to connect Haurvatāt and Amərətāt to certain Vedic deities, which would imply a very archaic origin to this pairing. Georges Dumézil, for example, has drawn a functional correspondence between these two *Aməša Spəntas* and the Vedic Nāsatyas. Jacques Duchesne-Guillemin and Geo Widengren have supported this hypothesis, while others, such as Ilya Gershevitch, Johanna Narten and Gherardo Gnoli, have rejected it.[29] Narten, meanwhile, has pointed out that in the list of provided in the *Yasna Haptaŋhāiti*, Dāenā and Fsəratū occupy the place of Haurvatāt and Amərətāt.[30]

Echoes of Haurvatāt and Amərətāt are found in Gnostic–Manichaean, Christian, and Islamic traditions. They appear as Harwōt and Marwōt in a Sogdian glossary, as Arioch and Marioch in the book of Enoch, and the demons Hārūt and Mārūt in the Qur'an (2:96). The flowers referred to as *hawrot mawrot* in Armenian are another reflection of this pair. Most significantly for our purposes, however, the Zoroastrian texts provide no visual description of either Haurvatāt or Amərətāt.

## IRANIAN GODDESSES IN SOGDIAN ART

Certain frescos among the wall paintings which adorned the Sogdian-era buildings at Panjikent, Tajikistan are related to very old rituals. A painting in Temple 2 depicts a scene of mourning around a dead young prince, whom scholars have identified as the legendary Iranian hero Siyāvaš (Av. Syāvaršan).[31] A female figure in the same painting has been identified as Anāhitā.[32] If these identifications are correct, what we have in this scene is a fascinating example of convergence of deities between East and West, Semitic and Indo-European, Siyāvaš being merely a Central Asian reflex of the Mesopotamian Dumuzi.

Anāhitā and Siyāvaš are thus both connected with two of the central characters in Mesopotamian mythology: Anāhitā with Inana-Ištar, and Siyāvaš with the beautiful young man, son or lover of Inana-Ištar, known under Dumuzi and other names, who dies, or is killed, and reborn each year, symbolizing the annual regeneration of plant life so important in this agricultural society. One of the main components of the annual ritual cycle connected with this myth was mourning and lamentations over the death of this divine son, who was considered to have died the death of a martyr.

Women were prominent in these mourning ceremonies, screaming and beating themselves in grief just like the goddess herself, who has been deprived of her son. The role of the women in re-enacting the goddess's grief also helped her divine son to return, their tears symbolizing the rain needed to bring the soil back to life. Thus, these grief rituals, dramatic as they were, at the same time served as a kind of ushering in of the martyred god's subsequent rebirth. Groups of villagers with blackened faces, representing the martyred god, would appear to herald his return. (Siyāvaš literally means "black face.") In some cases the villagers would wrap a tree in a shroud, then raise it up and recite prayers and invocations.

The Mesopotamian vegetation god and his goddess mother-lover, his death, and descent into the underworld, symbolized winter, while his revival and return to the world signaled the coming of spring. At least some of the Iranian tribes who came into contact with Mesopotamian peoples by the end of the second millennium BCE adopted these mourning ceremonies, which is somewhat ironic, since mourning is frowned upon in Zoroastrianism. Nevertheless, such mourning rituals, which involve much crying and sometimes self-flagellation and recur every year, seem to have been borrowed from the Sumerian, Semitic, and Mediterranean cultures with whom Iranians came into contact, along with the myths and mythological figures associated with those rituals.

In eastern Iran the martyred vegetation god gradually evolved into Siyāvaš, who is known to have been the focus of an important cult in pre-Islamic Bukhara. He was an important figure among the Sakas and Sogdians, and came to be celebrated in some Iranian texts, most famously through his story in the Iranian national epic, the *Shāh-nāmeh*.

Returning to the mourning scene in Temple 2 at Panjikent, if indeed the goddess figure is Anāhitā, we may recall that by Sogdian times her cult had been deeply influenced by rituals associated with Ištar and other Mesopotamian goddesses. It is thus not unreasonable to interpret this scene as an Iranian version of Ištar and Dumuzi's story.

## FEMALE FIGURES IN THE SHĀH-NĀMEH

Many of the characters in the Persian national epic, the *Shāh-nāmeh* ("Book of Kings"), of Ferdowsi, a tenth-century epic poem which celebrates the glories of Iran's pre-Islamic past, are also found in the Avesta and in the Rig Veda. For example, Yama in the Vedas, Jam in the Avesta, and Jam-shīd in the *Shāh-nāmeh* are the same character. Yama and Jam-shīd are presented as rejected by the gods. Following the separation between Indo-Iranians into Iran and India during the second millennium BCE, most of their gods lost their prior mythological status, but their influence remained as many were reconceived as heroes. (The same analysis has been applied to other Indo-European mythologies including the Greek and the Roman.) In other words, such originally divine figures were reimagined as humans but with special, super-human features.

Zoroastrian symbolism is also deeply evoked in art from the Islamic period, such as "The Court of Gayumars" from the illustrated *Shāh-nāmeh* commissioned by Shah Esma'il in the early 1520s. Gayumars (Gayō Marətan), described in Yasht 13 of the Avesta as the "Primal Man," was created along with water, soil, the first plant, and the first cow. The sixteenth-century Muslim painter's depiction of "The Court of Gayumars" shows a garden scene of inter-species harmony and primordial bliss prior to disruption by the evil deity Ahriman, a well-known image from Zoroastrian mythology.

Although the *Shāh-nāmeh* was the most commonly commissioned book by all the Muslim dynasties who ruled Iran, the work is in fact a celebration of pre-Islamic Iranian culture which champions recognizably ancient proto-Indo-European patriarchal and militaristic values, and throughout which Zoroastrianism is the formal religious framework. Many of the "heroes" in the *Shāh-nāmeh* are originally Indo-European or other deities. As such, Zoroastrian, as well as common Indo-European mythological motifs and symbols, are predominant, though Mesopotamian, Byzantine, Indian, and other influences are present as well. Another example is Zahhak, portrayed as a human-dragon in both the Avesta and the Vedas, who in the *Shāh-nāmeh* is transformed into a tyrannical king with snakes coming out of his shoulders. Zahhak is depicted in this way in virtually every illustrated manuscript of the *Shāh-nāmeh*.

Another figure present in the Avesta, Hōšang (Av. Haošyaṇha), appears in the *Shāh-nāmeh* as one of Iran's first mythical kings. In contrast to Zahhak, Hōšang is a heroic character, and is most often depicted slaying a black demon. The Persian word for demon is *dīv*, from Proto-Indo-European *\*deiwo*. In ancient times the term seems to have only meant "deity," and was later given a negative meaning by Zoroaster or Mazdā-worshippers.[33] In modern Persian the word means a kind of monster. We can also see traces of characters from Greek mythology in the *Shāh-nāmeh*, such as Esfandīār, who shares a number of features with Achilles.

### Possible Connections between Goddesses and Some Women in the Shāh-nāmeh

Although the *Shāh-nāmeh* was written during the Islamic period, its female characters are very strong and behave freely, in a way that might seem inappropriately open-minded in the context of tenth-century Muslim society. Yet their free behaviour is usually mixed with obedience, which sends us some mixed signals. Can "good" women be both bold and obedient? Why are they sometimes able to freely choose their lovers, while at other times they appear to have little or no rights at all?

While a detailed analysis of women in the *Shāh-nāmeh* is beyond the scope of this chapter, it may be noted in passing that the epic is made up of stories and legends from eastern Iran. The *Shāh-nāmeh*'s greatest hero, Rostam, is from Sistan, earlier known as Sakestān which means "land of the Sakas." The Sakas, like other Indo-Iranian peoples of Central and West Asia, blended their culture with that of the earlier native peoples of the region, exchanging influences in both directions. In the case of Mesopotamia, we know that goddesses of the native peoples were more powerful and central to the pantheon than those of the Indo-Iranians, and the same may have been true of the pre-Iranian inhabitants of Central Asia. This could explain why the Sakas had an important mother-goddess, as evidenced by the Herodotus' list of Saka deities which interestingly begins with "Hestia" (giving the Greek equivalent for the chief Saka goddess), before continuing "Zeus," "Apollo," and so on.

Herodotus' account suggests that in his time Saka society was probably more matriarchal than in later periods of Iranian history, and in fact heroic female figures are common in the myths of other pastoral nomadic peoples of Central Asia including the pre-Islamic Turks. Since we know that many characters in the *Shāh-nāmeh* can be explained as deities who become transformed into human heroes, it is not strange to find strong, "open-minded" women in the *Shāh-nāmeh*.

Descriptions of women in the *Shāh-nāmeh* usually emphasize their tallness: they are said to be "as tall as a cypress tree," with long dark hair and "gazelle" eyes. Khojasteh Kia believes that this measure of beauty comes from an old tradition in eastern Iran, before the coming of the Turks. In support of her argument, Kia cites the Panjikent paintings mentioned above, which date to before the seventh century. She points out that in both paintings the female figures are exceptionally tall, have dark long hair and gazelle-like eyes, not Mongolian eyes, as is the convention in later Persian paintings. The goddess depicted in the Temple 2 painting wears a crown decorated with flowers known as *nenuphar*, literally "water flower." She also wears a belt. Kia therefore believes that this goddess is Anāhitā, reflecting standards of beauty of the time which served as a literary model for women in the *Shāh-nāmeh*, as opposed to the Chinese–Buddhist ideal of feminine beauty seen in later Persian paintings.[34]

This theory seems plausible, especially when we consider the influence of a society's cultural symbols and reference points on local artistic representation. Artists, like anyone else, are affected by and imbued with the myths and symbols of the culture in which they grow up. Whether knowingly or unknowingly, they often use mythological elements in their artistic production. The various art forms of Iran, past and present, offer ample evidence of this influence. The Persian miniature painting tradition is rich with reconstructed scenes from ancient Iranian myths. Often a divine figure from prehistoric times is reimagined as a hero or a mythical king, with the myth associated with that particular deity being transposed to a greater or lesser extent onto the hero.[35] Even so, the characteristics typically seen in portrayals of legendary figures in Persian paintings depict ideals of beauty that bear little relation to how real Iranians actually looked.

The depiction of Anāhitā detailed by the writer or writers of the *Ābān Yašt* represents an ideal of female beauty, which persisted over the centuries within the collective memory of Iranian society. Thus, certain female characters in the *Shāh-nāmeh*, who behave in ways not typical for real Iranian women of the time, are in some ways perhaps reflections of goddesses, and their visual representations could therefore contain elements of a distant memory of divine beauty. Such characters are invariably described as tall, despite the fact that the popular taste in pre-Islamic Iran appears to have been for women of "middle height" with "small feet" and "almond eyes," an ideal expressed in the Middle Persian text *Xosrau ud rēdag* ("Khosrow and the Page").[36]

We will focus here on two female figures in the *Shāh-nāmeh*, Sūdābeh and Rūdābeh, whose names could be related to water, and therefore possibly constitute reflections of the ancient Indo-European water goddess who became Anāhitā.

At first glance, Sūdābeh and Rūdābeh appear to have two very different personalities and roles, positive and negative, but they have some similarities, like two sides of the same coin. They both are very beautiful and have strong personalities. Moreover, their beauty is described in nearly identical terms; the same terms applied to other beautiful women in the *Shāh-nāmeh*. They are elegant, splendid, and tall, with dark long hair and black eyes. In their personality, they both are determined and resolved. They both try hard to obtain the person whom they love.

The two women are ethical opposites, however, representing very different female models. Rūdābeh's love had a positive result; she married her beloved and gave birth to Rostam's father. Rūdābeh thus initiated a blessed family line. Sūdābeh, on the other hand, through her unethical lust for her stepson, generated bad luck for her beloved, ultimately resulting in both her death and his.

### Sūdābeh

In the *Shāh-nāmeh* version of the legend of Siyāvaš (related to the mythological story of Dumuzi and Ištar), the goddess Ištar appears to have been replaced by a negative female figure, a woman of magician roots, named Sūdābeh.

The *Shāh-nāmeh*'s Siyāvaš is the son of the Iranian king, Kay Kāvūs (Av. Kauui Usan). Sūdābeh, the king's beautiful wife, is his stepmother. She desires Siyāvaš and attempts to seduce him, but he refuses her advances and avoids betraying his father. After a long story, in which Siyāvaš had to prove his innocence because of Sūdābeh's lies, he was finally exiled to Tūrān, where he was killed innocently by order of the Turanian king, Afrāsiyāb, the best-known enemy of Iran in the *Shāh-nāmeh*. He is later avenged by his son.

Sūdābeh's love story with Siyāvaš is reminiscent of the Inana/Ištar story of a goddess's tragic love for Dumuzi, which led to the young hero-god's death. Interestingly, the contemporary Iranian writer, Simin Daneshvar, has observed the survival of a ritual connected with Siyāvaš into the twentieth century. In her novel *Sāvūšūn*, Daneshvar describes a mourning ritual practiced by women of Shiraz who have lost a son: they cut off their hair and hang it from a special tree (which reminds us of the vegetation god).[37]

Moreover, Sūdābeh's lustful behavior towards Siyāvaš bears many similarities with the story of Ištar and Gilgamesh. When Sūdābeh saw Siyāvaš, she desired him and "her heart beat faster." After a series of events, she manages to see him in private. She tells him he could be the king after his father dies and that he could possess her. Then, in an attempt to seduce him, she removes her veil and invites him to be her lover:

> ... Take any thing you want from me ...
> She clutched his head and ripped her dress, as though
> All fear and shame had left her long ago
> But Siyāvaš's cheeks blushed rosy red,
> Tears filled his eyes and to himself he said,
> My God who rules the plants succor me
> And save me from this witch's sorcery.[38]

An incident from the Epic of Gilgamesh is strikingly similar:

> ... And Ištar the princess raised her eyes to the beauty of Gilgamesh.
> 'Come to me, Gilgamesh, and be my lover!
> She tries to tempt him:
> When you enter our house
> The wonderfully-wrought threshold shall kiss your feet!
> Kings, nobles, princes shall bow beneath you.[39]

But Gilgamesh refuses Ištar's advances, reminding her of the fate of her previous lovers, including the vegetation god, Dumuzy:

> ... For the Dumuzy the lover of your youth
> you decreed that he should keep weeping year after year.

Thus, in both cases, Gilgamesh and Siyāvaš refused the advances of aggressive women.

Certain texts from the Islamic period, including the *Fārs-nāmeh* of Ebn Balkhi and the *Tārīx-e Tabarī*, describe Sūdābeh as a witch who uses magic.[40] That may therefore remind us of the Indo-Aryan goddess Diti, who used magic in order to obtain a son more powerful than Indra. Her uncontrolled lust for Kasyapa, the father of humanity, is strikingly similar to that of Sūdābeh's for Siyāvaš. Ištar, too, is a lustful woman more interested in sex than love. It seems that Sūdābeh represents just one side of the goddess Ištar: a strong personality with sexual desire, vengeful, and not faithful to their husbands or lovers. Her passion for Siyāvaš, being illicit, is devoid of fertility. Instead, it brings only bad luck and death.

## RŪDĀBEH

Rūdābeh is also associated with water, as her name attests: "she of the river water."[41] Rūdābeh's parents' names may possibly connect them to water as well. Her mother's name is Sindoxt, (possibly: Sin = Sind, a sacred river + *doxt* = girl). Her father, Mehrāb (Mehr + Apa), is a king descended from Azi-Dhahhāka, a demonic dragon who guards the water.

In the *Shāh-nāmeh,* Rūdābeh is the lover of Zāl and the mother of the hero Rostam. She is a brave, beautiful woman who lives a long life, as is typical for demi-gods. She is not shy to talk about her love for her parents, she fights to obtain her beloved, Zāl, and in the end she is successful. Her story is a beautiful, free, love story which is Islamized by Ferdowsi. It contains highly romantic scenes, such as when she lets down her hair, Rapunzel-like, so that Zāl may ascend it as a rope. Her pregnancy with Rostam is extraordinary as well: as a fetus Rostam grew too big to be born in the normal way, so the mythological bird, the Sīmorgh, prescribes a Caesarean section.

Another woman in the *Shāh-nāmeh*, Katayūn, is apparently a reflexion of Anāhitā. She is actually named in one passage as Nāhīd (Anāhitā), Katayūn being the name bestowed on her by her lover Goštasp. Her story resembles that of an older tale from Media, the romance of Zaryadres and Odatisse, from which it may ultimately be derived. Mary Boyce has suggested that this myth may have been originally connected with a love goddess such as Anāhitā.[42]

All of these connections are of course speculative, but taken as a whole they suggest a compelling pattern. In Iran's tenth-century society, which had become patriarchal and monotheist, popular culture retained and preserved echoes of earlier goddess-centered worship connected with water.

# Part 2

# FOREIGN RELIGIONS IN IRAN

# 6

# Judaism

One could make the case that Judaism, while being the religion of a people who self-identify as Semitic, is to a large extent a product of Iran. The religion of the Israelites prior to their contact with Iranians was not Judaism; it might be better characterized as a sacrificial Yahweh cult. The word from which the very term "Judaism" is derived, the Greek Ἰουδαῖος, emerges only in the Hellenistic period, by which time the dispersed Israelites and Judeans had begun to absorb a number of Iranian religious ideas. Centuries later the Babylonian Talmud, which gave shape to Judaism as it is known today, was composed within the confines and cosmopolitan context of Sasanian Iran; not surprisingly, this important text shows much evidence of interaction with Iranian cultural norms.

Moreover, it has rightly been observed that the Jewish diaspora, spanning twenty-seven centuries, begins in Iran. In fact, it has been argued that Iran is second only to Israel in historical importance for the Jews.[1] The religious and cultural tradition now known as Judaism underwent one of its most radical transformations as a result of contact with Iranians. This influence, which is felt in the later development of Christianity and Islam, reverberates throughout the cultures of more than half the world today.

Modern Judaism is largely a product of the Talmudic period—that is, the second through the seventh centuries of the Common Era. But of course, the roots of Judaism are much older. The traditional chronology, which is based on the genealogies of the Hebrew Bible, goes back to a purported date of Creation in 3760 BCE. Abraham, who is considered by Jews (and, for that matter, by Muslims as well) to be the founder of their religion, may have lived sometime around the eighteenth century BCE. But as is the case with all human cultures, the history of Judaism is a dynamic one, sometimes undergoing dramatic changes and developments. The Jewish faith as practiced today scarcely resembles the sacrificial religion of ancient times, and yet a distinct thread of continuity connects them through time and space.

## THE BEGINNINGS OF DIASPORA

One of the watershed periods of Jewish history is the reign of King David in the tenth century BCE, when the Israelites controlled a kingdom between the Sea of Galilee and the Dead Sea in the region of Palestine. Following the reign of David's son Solomon, the Israelite state split into two kingdoms, the northern kingdom of Israel and the southern kingdom of Judea. Although in the Bible these kingdoms are naturally treated as the center of the world—which, for Israelites, they were— from the perspective of the great contemporary civilizations based in the Nile valley and Mesopotamia, Palestine was hardly more than a small, remote place of little economic value or strategic importance. Not surprisingly, the Israelites do not figure prominently in the records of their larger imperial neighbors.

We know from both Hebrew and Mesopotamian sources that the northern kingdom of Israel was overrun by the armies of Assyria in 722 BCE. It was the custom of the Assyrians to uproot the survivors in all the regions they conquered, and resettle them elsewhere within their empire. The Bible states in the second book of Kings (18:11) that Israelites were sent to live in "Halah and Habor by the River Gozan and in the cities of the Medes"; that is, in western and northern Iran. This can be taken as evidence for an Israelite presence in Iran from the eighth century BCE at the latest. Some may have gone even further east. There is a legend among the Pushtuns (Pathans) of modern Afghanistan that they are themselves descended from the ten "lost" tribes of Israel, and the story may have some historical substance. Although most of the Pushtuns converted to Islam many centuries ago, small Jewish communities (likely descended from later arrivals rather than the original ten tribes) survived in Afghanistan into the 1990s.

In 586 BCE the southern kingdom of Judea succumbed as well, this time to the Babylonians (who were also Semitic) under King Nebuchadnezzar. The Babylonian soldiers utterly destroyed the Judean capital, Jerusalem, including the Temple built in the time of King Solomon, which was the center of the Israelites' sacrificial religion. In a sense, by destroying the Temple the Babylonians rendered the religious life of the Israelites non-functional, since the required sacrifice could only be performed there.

Like the Assyrians, the Babylonians had a policy of resettling conquered peoples. The Bible describes this process and its consequences from the point of view of the Israelites, whose Babylonian captivity is interpreted as Yahweh's punishment for their failure to keep the covenant established on Mount Sinai.

A few decades later, in 539 BCE, the armies of a new power to the east, the Persians in southwestern Iran, entered Babylon and liberated all the captive peoples, Israelites included. While, again, it is important to keep a sense of perspective—to the Persians, the Israelites cannot have seemed significantly different from any of the other captive groups—the biblical version of events places the Hebrew god at the center of this great historical occasion, describing the Persian emperor Cyrus as "God's anointed" who has been brought for the purpose of saving the Israelites (Isaiah 44:25–28 and 45:1–4). In other words, whereas to most peoples of the time Cyrus was simply the latest in a long line of empire-builders, seeking his own glory above all else, in the Bible his success is seen as a sign of the glory of the Hebrew god, Yahweh. It is interesting that of all the foreign rulers mentioned in the Hebrew Bible, only Cyrus is described in positive terms.

The Persian conquest represented the beginning of Iranian influence in Mesopotamia. This was a region which had long possessed an enormous diversity of ethnicities, languages and cultures (think "Tower of Babel"), though Semitic peoples predominated. When Cyrus liberated the captive peoples of Babylon he granted them what might be described today as "citizenship" in his empire and the freedom to settle anywhere they would choose. At the time, few Israelites felt the desire to return to their ruined homeland in Palestine. Instead, many remained in Babylon as free citizens, while others sought new lives elsewhere. (The Temple in Jerusalem was not rebuilt until the following century, with Persian assistance.) Significant numbers appear to have gone to live in the cities of the Iranian plateau, perhaps making contact with Israelites already living there from Assyrian times. Hence the observation that, "the diaspora begins in Iran."

From the beginning of the diaspora twenty-seven centuries ago the dispersed Israelites maintained connections with family and friends in other locations that formed the basis of long-distance trade networks. Israelites likely played a role in the silk trade which linked China to the West.[2]

These diaspora networks not only served to sustain family ties and business contacts, but were also conduits for goods and ideas. Thus, the experiences and achievements of one community could be easily transmitted, over time, to other related communities far away. Since in Achæmenid times the Persian Empire, of which the Israelites were citizens, stretched from Egypt and Greece to the borders of China and India, different Israelite groups found themselves living in very diverse cultural and physical environments. Of course Iranians settled in all of these areas too, with the result that the whole range of products and technologies, lifestyle and customs, art forms and philosophies could travel readily from one locale to another within this far-flung and cosmopolitan empire. Among the actual transmitters of all these cultural artifacts, the ancestors of Iranian Jews were prominent.

At the same time, the influences absorbed from Iranian culture by the Israelites themselves were enormous. In order to assess the extent of these influences, it is necessary to consider the religio-cultural system of the Israelites prior to their encounter with Iranians.

## THE INFLUENCE OF IRANIAN IDEAS

The religion of the ancient Israelites could be characterized in one sense as a "Yahweh-cult." That is, they were a group distinguished from neighboring Semitic tribes mainly by their adherence to a particular god, Yahweh, with whom they established a covenant through Moses on Mount Sinai (probably some time in the thirteenth century BCE). That is, the role of Moses among the Israelites can be seen as analogous to that of Zoroaster among the Iranians, in that they both elevated a god already existing within the pantheon of their peoples to a position of supremacy.

In neither case are we dealing with monotheism, strictly speaking. The First Commandment delivered on Mount Sinai is "Thou shalt have no other gods before me" (Exodus 20:3), an implicit admission that other gods exist (henotheism). Likewise, Zoroaster merely demoted some gods to the level of servants or emanations of Ahura Mazda, and others, like the *daēva*s, to the status of demons. As in the Iranian world, the Israelite holy texts were memorized and passed on by the priestly class, which alone knew the correct sacrificial formulas. And just as with the Avesta and the Rig Veda, by the time these texts were written down the sacred language—Hebrew in this case—was no longer spoken or perhaps even fully understood by the people, who had adopted regional vernaculars.

But there are many ways in which the Israelite vision of the universe and their place in it differed dramatically from that of the Iranians. The Israelites seem to have had little clear notion of the afterlife, assuming that souls merely went to reside in a murky underworld, known as Sheol. They lacked the elaborate angelology and demonology of the Iranians, and they had no notion of "the devil," only the gods of others whom the Israelites were forbidden to worship (but whom, as the biblical prophets endlessly complain, they often did anyway). The Israelites' conception of time, like that of most ancient peoples, was cyclical, based on the seasons and the agricultural year. The linear time and eschatology described in Zoroaster's cosmos is absent from the pre-Babylonian Israelite worldview. The Israelite sense of ethics was based on the community, rather than on the individual. Whereas the Torah speaks of Yahweh's covenant with an entire people and collective guilt and punishment, the Gathas attributed to Zoroaster are usually taken to focus more on the individual's responsibility for choosing good over evil.

Morton Smith considers that the notion of a Creator god may have been an Iranian influence on Judaism, with Genesis 1 being "a late preface" to the Bible, "most likely after 530 [BCE]." Smith sees a connection between certain passages in Deutero Isaiah (40–45) and Yasna 44 in the Avesta, which asks, "Who set in order justice, the sun and stars, earth and sky, waters and plants, right thought, light and darkness?"[3] The book of Isaiah also marks the first appearance in Hebrew texts of the notions of the resurrection of the dead (26:19) and posthumous punishment for evildoers (66:24).

The apocalypticism of biblical prophets such as Daniel dates from the post-Babylonian period, after Israelites had come into contact with Iranian ideas. Whether the notion of apocalypse originated with the Iranians or with the Israelites remains a contentious issue; some scholars, such as Mary Boyce and Geo Widengren, consider it to have very ancient origins in the Iranian tradition and find traces of it in the Avesta. Others, notably Philippe Gignoux, take the late date of the surviving Zoroastrian apocalyptic texts (principally the *Zand-i Vohuman Yasn* and the *Jāmāsp-nāma*) as evidence that the Iranian tradition derives from the Jewish one. The question may hinge partly on how one defines apocalypticism; at the very least, it may be conceded that Iranian notions of eschatology—both individual and collective—are found in the Avesta and predate Jewish ones. And as Touraj Daryaee has pointed out, some elements, such as the division of history into four ages which is found in Daniel, as well as the Final Battle and the Restoration/Resurrection, are not just Iranian but Indo-European, and therefore very ancient indeed.[4]

A more clear Iranian influence would seem to be the Jewish concept of a Messiah (literally, "anointed one"), who will come to save the righteous at the end of time. This notion would appear to derive from the Iranian belief in the Saošyant. The figure of *ha-Satan*, literally "the adversary," appears no earlier than in the book of Job, which was composed in the post-exilic period as well. Thus, the Satan reviled by Christians and Muslims alike clearly evolved from the Zoroastrian evil deity, Ahriman, a notion most likely transmitted to the Semitic world by the Jews of Iran.

The book of Esther is entirely set in Iran, being the story of a Jewish orphan girl, Hadassah (Esther), who marries the Persian ruler and becomes queen. It is interesting to note that, reflecting the mixed culture of the times, both Esther and her adoptive father, Mordecai, are named for Mesopotamian deities, Esther for Ištar and Mordecai for Marduk.[5]

The Esther story tells a familiar tale of persecution and revenge. The Iranian Jewish community is put into danger by the Persian king's jealous prime minister, Haman, who warns his sovereign that the Jews are a people "whose laws are different from those of any other people and who do not obey the king's laws" (3:8). Fortunately for the Jews, they have a protector in the queen, through whose intervention they are spared, and the evil prime minister is punished.

The final section of the book of Esther describes how the Jewish festival of Purim came into being:

> For Haman son of Hammedatha the Agagite, the foe of all the Jews, had plotted to destroy the Jews, and had cast *pur*—that is, the lot—with intent to crush and exterminate them. But when [Esther] came before the king, he commanded: "With the promulgation of this decree, let the evil plot, which he had devised against the Jews, recoil on his own head!" So they impaled him and his sons on the stake. For that reason these days were named Purim, after *pur*.
>
> In view, then, of all the instructions in the said letter and of what they had experienced in that matter and what had befallen them, the Jews undertook and irrevocably obligated themselves and their descendants, and all who might join them, to observe these two days in the manner prescribed and at the proper time each year. Consequently, these days are recalled and observed in every generation: by every family, every province, and every city. And these days of Purim shall never cease among the Jews, and the memory of them shall never perish among their descendants.[6]

In reality, the Jewish Purim seems to have been adapted from the Iranian springtime celebration of Fravardigān, much as European Christians would later transform the pagan Yule into Christmas. Esther and Mordecai are said to have been buried in the Iranian city of Hamadan, where their purported tombs have long been a destination of Jewish pilgrims who wish to honor their memory. The tombs of two other Hebrew prophets, Daniel and Habakkuk, are also believed to be in Iran, the former in the southwestern city of Shush (Susa) and the latter in the town of Tuyserkan south of Hamadan. The shrine buildings associated with all three sites date to recent centuries, and scholars have doubted whether they actually house the remains of the figures they are named for.

Given the extent of apparent Iranian influences on the culture of the post-exilic Jews, it is somewhat surprising that they have been generally overlooked in histories of Judaism. Biblical scholars have for the most part been slow to show interest in the ancient Iranian sources in comparison to Akkadian, Ugaritic, Egyptian, and even Hittite ones.

The late James Barr was exceptional among Bible scholars in taking a serious look at what experts on ancient Iran had to say about early Judaism, but concluded that the question of Iranian influence remains open.[7] Like other skeptics, however, Barr does not account for how so many ideas associated with Iranian religion came to be found in

Judaism, beyond hinting that they may have already been percolating independently within Israelite society before emerging into the textual tradition. Be that as it may, that the mutual encounter of Iranians and Israelites dramatically expanded the pool of symbols and ideas available to both groups can hardly be denied.

## THE INFLUENCE OF HELLENISM

The language chosen by the Achæmenids to rule their western provinces was Aramaic, which was the lingua franca of most Semitic peoples, including the Jews. In the last third of the fourth century BCE, however, Alexander of Macedon led his armies from Greece into Egypt, Persia, Central Asia, and even northwestern India, bringing all the Achæmenid-ruled lands under his control and opening up the way for centuries of Greek influence to penetrate throughout the region. The effects of Greek culture, called "Hellenism" (after Hellas, the ancient name for Greece) were felt on language, philosophy, and the arts, among other things.

Among the cities where Jews lived, Alexandria in Egypt (one of many cities founded by the conqueror and named after himself) came to rival Babylon both in terms of overall Jewish population and as a center for Jewish culture. The first translation of the Hebrew Bible, known as the Septuagint (from "seventy," the number of translators supposedly involved), was made into Greek by Alexandrian Jews, making the holy scriptures available for the first time to a non-priestly audience.

Hellenized Jews, connected by trade networks with Jewish communities in Iran, acted as cultural filters, transforming and transmitting Iranian stories and concepts throughout the eastern Mediterranean world. Fueled by Iranian eschatologies, Jewish messianic and apocalyptic movements arose in Mesopotamia and elsewhere. One typical end-of-the-world tale, originally from Parthia in eastern Iran, was rewritten into Greek by a Jewish author and circulated as *The Oracles of Hystaspes* (Vištaspa), purporting to be an ancient Iranian prophecy foretelling the destruction of Jerusalem.[8] The Greek work in turn served as a major influence on the later Christian book of Revelation.

Around two thousand years ago, the blending of Greek, Semitic, and Iranian elements also constituted the foundation for an emerging mystical movement which came to be known as Gnosticism. Gnostics— literally, "those who know"—often symbolized their spiritual rebirth by undergoing ritual baptism, a practice possibly evolved out of the "trial by water" prevalent among the ancient Iranians. Various messianic and Gnostic-baptist sects emerged all throughout the Near East, especially in Mesopotamia. Some of these groups apparently considered themselves Jewish, further complicating existing claims to authority between the hereditary Jewish priests and the scholarly rabbis.

## THE RABBINIC PERIOD

The translation of the Bible into Greek symbolized a sort of democratization of the Jewish tradition, in the sense that the traditional monopoly of priests over the religious practice of the Israelites could now be accessed by anyone literate in Greek. The strongest claim of the priests, once their unique possession of the sacred texts was taken away, was that they alone could perform the prescribed sacrifice at the Temple in Jerusalem, on which the Hebrew religion was based. However, since from the sixth century BCE most Jews lived outside Palestine, they began to derive their own metaphorical means of practicing their religion, congregating in synagogues and following interpretations of the holy texts made by non-priestly scholars, one group of whom came to be known as the Pharisees. This term may be derived from the Aramaic *pārsāh*, in the sense of "persianizer," as many of their interpretations show Iranian influences.[9]

In the year 70 CE, following a Jewish revolt in Palestine, the Roman army destroyed Jerusalem and razed the Temple, just as the Babylonians had done six centuries earlier. This time the Temple was not rebuilt. Since the ritual sacrifice could not be performed elsewhere than at the Temple in Jerusalem, the priests were deprived of their principal claim to power, leaving the rabbis to emerge as the main source of spiritual guidance for Jews everywhere.

The rabbis were not the only group vying for this authority, however. Various Jewish sects followed leaders and texts of their own, challenging the rabbinical interpretations. The most significant such sect, of course, was the Christians, whose interpretation of biblical prophecies and laws radically differed from that of the rabbis. Since many of the Gnostic and apocalyptic sects mentioned earlier also rejected the rabbis' supremacy, it became increasingly necessary for the rabbis to establish a tradition that they could claim as normative for all Jews.

One specific claim the rabbis had been making since at least the third century BCE was that they had received a large body of revelation handed down orally since the time of Moses, what they called "the oral Torah," which supplemented and exceeded in quantity the written Torah of the priests. Following the model of the Christians, and eventually the Manichaeans and Zoroastrians, the rabbis began to write down the oral Torah, as a text they called the Mishnah. They developed a highly sophisticated form of scholarly debate over the meanings and applications of this text, which in turn they wrote as a commentary on the Mishnah, called the Gemara. Taken together, the Mishnah and its commentary came to constitute what Jews now know as the Talmud, which is the basis for modern Judaism.

This process, which began in the third century CE and lasted until the end of the fifth, occurred in two locations, resulting in two Talmuds. The first, completed by around 400 CE, was the work of scholars in the

Galilee region and is known as the Palestinian (or Yerushalmi) Talmud. The second, longer work, completed by 600, was compiled in Babylonia, which was the main center of Jewish culture, and is referred to as the Babylonian Talmud (also as the Bavli). Since Babylonia was a part of the Iranian world and, as one scholar has noted, "Iranian cultural influences are manifest" in it, the Babylonian Talmud might, without too much exaggeration, be called an "Iranian Talmud."[10] Many of these Iranian cultural influences were conceived in negative terms, since it was a goal of the rabbis to maintain community identity through the discouraging of interactions between Jews and non-Jews. Nevertheless, it stands to reason that in the cosmopolitan environment of Babylonia Jews must have interacted substantially with Persians, a fact that those studying the history of Judaism largely neglected until quite recently.

Jacob Neusner, in his multi-volume *History of the Jews in Babylonia* published nearly half a century ago, summed up a long-held view when he claimed that, " . . . the doctrines of competing cults made no impact whatever upon those of Judaism known from the Talmud and cognate literature."[11] More recently, however, other scholars such as Yaakov Elman and Maria Macuch, more familiar with Sasanian legal texts in Middle Persian, have challenged this assumption by demonstrating the extensive influence of Sasanian law on the Talmudic project. This emerging awareness is summarized by Carol Bakhos and Rahim Shayegan in their introduction to a collection of essays titled *The Talmud in its Iranian Context*, in which they write:

> . . . mounting evidence demonstrates that in order to comprehend Sasanian Jewry more fully, in particular the rabbis and the heritage they have bequeathed in the Babylonian Talmud, scholars must immerse themselves in the language, culture, society, and religious ethos of the Sasanian Empire.[12]

Rabbis and magi, along with religious leaders of other Babylonian communities, tended to be valued by the general population in terms of their effectiveness with spells and incantations, and people would often consult whichever figures they believed most skilled in this regard whatever their religious affiliation. Like the magi, the rabbis had to wage ongoing battles against syncretism in an effort to keep the religious identities of their communities distinct. The rabbis were also concerned by conversions of Jews to Christianity, especially since many Jewish-Christians continued to live in Jewish society and even worshiped in synagogues.[13]

During most of the Talmudic period Babylonia was under the control of the Sasanian Persian dynasty, which had made Zoroastrianism the official state religion. A stone inscription left at Naqš-e Rostam (near Persepolis) by the magus Kerdir in the late third century boasts of punishing all those who refused to worship Ahura Mazda, including the Jews (*yāhūd*).

But the Sasanians' treatment of non-Zoroastrian communities varied according to time and circumstance.

For example, according to some stories in the Talmud, the Sasanian ruler Yazdigerd I (reigned 399–421) had close relations with a number of rabbis and was generally helpful to Jewish communities in Esfahan and elsewhere.[14] On the other hand, by the time of Yazdigerd II (reigned 439–457) the agitations of Jewish messianists seem to have aroused the concern of the Sasanian government, who outlawed the observation of the Sabbath, closed Jewish schools, and executed Jewish leaders. The Jews of Esfahan responded by killing two Zoroastrian priests, and in turn the Sasanians massacred much of the city's Jewish population.

### The Juhuro of the North Caucasus

At some point during the Sasanian period a number of Iranian Jews migrated to the northeastern Caucasus, perhaps to escape persecution. They settled mainly in the regions of what are now known as Daghestan, Azerbaijan and Chechnya. During later centuries these communities were augmented by Jewish immigrants from Gilan, Georgia, and Eastern Europe. Nineteenth-century ethnographers portrayed these "Mountain Jews" (Russian *gorskie evrei*), otherwise known as Juhuro, as both "primitive" and Asianized, preserving ancient traditions and cut off from the Jewish diaspora.[15] Russian Jews saw them as backward and in need of corrective religious education.

The Juhuro speak a dialect of Persian, called Juhuri, which is similar to the Tat language of the so-called "Caucasian Persians." Historically the Juhuro were farmers, and played an important role in wine production. From the late nineteenth century the majority resettled in towns along the western Caspian coast, where they continue to be known as Mountain Jews.

Today most Juhuro have emigrated to Israel, where they number upwards of 100,000 individuals, and others to the United States. Another 30,000 or so live in the Russian Federation, with a remnant group of perhaps 12,000 living in the Republic of Azerbaijan. This little-known community provides an intriguing footnote to the history of Iranian Judaism.[16]

## THE COMING OF ISLAM

By the time Arab armies conquered the Sasanian Empire in the 640s of the Common Era, Jews may have constituted the majority in some parts of Mesopotamia. This region would become the heartland of the Islamic Caliphate, and it seems likely that many converts to Islam there had originally been Jews. Certainly the influence of Jewish traditions on the emerging Islamic civilization is very clear.

It is surely no accident that the Islamic legal code, the *sharī'a*, so closely resembles that of the Talmudic tradition, as does the process by which Muslim scholars debated and formulated it. The *sharī'a* was mainly a product of the heavily Persianized Islamic culture of Baghdad and elsewhere in Mesopotamia, where the majority of Muslims came from Jewish or Christian backgrounds. Probably many of the lawyers who codified the *sharī'a* were themselves descended from Jews, and Arab scholars as well as Iranian converts from Zoroastrianism or Buddhism learned to use the rabbis' techniques of argumentation and scholarship. In the cosmopolitan atmosphere of the High Caliphate, furthermore, Jewish and Christian scholars regularly mixed and debated with their Muslim counterparts. The Jewish academies (*yeshivot*) at Pumbedita and Sura in Babylonia continued to flourish well into the Muslim period.

Many Jewish physicians, mathematicians, and astronomers found employment at the court of the Muslim Caliph. Jewish scholars were prominent among those translating works of classical science and philosophy from Greek into Arabic. Due to their international connections they were sometimes used as ambassadors. Though Jews, like Christians and other non-Muslims, were required to wear distinctive clothing and were subject to numerous restrictions, for the most part they were left to run their own affairs. Jewish communities throughout the Muslim world were represented by the *Reš galuta*, the Exilarch at Baghdad, who was answerable on their behalf and responsible for collecting and passing on taxes to the Caliphal government.

Jewish trade networks flourished during the early Islamic period, extending from the Mediterranean and northern Europe as far as India and China. It is interesting to note that although the written Persian language was replaced by Arabic following the Muslim conquests, Jews played a role in its re-emergence in the eastern Iranian world two centuries later. A Jewish merchant's letter from the eighth century, found in the Tarim desert of what is now western China, is the oldest known written example of the Arabized "New Persian" language, which is the basis of standard Persian today. In 2011 a major find of some hundred and fifty Judeo–Persian fragments, likely dating from more than a thousand years ago, was discovered in Samangan, Afghanistan.

### Radical Jewish Resistance Movements

Times of crisis tend to produce radical movements and ideas, and the mass conversions of Jews to Islam constituted a crisis for Jewish communities everywhere. In Iran, one such movement in the 740s rallied around a figure by the name of Abu 'Isa Esfahani, whose followers believed him to be the promised messiah. They practiced vegetarianism—a possible influence from Manichaeism which was then widespread—and their approach was characterized by an attitude of mourning which, though it ostensibly centered on the loss of the Temple in Jerusalem, would seem to echo the tragic ethos of Shi'i Islam, a popular underground movement at the time. At its peak Abu 'Isa's sect counted upwards of ten thousand followers, and it persisted for several centuries.

Around the same time and place, another Iranian Jewish movement arose in opposition to the authority of the rabbis. The Karaites, as they were known, rejected the Talmudic laws and advocated the observance only of laws present in the original Torah. They too adopted an attitude of mourning reminiscent of the Shi'ite Muslims, banning heat and light on the Sabbath and all other normally joyous Jewish holidays. The Karaites observed a fast which resembled the Islamic Ramadan. Intellectually, they practiced a philosophical rationality similar to that of the Muslim Mu'atazilites. The Karaite philosophy played a role in the conversion to Judaism of the Turkish Khazar rulers of the north Caspian region in the mid-eighth century.

A few decades later, in the 830s, an Iranian Jew by the name of Abu Amran led a sect that rejected the belief in a bodily resurrection (which, it will be remembered, was an Iranian idea in the first place, not a Hebrew one). His followers referred to him as "the Iranian Moses."

In the eastern Iranian city of Balkh, a Jewish scholar by the name of Hiwi wrote the first commentary on the Bible from the standpoint of literary criticism, preceding the famous rationalist Benedict de Spinoza by eight centuries. Though Hiwi's work is lost (possibly destroyed), his "Two Hundred Criticisms" are known through the refutations of the tenth-century rabbi Saadia Gaon.

By the tenth century the center of Jewish learning had moved from Babylonia to Andalusia (Spain). Nevertheless, as late as the twelfth century, messianic figures were still appearing in Iranian Jewish communities. Beginning in 1121 a charismatic individual from the region of Azerbaijan, David Ruy, who was apparently a skilled magician, tried to assemble a Jewish army to retake Jerusalem, which was then in the hands of the Christian Franks. The movement was unsuccessful, but David's example continued to inspire later Jewish groups.

## IRANIAN JEWS IN THE MONGOL PERIOD

With the relocation of the Jewish culture's center of gravity to Spain, eastern Jews became somewhat marginalized. Even so, significant Jewish communities persisted throughout the Muslim world and beyond. Jews continued to play important roles in trade, establishing networks all across Asia. Though the origins of the Jewish community in China— which persisted until the 1950s—cannot be dated or traced with any certainty, it seems likely that they came originally from Iran. Silk Road cities such as Samarkand and Bukhara had large Jewish quarters, though in recent times most Central Asian Jews have migrated to Israel.

When the Mongol armies erupted from Inner Asia and took control of much of Eurasia throughout the thirteenth century, one of their major aims was to control the long-distance trade routes; what might be called in modern-day parlance "the elimination of trade barriers." Since Iranian Jewish businessmen were prominent players in the trade networks which linked the Mediterranean world with China, and since Jewish communities were too small to constitute a political threat, some Jews were able to benefit from Mongol patronage and attain important commercial and political positions.

In the 1280s, for example, a Jewish physician by the name of Mordecai, gained the attention of the Mongol governor of Tabriz, Arghun Khan, who appointed him prime minister over all Iran. Though Mordecai had ostensibly become a Muslim, earning the title Sa'd al-Dawla, or "fortune of the State," the fact that Muslim sources refer to him as "the Jewish vizier" suggests a mainly pragmatic conversion. Once in power Sa'd al-Dawla appointed many of his Jewish relatives to governorships throughout the realm, causing intense resentment among the Muslims. Rumors began to circulate that he intended to take Jerusalem (echoes of David Ruy) and give it back to the Jews, and turn the *ka'ba* in Mecca into an idol temple. In 1291 he was executed.

Only a few years later, however, in 1298, another Jewish physician rose to the position of prime minister in Tabriz. Again a convert to Islam, he is known only by his Muslim name, Rashid al-din Fazlollah. Rashid al-din wrote books on medicine and other subjects, and is best known as the author of the encyclopedic world history *Jāmi' al-tavārīx* ("Collection of Histories") which was commissioned by the Mongol court.

An able administrator, Rashid al-din reformed the fiscal, commercial, legal, and postal systems of the Mongol state in Iran. He oversaw the construction of roads and the strengthening of public security. Like his predecessor, however, his power won him many enemies and in 1316 he too was executed as a result of intrigues at court. The downfalls of both Jewish premiers were followed by pogroms against Jews. Yet Rashid al-din's successor, Ghiyas al-din Muhammad, was also a Jewish convert. In 1327 he was executed as well.

Never again would the Jews of Iran have the benefit of powerful benefactors in government. The latter half of the fourteenth century saw the rise of Tamerlane (Teymūr-e lang, "Lame Timur," on account of a childhood accident), a Central Asian Turk who saw himself as a conqueror in the mold of Chinggis Khan but with the religious zeal of a ruthless Islamic reformer. He championed mainstream Sunni Islam against enemies of all kinds, whom he would accuse of heresy; the Jews were not spared his "ethnic cleansing." According to one story, Tamerlane was riding past a synagogue in Esfahan when the chanting from within startled his horse and threw the emperor. Furious, he ordered the massacre of the entire congregation. Habib Levy estimates that some 350,000 Iranian Jews were killed, converted, or fled Iran during Tamerlane's rule.[17]

Iran's best-known Jewish poet, Shāhīn of Shiraz, flourished during the Mongol rule in the early fourteenth century.[18] Shāhīn is famous for having rendered a number of the books of the Hebrew Bible into Persian verse, including much of the Torah (that is, the first five books, otherwise known as the Pentateuch) and the books of Job, Esther, and Ezra. The influence of the Iranian heroic epic, the Book of Kings, is particularly evident in Shāhīn's portrayal of Moses in the *Mūsā-nāmeh*. His treatments often mirror those of Muslim poets drawing on the same themes, such as the fall of the angel Azazel (the future Satan) from heaven after refusing to bow down before Adam—a popular story among Sufis—or that of the Joseph story, which in Shāhīn's version bears as much resemblance to the Qur'anic account as it does to the biblical version.[19] In another work, the *Ardešīr-nāmeh*, Shāhīn attempts to elevate the Jewish place in Iranian history by making Queen Esther the mother of Cyrus the Great (see Figure 4).

A blending of Iranian and Jewish identities characterizes much of Judeo–Persian literature. The seventeenth-century writer Bābā'ī son of Lutf, best known for his accounts of persecution and forced conversion suffered by Esfahan's Jews, also wrote poetry in which he incorporated Iranian themes into Jewish subjects, as in the following verse in praise of the prophet Elijah:

> Peacock of Mercy's oasis
> Simorgh of the tower of gnosis
> Toll gatherer on the road to finis
> O Elijah, take my hand.[20]

The peacock is a motif imported from the Persian poetry of India, whereas the Simorgh is a mythical bird from ancient Iranian legends. The term translated here as "gnosis" is *ma'rifa*, a central theme in Sufism. Later in the same poem Bābā'ī refers to Elijah as the *mahdī*, or Islamic messiah, and "our intercessor," a role attributed in popular Islam to Muhammad. Such examples vividly illustrate the degree to which writers like Bābā'ī felt both Iranian and Jewish.

## THE SAFAVID PERIOD

A Turkish group, led by the Safavī family of Ardebil in Azerbaijan, conquered Iran in 1501 and began a century-long process of forcing the country's Muslims, most of whom were Sunnis, to the Twelver Shi'i branch of Islam. Although the brunt of the Safavids' ideological force was directed at Sunni Muslims, the Shi'ite clerics who supported the government considered non-Shi'ites, including Jews, to be ritually unclean (*najes*), an attitude possibly inherited from Sasanian Zoroastrianism. This attitude on the part of Iran's Shi'ite Muslims, which extended to Christians and Zoroastrians as well, intensified the marginalization of the Jewish communities throughout Iran. Non-Muslims were required to wear distinctive headgear and clothing, and Shi'ite clerics occasionally ordered the public burning of Hebrew books. According to a set of restrictions compiled by a leading Shi'ite cleric, Mohammad Baqer Majlesi, in the late seventeenth century, Jews were not even allowed to go out in the rain for fear that they might splash Shi'ites, thereby causing contamination.[21]

As a result of tensions between the Safavids and the Sunni Ottomans who controlled Mesopotamia, relations between Iranian Jewish communities and those further west were dramatically reduced. Many Jews converted to Islam during this period, at least outwardly, though like the members of other religious minority communities some of them continued to practice their original faith in private. This was in contrast to the situation in the Ottoman world, where Sephardic Jews expelled from Spain had been welcomed and where Jewish communities thrived.

During the 1660s Jews throughout the Middle East were roused by an Ottoman Jew, Shabbatai Zevi, who claimed that he was the promised messiah. In response to this development, the Safavid ruler Shah Abbas II (reigned 1642–1666) issued a decree that all Jews under his rule must convert to Islam. Many Jews continued to practice their faith in private, while others chose to emigrate instead, mainly to the Ottoman lands. Those who practiced their religion openly were subject to all manner of discriminatory restrictions and lived under the constant threat of harassment and torture.

Jewish poets of the Safavid period continued the tradition of setting biblical stories into Persian verse. Among these one may count the *Fath-nāmeh* ("Book of Victory"), which draws upon the books of Joshua, Judges, Ruth, I Samuel and II Samuel, and the *Shoftim-nāmeh* (book of Judges) of Aharon ben Mashiah (active in the late seventeenth century). Jewish painters of the time also illustrated books of Persian literature, rendered into Hebrew letters, with paintings in the Persian miniature tradition.[22]

## THE MODERN PERIOD

The Safavid dynasty was brought to an end when the Afghan tribals conquered Esfahan in 1722. The Afghans, who were Sunnis, continued the policy of forcing Iranian Jews to convert to Islam. Under the Afšārid dynasty established by Nader Khan in 1732, the subsequent Zand dynasty during the second half of the eighteenth century, and the Qajars throughout the nineteenth, Iran's dwindling Jewish communities were characterized mainly by poverty and their marginal status. Frequent riots and other forms of civil unrest, which marked the reign of the weak Qajars, often resulted in unruly mobs looting Jewish shops and attacking Jews. The year 1839 saw the forced conversion of the entire Jewish community of Mashhad, numbering some 2,400 people.[23]

The revolutionary Bābī movement of the 1840s, led by a self-proclaimed prophet who extended the promise of equal consideration to Jews, attracted a number of Jewish followers. Although the Bābīs were ruthlessly crushed following their attempt to assassinate the Qajar king Naser al-din Shah in 1852, a remnant of the movement emerged a decade later as the newly pacifist Bahá'ís. Many Iranian Jews were among the converts to this new world faith. During the latter half of the nineteenth century European missionaries, who were prohibited from proselytizing among Iran's Muslims, also won converts from Judaism.

From the 1870s European Jews began to take an interest in the plight of Iranian Jewry. In 1898 the Paris-based Alliance Israélite Universelle opened a school in Tehran, followed by others in different parts of the country.[24] The Jews were granted one seat in Iran's new parliament following the Constitutional Revolution of 1906, although their "representative" was a Muslim, and therefore really more of an ombudsman.

Reza Shah Pahlavi's pro-German policies of the 1930s created an uncomfortable climate for Iranian Jews, who were often vilified in the press. With the founding of the state of Israel in 1948 over one-third of Iran's Jews emigrated there. Many settled in Jaffa and Holon, where today one can often hear Persian spoken in the shops and streets.

Under Shah Mohammad Reza Pahlavi in the 1950s and 1960s, the situation of Iran's remaining Jews improved markedly. The Shah established close relations with Israel, which became a major ally. Jewish children were allowed to attend Hebrew schools, and Jews figured prominently in Iranian academia and medicine. All of these factors led to a severe backlash after the 1979 revolution, however, since Jews were seen by the resurgent Islamists as being simultaneously in league with a corrupt king and an illegitimate foreign state.

### Iranian Jewry Since the Islamic Revolution

Iranians are a conspiracy-minded people, and Jews have long been seen as conspiracy's prime agents. Ruhollah Khomeini, during his years of exile in the 1960s and 1970s, often referred to the Pahlavi regime as being controlled by Zionists. Since the founding of the Islamic Republic the rhetoric on Jews has been highly mixed. On the one hand, religious leaders are generally quick to assert that Islam respects Judaism and that Jews are protected under Islamic law. At the same time, the impulse to see Jews behind every purported plot has continued. In principle Iran's religious leaders claim to distinguish between Iranian Jews who are honest and loyal to their country and those who secretly act on behalf of Israel, but in practice the distinction is not so clearly made.

In reality, among the recognized religious minorities in the Islamic Republic Jews have fared the worst. Nor has the government's animosity towards Jews been restricted to suspected Israeli spies within the country or its support for radical Palestinian groups abroad. In March 2003 the government of Argentina released the details of an eight-year investigation into the 1994 bombing of a Buenos Aires Jewish center that killed eighty-five people. The investigation found that this attack, together with an earlier one in 1992 and a foiled attempt in 1996, were orchestrated through the Iranian embassy in Buenos Aires.

Even under the comparatively liberal presidency of Mohammad Khatami (1997–2005) Jews in Iran continued to suffer various forms of repression, though it is likely that such acts were carried out by Khatami's hardline opponents. In 1999 a group of thirteen Iranian Jews were arrested on charges of spying for Israel, once again bringing Iran the unwanted attention of international human rights groups. The strongly anti-Israel rhetoric of Khatami's successor, Mahmud Ahmadinejad, has generally been seen as having a negative impact on Iran's Jewish population, though the regime officially continues to claim it distinguishes between Jews and Zionists. It is likely that fewer than 20,000 Jews remain in Iran today; their numbers continue to shrink through emigration.

# Buddhism

The Iranian world played an important role in the development and transmission of Buddhism, especially during the early centuries. Like other world religions, Buddhism spread via trade routes and absorbed local influences along the way.[1] A Pali legend suggests that the first individuals to spread the Buddha's teaching outside India were a pair of travelling businessmen from Balkh, Tapassu and Bhallika, who were present at the Buddha's famous sermon at the deer park near Benaras; as natives of the east Iranian province of Bactria, these men would likely have been ethnic Iranians. Whether or not this particular legend has any historical validity, the region in question (now Afghanistan) became one of the main centers of Buddhism and remained so up to the Islamic conquests in the seventh century. The process of Islamization took several centuries, and since the population of eastern Iran was mostly Buddhist, this meant that many converts to Islam brought with them a Buddhist cultural background.

## THE RISE AND SPREAD OF BUDDHISM IN EASTERN IRAN

The Indian emperor Ashoka Maurya (reigned 273–232 BCE) commissioned a number of Buddhist inscriptions on rocks and pillars throughout his realm, stretching across northern India to the eastern fringes of the Greek Seleucid Empire, which had replaced the Persian Achæmenids only half a century earlier. At least six of Ashoka's inscriptions in northwestern India included translations into Aramaic, the language of the erstwhile Achæmenid bureaucracy, and were thus presumably aimed at Iranians. His royal edicts explicitly call for missionaries to spread the *dharma* to the Kambojas (Iranians) and the Yonas (Greeks). The Aramaic translations of Ashoka's edicts show some conscious attempt to add an Iranian flavour, such as frequent insertions of the qualifier "good" (a likely reference to "the good religion" of the

Zoroastrians) and the deletion of references to *deva*s, considered minor deities by Indians but abhorred as devils in Zoroastrianism.

This northwestern region of the Indian subcontinent—roughly what is now Pakistan—was the transition zone between Iran and the Indian world, just as Mesopotamia was between Iran and the Semitic sphere. In the wake of Alexander's conquest, Greek culture was added to the mix. Later the region would succumb to successive waves of Iranian and Turkish Central Asians seeking to control the trade networks, thereby bringing yet more cultural elements into this cosmopolitan environment. Buddhism, strengthened by its involvement in the long-distance trading economy, became the major religion in the area and would remain so up to the Arab conquests in the seventh century CE. But as a developing worldview, Buddhism in northwestern India was subject to influences emanating from all the diverse peoples of the region.

After the fall of the Maurya dynasty in the early second century BCE, the eastern Iran–northwestern India border zone became an often unstable playing field on which various groups competed for power. These were mainly the Parthians from northeastern Iran; the Sakas (Scythians), an originally nomadic Iranian people from the Eurasian steppes; and the Kushans, who also spoke an Iranian language (Bactrian) but were originally from the eastern part of Inner Asia and may have been partially descended from the Indo-European-speaking Tokharians. Each of these groups exercised religious tolerance, facilitating the commingling of ideas and the blending of traditions.

Buddhism's flourishing and development was due mainly to the support of travelling merchants who would make donations to Buddhist monasteries (*vihara*s), and shrines (*stupa*s), which usually contained relics associated with the Buddha. The economic and religious significance of the stupas carried over into the Muslim period and continues to the present day in Afghanistan and Central Asia. Muslim shrines to Sufi saints, like the stupas before them, are sites for pilgrimage and the main centers of popular religion. A symbol of this continuity can be seen in the banners once flown by Iranian Buddhists from the tops of the stupas, which continue to adorn the cupolas of Sufi shrines in the region today.

In the centuries before the Arab conquests Buddhism was spread throughout the eastern Iranian world. Buddhist sites have been found in Afghanistan, Turkmenistan, Uzbekistan, and Tajikistan, as well as within Iran itself. It has long been known that the region of Bactria—what is now the northern part of Afghanistan and which remains largely Persian-speaking—was an important Buddhist center in the pre-Islamic period. The valley of Bamiyan in eastern Afghanistan is famous for two colossal Buddha statues, which were destroyed by the fanatical Taliban in 2001. A seventh-century Buddhist temple at Ajina-Teppe in southern Tajikistan contained another important statue, a reclining

Buddha twelve meters long; the statue is now in the National Museum of Antiquities in Dushanbe (see Figure 5).

What is only recently emerging, mainly from archaeological work in Turkmenistan, is the important role played by Parthians in transmitting Buddhism to China. Although Chinese sources mention a number of important Buddhist monks who came from Parthia, such as the second-century translator of Buddhist texts, An Shigao, most western Buddhologists have considered that Buddhism only caught on in a minor way in Parthia itself.

Archaeological work during the Soviet period tells a different story, however. Both the volume and distinctiveness of Buddhist artefacts from Parthian sites suggests a strong Buddhist presence during Parthian and Kushan times, from around the first century until the third century, when Sasanian power brought an increased support for Zoroastrianism.

Only since 1991 have Western scholars become aware of the extent of these Soviet-era finds. The Museum of Turkmen History in Ashgabat, Turkmenistan is full of Buddhist objects excavated from the Marv region, a once-important trading center along the Silk Road until its destruction by the Mongols in the thirteenth century. Some one hundred Buddhist rock inscriptions—mainly dedications—have been found in Margiana, dating from the first century BCE through the fifth century CE. Sanskrit texts of the Sarvastivadin school, dating to the fifth century, have also been discovered there. Unfortunately, because scholarly work in Turkmenistan has slowed dramatically since the country's independence in 1991, most of this material remains unstudied and its significance poorly understood.

Western scholars have tended to see Buddhism as having been transmitted from Gandhara (northwestern India) directly to China via cities such as Khotan and Kucha in the Tarim Basin. Although one vector of transmission appears indeed to have gone this way over the rigorous passes of the Karakorum Mountains, there is evidence of a western "detour" through Parthia as well. Though there are no surviving Buddhist texts in Parthian, the evolution of Buddhist terms in other languages suggests that at least in some cases, Buddhism was transmitted to China via Parthia. This would help explain why so many important Buddhist translators in China were of Parthian origin.

If Buddhism was prevalent in Parthia, which was centered on the northeastern part of the Iranian world, it is not clear how far its influence penetrated into the areas further west. Echoes of Buddhist ideas have been seen in some aspects of Christianity, and though the evidence for this is still rather foggy it is a fact that India and the Mediterranean were culturally connected (mainly through trade), and that this connection passed through Iran. Since Buddhism was strongly associated with trading activity, communities of Buddhist merchants from India lived in or traveled through western Iran. It is not known how successful the expatriate Indians were in winning converts to Buddhism in western Iran and Mesopotamia, but it would seem that the overall numbers of Buddhists in the west were far less than in the east.

## Buddhism in Western Iran

The evidence for Buddhists in western Iran is limited. In two official inscriptions the fanatical Sasanian high priest Kerdir, who lived in the third century, mentions *sramanas* (Buddhist monks) among those non-Zoroastrians he hopes to eliminate throughout Iran—a clear indication that such people existed in the country at the time. There are elements of Buddhist iconography in some Sasanian-period art. At Taq-e Bostan, for example, Mithra is seen standing on a lotus. Buddhist rock-cut monuments have been identified at Chehel-khāneh and Haidari in the southwestern Iranian province of Fars, and recently nineteen Buddha statues, in the Gandhara style, were discovered there.[2] Similar caves at Rasat-khāneh and Varjuvi in Azerbaijan may have been Buddhist sites as well, most likely later during the Mongol period.[3]

Place names give a further clue. A number of villages in western Khorasan—and even as far west as Rayy near modern Tehran—bear the name Nō Bahār, which is derived from Sanskrit *nava vihara* or "new [Buddhist] monastery."[4] Along the southern Iranian coast, the names Chāh Bahār in Baluchistan and Bot-khāneh ["Buddha-house"] and Bahārestān in Fars attest to the passage of Buddhist traders from India. Tiz, on the Baluch coast near the border of Pakistan, is mentioned in the *Čač-nāmeh* (a thirteenth-century history of Sind) as having had a substantial Buddhist community as late as the twelfth century, and may even have had a Buddhist administration in early Islamic times.

# IRANIAN BUDDHISM

The considerable differences between Indian and Chinese Buddhism can be attributed in large part to the introduction of Iranian ideas and symbols into the Buddhist pool. One of the most striking examples of Iranian–Buddhist syncretism is an image of the Buddha found in Qara-Teppe, Uzbekistan which bears the inscription "Buddha Mazda." This Kushan period wall painting shows the Buddha surrounded by flames, the ancient Iranian symbol of divine blessing ($x^v$*arənah*), which became standard in the iconography of Buddhist, Islamic, and (as a halo) Christian art.[5]

The archaeological remains of Buddhist stupas and monasteries throughout Bactria are supplemented by the many descriptions of Iranian Buddhist sites in the accounts of Buddhist travellers from China and elsewhere. The most famous of these is undoubtedly Xuanzang (died 664), a Chinese Buddhist monk who travelled via Central Asia to India in hopes of finding authentic Sanskrit texts and bringing them back to China. Xuanzang states that in his time Balkh had about one hundred Buddhist monasteries and some three thousand monks, all belonging to schools of the "Lesser Vehicle" (Hinayana). His account takes note of the economic importance of these monasteries, which were often raided by nomadic armies:

> Outside the city, towards the southwest, there is a monastery called Navasangharama, which was built by a former king of this country. The Masters, who dwell to the north of the great Snowy Mountains, and are authors of the Shastras, occupy this monastery only, and continue their estimable labours in it. There is a figure of the Buddha here, which is lustrous with noted gems, and the hall in which it stands is also adorned with precious substances of rare value. This is the reason why it has often been robbed by chieftains of neighbouring countries, covetous of gain.

> This monastery also contains a statue of Vaishravana Deva, by whose spiritual influence, in unexpected ways, there is protection afforded to the precincts of the monastery. Lately the son of Khan Yeh-hu, belonging to the Turks, becoming rebellious, Yeh-hu Khan broke up his camping ground, and marched at the head of the horde to make a foray against this monastery, desiring to obtain the jewels and precious things with which it was enriched. Having encamped his army in the open ground, not far from the monastery, in the night he had a dream. He saw Vaishravana Deva, who addressed him thus: "What power do you possess that you dare to overthrow this monastery?" and then hurling his lance, he transfixed him with it. The Khan, affrighted, awoke, and his heart penetrated with sorrow, he told his dream to his followers, and then, to atone somewhat for his fault, he hastened to the monastery to ask permission to confess his crime to the monks, but before he received an answer he died.[6]

Xuanzang then goes on to elaborate on the valuable relics contained in the monastery, which were objects of veneration for local Buddhists:

> Within the monastery, in the southern hall of the Buddha, there is the washing basin which Buddha used. It contains about a peck, and is of various colours, which dazzle the eyes. It is difficult to name the gold and stone of which it is made. Again, there is a tooth of Buddha about an inch long, and about eight or nine tenths of an inch in breadth. Its colour is yellowish white; it is pure and shining. Again, there is the sweeping brush of Buddha, made of the kasha plant. It is about two feet long and about seven inches round. Its handle is ornamented with various gems. These three relics are presented with offerings on each of the six

fast-days by the assembly of lay and monastic believers. Those who have the greatest faith in worship see the objects emitting a radiance of glory.[7]

Clearly the Buddhist community of Balkh was more taken with miracles and ritual than with the sort of individual mental discipline originally taught by the Buddha a millennium or more earlier, but this was surely not atypical. It is hardly surprising that according to Xuanzang, the monks of Balkh were so irregular in their observance of the monastic code (*vinaya*) "that it is hard to tell saints from sinners."

The close ties between Buddhist monks and government officials is also attested in an inscription which adorned the entrance to the No Bahar shrine, no longer extant but reported by the tenth-century Muslim historian Mas'udi in his book *Meadows of Gold*: The Buddha said, "The courts of princes require three qualities: intelligence, reliability, and wealth." Beneath this inscription, according to Mas'udi, someone had written in Arabic: "The Buddha lied. What any free man possessing one of these qualities must do is avoid the court at all costs."[8]

A memory of the fabulous riches and adornment associated with the Buddhist shrines and statues of eastern Iran is preserved in the tradition of Persian Muslim poetry, which first took shape in precisely that part of the Iranian world where Buddhism had prevailed until the coming of Islam. The idealized "beloved" about whom the poets write (normally conceived of not as a girl but as an adolescent boy) is often described as a "moon-faced idol" (*bot*—literally, a buddha), and sometimes in terms of other details such as having "a body of silver," recalling the fact that buddha statues were often covered in silver paint. According to A. S. Melikian-Chirvani, "the poetic archetype of the idol [in Persian poetry] responds trait for trait to the artistic archetype of the eastern Iranian buddha."[9] Likewise, the poetic expression *ey bot* ("oh, beauty!") is a secular survival of the sacred Buddhist invocation *aho Buddho*.[10]

## *Iranian Influences in Buddhism*

The subtle infusion of Iranian ideas into the spreading Buddhist tradition is most apparent in the contexts of Central Asian Iranian peoples such as the Sogdians of Transoxiana and the Sakas of Khotan. For example, Khotanese translations of *dharma* used the Iranian term *data* when referring to the Buddha's law. The term *Buddha-datu*, or "Buddha-law," may be compared with the earlier Zoroastrian *mazdo-data* (Mazda's law). Khotanese texts likewise employ the Iranian notion of *x$^v$aranah/farr* (Khotanese *pharra*) to mean "good fortune resulting from following the Buddha's path." Buddhist art from Gandhara to Bamiyan employs the *x$^v$aranah* symbolism of flames rising from the

Buddha's shoulders or encircling his head, which Frantz Grenet sees as an iconographic substitution of the Buddha for Mithra.[11]

As in the Aramaic Ashokan inscriptions, Khotanese and Sogdian Buddhist writers avoided the term *deva*. In Khotan the Indian goddess of prosperity was replaced by her Iranian equivalent Shandramata (the Zoroastrian Spenta Armaiti). Mithra appears in Sogdian Buddhist texts and as a statue accompanying the smaller of the two colossal Buddhas which existed at Bamiyan, Afghanistan. Zurvan, the Iranian god of time, replaces Brahmana in a Sogdian *jataka* tale (a story about the Buddha in his prior incarnations), while in some texts the Indian god Indra becomes Ohrmazd. The Buddhists were not entirely accommodating of Zoroastrianism, however. They were deeply critical of a number of Zoroastrian practices, including consanguinal marriage, the habitual killing of "Ahrimanic" animals such as snakes and scorpions, and the exposing of corpses.

The square form of stupa-building was adopted by the Buddhists of eastern Iran from the region's pre-existing tradition of sacred architecture, eventually becoming the norm throughout the Buddhist world. Another Iranian contribution to Buddhist architecture was the carving out of sacred grottos from rock—a technique inherited from Achæmenid funerary architecture—which spread to Buddhist sites throughout India and China. The most famous Iranian examples are the two colossal rock-cut Buddha statues of Bamiyan, one measuring one hundred feet in height and the other one hundred and fifty, which dated to the sixth century CE. The taller one, which was apparently painted red, is referred to in medieval Muslim sources as "the Red Buddha," and the shorter one as "the White Buddha," presumably painted white. The two colossi survived until recent times when they were tragically destroyed by Afghanistan's fanatical Taliban regime in 2001. (The Taliban period also saw the destruction of many other Buddhist sites, as well as the pillaging and dispersal of Buddhist artefacts from Afghan museums.)

Iranian influences are also present in the Buddhist art of the so-called Gandhara School, which arose under the Kushans in the first and second centuries CE. Representations of the Buddha in statues and paintings appear from this time onwards and are generally considered to emerge from Western forms, especially Greek but to some extent Iranian as well.

One distinctive feature in Gandhara art is the new prevalence of *bodhisattva* figures. The bodhisattva ideal is associated with the emergence of Mahayana ("Great Vehicle") Buddhism, a movement that arose in northwestern India and began to challenge the established schools (*nikaya*s, called Hinayana or "Lesser Vehicle" by the Mahayanists) some time shortly before the Common Era. The Mahayanists are characterized mainly by their identification with certain texts, many of which were apparently composed in the multicultural Indian–Iranian border region.[12]

Finding Iranian figures and notions in the Mahayana system therefore comes as little surprise. Probably the most obvious is the bodhisattva Maitreya, the future Buddha who will come as a saviour figure at the end of time—a clear parallel to the Zoroastrian Saošyant, and entirely absent from the "do-it-yourself" salvation of the earliest Buddhist texts. Maitreya is the most common bodhisattva figure occurring in Gandharan art, demonstrating his immense popularity in the Indo-Iranian border regions.

Another bodhisattva, Amitabha (which means "infinite radiance"), the Buddha of Light, bears many features associated with the Iranian god of time, Zurvan.[13] A third, Avalokitesvara, shares certain elements in common with Mithra, originally the Iranian god of covenants, identified with the sun. In Khotanese Buddhist mythology we find the figure of Ksitigarbha, non-existent elsewhere in the Buddhist world, who conducts souls across a "bridge of death" strikingly reminiscent of the Zoroastrian Činvat.

Just as some elements of Buddhist iconography appear in western Iran, numerous Sasanian features are found in the Buddhist art of the Iranian east. One such image is that of the griffin; another is that of a duck holding a necklace. In a seventh-century statue at Bamiyan, Maitreya is depicted wearing a crown identical to that of the Sasanian ruler Khosrow II. Many Bamiyan buddhas also wear hair ribbons of the Sasanian style.

Beginning in the Kushan period, Central Asian Buddhists began to build stupas to house relics of the Buddha. The architecture of many of these shrines, which allowed for circumambulation by pilgrims, seems to have been borrowed from that of Zoroastrian fire temples. The practice of adorning the shrines with flower garlands, prevalent in Bactria, was apparently carried over from a ritual associated with the Iranian goddess Anahita.

The merchants and missionaries who carried Buddhism to Central Asia and China were mostly of Iranian background. Many were Parthians, while others were Sogdians from what is now Uzbekistan, or Sakas from Khotan in what is now western China. Merchants and other travellers tended to be multilingual, and often applied their skills to translating texts. Many translations of Buddhist works from Indian languages into Chinese were done by translators with Iranian names.

From the T'ang period onwards one of the most popular forms of Buddhism in China was the so-called "Pure Land" school, which taught that to be saved, one merely had to be pronouncing the Buddha's name at the moment of death. Amitabha, the Buddha of Light, would then transport the devotee to a Pure Land of bliss, called Sukhavati, located somewhere in the West. As noted above, this markedly soteriological faith is at odds with the "do-it-yourself" approach of early *nikaya* Buddhism in India, and seems to owe far more to Iranian tradition.

In another example, an annual ritual widely practiced in T'ang China, in which the "hungry ghosts" of departed ancestors are fed, resembles the Iranian "all souls" festival of Fravardigān, from which it may be derived. This is the contention of Iwamoto Yutaka, who proposes that the Chinese name for the festival comes (via Sogdian) from the Iranian word for "soul" (*ravān*) and suggests that the salvation story associated with it—in which the virtuous monk Mu-lien willingly descends into hell to save his sinful mother—is a form of the Greek myth of Dionysos and Semele which was transmitted by Iranians to China.[14]

Iranian influence can be seen in Tibet both in the pre-Buddhist Bön religion and in Tibetan Buddhism. Bön texts speak of the religion as having originated in the West, from the "land of the Tajiks."[15] In Tibetan Buddhism, the famous *Book of the Dead* (*Bardo-Thodol*) shows a number of Iranian features, including the symbolism of light and the description of individual eschatology.[16] Similar to the Zoroastrian tradition, in the Tibetan *Book of the Dead* it is said that after three days the soul of the deceased passes along a precipice where it encounters either a radiant light or ghastly demons, depending on whether one has lived a good or evil existence.

## THE DISAPPEARANCE (SUBMERSION?) OF IRANIAN BUDDHISM

Buddhism's spread to the West during Sasanian times was impeded by the state-supported power of the Zoroastrian magi. Iranian Buddhism was strongest in the East, in what is now northern and eastern Afghanistan, far from the center of Sasanian control. In the seventh century these territories were conquered by the Muslim Arabs, whose interest in controlling trade routes put them in direct economic competition with Buddhist merchants and monasteries.

Hostile references in the Qur'an to the "idol-worshiping" Meccan Arabs of Muhammad's time were easily transformed into ideological weapons against the Buddhists, who, unlike Christians, Jews, and Zoroastrians, were not offered the protection accorded under Islamic law to "peoples of the Book." At first during the Umayyad period (661–750), the Arabs were content with submission to their overlordship and converts mostly sought to join the Islamic community of their own accord. Over time, however, as the Muslims consolidated their power in eastern Iran, anti-Buddhist attitudes became more prevalent, and while small Buddhist communities in some remote areas may have survived as late as the twelfth century, by the ninth century it would seem that most Iranian Buddhists had abandoned their religion in favor of Islam.

Yet, as is most often the case with religious conversions, Iranian Buddhists who joined the Islamic community brought a number of influences. The Barmak family (their name likely derived from the Sanskrit *pramukha*, "chief"; they are known in European literature as the Barmecides), who held the reins of power as ministers in the Islamic Caliphate during the first half of the ninth century, had originally been in charge of a major Buddhist shrine in the city of Balkh and may have remained unofficial patrons of Buddhist communities even after their supposed conversion to Islam. Richard Bulliet has suggested that their inherited position both provided the Barmaks with a regional power base of former Buddhists and enabled the central government in Baghdad to exercise control over eastern Iran through the Barmaks' influence.[17]

Popular legends associated with the early Sufi saint Ibrahim ibn Adham (who died around 790), born in Balkh to a family of Arab settlers, show the Buddhist color of the region. The story of Ibrahim's spiritual journey in some respects almost exactly mirrors that of the Buddha's, clearly an attempt to reach a Buddhist audience. One of the first of the so-called "intoxicated" (that is, ecstatic) Sufis, Abu Yazid (Bayazid) of Bistam (died 874), was originally a disciple of an Indian teacher from Sindh, still a heavily Buddhist area at that time. Certain Buddhist ideas are detectable in the mystical philosophy of these and other eastern Iranian Sufis. The notion of *fanā'*, for example—interpreted in Islamic terms as "annihilation in God" as the ultimate goal of the mystic—bears a strong resemblance to the Buddhist concept of nirvana.

In another possible example of Buddhist influence, certain heterodox sects such as the Yaresan in western Iran, like earlier Iranian movements such as Manichaeism, Mazdakism, and the Abu Muslimiyya, retain a belief in reincarnation.

## THE MONGOL REVIVAL

Buddhism experienced a brief revival in Iran during the second half of the thirteenth century under the Mongol dynasty known as the Il-khans. The founder of this dynasty, Hülegü Khan (reigned 1256–1284) and his successor Arghun Khan (reigned 1284–1291) were at least nominal Buddhists, and for four decades Buddhism held the status of something like state religion in Iran. The first two Il-Khanids favored foreign Buddhist merchants over local Muslim ones, and allowed for the building of Buddhist institutions and the transfer of assets (a nice way of saying "looting") from Muslims to Buddhists.

Needless to say, these practices aroused the resentment and hostility of Iran's Muslim majority. After the conversion of the Mongol ruler

Ghazan Khan to Islam around the turn of the fourteenth century, Buddhist activity in Iran was quickly extinguished, and the newly built Buddhist monasteries and stupas were either destroyed or converted into mosques. Buddhism essentially disappeared from Iran, reappearing only in the twentieth century in the context of some modern poetry and an emerging popular new age movement.

## BUDDHISM AND '*ERFĀN*[18]

There are subtle similarities with Buddhist ideas in the distinctly Iranian form of Islamic mysticism known as '*erfān*. Indeed, the first flowering of '*erfān*, seen especially in Sufi poetry and in the contemplative idealism of Persian miniature painting, occurred in the period following the Mongol devastations of Iranian territory in the thirteenth and fourteenth centuries, perhaps reflecting a need among Iranians to find inner peace amid external turmoil.

A similar set of conditions may have been at work in the twentieth century, when Iranians were first confronted with a despotic monarchy many found spiritually lacking, then by a professedly religious regime many saw (and see) as spiritually bankrupt. During the period of the last monarch, Shah Mohammad Reza Pahlavi (reigned 1941–1979), several of Iran's best-known poets, including most notably Sohrab Sepehri (1928–1980), drew overtly on Buddhist inspiration in their work, likely seeking a more peaceful alternative to the spirituality offered by militant Shi'ism. Sepehri's poem "Bodhi" is a good example:

> It was a moment; the doors opened
> Not a leaf, not a branch, the garden of nirvana (*fanā'*) appeared
> The birds of the place are silent
> This is silent, that is silent, it seems all has been silenced
> What was this scene? Beside a lamb, a wolf stood
> A weak voice, a weak echo
> Has the curtain been pulled aside?
> I've left, it has left, no more us
> Beauty has been left alone
> Every river has become the sea
> Every being has become a buddha[19]

Another well-known contemporary poet, Ahmad Shamlu (1925–2000), had some interest in Japanese Buddhism. He dedicated one of his poems to the Japanese poet Kobayashi Issa (1763–1828), and translated a book of haiku poetry into Persian. His collaborator on the haiku volume was Askari Pasha'i (who has also written three books on Shamlu), one of Iran's most accomplished translators, who has a longstanding interest in Buddhism. Pasha'i has lived in Japan and has published Persian editions of a number of books on Buddhism.

In the post-revolution period Buddhist ideas and practice, often as part of a broader, new-age type spirituality, have exerted an increasingly visible and explicit influence within Iranian society. Scholarly and popular books on Buddhism, both translations of works by westerners and original studies in Persian, are bestsellers in Iran today. Meditation centers do a thriving business, and seminars draw large audiences.

While some Iranians today, such as the Oscar-nominated actress Shohreh Aghdashloo, go so far as to overtly self-identify as Buddhists,[20] more often they merely incorporate aspects of Buddhist philosophy into their existing Muslim identity, for example practicing meditation. Like the Catholic monk Thomas Merton (1915–1968), they appear to see no fundamental exclusiveness between Buddhism and their own inherited religious tradition.

Even within some traditional circles of Shiʻi scholarship, intellectual interest in other religions, which formerly focused only on Islam's "Abrahamic" relatives Judaism and Christianity, now extends to Buddhism. This is particularly evident in the city of Qom, Iran's major center of Shiʻite learning, where a recently established "University of Religions" (Dānešgāh-e adyān) provides perhaps the only official academic setting in Iran where the comparative study of religion is actively pursued in a relatively non-polemical manner.

On the other hand, in the present tense political climate, Buddhism sometimes finds itself dragged into the ongoing tug-of-war between various ideological factions vying for power. The combative and controversial president Mahmud Ahmadinejad, for example, threatened on several occasions to "look into" the activities of meditation centers to verify their Islamic acceptability, and publishers of books on "alternative spirituality" found it increasingly difficult to get clearance from the Ministry of Islamic Guidance or to have their publications included at book fairs.

Thus, there would seem to be a certain historical continuity in the ways that Iranian Muslims relate to Buddhism. One might say that in Iranian culture, beneath an outward profession of officially sanctioned religion, the underlying norm is that of a deep, personal, often mystical spirituality that at the individual level feels free to draw on an almost unlimited range of tools and influences. On this deeper level, Buddhism has played a subtle, albeit often obscured role for many centuries, and may well continue to do so in the future.

# 8

# Christianity

Iran was the springboard from which Christianity spread throughout Asia. The first Christian missionaries who brought their faith to China in the seventh century were from Iran, and for the next hundred years, Chinese sources continued to refer to Christianity as "the Persian religion." The Christians of southern India, who traced the origin of their community to the apostle Thomas, were connected to Iran via sea routes and remained under the authority of the Iranian church based in Mesopotamia. The history of Christianity's first millennium is as rich in the East as it is in the Mediterranean region, but it is a history that is scarcely known today.

Given the central importance of Iran in Eastern Christianity, why is Iran's role generally neglected? One reason is that in a broad sense, the Christian mission in Asia was not a lasting success, since the overwhelming majority of the continent's inhabitants today belong to other faiths. Because Christianity became the dominant religion in Europe and in the Western Hemisphere, it is most often thought of as a Western religion. Yet there were many Christians in Asia long before the faith caught hold in Europe, and their contributions to the histories of Asian cultures are vitally important.

Another factor is that Eastern Christianity differs in many points of doctrine and practice from that of the West. The major forms of Christianity in Iran, Nestorianism and Jacobism, were both deemed heretical by the leaders of the state-supported Roman church during the course of ecumenical councils in the fourth century. Ever since that time, Western Christians have written of their Asian counterparts as misguided inferiors. To an objective historian, "heresy" is not a value judgment but merely describes a minority opinion. Unfortunately, an objective history of Asian Christianity has yet to be written.

## THE ESTABLISHMENT OF AN IRANIAN CHURCH

Christian legend has three "wise men"—presumably Zoroastrian magi (Gk. μάγος)—following a star to the baby Jesus' manger in Bethlehem.[1] Even leaving this unproven story aside, Iran was surely one of the earliest places to hear the Christian gospel. The book of the Acts of the Apostles (2:9) lists Jews from various regions of Iran among the witnesses to the miracle of the Pentecost, and it can be guessed that they did not hesitate to tell of this experience once they returned home.

For the first three centuries after the life of Jesus of Nazareth, Iranians could embrace and practice Christianity far more easily than could their counterparts in the Roman world. In the Roman Empire, Christians were seen as a deviant offshoot of Judaism, lacking official status and legal protection. The persecutions of early Christians throughout the Mediterranean basin are well known.

Iran, meanwhile, was under the rule of the Parthians, whose religious policy was one of non-interference. Not until after the elevation of Zoroastrianism by the Sasanian government in the late third century would Christianity be treated in Iran as a suspect faith. But even the Sasanians recognized Christianity as a legitimate religion well before Emperor Constantine legalized it in the Roman Empire in 313 CE.

The favorable circumstances of Parthian rule allowed Christianity to spread and grow throughout Iran, apparently from missionary bases in northern Mesopotamia (Arbela and Edessa, modern Irbil in northern Iraq and Urfa in southeastern Turkey). There was a Christian bishop at Arbela by the year 104, and Christians are attested as far east as Bactria by 170.[2] The Iranian church also maintained authority over Christian communities along the southern sea routes, from Socotra off the coast of Yemen to southern India and Ceylon, where a number of documents and inscriptions in the Middle Persian language (Pahlavi) attest to the presence of Iranians, presumably for the most part merchants, throughout the Sasanian period. From the early fifth century onward, the Indian Ocean dioceses were under the jurisdiction of the metropolitan of Rev Ardashir on Iran's southern coast.

Refugees from the Roman Empire swelled the ranks of native Syriac Christians and Iranian converts, and by the year 225 twenty bishoprics had been established throughout the Parthian-held lands. A group of sixty Christian tombs on the small island of Kharg in the Persian Gulf has been dated to 250, and a Christian church has been excavated there as well; a monastery survived on the island up to the eleventh century. Resettlements of civilians following Sasanian victories over the Romans in 256 and 260 brought both Syriac- (*nasrāyē*) and Greek-speaking Christians (*kristyānē*) to live in Iranian territories. Indeed, M.-L. Chaumont considers that "these massive transfers of foreign populations into Iranian territory were the major factor in the astonishing progress of Christianity in the Sasanian Empire during the second half of the third century and the beginning of the following century."[3]

By the late third century Christians had become so numerous that the zealot Zoroastrian chief priest Kerdir felt threatened enough to include several Christian sects in his attempts to suppress religions other than his own. At first, under Vahram II (reigned 276–293), Christians seem to have suffered from associations with Manichaeism, whose prophet, Mani, was executed in 276 at Kerdir's instigation. As related in the *Chronicle of Seert* and other sources, the Christians complained to the king about this confusion, explaining the differences between Mani's religion and their own, after which the persecutions abated.[4]

With the rise in status of Christianity to state religion of the Roman Empire in the fourth century and military setbacks inflicted by Rome on the Sasanians, Iranian Christians were saddled with the additional suspicion of belonging to the faith of the enemy. This was especially the case from 340–379, during the latter part of the reign of Shapur II, when they were severely persecuted. Regularly denounced by Mazdaean priests as a potential fifth column for the Romans, Iranian Christians were arrested in great numbers and subjected to all manner of tortures to force them to apostatize. A royal decree enumerates the "crimes" of which they were accused:

> The Christians destroy our holy [Zoroastrian] teaching, and teach men to serve one God, and not to honour the Sun, or Fire. They defile Water by their ablutions, they refrain from marriage and the propagation of children, and refuse to go to war with the King of Kings. They have no rules about the slaughter and eating of animals; they bury the corpses of men in the earth. They attribute the origin of snakes and creeping things to a good God. They despise many servants of the King, and teach witchcraft.[5]

Even more significantly, perhaps, the Christians refused Shapur's demand that they pay double taxes.

After Shapur's death in 379, however, the persecution of Christians abated and doctrinal disputes within the Roman church caused many followers of non-authorized Christian sects to seek refuge in Iran. One of the thorniest disagreements in the early church was over the nature of Christ. Some held that in Jesus both a divine nature and a human one were fused. This was the "miaphysite" position, whose adherents came to be known as Jacobites, after Bishop Jacob bar Addai who was one of its later proponents.[6] Others believed that these natures remained separate and that two distinct persons, one human and one divine, inhabited the historical Jesus. This so-called "diophysite" view was associated with the Bishop of Constantinople, Nestorius of Antioch, and its followers came to be called Nestorians.[7]

The miaphysite dogma prevailed at the Council of Ephesus in 431 (which Nestorius boycotted), but at the Council of Chalcedon in 451, both positions were rejected in favor of a compromise belief, that of "one person, two natures," which became the orthodoxy of the Byzantine church. Armenia, which was under Sasanian rule much of the time, became officially miaphysite Christian in the early fourth century, around the time that Christianity was recognized in the Roman Empire.[8] Following the Arab conquests in the mid-seventh century groups of Jacobites were deported from Edessa to Herat and elsewhere in eastern Iran, where they became numerous enough to establish two bishoprics.

Reduced to the status of heretics in the Roman world, diophysites and miaphysites alike found greater freedom in Iran. The Persian church broke away definitively from Byzantium following the Council of Ephesus in 431, establishing its new seat at the Sasanian capital of Ctesiphon in Babylonia under the leadership of an autonomous Patriarch, whom they called the Catholicos. This break represented a rejection of Byzantine religious authority, but also of its political authority over Iranian Christians and by extension Christian communities throughout Asia.

An Iranian synod held in 486 rejected (though did not eliminate) the asceticism and monasticism which were central to Byzantine and Syrian Christianity, abolishing the practice of celibacy, and made diophysitism the official doctrine of the Persian church. Thus, the theology and ascetic tendencies of the miaphysites were marginalized, but did not disappear from Iran. Diophysitism, following Pelagius of Rome and Theodore of Mopsuestia, also rejected the doctrine of original sin promulgated by the ex-Manichaean Augustine of Hippo. It shunned the crucifix as inappropriately emphasizing Jesus' suffering, in favor of the cross as a symbol of his resurrection and abiding life. The Nestorian perspective on hell and the afterlife was generally less severe than in Western Christianity, and in the case of the late seventh-century mystic Isaac of Nineveh, actually approached the Zoroastrian position. Specifically, Isaac taught that for sinners and demons alike hell would be only temporary, followed by a "restoration of all" (αποκαταστασις ϖαντων) to its original state of perfection, a notion earlier articulated by Origen (died 253) and which sounds strikingly similar to the Zoroastrian *Frašo-kərəti*.

The treatment of Christians by the Sasanian state varied greatly depending on changing circumstances. They were tolerated by most Sasanian governments, but there were three periods of major persecutions. During the reign of Shapur II, mentioned above, an estimated thirty-five thousand Christians were killed. A second wave, instigated by the prime minister, Mehr Narseh, took place during the

420s under Vahram V. The persecutions of Yazdigerd II (reigned 439–457) took the highest toll, resulting in the deaths of as many as 150,000 Christians. In many cases, though, it should be noted that Iranian Christians seem to have sought out their martyrdom, deliberately provoking Zoroastrians by putting out or defiling their sacred fires and committing other acts of sacrilege. Still, even at the worst of times Christianity was never actually a banned religion in Iran, as it had been in the Roman Empire for three centuries.

Though sporadic persecutions of Christians occurred throughout the Sasanian period, certain rulers were more sympathetic. Yazdigerd I (reigned 399–421) was hailed in Christian documents as "the victorious and glorious king"—some even claimed that he was a Christian. (Zoroastrian texts, by contrast, refer to him as *winahgar*, "the sinner.") Khosrow II (reigned 591–628) had two influential Christian wives and a Christian court physician. The last Sasanian emperor, Yazdigerd III, fleeing the Arab armies in the mid-seventh century, is said to have had a Christian burial following his death at Marv in eastern Iran in 651. His son, Peroz II, appears to have embraced Christianity as well, since after fleeing to China and securing a position in the Tang administration he established a Nestorian monastery in the capital, Chang'an.

By the late Sasanian period Christianity came to rival Zoroastrianism in terms of its number of adherents within the empire. Christians—most of whom were ethnically non-Iranian Aramaic speakers—constituted the majority within the heavily populated and economically important western provinces in Mesopotamia. (Native Iranian Christian communities existed, especially in the east, but they represented a much smaller portion of the population.) Christian support, therefore, was vital to maintaining the empire's stability. Thus, in the late sixth century the emperor Hormizd IV (reigned 579–590) wrote a letter to his Zoroastrian priests instructing them to end their persecutions of Christians and others, whom he refers to as the "hind legs" of the empire:

> Even as our royal throne cannot stand upon its two front legs without the back ones, so also our government cannot stand and be secure, if we incense the Christians and the adherents of other religions, who are not of our faith. Cease therefore to harass the Christians, but exert yourselves diligently in doing good works, so that the Christians and the adherents of other religions, seeing that, may praise you for it and feel themselves drawn to our religion.[9]

Hormizd IV's declaration likely reflects the additional fact that by the late Sasanian period Christians had increasingly come to figure among the imperial elite, as attested by their personal seals. Many of these seals bear inscriptions in Middle Persian, indicating a gradual acculturation of Iranian Christianity.[10] Widengren, and later Weissner, took this trend as evidence that at the time of the Arab conquests Iran was on the verge of becoming Christian, but their assessment is almost certainly overstated since the majority of Christians were not ethnic Iranians; rather, it was the empire's Christian elites who were adopting Iranian cultural practices.[11]

Whatever the actual numbers of Christians in Iran, their importance was disproportionately high, especially in the realm of higher learning. Like the Jews, Christians, with their cosmopolitan influences and knowledge of languages, were in a position to act as transmitters of culture across and beyond the Iranian world. Having access to the wisdom of ancient Greece, they often served as physicians. As the "pagan" knowledge of the Classical Mediterranean became increasingly rejected in the now Christian West, those who possessed such knowledge found refuge in Iran. The Nestorians were ejected from their academy at Edessa (now Urfa in eastern Turkey) after Nestorius was anathematized by the Council of Ephesus in 431. As a result of this many Nestorian scholars relocated further east to Nisibis in Sasanian Mesopotamia (Nusaybin in modern southeastern Turkey) to teach at the academy there.

The most important academic institution of the Sasanian and early Islamic periods was the school at Gondešapur in the southwestern Iranian province of Khuzestan. The Gondešapur academy, originally established as a Nestorian seminary by Shapur I in 260, was built by Roman prisoners of war. The original curriculum included biblical exegesis, theology, and Greek medicine. Later, Greek philosophy was added as a subject. During the reign of Khosrow I (531–579) the curriculum was expanded to include mathematics, astronomy, finance, jurisprudence, civil administration, and agricultural sciences; Zoroastrian and Indian approaches were added to Greek ones. Its hospital and observatory were famous throughout the world.

The Gondešapur school was largely unaffected by the Arab conquests of the mid-seventh century, since the conquerors saw its value and left it undisturbed. Indeed, its reputation was such that many elite Muslim families sent their sons there to be educated by Christian teachers. Throughout the early Islamic period the academy was under the directorship of the Nestorian Boxtišo family, who from the mid-eighth to early eleventh centuries held a virtual monopoly over the practice of medicine at the Abbasid court.

It was mainly the Iranian Nestorians who brought Christianity to Central Asia and China via the Silk Roads, although Jacobite and Melkite (Byzantine) communities were also present. Iranian missionaries, working in tandem with (or at times identical to) traveling merchants, made contact with the nomadic Turkic-speaking peoples of Inner Asia by the sixth century, apparently using their charisma and perhaps magic to persuade them to accept Christian priests as substitutes for their traditional shamans. One story has a Christian missionary stopping a thunderstorm where local shamans had been unable to do so.

The Nestorian Patriarch of Baghdad Timothy I (780–823) expanded the missionary effort to Central Asia, which in his time lay at the fringes of Muslim power. Recent excavations near Samarkand (in present-day Uzbekistan) have uncovered a Christian monastery complex, presumably Nestorian, which was in use from the eighth to the twelfth centuries.[12] A Christian king, Khunak, briefly ruled Bukhara after 689, and Nestorian ruins and relics have been found in the southern Uzbek city of Termez, at Pandjikent in Tajikistan, and in Kyrgyzstan as well. Patriarch Timothy established a mobile metropolitan see for the nomadic Turks in Central Asia and another in Tibet. In all cases the spread of Christianity was associated with activity along the Silk Roads, which brought the religion to China by 635 at the latest. The first Christian visitor mentioned in the Chinese records was an Iranian monk referred to as "A-lo-pen" (Abraham?), who may have been part of an official Sasanian delegation.

The so-called Nestorian monument at Xian, which tells the early history of Christians in China, was erected in 781 under the direction of an Iranian named Yazd-bozed.[13] Because Christianity was introduced to China by Iranians, Chinese sources at first referred to it as "the Persian religion." For centuries thereafter the Christian community of China maintained its connections to Central Asia and Iran. As late as the Mongol period, Marco Polo mentions a native of Samarkand named Mar Sargis who was appointed vice-governor of Zhenjiang district in central China, where he is said to have established seven monasteries. In Central Asia itself Christianity continued to exist among the Iranian and Turkic-speaking peoples well into the fourteenth century, when it was extinguished by the campaigns of the Sunni Muslim fanatic Temür Barlas (Teymūr-e lang; Tamerlane).

The liturgical languages of Iranian Christians were Syriac and, in Central Asia, Sogdian, an Iranian dialect formerly spoken in what is now Uzbekistan and which was the lingua franca of the Silk Roads in pre-Islamic times. (A modern variant of Sogdian is still spoken in the Yaghnob valley of Tajikistan.) There is some evidence that Pahlavi (Middle Persian) was used as a secondary liturgical language in western Iran, which would indicate the existence of Christians who were ethnic Iranians.[14]

Christian texts in Sogdian and Chinese dating to the ninth century and later have been found at Dunhuang in western China, and inscriptions in the upper Indus region (Ladakh, or western Tibet) attest to the passage of Christian travelers there. Excavations in the early twentieth century in western China uncovered a tenth-century Christian monastery at Buyalïq near Turfan, containing a library with many texts in Syriac and Sogdian. Slightly later Christian texts from nearby sites are in Turkic; Nestorian Christianity took hold among several steppe tribes prior to the Mongol period.

### Iranian Christian Polemics Against Other Religions

Christian writings in Syriac from the Sasanian period reflect themes consistent with the view of an embattled minority. In the fourth century, at the time of Shapur II's persecutions, there is a flourishing of martyr literature. There are polemics against the Zoroastrian reverence for the sun, fire, and water as representing worship of Creation instead of the Creator. To a Christian such could indeed appear to be the case, although as described earlier, the traditional Iranian view (that is, of *mainyus*) did not make such a radical disjunction between a deity and the substance associated with it, the doctrine of God's absolute transcendence being a more recent innovation.

Christian writers mock the "mumbling" recitations of the Zoroastrian magi, who perhaps understood little of their own formulas. By contrast, Christians of the period are often characterized by their literacy, which was based on being able to read the Bible. Christian texts also criticize the Zoroastrian preference for marriage among close relatives. In return, contemporary Zoroastrian works, including the *Dēnkard* (the "Acts of Faith") and the *Škand-gumānīg wizār* (the "Doubt-Destroying Exposition"), accused Christians of depopulating the world through the practice of celibacy, and ridiculed them for claiming that a good God could create evil things (such as snakes), that he was born of a woman, and that the Supreme Being could have been crucified and killed. Despite these ongoing exchanges, however, it has been noted that in Sasanian times Christians and Jews devoted more energy to refuting each other than they did to criticizing Zoroastrians.[15]

One of the most vociferous defenders of Iranian Christianity was the fourth-century monk Aphrahat (that is, Farhad) of Mar Mattai near Nineveh, a convert from Zoroastrianism, whom Jacob Neusner has called "the first Iranian church father." Aphrahat wrote long polemics against Iranian Jews, whom he saw as having irredeemably relinquished their status as chosen people to the Christians. Though there is nothing unique in this position, what is distinctive about Aphrahat's argument is his insistence that the Jews' observation of God's commandments had *never* brought them salvation, even in pre-Christian times.

Aphrahat was disturbed by what he perceived to be an undue concern by Iranian Christians with the beliefs and practices of their "misguided" Jewish neighbors. This explains his deep obsession with distinguishing the Christian Easter celebration from the Jewish Passover in the following passage:

> You have heard, my beloved, concerning this paschal sacrifice, that I said to you that it was given as a mystery to the prior people [i.e., the Jews], and its truth today is known among the peoples. Greatly troubled are the minds of foolish and unintelligent folk concerning this great day of festival, as to how they should understand and observe it.
>
> . . .
>
> The paschal sacrifice of the Jews is the day of the fourteenth [of Nisan], night and day. But for us the day of the great passion is Friday, the fifteenth, night and day. Then after the paschal sacrifice Israel eats unleavened bread seven days until the twenty-first of the month. But we observe as the festival of unleavened bread the festival of our redeemer. They eat unleavened bread with bitter herb. But our redeemer rejected that cup of bitterness and removed all bitterness from the peoples when he tasted but did not wish to drink. The Jews recall concerning themselves their own sins from festal to festal season, but we recall the crucifixion and the pain of our redeemer.
>
> They on the paschal sacrifice went forth from the slavery of the Pharaoh, but we on the day of His crucifixion were redeemed from the slavery of Satan. They sacrificed a lamb from the flock, and with its blood they were saved from the destroyer, but we through the blood of the Chosen Son were redeemed from the works of destruction which we were doing.
>
> . . .
>
> Now be persuaded by this small essay which I have written to you, for you are *not* commanded to be vexed with word-games, matters in which there is no profit, but [to preserve] a pure heart which keeps the commandment and the festival and the times of the observances of each day.[16]

It would seem from this and other examples that in the mixed cultural environment of northern Mesopotamia, the lines between religious communities in the Sasanian period were not so clearly drawn. A church synod in 585 drew attention to this fact:

> We have learned that some Christians, either through ignorance or through imprudence, are going to see people of other religions and taking part in their feasts, that is to say, going to celebrate feasts with Jews, heretics [that is, non-Nestorian Christians] or

pagans [Zoroastrians], or even accepting something sent to them from the feasts of other religions. We thus prescribe, by heavenly authority, that a Christian must not go to the feasts of those who are not Christians, nor accept anything sent to Christians from those feasts, for it is part of the oblation made in their sacrifice.[17]

More serious still, perhaps, was the threat of eroding communal boundaries through sexual relationships and marriage, a concern shared by Christian, Zoroastrian, and Jewish leaders alike. A seventh-century church text shows the extent of the priests' fears:

Women who have a faith believing in Christ and who wish to live the Christian life must guard themselves with all their might against union with pagans [that is, Zoroastrians], seeing that the union with them creates for them usages contrary to the fear of God and drags their will into laxity. So Christians should absolutely avoid living with pagans; and he who would dare to do so would be expelled from the church and from all Christian honour, by the word of Our Lord.[18]

It may be noted that the preoccupation of church leaders with what might seem minor details (such as the disagreements over dates or the sharing of meals with unbelievers), as well as with the prevention of miscegenation, is typical of priestly types in all religions, who more than any other social group are concerned with creating and maintaining distinctions between "us" and "them." Laypeople, by and large, are less concerned under normal circumstances with the blurring of boundaries, although in times of social stress, when scapegoats are needed, such differences are more readily perceived and acted upon.

Sacred art is another domain in which such boundary-crossing frequently occurs. Notwithstanding their ideological hostility to other faiths, Christians in the Sasanian world were not above appropriating certain aspects of Zoroastrian iconography. The old Iranian symbol for glory *(farr)* was often expressed in Sasanian times by framing an image in a ribbon with its loose ends fluttering upwards. In Christian Georgia, which was a Sasanian province, a sixth-century church has a cross framed in this manner. Georgian coins of the same period were struck in imitation of Sasanian ones, with the exception that they replaced the image of a fire on the Sasanian coins with one of a cross. Iranian Christian seals from the period often bear Sasanian symbols such as the winged lion (associated with St. Mark).

Another documented Iranian Christian apologist of the Sasanian period is Mihram Gušnasp (died 614), a convert from Zoroastrianism who served at the royal court. The *Acts of the Persian Martyrs* records the following dialogue between Mihram (also known by his Christian title of St. George) and a Zoroastrian priest:

Priest:    We in no way hold fire to be God, but only pray to God through fire, as you do through the Cross.

Mihram:    But we do not say, as you do to the fire, "We pray to you, Cross, God."

Priest:    That is not so.

Mihram:    So you have it in your Avesta that it *is* a god.

Priest:    We reverence fire because it is of the same nature as Ormazd.

Mihram:    Does Ormazd have everything which fire has?

Priest:    Yes.

Mihram:    Fire consumes dung and horse-droppings, and, in brief, whatever comes to it. Since Ormazd is of the same nature, does he also consume everything like it?[19]

As the source in question is a Christian text, the priest's reply to this challenge, if he offered one, is not recorded.

Mihram's sister, whom, following Zoroastrian tradition, he had married, proved an even more zealous convert to Christianity. Following her miraculous cure from a severe illness, she demonstrated her rejection of Zoroastrianism by defiling a sacred fire, handling it while in an impure state of menstruation, casting it to the ground, and stamping it out with her feet. It would be hard to imagine a way of combining insults that would be more horrifying to the Zoroastrian priests of the court.

Given the mutual hostility between Christian and Zoroastrian religious leaders in Sasanian Iran, it is curious that the Syriac Christian tradition preserves a work known as the *Prophecy of Zardušt*. In this strange text, Zoroaster is said to be the Jewish scribe Baruch, who foretells the future birth, crucifixion, and ultimate triumph of Jesus, who is none other than Zoroaster himself. According to John Reeves, the Syriac *Prophecy of Zardušt* is most likely a relic of an earlier Gnostic text employing both Mandaean and Manichaean terms and imagery.[20]

## IRANIAN CHRISTIANS UNDER MUSLIM RULE

By the early seventh century it would appear that western Iran, particularly the heavily populated Mesopotamian provinces, was largely Christian, accounting for perhaps half of the total population under Sasanian rule. Of Iran's Christians, an estimated seventy-five percent were Nestorian, twenty percent Jacobite, and five percent Melkite.[21] Most of the Christian population was of Aramaic-speaking Semitic stock, but as indicated above, their attempts to convert ethnic Iranians were sometimes successful. While the Arab conquests did not put an end to the expansion of Christianity in Iran, they slowed it down considerably.[22] Like the Zoroastrians and the Jews (but not the Buddhists or Manichaeans), under Islamic law Christians constituted a recognized religious community (*dhimmī*), a "people of the Book" (*ahl al-kitāb*) granted the protection of the Muslim state in return for payment of a special tax, the *jizya*. (The *jizya* was a survival of a similar Sasanian tax known as the *gazidag*.)

But as a religious minority the Christians were also subject to restrictions and discrimination, and were often singled out as scapegoats in times of social unrest. They were not supposed to build any new churches, on the assumption that while they were free to follow an "obsolete" religion if they chose, since "rational" people would inevitably come to see that Islam was a superior religion it was inconceivable (from the Muslim point of view) that the numbers of Christians would grow— hence no need for more churches. Actually they did continue to grow, albeit at a reduced rate, until the fourteenth century.

Under Islamic rule Christians were not supposed to erect any structures taller than those built by Muslims. They should not ring church bells, and they were forbidden from drinking alcohol in public or allowing their pigs to be seen by Muslims. They were not to ride horses (though donkeys and mules were permitted), and they should wear a distinctive mark and belt. They could not insult Islam or its prophet, proselytize to Muslims, or marry Muslim women. Muslim men, however, could marry non-Muslim women, on the somewhat dubious premise that the children of a Muslim father would thereby receive a proper Muslim upbringing.

Thus, though in many ways Arab rule was an improvement over that of the Sasanians, Christians and Jews lived amid a plethora of reminders that they were still second-class citizens. Christian sources of the seventh century are heavy with themes of apocalypse and retribution. Many saw the Muslim conquests as a form of divine reckoning against the corrupt Zoroastrians, while others interpreted them as punishment for the Christians' own laxity, for example, embracing the "heresy" of miaphysitism or converting to Islam. The Persian monk John of Phenek wrote of the Arabs in the 690s:

> We should not think of their advent as something ordinary, but as due to divine working. Before calling them, God had prepared them beforehand to hold Christians in honour; thus they had a special commandment from God concerning our monastic station, that they should hold it in honour . . . How otherwise, apart from God's help, could naked men, riding without armour or shield, have been able to win; God called them from the ends of the earth in order to destroy, through them, a sinful kingdom (Amos 9:8), and to humiliate, through them, the proud spirit of the Persians.[23]

Like the Jews, the Christians were left to run their own internal affairs
in their own way and were represented by the recognized head of their
community, the *Reš galuta* or Exilarch in the case of the Jews and the
Nestorian Catholicos in the case of the Iranian Christians. This set a
longstanding precedent whereby various non-Muslim communities
under Muslim rule would be treated as a "nationality" (*millet*)
under the direct jurisdiction of their own religious leader who was
answerable on their behalf to the Muslim authorities. The Christian
hierarchy in Iran thus became responsible not only for tax collection
but also the range of internal legal matters and social organization
within the Christian community—a kind of state-within-a-state. Only
when conflicts transgressed community boundaries were the Muslim
authorities supposed to become involved.

The Arabs, who lacked prior experience in administering an empire,
employed many Christians to serve in their bureaucracy. They also
gave their support to the Christian academies of Nisibis, Gondešapur
and Marv, which continued to provide trained civil servants and also
began accepting Muslim students. Christians and Jews were favored
as court physicians, secretaries, and astronomers. When the capital of
the Caliphate was moved from Syria to Mesopotamia following the
Iranian-led Abbasid revolution in 750, Iranian Christians began to
play an even more central role in government. The Nestorian Patriarch
Timothy I in particular was very close with the Abbasid Caliph al-
Mahdi, and together the two sponsored a number of inter-religious
dialogues between scholars. One thing they could agree upon was their
dislike of the Jews.

In the early ninth century the caliph Ma'mun founded an institute
at Baghdad called the *bayt al-hikma* (the "House of Wisdom") and
appointed a Nestorian, Hunayn ibn Ishaq, to head it. Hunayn himself
translated over one hundred books from Greek and Syriac into Arabic,
and presided over the translation of many others. Christians thus played
a major role in transmitting Greek knowledge to the Muslim world, just
as Andalusian Jews would do in passing that knowledge back to Europe
several centuries later.

Over time the influence of prominent Christians within the Caliphate
led to a degree of Muslim resentment, and in the ninth century increased
efforts were made to "Islamicize" the administration. Many Christians
and others maintained their positions by embracing Islam. The Crusades,
though they did not affect Iran directly, were an additional cause of
resentment towards Christians among Iranian Muslims.

Christians in Iran experienced a brief improvement in status following
the Mongol conquests in the thirteenth century. The Mongols had an
opportunistic approach to religion—whatever seemed to work, they
would approve and try to use for their benefit. They were, accordingly,
reluctant to privilege any one religion for fear of losing access to others.

Under Mongol rule certain factors did work to the advantage of Christians, however. Most of the rulers who had resisted the Mongol armies had been Muslims. This, combined with the fact that Muslims controlled the long-distance trade across much of Asia, left a residue of distrust on the part of the Mongols. Also, within the ruling Mongol family a number of important women had learned about Christianity from Nestorian missionaries. Finally, the Mongols had hopes of establishing alliances with Christian Europe against the Muslim states of the Near East. After the Mongol army sacked Baghdad and killed the Caliph in 1258, those of Iran's Christians who were fortunate enough to survive the initial slaughter found they often had a sympathetic ear at the Mongol court.

Muslims, for their part, found the Mongols barbaric and were initially reluctant to serve them. As a result, Christians were once again able to find important posts in the new government bureaucracy, especially once the Mongols in Iran, the Il-khans, set up their capital at Tabriz in heavily Christian Azerbaijan. The second Il-khan ruler, Abaqa (died 1282), actually decreed that government clerks had to be either Christian or Jewish. Unfortunately, many Iranian Christians were less than gracious in taking advantage of their improved status, using it to settle scores with Muslim rivals and offending them by drinking and carousing in public. Worse, in Baghdad the Patriarch Mar Denha I had a number of formerly Christian Muslims drowned in the Tigris River. During this time Roman Catholic monks from Europe arrived in Iran and set up missions throughout the northwestern part of the country.

The Christians' new-found status was short-lived, however. The Il-khans eventually saw fit to align themselves with Iran's Muslim majority, beginning with Ghazan Khan who embraced Islam after his accession in 1304. No longer protected by the favor of their Mongol overlords, Iranian Christians were devastated by Muslim pogroms during the first decades of the fourteenth century. The Central Asian Turkic conqueror Tamerlane, who saw himself both as a second Chinggis Khan and as a restorer of mainstream Sunni ("traditionalist") Islam against Shi'ites and other "heretics," delivered the *coup de grâce* when he conquered Iran in 1394, destroying churches and monasteries and massacring Christians as he went.

Though Christian communities survived in Iran, after the tribulations of the fourteenth century their numbers became greatly reduced—mainly, one may suppose, through conversion to Islam—and largely restricted to the region of Lake Urmia in the northwestern part of the country. As a result of Catholic missionary efforts in the mid-seventeenth century some of the Nestorian Christians in western Iran and northern Mesopotamia accepted the authority of the Pope in Rome; from 1844 these Uniates were formally designated by the Ottoman government as

"Chaldeans," a title that the Nestorians (who most often referred to themselves simply as "Syrians") had occasionally claimed as well.

## ARMENIAN CHRISTIANS IN IRAN

The Indo-European-speaking people of Armenia, a land stretching southwards from the Caucasus Mountains, have a long history of interaction with their Iranian neighbors. Armenia was under the rule of Iranian dynasties for much of its history, beginning with the Achæmenids in the sixth century BCE when the province is first mentioned. The pagan beliefs and practices of pre-Christian Armenia were heavily infused with borrowings from ancient Iranian religion, though the Armenians apparently did not possess the Avesta. Their chief deity was Aramazd— that is, Ahura Mazda. The goddess Anahita and the god Mithra were also highly revered.

Following their adoption of Christianity as state religion in the early fourth century, Armenians became a major Christian presence on the northwestern fringes of the Iranian world. Armenian Christianity preserves many ancient Iranian features, however, even to the present day. For example, on the eve of the Christian Ascension, Armenians go out to collect flowers they call *hawrot-mawrot*, which are named for the *Aməša spənta*s of health and immortality, Haurvatat and Amərǝtat. The Armenian cross has a solar symbol at its center and rests upon a bed of flames. Small numbers of Armenians, known as the Arewordik' ("Children of the Sun"), never converted to Christianity but maintained a religious culture heavily infused with Zoroastrian rituals and elements up to the early twentieth century.[24]

Throughout the Muslim period Armenia was an oft fought-over middle zone, occasionally independent but mostly under the rule of various Muslim dynasties. Armenians frequently served as the go-betweens among the rival powers of Christian Europe, the Muslim world, and even China and India.

By the early seventeenth century the Armenian lands were being devastated by endless battles between the empires of Safavid Iran and Ottoman Turkey. In 1605 the Safavid king Abbas I, as part of a scorched earth policy aimed at the Ottomans, uprooted over three hundred thousand Armenians from the region of Jolfa on the Araxes River and resettled them in his capital of Esfahan in central Iran.[25] Armenians became the leading craftsmen, bankers and businessmen of the city, and played a major role in Iran's silk trade. In 1638 an Armenian of Esfahan published the first-ever printed book in the Middle East.

Armenians have been the most numerous and significant Christian minority in Iran since their forced transplantation in the seventeenth century. New Jolfa, on the southern bank of the Zayandeh River, remains a visibly Armenian enclave, though Armenians now live all throughout the country. Most Armenians in Iran belong to the Armenian Apostolic Church (which is miaphysite), although there are small numbers of Armenian Catholics and Protestants as well.

## EUROPEAN CHRISTIAN MISSIONS

After a three hundred year hiatus, Roman Catholic emissaries were sent to Iran from the early seventeenth century as European states sought alliances against the Ottomans. Shah Abbas I granted certain concessions to European Christians who came to live or do business in Iran, although they were not allowed to proselytize among Muslims. According to Islamic law apostasy is a capital offense, reflecting the Islamic notion that while Judaism and Christianity are legitimate revealed religions, Islam supersedes them and having understood this, a Muslim could not conceivably "go back."

When France, England, and the United States began sending missionaries to Iran in the early nineteenth century, this policy continued. As a result, European missionaries competed with each other to "convert" Iranian Christians to their own denominations. The French in particular took to opening schools, and increasing numbers of young Iranians learned French as their gateway to the world of European science and letters.

Efforts by Protestants from England and the United States were spurred by the translation of the Bible into modern Persian by the Englishman Henry Martyn in 1812. The first American missionaries, a Presbyterian minister named Justin Perkins and his wife, settled in the heavily Nestorian region of Urmia (Azerbaijan) in 1834. The Perkinses somewhat misleadingly described the Nestorian communities to be living a generally comfortable life, free to remain home and tend their fields while their Muslim neighbors got conscripted for military service. (In fact they were mostly poor tenant farmers.) Although the Nestorians did not proselytize, sick Muslims often came to their churches seeking the prayers of the priests and hoping to be cured. These Muslims would frequently kiss the cross and the Bible and leave offerings to the Christian saints.

Over the next fifty years the American missions established eighty-one schools throughout Iran. The Presbyterians brought modern medicine to the country, setting up their first hospital in Urmia in 1882. Scholars have generally considered that it was the Western missionaries who created the historical association, based mainly on geography, by which Iran's Nestorian Christians came to call themselves "Assyrians," the name they are generally known by today (*Āsūrī* in Persian). Assyrians themselves, however, contest this interpretation, claiming much older roots for their modern self-designation.

Apart from access to schools and hospitals, part of the appeal for Iranian Christians to embrace Western forms of Christianity was to secure the protection of Western governments. And indeed, throughout the nineteenth century American, British and French officials frequently intervened with the Iranian authorities on behalf of their Iranian converts, for example in mitigating some of the customary legal discriminations to which Christians were subjected in Muslim society. One such case was in 1881 when the British ambassador was able to pressure the Iranian government to rewrite a number of laws, including one which specified that if a Christian converted to Islam he would inherit the property of all his relatives. (The law nevertheless continued to be applied until the 1940s.)

Although the Presbyterian and Anglican missions were the most visible, by the end of the nineteenth century nine different Christian denominations were competing to convert the Iranian Christians. Throughout the country efforts were made to win over Jews and Zoroastrians as well. A number of Iranian Muslims also made use of the missionaries' medical and educational facilities, and despite the Islamic prohibition at least some Muslims converted to Christianity. Obviously all these developments, from the interference of foreign powers to the conversions of Muslims, aggravated relations between Iranian Christians and their Muslim neighbors on the local level.

In 1932 the Pahlavi government nationalized all elementary education, and two years later American missionaries were expelled from Urmia. Under the nationalist Mosaddeq regime in the early 1950s the activities of foreign missionaries were further curtailed. But by that time Iranian converts were numerous enough to maintain the work of the missions on their own, now using the Persian language rather than Aramaic. Christian missionary work was definitively halted, however, following the revolution of 1979.

## CHRISTIANITY IN IRAN SINCE THE REVOLUTION

Under the Islamic Republic Iran's Christian population, mirroring that of other religious minorities, has dropped dramatically through emigration. Armenians, who numbered over 300,000 before the revolution, now stand officially at 150,000, but the real figure is probably far less, possibly even as low as 35,000. (Armenian leaders are reluctant to say, as they fear jeopardizing their two seats in parliament.) Even so, they remain the country's largest recognized non-Muslim community.

The smaller Assyrian and Chaldean communities have dwindled even more sharply, and their combined number in Iran is less than 20,000. All three Christian groups have lost considerable numbers through emigration, mainly to California. They have also seen a decline in birth rates, in keeping with the overall national average. With the advent of an independent Armenian state following the collapse in the former Soviet Union in 1991 there has been an increase in travel and business networks between Armenians in Iran and Armenia.

While overall, Armenians have suffered less discrimination than other non-Muslim groups since the revolution, they have had to struggle to maintain their rights to linguistic and religious education which the government has made occasional attempts to compromise. On the other hand, thanks to their historical cosmopolitanism and access to international networks, their special role in trade has been preserved. Many shops selling tourist items or international foods, for example, are Armenian-owned. Even so, the decline in numbers of foreign tourists since the revolution has hit Armenian merchants and craftspeople particularly hard. Recently some Armenians are said to have obtained government jobs, from which they were excluded after the 1979 revolution.

Because as Christians the Armenians are legally allowed to produce, sell, and consume alcoholic beverages among themselves (in principle because it is required for Holy Communion), they have tended to control the illegal traffic in alcohol among Muslims as well. Once, before a party in Tehran, I was mystified by the hostess's frantic complaints that "the Armenian plumber" hadn't arrived yet. Not seeing signs of a water leak anywhere, I failed to understand why she was so concerned. Then the "plumber" finally arrived; he opened his "plumber's kit," and began to stock the bar in time for the party.

### Unrecognized Christians

The small numbers of Armenian Protestants—a legacy of European and American missionary efforts—have fared less well. Unlike the country's recognized Christian communities, Protestant and Catholic groups in Iran continue to proselytize (often conducting their services in Persian), and because they are under the jurisdiction of church administrations in Europe or the United States, they are often accused of serving foreign interests. In 1994 the Armenian head of Iran's Council of Protestant Churches, Tateos Mikaelian, was murdered under mysterious circumstances.

Although Western missions of the nineteenth and twentieth centuries were technically allowed only to proselytize among non-Muslims, small numbers of Iranian Muslims did convert to Catholic and Protestant Christianity. Since Islam does not allow for apostasy, these conversions have not been recognized by the Islamic Republic. Thus, like the Bahá'ís, Christian converts have been denied the rights and protections theoretically afforded to recognized religious minorities. Furthermore, because of their foreign connections, Catholic and Protestant churches in Iran have been perceived as centers of espionage. Many have been closed down by the government.

In 1979, an Anglican minister (an Iranian) was murdered in Shiraz, and church properties were confiscated all over the country. Catholic missionary schools were likewise seized by the government. The case of Mehdi Dibaj, an Iranian convert to Protestantism who was arrested in 1983 and held for ten years before his trial for apostasy, gained international attention, but in 1994 he was assassinated nevertheless.

More recently, in 2009, a young evangelical pastor by the name of Yusef Naderkhani was arrested in the northern city of Rasht and charged with apostasy. He was convicted the following year and sentenced to death, bringing official protests from several Western countries as well as Christian organizations throughout the world. His prosecutors attempted to deflect this criticism by bringing new charges of "banditry and extortion" in August 2012. At his trial several weeks later Naderkhani was acquitted of apostasy charges but found guilty of evangelizing Muslims and sentenced to three years in prison, but immediately released because of time served.

Figures such as Naderkhani are targeted because they are ethnic Iranians and actively proselytize Muslims. Generally speaking, any church that uses Persian in its services is suspect, since it is formally assumed that Christianity is a religion of ethnic non-Iranians. In 2012 Iran's Revolutionary Guard Intelligence Organization took over control of Iran's churches and immediately began shutting down Protestant churches throughout the country. No new churches have been issued operating licences since the revolution in 1979, but an estimated 40,000 people attend underground churches and estimates of recent converts reach as high as 500,000.[26]

# 9

# Mandaeism

Iran played an important, though not necessarily central role in the
history of Gnosticism, an esoteric religiosity that began to emerge
in the Near East a little before the beginning of the Common Era.
Gnosticism was not a religion per se, but rather an *approach* to religion,
which could be expressed from within the matrices of diverse faith
systems. The term itself derives from the Greek word γνῶσις, meaning
"knowledge," in the experiential rather than theoretical sense (as opposed
to σοφία, meaning "wisdom"). Thus, it could also be defined as "special
insight." Gnosticism's basic premise is that salvation can be attained
through acquiring the right kind of knowledge—specifically, regarding
the "true" nature of the physical world, the human predicament, and
how to get out of it.

The Gnostic approach is characterized by a number of recurring
themes and perceptions. One is a radically dualistic view of the
universe, in which good is associated with spirit and evil with matter.
Spirit is symbolized by light, and matter by darkness. Humans are
seen as being in a wretchedly fallen state, their inner "divine spark"
being entrapped within a repulsive and impure material existence. The
Gnostic, having understood the true, pitiful condition of humankind,
seeks to transcend it through various forms of self-purification in hopes
of ultimately returning to his or her original, spiritual existence. It is
generally understood that this salvation will be the privilege of only a
select few who are able to apprehend deep truths beyond the ken of the
many. The ritual of baptism is often central, representing one form of
initiation into the Gnostics' esoteric world.

In the Gnostic worldview—expressed through an elaborate and
syncretistic mythology drawn from a range of mythical traditions—
Greek, Semitic, and Iranian influences can all be detected. Its spirit–
matter dichotomy echoes Platonic thought, while the dualism of good
and evil and its light–dark symbolism are drawn from Iranian religion.
The practice of baptism and its association with notions of purification,

renewal, and sublime insight is very old, being found among the ancient Egyptians, the Greeks, and others. Gnostic cosmologies, together with a strong interest in astronomy and numerology, show continuities from the knowledge systems of ancient Babylonia.

The origins of Gnosticism are hopelessly buried amid the underground activities of a plethora of secretive sects from around the beginning of the Common Era. Kurt Rudolph considers it to have originated as "a relatively independent Hellenistic religion of later antiquity" that was "enriched with Christian concepts until it made its appearance as an independent Christian Gnosis."[1] Specific Gnostic groups are first mentioned in the polemics of their enemies (mostly Christian), but a clear picture of their beliefs emerges only much later in the recent period, from Gnostic texts themselves. Among these long-lost primary sources the most notable are those discovered at Nag Hammadi in Egypt in 1947.

Most early Gnostic movements were associated with Christianity. Simon Magus, for example, a figure known from the Acts of the Apostles, is identified by later Christian heresiographers as an early Gnostic. It should be remembered, however, that during the early Christian era, when Christianity itself was considered by the Roman authorities to be merely an unauthorized version of Judaism, religious distinctions were often clouded. In fact, consistent with the Pool Theory mentioned in the Preface, the various Near Eastern sects now identified as Gnostic drew from the complete range of available traditions at the time, giving to each their own distinctive interpretation.

Rudolph considers the principal Iranian contributions to lie in the realms of eschatology—including a final judgment and the resurrection of the dead—mythico-historical periodization, and dualism. While Rudolph sees many of these ideas as having come through a Jewish filter, he points out that some are not found in any Jewish tradition. He goes on to state that moreover, "The distinction between soul and body, combined with the notion that the former enters the heavenly realm of light after death, is to be met with in the Orient only in Iran."[2]

## THE MANDAEANS

The Mandaeans are the only surviving Gnostics in Iran, and they were likely the first. Their name is said to be derived the Aramaic *manda*, "knowledge," which would make it a perfect calque on the Greek term, though other etymologies have been proposed. The sect traces its origins to a Jewish community, originally from the Jordan valley, prior to the time of Jesus. They revere John the Baptist as their prophet, considering Jesus to be merely one of John's disciples who went astray.[3] Their origin myth is preserved in a work known as the *Haran Gawaita* ("Inner Harran").

Like other unrecognized religious groups in Roman Palestine, the Mandaeans suffered persecution both from provincial administrators and from the local Jewish authorities. As many others had done and would continue to do, they eventually chose exile under the more tolerant rule of the Parthians further east. Exactly when this migration took place is unclear, but it probably occurred sometime between the first and third centuries of the Common Era.

The particular history of the Mandaean community is difficult to follow, and it is sometimes difficult to disentangle them from the many diverse Gnostic–baptist sects existing in Mesopotamia during the Parthian period. (One such sect, the Elchasaites, gave birth to Manichaeism.) There are some commonalities between Mandaean ideas and those found in the Coptic Nag Hammadi texts, and Manichaean hymns to Thomas have been shown to have been based on Mandaean originals found in their sacred book, the Ginza.[4]

The Mandaeans have been connected with the pagan Sabeans of Harran mentioned in Muslim sources, but Jorunn Buckley insists that the religions of the two groups are "at best, only distant relatives."[5] The Arabic and Persian term for them, *subbī*, means "baptizers," and their migration path from Palestine to Khuzestan in southern Iran may have taken them through Harran, though this is not established. Like the Mandaeans today, the Sabeans possessed a highly sophisticated cosmology and astronomical knowledge based on that of ancient Babylonia, which often earned them positions as advisors at court or teaching in academies.

The Mandaean sacred text, called the Ginza ("The Treasure"), was apparently compiled from the community's oral tradition shortly after the Arab conquests of the seventh century, though parts of it may have been written down by the third century or even earlier.[6] The Qur'an instructed the Arabs to accord protection to "peoples of the [revealed] Book," and the Mandaeans were quick to prove to their new overlords that they possessed one. Nevertheless, in actual practice the Mandaeans would often suffer the same types of discrimination and occasional persecutions to which other "protected communities" were subjected under Muslim rule.

European mentions of the Mandaeans date to the sixteenth century, when Portuguese missionaries mistakenly identify them as "Christians of St. John." They appear in the records of the English East India Company as well. During the Qajar period the community in Iran suffered both persecution and disease, being nearly wiped out by a cholera epidemic in 1831. More recently, Mandaean communities were severely affected by the Iran–Iraq war of 1980–1988 and by subsequent conflicts in the Gulf region.

### Beliefs and Practices

Typical of Gnostic traditions, Mandaeism sees humans as existing in a fallen state, striving to regain their true home in the heavenly "World of

Light" (*alma d-nhura*) above. This world, called Tibil, and the World of Light are connected, principally through the activities of supernatural beings called *'utra*s ("angels" or "guardians") who remain in contact with Mandaeans. The three most prominent *'utra*s are Hibil (Abel), Šitil (Seth), and Anuš (Enos), who are regularly invoked in Mandaean prayers. Šitil, the biblical Seth, is "the purest of souls," against whom deceased Mandaeans are weighed so as to determine if they may enter the World of Light or require further purification.

As in Manichaeism and a number of other belief systems, Mandaeism posits that each human has a heavenly twin (*dmuta*). Thus, the aim of Mandaeans is to ascend to the World of Light and attain reunion with their idealized, spiritual counterparts. There is an underworld of darkness in opposition to the World of Light, but bad Mandaeans do not go there; rather, they experience a series of posthumous purifications so that they may ascend to the World of Light.

The *'utra*s, or "Lightbeings," are ruled over by a supreme deity referred to as the First Life, also known as the King of Greatness or the King of Light. He is described in the Ginza (the sacred book of the Mandaeans) as light itself, the eternal embodiment of all that is good:

> Nothing was when he was not and nothing would be were he not to be; he is under no obligation to death, and destruction means nothing to him. His light illuminates and his radiance irradiates all the worlds . . . Light which is inextinguishable, Beauty, Lustre, and Glory, in which there is no fault . . . He is the Light, in whom is no darkness, the Living One, in whom there is no death, the Good One, in whom there is no malice, the Gentle One, in whom there is no confusion and anger, the Kind One, in whom there is no venom or bitterness . . . and he outshines everyone, as the sun [outshines] lamps, and he is brighter than everyone, as the moon [is brighter than] the stars.[7]

In opposition to this god of goodness and light, the Ginza also describes his evil, shape-shifting counterpart, the King of Darkness:

> That King of Darkness assumed all the forms of earthly creatures: the head of a lion, the body of a dragon, the wings of the eagle, the back of the tortoise, the hands and feet of a monster. He walks, he crawls, creeps, flies, screams, is insolent, threatening, roars, groans, gives [impudent] winks, whistles, and knows all the languages of the world. But he is stupid, muddled, his ideas are confused, and he knows neither the first nor the last, but he does know what happens in all the worlds . . . When he pleases he magnifies his appearance, and when he pleases he makes himself small. He moves his membrum in and out and thus possesses men and women.[8]

The universe also includes evil spirits associated with the planets and the zodiac, who are the children of the evil female spirit Ruha who is associated with lust, emotions, and—presumably by association—music. Her name means simply "spirit," and she is sometimes referred to as *ruha d-qudsa*, suggesting that she is a demoted version of the Christian Holy Spirit or the Gnostic Sophia.[9] The Mandaean view of physical existence is typically Gnostic, as in the following account of Adam's death found in the Ginza:

> When the project of the house of the great Life was carried out, he sent the messenger to Adam, to free him and bring him out of his body, out of this world, from the shackles, from the chain, from the noose, and the bonds, to bring him away from the earth, that Ptahil and the seven planets had built, into which they had led him and had made him live and remain, to liberate him and lead him out of his filthy, stinking body, the destroyer, corruptible, from the heart-rending lions, from the flames of fire, pernicious, from the [body] that disintegrates and is reduced to pulp, from the sea, that cannot be sounded, from the abyss, that cannot be closed up again, from the serpentlike beast that surrounds the world, from whose force no one has grown . . .[10]

Mandaean rituals are mostly associated with water, which is seen as a form of light and thus as a life-giving fluid with magical properties. As in Zoroastrianism, there are three levels of ritual ablution. The first, called *rišama*, is to be performed daily at dawn, following defecation; this corresponds to the *pādyāb* ritual in Zoroastrianism. The second, the *tamaša*, must be performed after contact with a corpse, sperm, or a menstruating woman. Finally, there is the "full" baptism, the *masbuta*, in flowing water, which is seen as a manifestation of the World of Light on earth; this ritual thus forms a temporary bridge between the two worlds. Mandaeans are baptized not just once but countless times throughout their lives; practicing Mandaeans should perform the ritual every Sunday. It is interesting that the prayer uttered during the *masbuta* includes the phrase, "I have baptised myself with the baptism of the great Bahram . . ." E. S. Drower considers that "The use of this name shows the essentially Iranian nature of the rites grafted onto an old and aboriginal water-cult.[11]

Indeed, Mandaean notions of ritual impurity have much in common with those found in Zoroastrianism, Judaism, and Islam (especially Shi'ism), and are characteristic of the Mesopotamian environment. As Drower observes,

> In the ethical system of the Mandaeans, as in that of the Zoroastrians, cleanliness, health of body, and ritual obedience

must be accompanied by purity of mind, health of conscience, and obedience to moral laws. This dual application was characteristic of the cults of Anu and Ea in Sumerian times and Bel and Ea in Babylonian times, so that, if Mandaean thought originated or ripened under Iranian and [Near] Eastern influences, it had roots in a soil where similar ideals were already familiar and where ablution cults and fertility rites had long been in practice.[12]

The Mandaean food laws proscribe the eating of a range of animals and frown on meat-eating in general, to the extent that some observers have labeled them as vegetarians. Bulls are considered sacred and Mandaeans consider it a crime to kill one, although they were used for work. (In recent times, however, Mandaeans have abandoned agriculture.) While the Mandaeans are not in fact vegetarians, their negative attitude toward killing and the consumption of animal flesh recalls the vegetarianism of such ancient Mesopotamian sects as the Elchasaites, from which Manichaeism emerged. The Mandaean ethic may also hearken back to the view found in the Zoroastrian *Bondahešn*, where the advent of meat-eating is depicted as a sign of the world's degeneration. On the other hand, the Mandaeans consider it acceptable to kill certain "evil" animals such as flies and scorpions, although this is not a religious injunction as in Zoroastrianism.

The Mandaean calendar, like that of the Zoroastrians, inserts a five-day period every year to compensate for the fact that the months all contain thirty days. Called *Panjeh* in Persian (meaning "the five"), it is a period of special celebrations. According to Lupieri, "Even those who happen to die during these days are considered particularly fortunate, for the gates of heaven are open to their souls. On their voyage toward the realm of light they do not have to fear attacks from the forces of evil."[13]

Another important ritual, the *masiqta* ("elevation"), is performed three days after death to ensure that the soul of the deceased is able to rise into a new, heavenly "light body," called the *'ustuna*. The soul's journey towards the realm of light is considered a dangerous one, since it must first pass through several levels that are inhabited by demons. Sinful souls must pass a period of time in these purgatories so as to be purified through suffering.

As in Zoroastrianism, displays of mourning are supposed to be avoided. (Mandaeans refer to a metaphor, also found in the Zoroastrian *Arda Virāz Nāmag*, that mourners' tears create a river that the deceased must then cross.) Three days after a Mandaean's burial, a furrow is traced three times around his grave. Zoroastrians do the same, drawing a *kaša* (furrow) three times around the exposed corpse of the deceased.

The seal-ring used in Mandaean ceremonies, called a *skandola*, is interesting for its iconography, which includes a lion, a scorpion, a wasp, and a circular snake. Drower sees these as being parallel to similar symbols in Mithraic temples, and suggests they are of Iranian origin. The snake, which Mandaeans call "the dragon without hands and feet," symbolizes water and life, and is often found over the doorways of Mandaean homes. A similar snake symbol appears beside the entrance to the principal Yezidi shrine at Lalish in northern Iraq (See Figure 10).[14] In another parallel with the Yezidis, Mandaeans will not wear blue clothing, since they associate the colour with the material world and its impurity.

Ritual meals play an important role in Mandaeism, as in other religions. The parallels with Zoroastrian food ritual are particularly striking, however, and have been outlined in detail by Drower.[15] In both traditions consecrated food and clothing are intended for the dead as well as the living. The preparation of the sacred beverage, *haoma*, in Zoroastrianism resembles that followed for the Mandaean *miša*. Drower also detects parallels in the use of fruits and other times such as the *barsom* (metal rods meant to symbolize twigs), water for ritual purification, and the layout of sacred space.

## Mandaean Texts

Written texts have long been central to the Mandaean tradition, and to copy one by hand—a task usually done by priests—is considered a meritorious act which can propitiate one's sins.[16] The principal Mandaean sacred text, the *Ginza*, is claimed to date back to the community's origins some two thousand years ago, but was actually printed for the first time as recently as 1998.[17] The text is divided into two halves, the "Right Ginza" and the "Left Ginza," which face each other upside down like two bowls. Indeed, Jorunn Buckley has pointed out that Mandaean inscribed clay bowls have been found placed together in exactly this manner. "In this way," she explains, "the text does not escape but remains within its confines."[18] The text contains creation myths, eschatology, moral teachings, polemics against other religions (particularly Judaism and Christianity), and teachings attributed to John the Baptist.

Written versions of Mandaean liturgies and prayers were collected and published during the first half of the twentieth century by scholars such as Mark Lidzbarski and Ethel Drower. Another important Mandaean text is the *Book of John*, which is actually more concerned with the *'utra*s than with the Mandaean prophet. Other surviving texts include exegetical works, stories such as the *Haran Gawaita*, and a treatise on astrology.

## Women's Roles

Whereas other Gnostic systems generally view the female negatively, Mandaeism has many positive women figures. Mary, the mother of

Jesus, is a prominent figure in Mandaean legendary history.[19] In the Mandaean Book of John, it is she who brings the fledgling community together in the face of persecution. Mandaeism allows for women priests, and this tradition may be very old. Women have also played an important role in the transmission of Mandaean texts, as "copyists, book-owners, library-owners, editors, and beneficiaries of copied manuscripts."[20]

Against the backdrop of other Near Eastern religious traditions, the visibility of women figures in Mandaeism is striking. Still, as in other Gnostic traditions, the female is associated with the impure material world, while the heavenly World of Light is conceived as male. The major demonic figure, Ruha, is female, and she bears some similarity with the Manichaean demoness Az ("greed"). Still, Buckley emphasizes that Ruha is not necessarily purely evil, but rather more of a fallen figure. Indeed, a prayer included in the text known as the *Scroll of Exalted Kingship* seems to invite sympathy for Ruha's plight:

> Ruha lifted up her voice
> She cried aloud and said "My Father, My Father
> Why didst thou create me? My God, My God,
> My Allah, why hast thou set me afar off
> And cut me off and left me in the depths of the earth
> And in the nether glooms of darkness
> So that I have no strength to rise up thither?"[21]

In light of the Gnostic elements in Mandaeism, it is also interesting to note that the primordial "wellspring" of creation, the *aina*, is female. Curiously, this creative force is believed to have first brought into being the letters of the alphabet, prior to the creation of the universe or anything in it. According to this cosmology, creation presupposes speech and writing. The exalted status of these is reflected in the Mandaeans' reverence for their texts and in the attention given to copying them.

### Iranian–Mandaean Identity

Despite their presumed Palestinian Jewish origins, Mandaeans in Iran have to a degree appropriated Iranian culture for themselves. Reflecting the numerous parallels between their religion and Zoroastrianism, Mandaeans claim that "The Pahlawan religion and ours followed the same road at first, but we discovered new light and followed it, whilst they kept on as before."[22]

In a similar vein, Mandaeans claim to possess the "true" versions of legends about Iranian heroes. Relating the story of Rostam killing his son, a Mandaean informant told Drower that "the Persians wrote of this in the *Shāh-nāmeh*, but their history is not the true one. Only we

Subba know the true story and have told it from father to son." In the Mandaean version the son's name is Yazd, not Sohrab, and after being killed by his father he is brought back to life by the Simorgh.[23]

## Mandaeism Today

The modern Mandaean community—the only ancient Gnostic group to survive up to the present day—has its roots in the provinces of Khuzestan in southwestern Iran (mainly the city of Ahvaz) and the marshes of southern Iraq. The older generation continues to speak its own language, a dialect of Aramaic called *ratna*, which appears to be dying out, despite efforts to revive it. Iranian Mandaeans, who currently number perhaps five thousand, lost their status as a protected community after the 1979 revolution. This was theoretically restored by a *fatwa* (legal opinion) from Supreme Leader Ayatollah Ali Khamene'i in 1995, but has not yet been put into practice. More than eighty percent of the original Mandaean populations of Iran and Iraq have emigrated to the West. The largest communities of the Mandaean diaspora are in the Netherlands, Sweden, and Australia. There are small groups of Iranian Mandaeans scattered throughout the U.S., notably in Texas, Idaho, Chicago, and in the suburbs of Washington, D.C. and Los Angeles.

Mandaeans are prominent in the gold and silversmithing trades in both Iran and Iraq, and now in other countries as well. The actual number of Mandaeans is unknown, but is probably fewer than one hundred thousand worldwide. The estimated five thousand who remain in Iran live mainly in the city of Ahvaz. Iraq, which was home to some seventy thousand Mandaeans prior to the US invasion in 2003, has also seen its population fall to a mere five thousand or fewer.[24]

Jorunn Jacobsen Buckley, a Norwegian–American scholar who has been working with Mandaeans for over forty years, has been instrumental in bringing their tradition into the public awareness even in Iran, where many scholars have told her they didn't even know such a religion existed in their own country. Buckley has also brought Mandaeans to the attention of the international community, arguing for their recognition by international refugee organizations.

The future survival of this ancient religious community, which Buckley fears to be in jeopardy, is threatened by several factors. It is not possible to convert to Mandaeism; one may only be born into it. Though Mandaeans have a long history of successfully keeping marriages within the tradition, endogamy has become increasingly difficult especially given the rate of emigration from their historical homelands.

There are other problems associated with emigration. Mandaean communities abroad lack both an adequate number of priests to perform their rituals, and consecrated places in which to perform them. Copies of Mandaean sacred texts are limited, and knowledge of the language is on the wane. Recently there have been attempts to remedy these problems, through the relocation of priests, the copying of texts, and the seeking out of appropriate locations for baptisms. The possibility of allowing conversions through marriage has been advocated by laypeople but is staunchly rejected by Mandaean priests.

Mandaeans believe that when their community ceases to exist, the world will come to an end. However, given the typically Gnostic negative view of the world, this teleology could be interpreted more in terms of hope than despair.

# Part 3

# CHALLENGES
# TO SASANIAN
# ZOROASTRIANISM

# 10

# Manichaeism

ithin the exceptionally rich hybrid religious atmosphere of third-century Mesopotamia arose what would for a thousand years be one of the major world religions, but which by the fortunes of history is no longer practiced by anyone in the world today. This was Manichaeism, perhaps the most maligned religion in history. For centuries it was known only through the polemics of its worst enemies, such as Augustine of Hippo in the Christian tradition and the various heresiographers and historians of Islam. Byzantine writers derisively termed it a "*mania*," punning on the founder's name, Mani. Even Chinese sources dismissed Manichaeism as a sect of "vegetarian demon-worshipers."

Yet for all the venomous attacks of its adversaries, Manichaeism must be ranked as one of the most influential religions in history, if for no other reason than that its proselytizing successes and extreme doctrinal positions forced apologists for other faiths to refine and strengthen their own views. It was largely opposition to the explosive popularity of Manichaeism that energized the Zoroastrian magi to lobby so aggressively for their own religion's official status in the Sasanian Empire. Augustine was a Manichaean for nine years before converting to Christianity, and his interpretation of the latter faith was greatly influenced by his rejection of the former. The resurgence of Manichaean tendencies during the High Caliphate of Islam in the late eighth century, particularly within the Persian bureaucracy, stimulated the active responses of Islamic theologians.

Perhaps the most significant impact of Manichaeism on competing faith traditions was the idea that a religion is defined by its scriptural canon. Indeed, John C. Reeves suggests that:

> Manichaeism may well be the earliest example of what Islam will later term a "people of the Book"; i.e., a scripturally based religious community . . . It does not seem far-fetched to view

> Mani's authorial efforts as catalytic in the eventual determination
> of the physical content and conceptual boundaries of Jewish,
> Christian, and even Zoroastrian scripture.[1]

It should be recalled that when Manichaeism arose in the third century
CE, the canons of these other traditions had not yet been established.

Mani, the prophet and founder of Manichaeism, was born in
Mesopotamia in 216 CE, of parents who had originated from Parthia.
At the tender age of four Mani was taken to live with his father in an
all-male religious commune of Elchasaites, one of the numerous Judeo–
Christian baptist sects that existed in Mesopotamia at the time, whose
traditions may be traced to those of the ancient Qumran community
in Palestine. Mani, visited by his "cosmic twin"—an ancient Indo-
European idea, as discussed in preceding chapters—received his first
revelation at the age of twelve. At twenty-four he received another,
which led him to see himself as the Paraclete (the twin) of Jesus and
inspired him to embark on his worldwide mission.[2]

Inspired by the example of the apostle Thomas, for whom he felt a
special affinity—having apparently read the *Hymn of the Pearl* which
is found in the apocryphal Acts of Thomas—in the year 240 Mani set
off to Sind in northwestern India. There, he is said to have converted
a local Buddhist ruler to his new religion.[3] By performing a number
of "miracles," Mani appears to have persuaded the ruler that he was
an incarnation of the Buddha. Indeed, as for many religious figures of
the time, miracle-working would be a major factor in attracting the
masses to Mani's religion.[4] Matthew Canepa notes in this regard that
"Like Jesus and the Buddha, whom Mani considered his heralds and
predecessors, Mani performed many miracles, healings and exorcisms
which religious and political adherents and opponents each defined
differently as magical or religious according to their polemical bent."[5]

Returning to Iran two years later, Mani found an audience with two
princes of the newly established Sasanian dynasty. The king, Shapur
I, was sufficiently impressed by Mani's charisma that he granted him
the freedom to spread his teaching throughout Iran. Later in his career
Mani composed his sole work in (Middle) Persian, the *Šābūragān*, in
honour of the Sasanian monarch.[6] This text, which Mani claimed as the
authentic teaching of Zoroaster, together with his apparent popularity
at court, provoked the jealousy of the Zoroastrian magi, led by their
chief priest, Kerdir. The two remained rivals until the accession of
Vahram I in 273, after which Kerdir succeeded in getting Mani expelled
from favor, perhaps on the pretext of Mani's failure to heal an ailing
princess. Mani died in prison in 276, presumably tortured to death, at
the age of sixty.

The new ruler, goaded by Kerdir, launched a major persecution of Manichaeans. As a result of this a number of them fled to Sogdian Central Asia where Mani's chief missionary, Mar Ammo, had already spread their teaching. (Sogdian Manichaeans would later bring the religion to China.) Simultaneously, to the west, the Arab ruler of Hira offered them protection, facilitating the spread of Manichaeism into North Africa. From there the religion began to work its way across the Roman Empire, where it raised the alarm of Emperor Diocletian. In 302 the Emperor issued an edict against the religion as a corrupt teaching of Rome's Persian enemies:

> We have heard that the Manichaeans . . . have set up new and hitherto unheard of sects in opposition to older creeds so that they might cast out the doctrines vouchsafed to us in the past by divine favour—for the benefit of their own depraved doctrine. They have sprung forth very recently like new and unexpected monstrosities among the race of the Persians—a nation still hostile to us—and have made their way into our empire, where they are committing many outrages, disturbing the tranquillity of the people and even inflicting grave damage to the civic communities: our fear is that with the passage of time, they will endeavour, as usually happens, to infect the modest and tranquil Roman people of an innocent nature with the damnable customs and the perverse laws of the Persians as with the poison of a malignant serpent . . .[7]

By comparison with other figures considered to be founders of major religions, Mani's career appears exceptionally deliberate and successful. Rather than dismiss previous religions as "false," he claimed that they contained truth but had been corrupted. Thus, he was a keen student of other religions and took from each what he found appropriate. Mani claimed to be a perfecter of Christianity, but his understanding of Jesus differed dramatically from that found in any Christian sect. He took from Iranian religion its light–dark symbolism, its ethical dualism and much of its cosmic hierarchy, along with the commandment not to lie, but challenged the legalistic authority of the Zoroastrian priestly class, the magi. From Indian traditions he borrowed the principle of non-injury, a belief in reincarnation, the notion of good deeds acquiring merit, and the quadripartite social structure of monastic and lay men and women. The Manichaean ideal of worldly poverty was common to both the Christian and Buddhist–Jaina ascetic traditions. Mani taught Gnostic ideas such as the pairing of humans with their heavenly twins and the goal of ascension to a spiritual realm of light.

Mani saw himself as the fourth in a line of "apostles," after Zoroaster, Buddha, and Jesus. His approach could be considered intentionally syncretistic,[8] subsuming and subordinating the teachings of earlier religious figures. As he states in the *Kephalaia*:

> The writings and the wisdom and the revelations and the parables and the psalms of all the first churches have been collected in every place. They have come down to my church. They have added the wisdom that I have revealed, the way water might add to water and become many waters. Again, this is also the way that the ancient books have added to my writings, and have become great wisdom; its like was not uttered in all the generations. They did not write nor did they unveil the books the way that I, I have written it.[9]

Thus, Mani preached in whatever terms were most familiar to his target audience, initially presenting his message as a perfection of Christianity within his heavily Christian home environment of Mesopotamia, then refiguring it in Zoroastrian terms when writing for his royal Sasanian patron in the *Šābūragān*. Later Manichaean texts from Central Asia and China appear at first glance to be Buddhist. Mani explicitly enjoined his missionaries to take this "all things to all men" approach, borrowing the term "skilful means" directly from Mahayana Buddhism. In a further example of Indian influence, the *Kephalaia* mentions *aurentes* (*arhant*s) and *kebellos* (*kevali*, Jaina gnostics). Analyzed in terms of the Pool Theory, Mani appears to have made conscious use of the entire symbolic repertoire available to him.

Mani also hoped to avoid sectarian squabbles and prevent any possible misunderstandings about his teaching from the very start. Seeing how Christians were battling over which texts to include in their canon and which to reject as spurious, he undertook to write his sacred scriptures by his own hand—nine in all.[10] (He also devised his own alphabet, based on the Syriac.) The first seven of these books, *The Living Gospel*, *The Treasure of Life*, *The Book of Mysteries*, *The Book of Legends*, *The Book of Giants* (which draws heavily on the apocryphal Jewish *Apocalypse of Enoch*), *The Epistles*, and the *Psalms and Prayers*, he composed in Syriac–Aramaic, the Semitic language spoken by many Eastern Christians, Jews and others. An additional work, the aforementioned *Šābūragān*, was in Middle Persian. Parts of the latter text have survived in the original, whereas Mani's Syriac books exist mainly in translations.

Finally, there is the mysterious work known as the *Aržang* ("the Worthy"), of which no traces have been found, though apparently copies survived as late as the thirteenth century.[11] It was an illustrated volume of Mani's teaching, highlighting his talents as a painter. Mani realized that in a world where most people were illiterate, mere texts had limited pedagogical value. He therefore used his considerable artistic skill to create a "picture book" as a kind of visual gospel.[12]

Mani's didactic use of art likely influenced that found later in other religious traditions. Book illustrations and biblical scenes depicted on stained-glass windows in medieval Christian churches are one example. Another is Tibetan Buddhist art, which bears striking similarity to the description of Mani's *Aržang* in the following passage from Marwazi's *Kitāb tabā'ī al-hayawān*:

> He painted it with remarkable images, and he drew pictures of every (kind of) demon and crime, such as robbery, fornication, and so on, and beside the crimes the required punishments, and he drew underneath the illustration of each demon a picture of what it produces.[13]

Ironically, in Iran Mani's reputation as an artist has outlived that as an arch-heretic. By the Safavid period one could find in a treatise on painting the statement that if one wished to applaud a brilliant painter, the highest of compliments was to compare him to Mani.[14] The historian Mirkhwand, in his well-known work *Rawdat al-safā*, writes that:

> Mani was a painter without equal. They say for example he would draw a circle whose diameter was five cubits with his finger, and when they would examine it with a compass, none of its constituent parts ever fell outside the circumference of that circle . . . he could effect a consummate ornamentation because of the extraordinary pictures he could produce.[15]

Even today, Mani's name has a positive resonance among Iranian artists.

Another effective strategy employed by Mani was to encourage his missionaries to translate his scriptures into vernacular languages. Judaism had been slow to do this, and the Syriac used by Eastern Christians was understood either poorly or not at all by ethnic Iranians. Buddhism was slow to spread at first; only once translations began in earnest did it start to win large numbers of converts outside India. By contrast, Mani's chief missionary to the eastern lands, Mar Ammo, was highly effective in bringing Manichaeism to Khorasan and Central Asia, preaching in their local idioms.

Yet as part of the violent purges of Manichaeism under the Roman Empire in the West, and later by the Islamic Caliphate in the East, an attempt was made to destroy all Manichaean writings. For many centuries the particulars of the religion were known only through the polemics of its enemies, such as the ex-Manichaean Augustine, notably in his treatise *Contra Faustum*, and another fourth century anti-Manichaean tract called the *Acta Archelai*. Classical Muslim writers such as Ibn Nadim and Abu Rayhan Biruni were somewhat less polemical, and even included some quotations from Manichaean texts in their own writings (as did the Christian writer Theodore bar Konai), but they still treated the religion as a heresy. Thus, for centuries all knowledge of Manichaeism was based solely on non-Manichaean sources, until archaeological expeditions in the twentieth century turned up long-buried Manichaean libraries in the widely separated deserts of western China and Egypt. In the decades since then scholars have been busily translating and studying the newly discovered Manichaean texts and attempting to reconstruct the history, nature and practice of this extinct world religion.

The following passage, from an undated Parthian text, demonstrates the Manichaean technique of incorporating names and symbols from diverse religions. It consists of a dialogue between a "boy" (representing the soul that seeks salvation) and "Jesus," the Redeemer:

> [Jesus]: . . . the garment of the beings of Light. [For] out of stupefaction the four quarters of the world were plunged into turmoil. But you, beloved one, endure here (in the world) for the sake of the souls, so that (their) salvation may be attained through you.[16]
>
> [Boy]: The love and service that you, O God, have always shown to me are manifest. But I suffered this one time when you ascended and left me behind like an orphan.
>
> [Jesus]: Remember, O Boy, how the chief of the battle-seeking ones (i.e., the First Man), the Father, the God Ohrmizd, left his sons behind in the depths when he ascended from the Dark for the sake of great gain.
>
> [Boy]: Hear my supplication, you most beloved of beloved names! If you do not free me (from the world) this time, send many gods so that I may gain victory over the evildoers.
>
> [Jesus]: I have instructed the Great *Nous* to send you messengers when . . . had come. Be patient, like the burdened beings of Light are.
>
> [Boy]: The world and (its) children were alarmed. For my sake Zarathustra descended into the realm of Persia. He revealed the Truth and he chose my "limbs" (i.e., elements of Light) from among the beings of Light of the seven regions.
>
> [Jesus]: When Satan saw that he had descended, he sent out the demons. Before the gods were able to return the attack, they had hurt you, o beloved one, and wisdom was distorted.

[Boy]: My suffering ceased at the time when I was . . . by Buddha Shakyamuni. He opened the door of salvation for the fortunate souls among the Indians which he freed.

[Jesus]: Because of the (skilful) means and wisdom that you received from the Buddha, Dibat (Venus), the great Virgin, envies you. When he (Buddha) entered into Nirvana, he commanded you: "Await Maitreya here".

[Boy]: Then Jesus had mercy for a second time. He sent the four pure winds (the Christian gospels) to help me. He bound the three winds (the Jewish scriptures); he destroyed Jerusalem with the steeds of the demons of wrath.

[Jesus]: The cup of poison and death . . . was poured out over you by Iscariot, together with the sons of Israel. And much further sorrow . . . (three lines illegible).

[Boy]: . . . [The number] of prophets is small and the numbers of the two armies attacking me are countless.

[Jesus]: Your great battle (is) like (that of) the God Ohrmizd, and your collection of treasures (redeemed Light) is like that of the Chariots of Light (the sun and the moon). You can also redeem the Living Self that is (trapped) in flesh and wood (i.e., plants) from Az (the demoness of Greed).

[Boy]: All three gods (Zarathustra, Buddha, and Jesus) protect this child, and they sent me Mar Mani as the saviour who leads me out of this servitude, in which I served the foes in fear against my will.

[Jesus]: I gave you freedom, my comrade . . .[17]

Virtually stamped out in the Roman Empire and vigorously persecuted by the Sasanians, Manichaeism moved east along the Silk Roads.[18] Its main purveyors, as had been the case with Buddhism and Christianity, were Iranian (mainly Sogdian) merchants and monks who travelled with them. All three religions, lacking state sponsorship in many or most cases, relied heavily on the economic support of their respective monasteries which were located along the trade routes. Manichaean communities took hold in such places as Samarkand and further east in the Tarim basin (what is now western China), beyond the easy reach first of the Sasanians and then the Muslims. The formal head of the Manichaean church, referred to as the Archegos, remained based at Baghdad until the early tenth century when he fled to Samarkand during an anti-Manichaean clampdown under the Muslim Caliph Muqtadir.

Manichaeism enjoyed one stint as official religion, under a state established by Uighur Turks in Central Asia from 763–840, and under some smaller remnant Uighur kingdoms for two and a half centuries after that. Otherwise Manichaeans remained a distrusted minority wherever they were, from Iran to China, often outwardly professing to be good Muslims, Christians, Buddhists, or Taoists. The last Manichaean community appears to have survived in southeastern China into the seventeenth century, when it became unrecognizably absorbed into popular Buddhism.[19]

In 1921 the Chinese scholar Chen Yuan found literary evidence of a Mongol-period Manichaean temple at Jinjiang in Fujian province near the city of Quanzhou (known as Zaytun in medieval times). During the 1980s, specialists in Manichaeism including Peter Bryder and Samuel Lieu were finally able to visit the site, where they saw a large number of Manichaean fragments found by local archaeologists, complete with inscriptions, as well as a statue that identified itself as a representation of "Mani, the Buddha of Light" (see Figure 7). In 1997 a smaller, much older, Manichaean shrine was identified in the north of the province.[20]

## MANICHAEAN BELIEFS AND PRACTICES

The basic Manichaean worldview was one of Gnostic dualism, in which humans were seen as being entrapped in matter, estranged from their true home in the World of Light. How this predicament came about and how it may be escaped were elaborately explained through a retelling and reweaving of familiar myths drawn from Zoroastrianism, Judaism, and ancient Babylonia, along with Christian and Buddhist parables. As in other Gnostic systems, God—conceived as the Father of Light, and called Zurvan in Iranian texts—was remote and unapproachable. Instead, humans dealt with a range of angels and demons, emanating either from the realm of Light or from that of Darkness. Mani rejected daily baptism, the central ritual of the Elchesaite sect in which he was raised, on the ground that "purifying the vessel" was useless unless one had first purified the soul.[21] This, he believed, could only be achieved through gnosis, a progressive perfection of one's own spiritual knowledge.

Certain aspects of Gnosticism have emerged throughout Iranian history in all manner of religious behaviours, from resistance movements such as the Mazdakites or the Babakites, to underground sects such as the Isma'ili Shi'is, to the elitist speculations of the Hellenistically-inspired philosophers Avicenna, Shehab al-din Sohravardi and others, and to the mystical teachings of various Sufis. None of these later expressions possesses the extreme anti-materialism of Manichaeism, though they all share to some degree Manichaeism's dualistic cosmology and its symbolism of light as a representative of goodness, purity, and the divine.

As mentioned above, Mani held Jesus to be a central figure, though his is a very different Jesus from that of the Christians. In fact the Manichaean Jesus has three aspects: he is Jesus the Splendor, the original purveyor of gnosis who imparts it to Adam at the beginning of time and continues to bring esoteric knowledge to humans; he is the historical Jesus—though a docetic one; that is, only appearing to be human and not dying on the cross—whose suffering symbolizes the predicament of goodness being trapped as particles of light encased in matter; and he is Jesus the Judge who will come again at the end of time.

The following Manichaean hymn, translated from the Parthian language, speaks of the original entrapment of Light by an evil figure who, not accidentally, is a female:

> Lo, that great Kingdom of Salvation [waits] on high,
> Ready for those who have gnosis, so that they may finally find
>     peace there.
> Sinful, dark Pesus [the mother of the first humans] runs hither
>     and thither brutishly,
> She gives no peace at all to the upper and lower limbs [of Light];
> She seizes and binds the Light in the six great bodies,
> In earth, water and fire, wind, plants and animals.
> She fashions it into many forms; she moulds it into many figures;
> She fetters it in a prison so that it may not ascend to the height.
> She weaves [a net] around it on all sides, she piles it up;
> She sets a watchman over it.
> Greed and Lust are made its fellow captives [i.e., inside the
>     human body].
> She mixes destructive air into those six great bodies.
> She nurtures her own body but destroys their sons.
> The powers of Light on high confuse all the demons of wrath,
> The sons of that Pesus, who is in a higher place.[22]

Several key themes are present in this hymn, including a feeling of revulsion toward the body, and a negative attitude toward women, who are blamed for the process of reproduction which is seen as degenerative, insofar as it results in light particles being further diluted with every generation. Manichaeism thus prescribed celibacy for the Elect, and *coitus interruptus* for sexually active Hearers. The latter instruction remained somewhat idealistic, however, since in practice the community's survival required that their lay followers (called "Hearers") produce new generations who could continue to support them.

The same was true of the Buddhist (and perhaps Jaina) communities upon which that of the Manichaeans was modeled. The Elect, like Buddhist and Jaina monks, were forbidden from killing any living thing (they believed plants as well as animals had souls), and they practiced vegetarianism as a lesser evil. But even so, the Elect were not to grow food, since disturbing the soil and harvesting plants were thought to be damaging to the light particles within them.[23] They were not even to prepare their own food, but relied on the Hearers to do this for them. Without a permanent and self-regenerating community of lay supporters, Manichaeism, like Buddhism, would have died out within a generation. Though Hearers could not hope for immediate salvation, they could aspire to be reborn as members of the Elect.

A late fourth-century text known as the *Book of Steps* (*Ketaba demasqata*) describes the Christian community in terms analogous to Manichaeism, with the "righteous" and the "perfect" mirroring the division between "hearers" and "elect." As in Manichaeism, the "perfect" were forbidden from performing manual labour, and depended on the support of the "righteous."[24] Similarly, a work called the *Cave of Treasures* describing the descent of the children of Adam's "perfect" son Seth to the "dark world" of Cain's descendants recalls the mixing of light with dark in Manichaean cosmology.[25]

Given the dependence of the monks on the laity for their very survival, it is not surprising that the daily ritual meal was the central component of Manichaean practice. The most important event of the Manichaean calendar, furthermore, was the feast of Bema, the "empty chair," which commemorated Mani's death and fulfilled a similar function to that of Easter in Christianity. Interestingly, paintings from manuscripts and monastery walls in the Turfan region of western China depict these ritual meals in a way that bears a striking resemblance to food rituals practiced by Zoroastrians today.

## Purifying the World

While much of contemporary Manichaean studies has focused on the cosmology and corresponding mythologies present in the recently discovered Manichaean texts, Jason BeDuhn has emphasized the action-based aspects of Manichaean practice, pointing out that the Manichaean lifestyle was more than merely a withdrawal from a disgusting world of material bondage. Rather, the aim of Manichaeans' life in this world was to strive actively to liberate particles of light through their rituals and practices.[26]

The proper use of food was a primary means of doing this. By purifying themselves through their rigorously regimented daily routine (consisting mainly of prayer and the singing of hymns), and thus separating out the evil which clung to them like tarnish on a silver vessel, the Manichaean Elect were thought capable of freeing the light particles within food by the very process of eating it. Fresh, uncooked produce was favored as possessing the highest proportion of light. Augustine ridicules Manichaean beliefs about food—what BeDuhn calls "metabolic salvation"—in the following passage:[27]

> All you promise (the Hearers) is not a resurrection, but a change
> to another mortal existence, in which they shall live the life of
> your Elect, the life you live yourself, and are so much praised for;
> or if they are worthy of the better they shall enter into melons
> and cucumbers, or some food which will be chewed, that they
> may quickly be purified by your belches.[27]

This is mere calumny, of course. According to the Manichaean texts, the Elect sent up the liberated light not in the form of "belches," but as hymns sung during and after the meal.

### What Made Manichaeism Attractive?

What was the appeal of Manichaeism, which brought so many converts from so many different cultural backgrounds to adopt its austere worldview?[28] Its esoteric cosmology and teaching could hardly have been accessible to large numbers from among the general population. Mani himself must have been a highly charismatic figure, as must some of his missionaries. They welcomed debates with proponents of other religions, but how did they win these debates?

While the persuasion of rhetoric and reason must have played some role, it would appear that other skills such as magic and healing were often instrumental in winning converts. Western Asia had long been home to a confusing plethora of religious sects, and historical accounts from all periods make mention of religious leaders who amaze people with miracles of one kind or another. Jesus of Nazareth is one well-known example, but similar claims are made about virtually all religious figures with popular appeal.

Like Jesus, Mani was known as a miracle-worker and a physician. Indeed, during his years at the royal court he seems to have been valued more for his medical knowledge than for his spiritual insights. A Manichaean church history in Sogdian tells of how one of Mani's disciples, Gabryab, challenged the King of Revan (possibly Yerevan in Armenia) to see whether the Christians at court could heal a sick girl:

> If I through the mercy of the Gods can heal the girl of the illness, then I shall require this of you: "Turn away from the Christian religion, and accept the religion of the Lord Mar Mani!" At that he turned around and said to the Christians: "Christ was a god who could work miracles. The blind as well as the lame and cripples he healed of their disease. Similarly he also revived the dead. And it is a rule, that the son has the traits of the father and that the pupil shows the mark of the teacher. If you really and truly are disciples of Christ, and the mark and trait of Christ are upon you, then all come here and cure the girl of her disease, just as Jesus said to the disciples: 'Where you lay your hand, there will I work improvement through God's hand!' If you do not do so, then I by God's power shall heal the girl of the disease, and then you Christians shall go from the kingdom of Revan." The Christians said: "We will not be able to heal her; you make the girl healthy instead."[29]

Gabryab naturally succeeds in healing the girl, and the king becomes a Manichaean. Once Gabryab moves on, however, the devious Christians persuade the king to return to Christianity.

Later, during the Abbasid period, many Iranians especially of the scribal class were accused of being crypto-Manichaeans (*zindīq*). For such individuals, Manichaeism—if that was indeed the heresy to which they subscribed—may have been primarily a kind of nativist reaction to Arab rule. In addition, its esoteric character may have appealed to Iranian intellectuals' sense of superiority. The following verse by Abo'l Faraj Esfahani gives an indication of this:

> O Ibn Ziyad! O Abu Ja'far!
> You affect a religion that is different from the one you conceal.
> On the outside, sounding like a *zindīq*;
> Yet inwardly, a virtuous Muslim youth.
> But you are not a *zindīq*!
> You just want to be regarded as clever![30]

## OPPOSITION TO MANICHAEISM

Of all the religions competing for the devotion of Iranians in the third century, Manichaeism was clearly considered by the Zoroastrian magi to be the greatest threat. This may have been partly to do with the direct personal rivalry of Mani and Kerdir, but presumably popular response played a role as well. For the Zoroastrian priests Manichaeism became the epitome of heresy. Indeed, the generic term they used for heretic, *zandīk*, is usually taken by contemporary scholars to mean "Manichaean." This usage, which was mirrored in Byzantine Christendom, continued into Islamic times.

Since *zand* means "commentary," the literal meaning of *zandīk* is "one who engages in [unauthorized] commentary [on the Avesta]." However, since the term could be applied to any wide range of religious figures seen as deviant by the Zoroastrian priesthood, it is not necessarily clear in most cases which particular sect the sources are referring to. Indeed, the Muslim writer Khwarazmi states in his *Kitāb mafātih al-'ulūm* that "the *zanādiqa* are the Manichaeans, and the Mazdakites are (also) designated with this name."[31]

Among the texts composed by Zoroastrian priests to refute Manichaean doctrines, one of the most significant is found in the *Dēnkard* (Book Three, section 200). In this work, which refers to Mani as "the Lie (*drūj*) Incarnate," the priests list twelve specific points on which Manichaeism and Zoroastrianism are fundamentally at odds. These points include such central doctrines as the essence of human nature—Zoroastrians believed people to be basically good, while Manichaeans believed the opposite—and a rejection of the world—which Zoroastrians believed was created by Ahura Mazda to be perfected, whereas Manichaeans believed it was created out of evil, that it cannot be otherwise, and that it must be escaped. Another point of difference was their respective views on agriculture, which Zoroastrians saw as life-giving and Manichaeans as life- [that is, light-] destroying. Zoroastrians saw the material world as infused with good spirits (*mainyus*) which should be drawn into oneself; Manichaeans saw these as evils to be expelled. Zoroastrians shunned celibacy, while Manichaeans celebrated it. It should be noted, of course, that the arguments in the *Dēnkard* against Manichaean doctrines are constructed in terms of Zoroastrian understandings of them which may have been less than accurate.

Manichaeism posed a somewhat different danger to Islam than it did to Zoroastrianism and Christianity. Despite its possession of sacred scriptures, Manichaeans were never granted the protected status of "peoples of the Book." The first Arab Muslim dynasty, the Umayyads (661–750), seem to have paid little attention to Manichaeism, as to other religions practiced among non-Arab subject populations. A rise in anti-Manichaean literature shortly after this period suggests that Manichaeism was spreading, however. With the geographical shift of the Caliphate to the Iranian world under the Abbasids after 750, and the new government's need to suppress the kind of heterodox forces that had helped bring them to power, Manichaeism came to be seen as a major threat.

The perceived menace of Manichaeism may have been tied to its role in shaping the emerging Shiʻism that provided the Abbasid revolutionaries their ideological support. One of the first rebel groups to successfully challenge Umayyad rule was the Kaysaniyyah, who arose from Hira in northern Arabia where Manichaeism had been strong. Following their conquest of Kufa in 685 their leader, Mukhtar al-Thaqafi, conducted a ritual featuring an "empty chair," which, in the words of Cyril Glassé, "looks so temptingly like the Manichaean Bema Ceremony that . . . it must be the Manichaean Bema Ceremony."[32]

Muslim theologians, following earlier critiques by Christian writers, accused the Manichaeans of being unwilling to interpret their fantastic cosmogonic myths allegorically—a position we today might associate with what we call "religious fundamentalism." Muslim philosophers, steeped in the tradition of Aristotle and other classical thinkers, disputed what they believed to be the Manichaeans' rejection of accidents and potentiality. Muslims claimed that the Manichaeans did not believe in spirits, but only in what they could experience through their senses, and that they believed the Father of Light is the very same light that is perceived in this world.

One of the major theological debates in monotheistic religions arises from the problem of evil—how a single creator god can be both all-powerful and entirely good—and the consequent problem of whether humans possess free will or are predestined to act as they do. Manichaeans, like other dualists, had a much easier time dealing with these issues, since they posited that evil was due to the interference of an evil deity. Some scholars have argued that the free-will debate among Muslims, which took shape under the Mu'atazilite school in the eighth century, began as an effort to refute the Manichaeans.[33]

Manichaeans operated secretly during Islamic times, and apparently had considerable success either in converting Muslims or keeping non-Muslim Iranians away from Islam. They are known to have circulated a number of false *hadith*s (reports) about the prophet Muhammad as part of their propaganda. In the eighth and ninth centuries a sort of dualism seems to have become popular among the literate bureaucratic classes of Iran as a form of nationalist reassertion against the ruling Arabs, the so-called *sho'ūbiyyeh* movement. It has even been argued that the famous Persian Sufi martyr Hallaj was a crypto-Manichaean.[34]

In fact, since as noted above the term *zindīq* used in the sources may have referred to any number of heretical sects, it is hard to know if the beliefs secretly followed by suspect bureaucrats and Sufis was in fact Manichaeism as such or some other kind of Iranian dualistic "heresy" such as Mazdakism. The dissimulation they practiced, in any case, was adopted by Shi'ites as the doctrine of *taqiyyah*.

## MANICHAEISM IN THE EAST

Manichaeism spread to the West from its base in Semitic Mesopotamia. Thus, throughout the Roman world Manichaean communities had little direct influence from Iran or Iranians. In the East, however, it was another story. The missionaries who spread Mani's message across Asia were mostly Iranians, as were many of the people they converted from among Persians, Parthians, Sogdians and others. The Sogdians, due to their presence and activity along the Silk Road, were the principal agents for spreading Manichaeism among the Turks and eventually the Chinese. It was Sogdians who converted the Uighur ruler Bügü Khan, who accorded Manichaeism the status of official state religion of the Uighur Empire, beginning in 759 CE.[35]

With Uighur support, Manichaean merchants, monks and others were able to establish trading communities and monasteries in China, even in the face of the occasionally harsh persecutions of foreign religions by Chinese governments. Though the attachment of Uighur elites to Manichaeism waned by the tenth century, by that time the faith had gained a following among the native Chinese population. True to its chameleon-like legacy, Manichaeism in China survived by appearing to be something else, cloaking itself in Buddhist and Daoist language and symbols.

# THE LEGACY OF A "DEAD" RELIGION

It is not possible to know in any given historical context what the numbers of Manichaeans were or even what proportion they represented of any particular society. But what can be said with confidence is that the popularity of Manichaean ideas in a wide range of cultural contexts presented a challenge to which proponents of other religious systems were forced to respond. Manichaeism was not a religion that could be ignored.

The major importance of Manichaeism in the history of religions may be precisely this: it compelled other religions to defend and articulate themselves, eventually resulting in their taking the forms by which we know them today. It would appear that it was by engaging in polemics primarily with Manichaeism that Christianity, Zoroastrianism and Islam staked out their own orthodoxies, since the interpretations and expressions of each of these other religions prior to that engagement were far more diverse than afterwards.

Eliminating the competition posed by Mani at the Sasanian court was the first step taken by Kerdir and the Zoroastrian priesthood in making their religious vision that of the Sasanian state. Augustine constructed his Christianity initially as a rejection of his prior Manichaeism. And the purge of suspected Manichaeans from the bureaucratic elite of the early Abbasid Empire went hand in hand with the emergence of the *'ulemā'* as the controllers of religious authority in the emerging Islamic society of the time. While the representatives of these other religions also engaged in debates with each other, their most vitriolic attacks were directed at Manichaeism, which, claiming their own sources as its own, posed the greatest threat.

## Mani Hayy! *Manichaean Revival in the Modern Age*

The Internet is now home to several self-proclaimed neo-Manichaean communities. On one site, the Church Revived and Triumphant of the Holy Prophet Mani offers the following invitation:

> Welcome Converts to the Sacred Light of Truth! In the name of the Father and the Light of Truth, Liberator of the Soul and Mind from the base Darkness of Sin, Materiality, and the Flesh— greetings! We, the Synod of Bishops of the Neo-Manichaean Church, declare our willingness to accept candidates for membership. To join, a dedicant must answer one question: Do you, dedicant, declare yourself an eternal servant of the Holy Light of Truth, as revealed to the Holy Prophet, Mani the Blessed, and an everlasting enemy of the Darkness of Materiality and Flesh? As Brethren of the Light, we shun the material world

that is Darkness and decay; therefore, we exist as a Body of
believers only on the Internet, which is composed, after all, of
pure Light travelling as electromagnetic radiation from computer
to computer.[36]

Another site, belonging to the Order of Nazorean Essenes, proposes a
revised form of Manichaeism ("A Synthesis of Buddhism, Zarathustrianism
and Gnostic Christianity") suitable to the modern age, complete with
gender equality and ecological awareness:

THE MODERN ORDER of MANI differs slightly from the
ancient Manichaean movement in that it allows female Electi to
openly hold office, and allows Electi to pluck from the Cross of
Light [that is, harvest the fruits of the earth] as well as openly
marry within the Bridal Chamber. It is therefore not "orthodox"
in the sense of the Eastern Denavar Manichaeism, but "orthodox"
in the sense of being an evolved restoration of Syrian, or Mihr
Manichaeism, mingled with older orthodox Nazorean roots.[37]

One assumes that Mani, who preached in whatever terms were most
familiar to his audience, would only have approved.

# 11

# Undercurrents of Resistance: Mazdak and His Successors

One of the most severe magi-led persecutions of religions other than Zoroastrianism during the Sasanian period occurred under King Peroz I (reigned 459–487). During this time the Kanthaeans (Arabic *kaynaniyya* or *kanthawiyya*), a Gnostic–baptist sect in Persian Babylonia, possibly related to the Mandaeans, sought to protect themselves by adopting Zoroastrian rituals associated with fire temples. Their leader, a priest named Battai, changed his own name to the more Zoroastrian-sounding Yazdani. The Kanthaeans seem to have adapted several Manichaean texts and rituals for their own use. They survived into Islamic times and apparently participated in theological debates with Muslims. Drawing from the same symbolic "pool" as the Manichaeans, some of them practiced vegetarianism and celibacy, and believed in the transmigration of souls.[1]

Beginning in the late fifth or early sixth century the state-supported religious authority of the Zoroastrian magi faced its most serious threat yet, in the form of a popular movement led by a religious leader named Mazdak son of Bāmdād. This movement, which Mazdak himself called the *drust-dēn* (the "right religion"), seems to have taken shape some time earlier under the leadership of Zardošt of Fasa, a contemporary of Mani and thus a fellow rival with the magi competing for "Zoroastrian" authority. The Kanthaeans may also have influenced him in some respects, but like his predecessor Zardošt Mazdak seems to have presented himself as an interpreter of Zoroastrianism, able to detect "hidden, inner meanings" in the Zoroastrian texts. To the magi, therefore, he was, like Mani, a heretical interpreter of the Avesta, a *zandīk*.

A passage in the *Siyāsat-nāmeh*, an eleventh-century political treatise, purports to describe how Mazdak won over the Sasanian monarch Kavād I (Ar. Qubādh; reigned 488–496 and 498–531), by performing a miracle. Called before the king to explain his unique teaching, Mazdak makes the following boast: "For the most part the people are wrong in their interpretation of the Avesta and the Zand; I will show them the true meaning." In response, Kavād asks by what miracle he will demonstrate that his teaching is correct. (Apparently performing miracles was more convincing than actual arguments.) Mazdak replies that he will make the sacred fire of the Zoroastrians speak and "bear witness to my prophethood, so that the king and everyone with him may hear." The following day Kavād and his entourage accompany Mazdak to the fire temple, and sure enough, from within the fire a voice is heard affirming Mazdak's prophecy. (This is later shown to be a trick.) From that time on, according to the story, the king would place Mazdak on the throne and sit at his feet like a disciple.

> Then people began to join Mazdak's religion, partly out of liking and sympathy, and partly for the sake of agreeing with the king. From various provinces and districts they came to the capital, and either openly or secretly entered Mazdak's religion. The nobility, the peasantry and the military for the most part had no great zeal for it, but out of respect for the king they dared not say anything; of the priests not one went over to Mazdak's religion; they said, "Let us see what [proof] he adduces from the Avesta and the Zand.

When Mazdak saw that the king had embraced his religion and that people from far and near were accepting his invitation, he introduced the subject of property, and said, "Wealth must be divided among the people, for all are God's slaves and children of Adam. Whatsoever people may need, the expense must be met from communal funds, so that no man suffers neediness and privation in any respect and all men are equal." After he had convinced Qubād [Kavād] and his other adherents on this point and they had agreed to the sharing of wealth, then he said:

> Your wives are like your other possessions; they too should be regarded as common property. If any man feels desire for a woman let him come together with her. There is no jealousy or intolerance in our religion and nobody is deprived of the pleasures and lusts of the world. The doors of satisfaction are open to everybody.
>    Then by reason of the sharing of women, people were more eager to adopt his religion, especially the common people. And he laid down the custom that if someone invited twenty men to his house not only would he provide bread and meat and wine and minstrels and other amenities, but all the guests would get up one by one and make use of his wife; and they thought it no wrong.[2]

Taking the more shocking aspects of the author's description with a grain of salt, the appeal of Mazdakism seems to have been one of social justice, indicating perhaps a worsening disparity between the elites—who included the Zoroastrian magi—and the impoverished masses. Factional rivalries at court and a desire on the part of Kavād to counter the power of certain priests likely played a significant role in Mazdak's rise to influence. Indeed, such a situation appears strikingly similar to that in Mani's time, when religious leaders allied with various royal contenders each conspired to bring their own patron to the throne.

Contemporary historians have tended to describe Mazdak's teaching as a sort of proto-communism: making available to the masses goods and women that had long been hoarded by the elite. The social program attributed to him was particularly threatening to the rich and powerful, including the Zoroastrian clergy, who supported Kavād's son Khosrow in his efforts to suppress the movement. Following Mazdak's arrest and execution, which likely occurred near the beginning of Khosrow's reign, the surviving Mazdakites went underground. Many of their ideas survived, however, resurfacing in rebellions such as that of Bābak three centuries later.

## MAZDAK'S LIFE AND TEACHINGS

All the surviving textual evidence about Mazdak's movement is from external, antagonistic sources, mainly later Muslim and Zoroastrian ones but also a number of sixth-century Christian texts in Greek and Syriac. A Middle Persian *Book of Mazdak* was apparently translated by Ebn Muqaffa' but has not survived. According to the poetically-embellished tenth-century account in the *Shāh-nāmeh* of Ferdowsi, Mazdak originally held a government post as keeper of the treasury. Seeing that many of society's ills were due to people being in want, he ordered the granaries opened and their contents freely distributed. Ferdowsi gives the following account of Mazdak's teaching to Kavād:

> There are five things that lead us away from justice, and the wise cannot add another to them. These five are envy, the longing for vengeance, anger, desire, and the fifth, which becomes man's master, greed. If you conquer these five demons, the way to God is open to you. It is these five that make women and wealth the ruin of the true faith throughout the world. If women and wealth are not to harm the true faith, they must be held in common.[3]

Kavād, according to this story, was swayed by Mazdak's message of justice, but his son, Prince Khosrow, the future king Anushirvan (reigned 531–579), was not. In Ferdowsi's account (which must be considered largely fictional), six months after the aforementioned encounter Prince Khosrow organizes a debate by summoning religious leaders from across the realm. At first the king remains impressed by Mazdak's wisdom, but then a Zoroastrian priest confronts his rival with the following words:

> You are a seeker after knowledge, but the new religion you have made is a pernicious one. If women and wealth are to be held in common, how will a son know his father, or a father his son? If men are to be equal in the world, social distinctions will be unclear; who will want to be a commoner, and how will nobility be recognized? If the labouring slave and the king are the same, when a man dies, who is to inherit his goods? This talk of yours will ruin the world, and such an evil doctrine should not flourish in Iran. If everyone is a master, who is he able to command? Everyone will have a treasure, and who is to be its treasurer? None of those who established religions have talked this way. You have secretly put together a demonic faith; you are leading everyone to hell, and you don't see your evil acts for what they are.[4]

Kavād is somehow persuaded by the priest's words, and hands over Mazdak, "along with 100,000 of his followers," to his son Khosrow to deal with according to his wishes. Khosrow has the Mazdakites buried upside down in a garden, "with their feet in the air, like trees." Mazdak is taken to see this gruesome orchard, and faints in shock at the spectacle. He is then strung up on a gallows upside down and riddled with arrows.

The version of Mazdak's fall from grace is depicted somewhat differently in the *Siyāsat-nāmeh*. In the latter text it is Khosrow who persuades his father that Mazdak is a charlatan, but fearing an uprising if they make him a martyr, father and son conspire to lure 12,000 of Mazdak's supporters (a significantly smaller number than in the *Shāh-nāmeh*) to court where they are captured and buried upside down in a field with their legs sticking out, as in Ferdowsi's version. Mazdak is then brought out to observe their fate, and he too is buried, but right side up, so that he can contemplate the scene as he dies. Khosrow then continues his treachery by imprisoning his father and seizing the throne for himself.

While neither of these accounts can be considered properly historical, earlier Christian sources suggest the backdrop of the incident they describe, which probably occurred in the late 520s or early 530s. At that time there were two major rival factions at the Sasanian court looking to the eventual succession of the aged king Kavād. Mazdak's supporters favored the king's eldest son, Kāvūs, but the party supporting Khosrow eventually prevailed. Khosrow, known as Anushirvan ("the immortal soul"), went on to become one of pre-Islamic Iran's most celebrated rulers.

History credits him with initiating an important series of social reforms, especially in the realm of taxation. In fact these reforms probably began under his father Kavād; ironically, they may have been what instigated the popular rebellion associated with Mazdak in the first place.

What little is known of Mazdak's religious doctrines comes mainly from later Muslim sources. His teaching is best considered as a reformed Zoroastrianism, and not a version of Manichaeism, as some have argued. Drawing from the common Iranian pool, he retained the dualism and light symbolism of both religions, but not the latter's anti-materialism; rather, he championed the world- and life-affirming approach of Zoroastrianism. His approach to combating greed (*āz*, considered Ahriman's most powerful tool) through the redistribution of desirables is highly un-Manichaean.

The most detailed description of Mazdakite beliefs is found in a twelfth-century work of heresiography, the *Kitāb al-mihal wa'i-nihal* (*Book of Religions and Sects*) of Mohammad Shahrestani (1076–1153).[5] Shahrestani describes a Mazdakian cosmology in which the God of Light presides over the world from a celestial throne, surrounded by the hypostatized powers of Distinction, Insight, Alertness, and Joy. They rule the world through seven ministers, themselves encircled by a ring of twelve spirits. The Realm of Light is opposed by the Realm of Darkness, as in Manichaeism and other Iranian traditions.

According to Shahrestani's account, Mazdak's cosmic system of the Two Realms and the Two Principles was "the same as the greater part of Manichaeans," differing only in that he taught that Light (goodness) works freely and deliberately, whereas Darkness (evil) works at random. And in contrast to Manichaean belief, the "mingling" of the two which characterizes the phenomenal world occurred not through the misguided choice of primordial beings but by chance; salvation, likewise, is by chance, not choice. This notion of salvation, which may be tied to that of sudden enlightenment in Zen Buddhism, was anti-elitist, in that even the lowliest person might fortuitously receive it.

Like Mani, Mazdak preached a pacifist lifestyle including vegetarianism, but unlike the former, he taught that suicide is an acceptable means to avoid mingling with Darkness. The mark of a righteous person was that he embodied "the Four Powers and the Seven [ministers] and the Twelve [spirits]," in which case he "attains the state of divine lord in [this] inferior world and can do without any religious obligation." In other words, Mazdak rejected any kind of formal religious duty or ritual.

As a self-proclaimed Zoroastrian reformer, Mazdak is condemned as an arch-heretic in Zoroastrian priestly texts. It is significant that these texts consider Mazdakism to be a corrupt form of Zoroastrianism, while they treat Manichaeism as a separate religion altogether.

The ninth-century Pahlavi *Dēnkard* contains the following interesting note about Mazdakite practices:

> They grant supplies of food, so that they may say the food is proportional to the hunger; they speak of procreation, and say that they say lineage is through the mothers; and they approve of wolfishness, so that they would act something like wolves in the performance of gratifying their desires, like that of the wolf's progeny behind the mother. Moreover, they form their lineage through the mothers; buying their women as sheep, they shall carry off for profit even that son or brother who is the progeny, those that we have produced for your companionship . . .[6]

This text makes explicit the information that the Mazdakites provided food for the hungry, which was certainly a central element in their attractiveness to the peasant classes. Moreover, the reference to their establishing matriarchal lineage was, as corroborated in numerous other texts, a major point of objection from the point of view of the highly patriarchal Zoroastrian clergy.

The tenth-century account of Ibn Nadim likewise emphasizes the social aspect of Mazdak's movement:

> [He] ordered them to partake of pleasures and to pursue carnal desires, food and drinks, social intercourse and mixing together, as well as to refrain from arbitrariness with one another. For they shared their women and families, as no one of them was excluded from the women of another, nor did he himself withhold [his own women]. But along with this they exemplified deeds of kindness, refraining from killing and causing people sorrow. They had a system of hospitality which no other people had. For if they received a man as a guest, they did not exclude him from anything he desired, whatever it might be.[7]

### Problems with the Later Accounts

Patricia Crone has pointed out that the Christian sources, which are much closer to Mazdak's time period than the Muslim and Zoroastrian ones, make no mention of Mazdak for the first reign of Kavād, whereas they are unanimous in attributing the king's "communist" policies regarding women to that period. It is precisely on the pretext of heresy that Kavād was dethroned in 496, and these same sources make no mention of heretical activities throughout his second reign from 498–531. At the same time, they are completely silent on the issue of property redistribution.

Crone therefore surmises that the two policies, one pertaining to women and the other to property, were conflated by the Zoroastrian and Muslim sources, which, in her opinion, wrongly attribute the former to

Mazdak whereas it was originally Kavād's policy alone, aimed primarily at reducing the power of the nobility. Crone posits that Mazdak's peasant revolt may actually have begun at the end of Kavād's reign, largely in response to his tax reforms which were unfavorable to farmers and amid the turmoil of succession disputes from which Khosrow ultimately emerged the victor. Once Khosrow had managed to put down his brother Kāvūs's rival claims to the throne, he was then free to turn his attention to the suppression of the Mazdakites, a process that may have taken several years. "We may accept," Crone concludes, "that Kavād was a heretic who tried to impose his views on a reluctant populace (reluctant nobles above all), while Mazdak was a rebel who stirred up a peasant revolt: they simply did not act at the same time, let alone in alliance."[8]

### The Communist Trope: Possible Antecedents

Mehrdad Bahar has explored the possibility that aspects of the "revolutionary" social programs attributed to Mazdak were not revolutionary at all, but rather traditional practices that had existed in rural societies in Iran from time immemorial.[9] In particular, the "sharing of wives," which is such a predominant theme in anti-Mazdakite polemics, may actually reflect an ancient fertility ritual, attested for numerous times and places even up to recent times, of an annual orgy meant to symbolize the regeneration of life every spring. Such rituals, which are reflected even in the pre-Lenten carnivals of Catholic tradition, represent a period of complete disorder which is then followed by a restoration of order.

According to Bahar's analysis, some ancient Iranian rural societies had such a ritual—the disorder/order aspect of which is preserved even today in the outdoor celebration of *Sīzdah be-dar* thirteen days after Nō rūz—which in Sasanian times the Zoroastrian clergy attempted to suppress. The peasant uprisings against Sasanian authority which occurred at the end of Kavād's reign or the beginning of Khosrow's may thus have combined resistance both to the government's attempts at tax reform and to the clergy's efforts to suppress a long-cherished annual ritual. Bahar further notes that some non-*Shāh-nāmeh* versions of the "evil tyrant" Zahhāk portray him as advocating the sharing of women and possessions. Since Zahhāk is considered by the tradition to be non-Iranian, the fertility ritual of an annual orgy may have originally come from pre-Iranian inhabitants of the Iranian plateau, a possibility corroborated by the existence of similar rituals among other ancient peoples of the Near East.[10]

## POST-MAZDAKITE REBELLIONS

During the late 740s an Iran-based rebel movement of expatriate Arab men and local Iranians arose in Khorasan. The rebellion was led by an

Iranian general, Behzādān known as Abu Muslim, whose charisma and success made him a threat to the very people he had brought to power. While ostensibly Shi'ite in its ideology, in fact the Abbasid movement included a wide range of groups, both Muslim and non-Muslim, who shared a hatred for the ruling Umayyads as well as a tendency to extremist beliefs (Ar. *ghulū*, literally, "exaggeration"). Mazdakites were likely among Abu Muslim's diverse supporters. A parallel uprising in Khorasan during the years 747–748 led by a neo-Zoroastrian prophet, Behāfarīd, was suppressed by Abu Muslim who had his rival captured and executed in 749.

Once in power the new Abbasid government executed Abu Muslim in 755, but his non-Muslim followers believed he would be reincarnated and they maintained their allegiance to him after his death. In Shahrestani's time (that is, the twelfth century) there were still Mazdakite communities scattered throughout Iran and Sogdiana, among which Shahrestani counts those he calls [*abū*] *muslimiyya*.[11] Certain Mazdakite groups thus continued to revere Abu Muslim and his descendants for several centuries at least.

Mazdakites participated in two major revolts against Abbasid rule in the wake of Abu Muslim's execution. The first, which was quickly put down, rallied behind a general named Sunpadh, a political figure from Nishapur who claimed that Abu Muslim's spirit had entered his body. According to the *Siyāsat-nāmeh*, Sunpadh gained the support of Zoroastrians by promising to expel the Arab conquerors, while urging the Mazdakites to join the revolt because Mazdak had been reincarnated as a Shi'ite Muslim.[12] After some initial victories over the Abbasid Caliph Mansur's forces, Sunpadh was defeated at Ray (modern Tehran) and his followers dispersed. Now known as the *khorram-dīniyyeh* ("those of the Happy Religion," reflecting Mazdak's teaching of a joyful and generous approach to life), they went underground once again only to re-emerge as a political force in Azerbaijan several decades later.

A second rebellion took place in Central Asia under the leadership of a self-proclaimed prophet known as al-Moqanna', "the Veiled One," who maintained control over much of Sogdiana from 766–780. According to Biruni, the religion taught by al-Moqanna' was "all the laws and institutes which Mazdak had established."[13] Like Mazdak, he is said to have been a master illusionist, winning people over through tricks construed as miracles. Narshakhi, a tenth-century Sogdian historian, states that al-Moqanna' used mirrors to direct sunlight into the eyes of his crowd, making them believe they had seen God.[14] Known as the *sapīd-jāmagān* ("wearers of white robes"; Ar. *mubayyida*), al-Moqanna''s sect still existed in Shahrestani's time.[15]

A few decades after al-Moqanna''s rebellion in Central Asia, the *khorram-dīniyyeh* reappeared in Azerbaijan under the leadership of Bābak, who launched a spectacularly successful rebellion against the Abbasid government in 816. His movement attracted a range of disaffected groups from across Iran, and managed to hold firm against Abbasid authority for more than two decades. A succession of generals was unable to defeat him, until at last he was betrayed by an Armenian prince who turned him over to the Abbasid commander Afshīn in 837. Bābak was taken to the capital, Samarra, where he was dismembered alive, reportedly rubbing his face with the blood of his severed wrists so as not to appear "yellow" from fear.[16]

In terms of belief, the *khorram-dīniyyeh* denied the Day of Judgment, an article of faith for Muslims and Zoroastrians alike, and considered that final authority in all matters of belief lay in the esoteric interpretations of the leader of the sect. Their rituals centered on purity and included the use of bread and wine. The tenth-century Muslim encyclopædist Maqdisī, claiming to base his account both on personal encounters and on a lost *Book of the Khorramites*, provides the following details:

> [The Khurramites] are unanimous in their belief in reincarnation. They accept the change in name and body. They claim that all the prophets, despite the differences among the laws and religions they have established, constitute but a single spirit, and that revelation has never ceased. Every religious man is, according to them, on the right path, from the moment he hopes for reward and fears punishment; they don't allow him to be insulted or accused of reprehensible acts, as long as he doesn't think of attacking their community and obliterating their doctrine . . .

> They have *imām*s whom they consult for resolving disputes and envoys who circulate among them whom they call *ferešteg ān* ("angels"); what sanctifies them the most is wine and [other] beverages. The basis of their religion is belief in the two principles, light and darkness; those we have seen in their country, that is to say the region of Masebedān, we found extremely preoccupied by questions of cleanliness and purification, filled with the desire to approach other men with kindness and beneficence.

> We found that they accept the sharing of women, on the condition that the women themselves consent, as well as the freedom to enjoy all forms of pleasure and to take advantage of all the attractions of nature, as long as it results in no harm to anyone.[17]

Thus, anticipating approaches such as that of the Bahá'ís in the nineteenth century and the perennial philosophers of the twentieth, the Khorramīs believed that all religions were basically true and that all prophets bring messages from the same source. They assumed that all religious people were essentially on the right path, as long as they did not harm the community of the Khorramīs. (This condition allowed the otherwise pacifist Khorramīs to kill many thousands of their Muslim persecutors.) They were said to be peaceful and cheerful except when in battle, and their ethic is echoed in the contemporary Wiccan Rede, "Do as you will but harm none."

Bābak's revolt seriously destabilized the Caliphate for many years, until his eventual capture and execution. Although Bābak's supporters continued to stage occasional rebellions following his death, the movement was greatly weakened, and over time Mazdakite doctrines, firmly established within the available pool of Iranian religious ideas, became absorbed into a range of esoteric Muslim groups. In the absence of a clear leader, many Khorramīs came to look to the Isma'ili Shi'i imams as their source of guidance and authority.

A twelfth-century Isma'ili source, however, indicates that some who outwardly professed allegiance to the Isma'ili imam continued to practice their Mazdakite faith in secret. Such people referred to themselves as "Parsis," reflecting their persistent attachment to Persian, as opposed to Arab tradition. Accordingly, they transposed Shi'ite notions of the imamate to the line of pre-Islamic Persian kings, and saw its passing to a few generations of Arabs as a temporary phenomenon. This made them heretics in the eyes of the Isma'ilis.

These "Parsis" (not to be confused with the Zoroastrians of India) maintained a number of Mazdakite beliefs, including an aversion to harming animals, plants, or men except those who would raise arms against them. They considered that women were "the water of the house from which it is licit for every thirsty man to drink," but apparently saw sexual freedom as independent from marriage, since they condemned as a sin the taking of more than one wife. The Parsis interpreted the resurrection in terms of reincarnation into another body, again putting them at odds with more conventional Islamic views. Ironically they considered other Isma'ilis, who Sunni Muslims called esotericists (*batiniyya*), as following a "superficial" interpretation of the truth.[18]

## SURVIVALS OF MAZDAKITE INFLUENCE

Iranian esotericism continued to exist, but in Islamic garb. Isma'ili Shi'ism would draw on much of the symbolism of pre-Islamic gnosis, as would illuminationist (*ešrāqī*) philosophy and some Iranian Sufi mystical traditions. The Sufi notion of '*erfān*, understood as sublime insight acquired through a combination of personal discipline and divine grace, has long held an attraction for Iranian Muslim mystics, and is now even studied in the seminaries of Qom as an academic subject.

A seventeenth-century Zoroastrian *ešrāqī* text, the *Dabestān-e mazāheb*, mentions a group of neo-Mazdakites living outwardly as

Muslims.[19] In 1844 an English missionary, Joseph Wolff, met a group of Persian Sufis while travelling in Central Asia. "The time will come," they told him, "when there shall be no difference between rich and poor, between high and low, when property shall be in common—even wives and children."[20] Hidden beneath a veneer of Islamic mysticism, the social platform of Mazdak had survived for thirteen centuries!

Bābak remains a popular figure in rural Azerbaijan. In recent years thousands of people have gathered every summer at the foot of his castle near the village of Kalibar in the eastern part of the province, ostensibly to celebrate his birthday. Local women say the reason the castle still stands is because the mortar holding it together was strengthened with eggs brought by women in Bābak's time.

# 12

# Islam

During the middle decades of the seventh century an army of Arabs, united for the first time by a new faith, Islam, stunned both the Roman (Byzantine) and Persian (Sasanian) empires by conquering the important Byzantine provinces of Egypt and Syria and the whole of the Sasanian realm. The Arabian peninsula, which was mostly sparsely inhabited desert, had never before been a region of political importance. The great empires only concerned themselves with controlling the coastal regions, where there were a number of towns which served as staging posts along the trade routes that linked the Mediterranean with the Indian Ocean. These towns had often been under the economic hegemony of Iran, and many were home to small Iranian trading communities.

Iranians thus had a long presence in Arabia, where prior to Islam, expatriate groups of Zoroastrians, Manichaeans, and Mazdakites existed. At the same time some Arabs, especially among the Tamim tribe, are said to have subscribed on some level to Zoroastrianism. The Arabs' longstanding familiarity with Iranians and their culture accounts for the numerous Iranian ideas, including a number of Persian loanwords, which appear in the Qur'an.

One of the first Meccan converts to Muhammad's new religion was a man known as Salman al-Farsi ("the Persian"). As the first Iranian to embrace Islam, Salman—who is often referred to as *Salmān-e pāk*, "Salman the Pure"—holds a special place in the hearts of Iranian Muslims. Salman was apparently the first to introduce the Arabs to trench warfare, enabling Muhammad and his companions to defeat the Meccans at the so-called Battle of the Trench in 627. He is said to have been one of the original supporters of 'Ali's succession, making him a foundational figure for Shi'ites. Reinforcing his spiritual credentials, Salman is reported to have been a member of the hereditary Zoroastrian priesthood prior to his conversion to Islam; among Iranian Shi'ites he is held up as an archetypical transmitter of esoteric knowledge.

On the political stage of the ancient Near East, neither the Persians nor the Romans had ever considered the Arabs to be a serious threat. Arabian society was small in scale and rather diffuse. Largely pastoral nomadic, it was made up of clans who could enter into pacts with each other but lacked any central organization. Muhammad ibn 'Abdallāh, the prophet of Islam, was the first Arab to win the allegiance of all the clans of the Arabian peninsula.

Muhammad's prophetic career did not get off to an easy start. The message he preached in Mecca posed a challenge to many of the city's inhabitants. His vision of monotheism was uncompromisingly radical: even the Christian trinity appeared to him as a kind of polytheism. Mecca, being a trading town, had temples to the various religions of local expatriate business communities, and pious donations were an important part of the local economy. Muhammad's teachings also contained a measure of social critique, warning that those who did not practice charity and justice would be judged by God for their acts. Since in Muhammad's time social disparities seem to have been on the rise, his message caused some discomfort among Mecca's wealthy and powerful elites.

Muhammad himself does not seem to have had direct contact with any Iranian religious community, but since Iranian ideas were part of the Arab culture of his time, it is not surprising to find them present in the Qur'an. Islamic beliefs in heaven and hell, a last judgment based on the weighing (*mīzān*) of good and bad deeds, a bridge of death, and angels, as well as tendencies toward millenarianism, messianism, and apocalypticism, along with notions of ritual purity, have all been argued to have Iranian origins.

The five daily prayers (Ar. *salāt*, NP *namāz*), which became the most visible expression of Islamic piety, mirror Zoroastrian practice. The popular Muslim story of Muhammad's miraculous night journey to heaven (the *mi'rāj*) is paralleled in the Middle Persian tale of "Righteous Viraz," which may also be the ultimate source for Dante's *Divine Comedy*. (A Jewish version, featuring Moses, was very popular among Iranian Jews.) The Islamic belief that Jesus' death on the cross was mere appearance is found earlier in Manichaeism, as is the Islamic tithe for charity (*zakāt*). The angels Harut and Marut (Qur'an 2:96) are clear reflections of the Zoroastrian Aməša Spəntas Haurvatat and Aməretat. The Qur'an mentions Zoroastrians (*al-majūs*) alongside Jews, Sabeans, Christians and polytheists in contrast to "those who believe" (Qur'an 22:17). The Qur'anic Arabic language includes numerous Persian loanwords, including 'afrīt ("demon"), junāh ("crime"), firdaws ("Paradise"), rawda ("well-watered garden") and many others.[1]

Muhammad was able to attract a growing number of followers in his native town of Mecca, largely among the disenfranchised. Eventually tensions with the Meccan elites reached a point where Muhammad felt compelled to accept an offer from the inhabitants of Yathrib, an agricultural town several days' journey to the north, to bring his group to live there. This migration, called the *hijra* in Arabic, marks the beginning of the Islamic calendar in 622 CE.

From his new base in Yathrib, which came to be known as *Madīnat al-nabī* ("the City of the Prophet") or Medina for short, Muhammad and his companions were able to launch raids against the caravans of the Meccans and build up their economic and political strength. Raiding was an accepted part of the economic life all throughout the marginally productive Arabian peninsula, hence the prevalence of pacts by which weaker clans would seek the support of stronger ones. As Muhammad's community grew in power, one by one the clans of Arabia sent emissaries to seek such agreements.

The traditional act of submission by the weak to the powerful, which is called *islām* in Arabic, can be read as having either a political or religious significance in Muhammad's case, since it is impossible to know whether the Arabs felt they were submitting to Muhammad's authority as leader of his group or to the authority of the one God, Allah, whose prophet he claimed to be. One may suspect that for many of the Arabs it may have been the former, since Arabic accounts of what translators have labeled "conversions" indicate that in most cases people "submitted" first and only afterwards learned about the Qur'an, its content, and the social codes of the Muslims. This is true not only of the initial period but of conversions throughout the early centuries of the Islamic caliphate.

Another fact which supports a socio-political, rather than primarily religious definition of *islām*, is that once word went out of Muhammad's death in 632 many of the Arab tribes rebelled. But by that time Muhammad's community, the *umma*, was strong enough that the recalcitrant Arabs were brought once again under the control of his successor (*xalīfa*, or Caliph), Abu Bakr.

With the entire peninsula bound by mutual allegiance to the *umma*, it was no longer possible for the Arabs to raid each other. Quite naturally, they therefore extended their raids to neighboring lands. Their unprecedented empowerment, buttressed by a new faith and combined with the weakness, exhaustion, and unpopularity of the Roman and Persian regimes, enabled the Arabs to expand their rule from Spain to the frontiers of China and India within only a matter of decades.

From a religious point of view Arab rule was less onerous for its subjects than the Roman or the Persian governments had been. For centuries each of the imperial states had sponsored one officially recognized religion—Chalcedonian Christianity in the case of the Romans and Zoroastrianism in the case of the Persians—and frequently permitted their established clergies to wage campaigns against any sect they deemed heretical. The Arabs, by contrast, allowed individual communities to run their own affairs and follow their own customs, requiring only that they pay a poll tax, the *jizya*, which was less than the extortionate taxes that had been extracted by previous regimes. For followers of minority or heterodox religious sects, this release from the persecution of ruthless magi or intolerant bishops must have come as an enormous relief.

During the first several centuries of Muslim rule in Iran the authority of the Zoroastrian priests slowly but steadily eroded. Their state support forever lost, the magi had to compete financially—subsisting as they did on fees charged for the performance of rituals and ceremonies— with Muslim governments who were levying the poll tax and other obligations on Zoroastrian citizens.

It may also be that in aligning their interests with those of the Sasanian government more than with the general population, the magi had ceased to serve the needs of many Iranians. The widespread popularity in Iran of Christianity, Manichaeism, and, in the East, of Buddhism, as well as the ease with which new movements such as that of Mazdak won large followings, can be taken as further evidence that the Zoroastrian priests had distanced themselves from the interests of the general population.

## FROM "THE RELIGION OF THE ARABS" TO UNIVERSAL FAITH SYSTEM

Richard Bulliet has suggested, based on his reading of family genealogies from Khorasan, that by the year 1000 about eighty percent of urban Iranians (albeit in a largely rural society) were Muslim.[2] Why so many Zoroastrians, Christians, Jews, Buddhists and others chose to embrace the new faith is open to consideration. Presumably many factors played a role.

Among these, forced conversion was apparently not foremost at least during the early period. The Arabs initially saw their military successes as a sign that God had favored them above all other peoples, and they were not for the most part overly eager to share the fruits of their success too widely. The conversions of subject peoples throughout the period of the Damascus-based Umayyad Arab dynasty (661–750 CE) appear to have been mainly a case of Arab society being overwhelmed by the popular demand of outsiders for inclusion in the privileged class. This led to tensions as non-Arab converts came to outnumber Arab Muslims, a transition that probably occurred by the early eighth century.

For the many peoples who had come under Arab rule, tribal norms constituted the formal basis for relations between the Arabs and their subject communities. Islam was initially perceived both by the Arabs and by their subjects as "the Arab religion" (*dīn al-'arab*), so "converting" to Islam literally entailed "going Arab." (This notion is preserved in the later Spanish term for Christians who embraced Arab culture, *mozarab*, from the Arabic *musta'rab*.)

Specifically, because Arab society was based on blood ties, it was necessary for any non-Arab who wanted to join the Muslim community to find an Arab patron who could give him honorary membership in a particular Arab clan. Obviously this gave the patron a certain amount of leverage over his client.[3] Thus, non-Arab converts often felt that despite the Qur'an's universalist message they were still being treated as second-class citizens. The growing disaffection of non-Arab converts merged with that of certain marginalized Arab clans, eventually giving rise to the so-called "Abbasid" movement that challenged and eventually overthrew the ruling hierarchy. The ideology chosen by the rebels to symbolize their struggle was drawn from an event that occurred before Muhammad's death in 632 CE.

## CHALLENGING THE BASIS OF TEMPORAL AUTHORITY

The passing away of God's Messenger brought about the first major crisis within the Muslim community. Muhammad's friend and father-in-law Abu Bakr, a man who was by all accounts widely respected, is said to have emerged from Muhammad's tent and told the anxious crowd, "O men, if anyone worships Muhammad, Muhammad is dead; if anyone worships God, God is alive, immortal."[4] Still, as transmitter of the divine revelation of the Qur'an, Muhammad's leadership had been vital and unquestioned. The problem of how the community was to decide on a successor was left unresolved, at least in the minds of many.

For others the issue had been settled during Muhammad's lifetime. According to a hadith included in the Sunni collection of Ibn Hanbal, toward the end of his life, at a place called Ghadir Khumm, Muhammad had taken 'Ali, his cousin and son-in-law (Ali was married to Muhammad's only surviving child, Fatima), by the hand in a traditional performative gesture and declared that "Of whomsoever I am the Lord (*mawlā*), then 'Ali is also his Lord. O God! Be Thou the supporter of whoever supports 'Ali and the enemy of whoever opposes him."[5] Most of those present assumed that Muhammad was referring to the management of his own household. A significant minority, however, understood him to mean he was designating 'Ali as his successor as leader of the Muslims. Over time these came to be referred to as the *šī'at 'Alī*, or "partisans of 'Ali"—known in English as the Shi'ites.

But at the period of Muhammad's death, the majority of his followers sought to resolve the issue of succession through the traditional means of their society. 'Umar ibn al-Khattāb, considered by many to be a contender for the role, pre-empted any dispute by taking Abu Bakr's hand in a formal gesture of allegiance and proclaiming his support for him. But those who felt that Muhammad had already chosen his successor were not satisfied, feeling that 'Ali had been unjustly deprived of his rightful position as leader of the Muslims. 'Ali himself seems to have held this view, though he did not protest at the time.

Eventually 'Ali was chosen to be the fourth Caliph, but the powerful Umayyad family, based in Damascus, refused to acknowledge his authority. After agreeing to arbitration with his rivals, in 661 'Ali was murdered by a disgruntled faction of his own followers (the Kharijites, from *xawārij*; lit., "those who withdrew" [their support]). His eldest son, Hasan, declined the leadership role 'Ali's supporters expected of him; 'Ali's younger son Husayn eventually stepped in. Buttressed by what appeared to be strong support in southern Iraq, Husayn challenged the rule of the Syria-based Umayyads. But when the Umayyad Caliph Yazid sent an army to put down the rebellion, Husayn found himself abandoned by all but a handful of supporters and was killed by Yazid's forces at Karbala in 680 CE. In the years that followed there arose a tendency for anyone in Muslim society who had any cause to feel marginalized—whether professionally, socially, politically, or otherwise—to see in the murders of 'Ali and his son Husayn a symbol for all those who had suffered injustice of whatever kind.

By the mid-eighth century the majority non-Arab Muslims of eastern Iran, in alliance with Arab garrisons which chafed at having been relegated to the backwaters of the empire, were strong enough to challenge the ruling Umayyads whom they collectively viewed as corrupt and un-Islamic despots. Led by the charismatic Iranian general known as Abu Muslim the rebels rallied in the name of a descendant of Muhammad's uncle Abbas, seeking to put him at the head of the Caliphate. In 751 CE they succeeded in overthrowing the Umayyads and the "Abbasid" empire was born.

## THE IRANIAN ROLE IN SHAPING ISLAMIC CIVILIZATION

From the first contact between the Arab Muslims and the Iranian population there were intermarriages, especially between the daughters of important Iranian families and the sons of Arab ones. Conquering armies almost always take the womenfolk of those they have vanquished, but in this case such marriages served a double purpose. For the Arabs, alliances with Iranian families helped improve their prestige among a subject people who still saw themselves as possessing the superior civilization. For Iranians, marital alliances were a way of holding onto their status and privilege under changed political circumstances. It is easy to forget that beneath an outward process of Islamization the children of such marriages, raised in Iran by Iranian mothers, would have grown up in many respects more culturally Iranian than Arab. There is a prevalent male fiction that fathers determine their children's education, but women know better. The role of Iranian mothers in maintaining and passing on Iranian cultural traditions after the Arab conquest is largely undocumented but was surely significant.

What is far better attested is the predominance of Muslim men of Iranian stock in working out all aspects of what would become the universal Islamic civilization, whether in law, theology, science, philosophy, history, geography, the arts—even in the realm of Arabic literature and linguistics. Although the Arabs brought peoples as diverse as Egyptians, Syrians, Greeks, Berbers, Visigoths, and Indians under their far-flung administration, none of these nations would rival the Iranians in contributing to the emerging Islamic culture. Indeed, within a little over a century Iranians would come to play a larger role than the Arabs themselves.

With the overthrow of the Umayyads in 751 the leaders of the Abbasid movement chose to move the capital eastward, closer to their Iranian power base. After initially establishing themselves at Kufa in Iraq, they built a new city near the former Persian capital of Ctesiphon, on the banks of the Tigris river. They called their new capital Baghdad, a Persian word meaning "given by God."

With the Muslim world's center of gravity shifted to the fringes of Iran, the new government soon took on the role of successors to the pre-Islamic Sasanians. While the Umayyad administration had been in many respects a somewhat superficially Arabized continuation of the provincial Byzantine government of Syria, the Abbasids adopted the institutional apparatus of the Sasanians. Indeed, the culture of the Abbasid court was so marked by Iranian norms that the famous ninth-century Arabic writer al-Jahiz referred to the Abbasid Caliphate as a "Persian" (*'ajamiyya*) government.[6]

Under the Abbasids the earlier Sasanian system of administrative departments (*dīvān*s) was kept more or less intact; this included the office of prime minister (*vazīr*), the postal and intelligence service (*barīd*), and the tax farming system of the landowners (*dehqān*s). The court system, in which judges (*qādī*s) were appointed from among the scholars of religious law, was a continuation of the Sasanian model. The first Abbasid coins placed Arabic inscriptions next to images of Zoroastrian fire altars. Sasanian court traditions such as poetry and music were maintained and embellished by Arab influences. The Abbasids retained the Persian solar calendar and the equinox festivals of Nō rūz and Mehregān, and adopted the Sasanian ideology of kingship whereby the ruler was considered to be the "Shadow of God on Earth" (*zillu-llāh* *fi'l-ard*)—a thoroughly un-Arab and un-Islamic notion. Finally, they dispensed with any lingering threats from their own rebellious past by initiating the persecution of suspected Shi'ites.

The door was opened to Iranian influence in every aspect of Muslim life and society. Both the codification of Islamic law and the collation of *hadīths*—reports about the words and deeds of Muhammad, which served as one of the basic sources of Islamic jurisprudence—occurred mainly in the Iranian cultural sphere. The compilers of all six hadith collections considered canonical by later Sunnis (that is, the majority of the world's Muslims) were scholars of Iranian background. The very impulse for collecting hadiths was due to the emergence of a whole new set of conflicts over how to order and maintain Muslim society, a society which was no longer monocultural but had become thoroughly cosmopolitan.

As long as the majority of Muslims had been Arabs, traditional Arabian cultural norms continued to be accepted wherever they were not altered or abrogated by the divine revelation of the Qur'an. And indeed, throughout the first century of the Islamic period under the Umayyad dynasty, descendants of the Arabs who had originally submitted to Muhammad's authority took this approach, resolving legal disputes through the "informed opinion" (*ra'y*) of an appointed judge, who was usually an Arab.

Once Arabs were in the minority, however, other sets of long-established social norms began to compete with Arab ones. If an answer could not be found in the Qur'an, the next recourse was to claim that one's position was vindicated in an example from the life of Muhammad. Obviously it was possible to invent stories in which Muhammad was said to have done this or that, and such inventions quickly became rampant. It was urgent for Muslims to find a way to authenticate stories about their prophet which could be used as a basis for establishing a universal social code. This project, which resulted in the formulation of *sharī'a* law, took at least two centuries, and was carried out largely in the Iranian world.

The early Abbasid period is known as "the Classical Age of Islam," and in this time scholars of Iranian background were everywhere pre-eminent. Famous figures such as the historians Tabari and Meskavayh, the mathematician Khwarazmi, the physician–philosophers Rhazes and Avicenna, the geographers Ebn Khordadbeh, Estakhri and Ebn Faqih, and the Sufi brothers Mohammad and Ahmad Ghazali, all had Iranian origins.

In the realm of language and literature Iranians again played a central role. That an Iranian linguist, Sibavayh, should have been the first to write down a systematic grammar of Arabic is no surprise. Arabs didn't need grammars—it was the Iranians who had to learn Arabic as a foreign language. As Iranian intellectuals sought to express their ideas in this new tongue, they found that many abstract philosophical or technical terms did not exist in Arabic and had to be invented. Neologisms were coined using the Iranian scholars' analysis of the grammatical rules of Arabic.

Beginning in the mid-eighth century a group of mainly Iranian scribes called the *sho'ūbiyyeh* (literally, "ordinary folk") translated many literary works from Middle Persian (Pahlavi) into Arabic, both for the benefit of their Arab superiors and to ensure a wider distribution throughout the empire. Perhaps too, in bringing so many classics back to life, there was a sense of asserting Persian cultural superiority. "Mirrors for Princes"-type literature, such as the eighth-century *Book of Companions* (*Kitāb al-sahāba*) helped to shape the Abbasid concept of rule, while semi-legendary royal chronicles like the *Book of Kings* (*Khwadāy-nāmag*, the principal source and model for Ferdowsi's later epic rendition, the *Shāh-nāmeh*) provided the historical framework into which Islamic rulers sought to situate themselves. Morality tales such as the animal fables of *Kalila and Dimna* (derived from the Sanskrit *Pañcatantra*) and the adventure stories of *The Tales of A Thousand and One Nights*—of widespread provenance but best known at the time from the Middle Persian collection *Hezār afsān* ("A Thousand Tales")—served both to entertain and instruct. Thus was the Sasanian literary tradition assimilated into the Islamic world.

Another form of Iranian reassertion that existed at this time, especially among the bureaucratic elites, took the form of crypto-religion. The best-known of the *sho'ūbiyyeh*, Rozbeh son of Dadoy, called Ebn al-Muqaffa', was perhaps a typical case. A government employee, his conversion to Islam was clearly opportunistic, and eventually he was accused of being an infidel and executed. Large numbers of Iranian intellectuals at the time secretly practiced some form of esoteric Iranian religion—as mentioned previously, the term used, *zandaqa*, usually meant "Manichaeism" but could refer to any dualistic heresy— which brought about a major official purge of suspected heretics. The movement was crushed under the caliph Mahdi from 775–785, but re-emerged in altered form during the following century in the form of various Shi'ite beliefs which spread among the same class of literate Iranians.

Throughout the first two centuries of Arab domination various resistance movements throughout Iran took on a religious character. One such attempt to throw off Arab rule was led by the magician Moqanna' ('the Veiled One") in Central Asia in the 780s. The best-known, however (and in the Islamic sources, the most abhorred), was the rebellion of Bābak in northern Iran from 816–837, discussed in Chapter 11.

Though these and other attempts to resist Arab domination ultimately failed, Iranian culture did succeed in reasserting itself throughout the ninth and tenth centuries as the eastern provinces of the empire, first the Tahirid governors of Khorasan and then the Saffarids of Sistan further south, successively freed themselves from many aspects of the Caliphate's centralized rule. The persistent attachment to Iranian identity throughout the eastern part of the Caliphate is evidenced by the tendency among local elites to give their children Persian, rather than Islamic names, and the fabrication of genealogies linking them to Sasanian families or even to mythical heroes.[7]

During this period written Persian, which had given way to Arabic for two centuries, began to re-emerge, first under the Saffarids, whose ruler reprimanded his Arabic court poets for composing in a language he couldn't understand. Persian formally regained its status as official language under the Samanid dynasty of Central Asia (875–998 CE). Persian was also championed by the Ziyarids, who ruled the southeast Caspian region from 928–1043.

The major type of institution for the propagation of Islamic higher learning, the *madrasa* (literally "place of study") arose in Iran during the tenth and eleventh centuries. By the time the Seljuk prime minister Nezam al-Molk (himself an Iranian) built the famous Nezamiyyeh madrasa in Baghdad in 1065, there were already some twenty-five madrasas functioning in Iran. The madrasas, with their regularized curriculum based on law and *hadīth* studies, were the primary mechanism through which a normative Sunni Islam was developed and disseminated throughout the Muslim world.

### The Persian Garden as Metaphor for Islamic Paradise

The very word "paradise" is of Persian origin. Its modern Persian form, *ferdows*, means simultaneously "heaven" and "garden." (The corresponding Arabic term, *jannat*, has the same double meaning.) Both the English and modern Persian words are derived from the Old Persian *paira daeza*, meaning a walled enclosure, borrowed into ancient Greek as παράδεισος and later into Arabic as *firdaws*.

One of the most pervasive yet subtle influences of Iranian culture throughout the world is the type of garden plan generally known as "Islamic." Such gardens are found not only throughout the Middle East, South Asia, and the rest of the Muslim world, but were also transmitted, via Spain, to much of the Western hemisphere. The basic design of an "Islamic" garden consists of a quadrangle, bisected (usually by channels of water) into quadrants, often with a pavilion or fountain in the middle, and with various plantings (consisting of trees, shrubs, flowers, and various groundcovers) throughout the quadrants. Such gardens are favored spots for picnics and lovers' trysts. The flowers, birds, and running water are all meant to evoke paradise.

In virtually all respects, however, this garden tradition is not "Islamic" as such, but has rather been Islamicized from the model of pre-Islamic Iran. Its precedents are very ancient: pottery bowls from as early as 4000 BCE show the familiar motifs of four quadrants with a pool at the center, the tree of life, and so on. By Sasanian times at the latest the garden quadrangle, called *čahār bāgh* in Persian, had become the established design in Iran. A typical variant is the *hašt behešt*, or "eight paradises." The garden itself is often known as a *bustān*, literally "aromatic place," or *golestān*, "place of flowers," and figures as the setting for much of classical Persian poetry. The Persian garden is also one of the most common motifs in the design of Persian carpets, whose influence spread to South Asia, China, and Europe.

The heavenly gardens described in the Qur'an both recall and embellish the ancient Iranian garden model. In all there are 166 Qur'anic references to gardens. As with nature in general, gardens in the Qur'an are meant to be taken as signs (*āyat*) of God's divine order and perfection. In other words, the function of nature's beauty is to lead humans to God. From prehistoric times Iranians revered the natural world for its divine qualities, paying homage to the various *mainyu*s inhering in natural phenomena. For Muslim Iranians, this nature-reverence became sublimated to the level of symbolism, but remains nonetheless profound.

The fifty-fifth chapter of the Qur'an, entitled *al-Rahmān* ("The Beneficent"), which describes the many beautiful gifts which God has bestowed on humans, contains the kind of rich imagery that evokes paradise in the minds of many Muslims. Verses 46–78 read as follows, in the translation of Muhammad Marmaduke Pickthall:

> But for him who feareth the standing before his Lord there are
>     two gardens.
> Which is it, of the favours of your Lord, that ye deny?
> Of spreading branches.
> Which is it, of the favours of your Lord, that ye deny?
> Wherein are two fountains flowing.
> Which is it, of the favours of your Lord, that ye deny?
> Wherein is every kind of fruit in pairs.
> Which is it, of the favours of your Lord, that ye deny?
> Reclining upon couches lined with silk brocade, the fruit of both
>     the gardens near to hand.
> Which is it, of the favours of your Lord, that ye deny?
> Therein are those of modest gaze, whom neither man nor jinni
>     will have touched before them.
> Which is it, of the favours of your Lord, that ye deny?

(In beauty) like the jacynth and the coral-stone.
Which is it, of the favours of your Lord, that ye deny?
Is the reward of goodness aught save goodness?
Which is it, of the favours of your Lord, that ye deny?
And beside them are two other gardens,
Which is it, of the favours of your Lord, that ye deny?
Dark green with foliage.
Which is it, of the favours of your Lord, that ye deny?
Wherein are two abundant springs.
Which is it, of the favours of your Lord, that ye deny?
Wherein is fruit, the date-palm and pomegranate.
Which is it, of the favours of your Lord, that ye deny?
Wherein (are found) the good and beautiful –
Which is it, of the favours of your Lord, that ye deny?
Fair ones, close-guarded in pavilions –
Which is it, of the favours of your Lord, that ye deny?
Whom neither man nor jinni will have touched before them –
Which is it, of the favours of your Lord, that ye deny?
Reclining on green cushions and fair carpets.
Which is it, of the favours of your Lord, that ye deny?
Blessed be the name of thy Lord, Mighty and glorious!

Such a paradise garden has long been a major theme for poets, painters, and architects throughout the Persian-speaking world. One has only to think of the quatrains of Omar Khayyam, known to the English-speaking world through the versions of Edward Fitzgerald, the *Rose Garden of Sa'di*, or the lyric odes of Hafez and other classical poets. The Mughal Emperor Jahangir (died 1627) had the following inscription placed on one of the pavilions of his Shalimar Garden in Srinagar, Kashmir: "If there is paradise on earth, it is this, it is this, it is this" (*Gar ferdows rū-ye zamīn ast, hamīn ast, hamīn ast, hamīn ast*).

Copies of the *Shāh-nāmeh* and other popular works of literature are often embellished with miniature paintings which depict scenes reminiscent of the Qur'anic passage quoted above. Persian painting goes back to pre-Islamic times and is one of the world's most important and influential artistic traditions. Garden and nature scenes have always figured prominently. To one trained to appreciate Western art, Persian paintings often look "unrealistic," even naïve. What is important to note is that in the Iranian artistic tradition, things are represented not as they are but rather as they "should" be. They depict an idealized world. In this sense they resemble Byzantine icons, which were intended to serve as windows from this world into the next.

The garden remains the essence of the Iranian notion of paradise up to the present day. This feeling is well-expressed in the following verses, composed by the nineteenth-century poet Fath 'Ali Khan of Kashan, in praise of a garden built at Tehran for his patron, the Qajar king Fath 'Ali Shah:

> A name to be inscribed on the surface of heaven,
> Still its height is loftier than the seven heavens,
> And its extent is greater than the original eight paradises.
> No wonder then that when Mani (the painter-prophet) and Azar
>     (the father of Abraham, a professional idol-maker) saw its
>     beautiful paintings,
> They broke their brushes from shame.
> . . .
> The clear water of that pool is like the life-giving breath of Jesus,
> And it seems that Mary may have washed her virgin-pure clothes
>     in it.
> . . .
> I asked, "Is this the life-giving water?" and the answer came, "Yes."
> I asked, "Is this garden paradise?" and wisdom replied,
>     "Certainly."[8]

## THE PERSISTENCE OF IRANIAN IDENTITY

One of the remarkable aspects of the history of Islamization is the survival of Iranian identity, especially the Persian language, when so many other ancient societies—Egyptian, Syrian, Babylonian—came to be Arabized. Certainly the transfer of Muslim power to Mesopotamia, and the revival of Sasanian political institutions played a role in this, along with the fact that Muslims of Iranian background were so active in defining what would constitute "Islamic" civilization.

Yet despite the eventual adoption of Islam by the vast majority of Iranians, ever since the time of the *sho'ūbiyyeh* in the eighth century a certain tension has existed between the "Iranian" and "Islamic" dimensions of their identity, a tension that can be observed even today. The celebration of Nō rūz, which was and remains the most visible means by which Iranians assert their cultural identity, has long been viewed with ambivalence by Islamic scholars from Mohammad Ghazali to Ruhollah Khomeini. The classical Persian poets often turned this tension to their advantage, making liberal use of pre-Islamic stories and symbols even when conveying Islamic messages.

In this sense, the *Shāh-nāmeh* and the Qur'an represent two literary expressions that epitomize the double-layered loyalties Iranians have typically experienced. At times the relationship between the two can appear to be almost seamless, as in the traditional gymnasia (*zūr-khāneh*s) where athletes exercise to the alternating rhythms of the two texts which are recited to accompany them. When Selim II acceded to the Ottoman throne in 1566, the Safavid ruler Tahmasp sent him twin gifts of a Qur'an and the illustrated *Shāh-nāmeh* which bears his name and is considered by many to be the greatest collection of Persian miniatures ever produced.[9]

On other occasions, Iran's ancient and Islamic literary heritages are clearly perceived as rivals, as in the following poem attributed to the fourteenth-century cleric Hasan Kashi who complains of Iranians' attachment to "useless lies" about "irreligious, corrupt" figures from the past:

> Dear son, do not read allegorical stories
> Beware of reading them!
> How long will you go on reading the *Shāh-nāmeh*?
> Remember promptly, this is a book of sin
> How much of this reminiscence of Vamig and 'Uzra?
> Remember instead your Creator
> How long will you go on reading about Vis and Ramin?
> The story of those corrupt and irreligious ones
> For how long will you speak about the tales of Rostam and Zal?
> Playful and useless imaginary lies
> The saying of the Zoroastrians and the people of myths
> How long will you recite them for Muslims?
> If you wish to read in Persian
> So that your spirit may sense comfort and familiarity
> There exist stories of Muhammad, the trusted one
> Just as glorious and exemplary as 'Ali
> There exists as well the praise of 'Ali and his kin
> Enough to recite night and day.[10]

# Part 4

# ISLAMIC IRAN

# 13

# Persian Sufism

Mysticism, an approach found in all religions, can be characterized as an individual's personal quest for direct personal experience of the Divine. Muslims following this type of religiosity came to be known as Sufis, likely in reference to certain early ascetics who, like Christian monks, wore cloaks made of wool (Ar. *sūf*). Key themes in Sufism are the overcoming of the lower self (*nafs*) and progressing through various stages of spiritual development (*maqāmāt*), usually under the guidance of a Master (*morshed*; also Ar. *shaykh*, Pers. *pīr*) to whom the disciple (*morīd*) professes complete obedience. During the early centuries Muslims attracted by the mystical quest tended to congregate around individual masters seen as having perfected specific techniques for advancing along the spiritual path; the most common such technique was *dhikr* (Pers. *zekr*; lit. "remembrance"), a mantra-like repetition of the Divine names or other formulas such as verses from the Qur'an. Over time the particular approaches of various Sufi masters coalesced into the established practices of diverse Sufi orders (*tarīqāt*).

The first Sufis were perhaps those Muslim mystics living in Syria and Egypt who were exposed to Christian monastic communities. But by the mid-eighth century a number of prominent Sufis had appeared in the Iranian world as well. Though Sufi orders are found in all Muslim societies today, the institutionalization of Sufi brotherhoods first took place predominantly in the Iranian east. Many of the foundational figures in Sufism were Iranians, including Hasan Basri, Abu Yazid Bistami, Yahya b. Moaz, Haris Mohasebi, Sari Saqati, Abo'l-Qasem Jonayd, Hosayn b. Mansur Hallaj, 'Abd al-Karim Qoshayri, Mohammad and Ahmad Ghazali, Abu Najib and Shehab al-din Sohravardi, 'Abd al-Qader Gilani, Najm al-din Kobra, Jalal al-din Rumi, and many others. Iranian Sufis were the major transmitters of Islam to India, China, and Southeast Asia—precisely, in other words, those parts of the world where most Muslims today reside. Thus, Sufis played a central role in the shaping of a Persianate Islamic civilization in the broadest sense.

## EARLY IRANIAN SUFIS

Hasan Basri (died 728), son of a Persian slave named Piruz, is one of the prominent founding figures of Muslim mysticism. He advocated an asceticism uncharacteristic of mainstream Islam, resisting the attachment to wealth and comfort that came as a corollary to the Muslim conquests. Hasan's unworldliness expressed itself in an ethos of mourning, perhaps influenced by the emerging popular Shi'ism of southern Iraq.

Abu Yazid, or Bayazid, of Bastam (died 874) was an early proponent of what is often called "intoxicated" Sufism (*sukr*). His teachings on the mystical goal of ultimate "annihilation" (*fanā'*) in the Divine may have drawn some influence from Indian ideas conveyed through his teacher, Abu 'Ali of Sindh. Bayazid used the story of the prophet Muhammad's miraculous night journey to heaven (*mi'rāj*) as a model for the Sufi quest, a trope that became very popular in later Sufism. Recall that the Islamic *mi'rāj* story most likely derives from a Zoroastrian source, the *Arda Viraz Nāmag*; Maria Subtelny has noted that in the Islamic version the role of the angel Gabriel is a reflection of the Zoroastrian deity of wakefulness and prayer, Sorūš (Sraoša), symbolized by a rooster.[1]

Another important theme, which begins to develop among Iranian Sufis during the tenth century, is that of intense love (*'ešq*) for the Divine; the mystic's condition is one of suffering caused by separation from the divine Beloved. In later centuries some even came to speak of the "Religion of Love" (*dīn-e ešq*; also *mazhab-e ešq*, or *dīn al-hubb*) in contrast to a religiosity based on merely following the injunctions of the *sharī'a*. This "Religion of Love" is particularly associated with poets such as Rumi and Hafez, discussed below.

Ahmad Nuri (died 907) and Abu Bakr Shebli (died 946) were among the first Sufis to describe the mystical experience as one of love, a theme that was central to the work of later Sufi writers such as Ahmad Ghazali (died 1123 or 1126), 'Ayn al-Qozat Hamadani (died 1131), and Sayf al-din Bakharzi (died 1261). Annemarie Schimmel sharply distinguishes this emerging "*eros*-oriented" spirituality among the Sufis from the "*nomos*-oriented" Islam of the legal scholars:

> On the one hand we find a religion which is bound by the law and where the law, the *shari'a*—and again we can bring in here the *'aql*, intellect—leads human beings on a strictly prescribed way in which salvation is guaranteed, God willing of course; and on the other hand, the Sufi way of feeling, of experiencing the immediate presence of God already here and now. It is a contrast known in virtually all religions, but in Islam it becomes particularly clear because the words of the loving intoxicated Sufis stand against the words of the scholars who intellectually explained the law and its minutest details.[2]

Sufi mystics had various ways of working themselves into ecstatic trances in which they came to feel a union with the divine. Some, the "sober" (*sahw*) Sufis, such as Abo'l-Qasem Jonayd of Baghdad (died 910), sought to attain such states through practices such as mantra-like repetition of prayer formulas or the names of God (*dhikr* or *zekr*, lit., "remembrance"). Others, the "intoxicated" Sufis, might dance and whirl, sometimes accompanied by music (*samā'*, lit., "listening"). In a general sense the "intoxicated" approach was more associated with the East (Khorasan) and the "sober" approach with the West (Baghdad), but there were "sober" Sufis in the East and "drunken" Sufis in the West as well.

Hosayn b. Mansur Hallaj is the paradigmatic example of the "intoxicated" approach. A student of both Jonayd and Nuri, Hallaj was known for his exuberant public displays, such as dancing about and proclaiming "I am the Divine Truth!" In 922 he was executed for blasphemy—or, as some Sufis would have it, simply because he too publicly revealed the path to union with the Divine, a secret ordinary people were not yet prepared to hear.

Hallaj's experience illustrates the attitude of a mystic so absorbed in love for the Divine he becomes indifferent to his reputation among human beings. This attitude could be seen among a range of Muslim mystics of the tenth century, some of whom went so far as to publicly behave in a way that would bring reproach, as proof that their piety was not meant for the eyes of men. Such individuals were known as *malāmatiyyeh*, "those who bring blame upon themselves." Later mystic poets such as Rumi and Hafez would make extensive use of a literary trope that contrasted the outwardly licentious "true lover" with the hypocritical religious puritan.

Sufis typically used verse as a way to express the ineffable nature of their spiritual quest, borrowing the symbolic language of love and wine from Persian court poetry and imbuing it with spiritual meaning. One seminal figure in this regard, Abu Sa'id Abu'l-Khayr (died 1049), is known both for his use of love poetry and for instituting ecstasy-inducing *samā'* sessions at his Sufi lodge (*khānegāh*—of which his may have been the first) in the city of Nishapur. When reciting the Qur'an, Abu Sa'id is said to have skipped over the passages referring to hell and punishment, focusing instead on verses emphasizing Allah's mercy. When criticized for his selective approach to the holy text, he reportedly replied with the following poem:

> O Saqi pour the wine! Minstrel strike the chord!
> Let me drink wine today, for now's my moment of rapture!
> There is wine; there's money, there are tulip-faced idols;
> There's no grief, and if there is, it's the lot of our foes' heart.[3]

The poetic themes of love and drunkenness as metaphors for the ecstatic experience made their authors suspect in the eyes of some, including certain "sober" Sufis. Such poetry, and the trance-inducing music that was often associated with it, could easily be conflated with the antinomian practices of the *malāmatiyyeh*. Thus, tensions began to develop not only between Sufis and non-Sufis but also among Sufis themselves. Ibn Munawwar reports the following complaint about his ancestor Abu Sa'id:

> He holds Sufi gatherings. He recites poetry on the pulpit. Commentary upon the Koran is not what he preaches. Nor does he tell of prophetic traditions. He makes grandiloquent claims. He sings and his young followers dance. They eat roasted chicken and cake, and then he claims to be an ascetic. This is not the manner of ascetics, nor is it the belief of the Sufis. The masses are attracted to him. They will be led astray. Most of the ignorant populace are already committing vices. If something is not done immediately, very soon public unrest will come.[4]

The tensions highlighted in the above passage did not arise solely because of differences in doctrine and practice. Also at play was the issue of authority and leadership; specifically, on what basis these should be derived. The legal scholars, who often served as advisors to government and played other important social roles, understandably felt that a lifetime of scholarship should serve as the primary basis for authority on religious matters. Sufi masters, more often than not, won followings largely through their personal charisma, though they were often well-studied in the formal religious sciences as well. This was the case for Shehab al-din Sohravardi and 'Ayn al-Qozat Hamadani, both of whom were executed at the instigation of their more legalistically minded rivals among the *'ulemā'*.

By the late eleventh century Sunni jurists were enjoying the support of the ruling Seljuk Turks, for whom the battle against heterodoxy was an important propaganda tool. The rift between Sufism and "orthodoxy" threatened to tear the Islamic community apart, but was healed somewhat by the celebrated Iranian scholar Abu Hamid Mohammad Ghazali (1058–1111), who has been called "the most influential Muslim after Muhammad."[5] Ghazali proved himself very early in life as a master of Islamic law in his capacity as professor at the prestigious Nezamiyyeh seminary in Baghdad, founded by the Seljuks' Iranian prime minister Nezam al-Molk. Following an intellectual and spiritual crisis in his thirties, however, Ghazali stepped down from his post and spent ten years exploring the Sufi path. On his return to teaching he developed an approach that reconciled legalism with mystical discipline, establishing the possibility at least that Sufism and Sunni orthodoxy could co-exist.

This reconciliation was achieved most notably in Ghazali's forty-volume work, *Ihya 'ulūm al-dīn* ("Enlivening of the Religious Sciences"), a comprehensive guide to the meaning of Islamic life that remains hugely popular among Sunni Muslims to this day.

The century following Ghazali saw the development of Sufi orders such as the Qaderiyyeh—after Shaykh 'Abd al-Qader Gilani—and the Sohravardiyyeh, established by Shehab al-din Sohravardi but named for his uncle, Ziya al-din Abu'l-Najib. Just as schools of Islamic law developed along lines laid down by certain founding figures, different mystical approaches became institutionalized as disciples of particular Sufi masters formalized and codified their teachings and practices. During this early period as well the Sufi code of ethical behaviour (*adab*) became strongly tied to the "spiritual chivalry" (*javānmardī*) advocated by the artisan guilds; S. H. Nasr describes this relationship as the "wedding of economic activity with ethics on the one hand and with beauty and art on the other."[6]

## PERSIAN SUFI LITERATURE

One of the great and lasting contributions of Iranian Sufis was in the realm of literature. The first major Sufi manual in Persian, *Kašf al-mahjūb* ("The Unveiling of Secrets"), was composed by Abo'l-Hassan Hojviri (died 1077). Originally from eastern Iran, Hojviri spent the latter part of his life in Lahore and is considered one of the founders of Sufism on the Indian subcontinent.

Several decades later Ahmad Ghazali, Mohammad Ghazali's younger brother, wrote a Sufi work titled *Savāneh* ("Inspirations"), which was innovative in its use of alternating prose and verse. This model would later be used by the thirteenth-century writer Sa'di of Shiraz in his famous book of wisdom literature, the *Golestān* ("The Rose Garden").

Ghazali's *Savāneh* is considered to be one of the seminal Sufi treatises on love. The work begins with a quotation from the Qur'an which states that "[God] loves [the people] and they love him" (5:54), and continues as follows:

> Our steeds started on the road from non-existence along with love;
> Our night was continuously illuminated with the lamp of Union.
> When we return to non-existence, you will not find our lips dry,
> From that wine which is not forbidden in our religion.[7]

### Persian Sufi Poetry

The Persian language began its resurgence in the face of Arabic during the tenth century, first as a court language under the Samanids whose most important poet was Ja'far b. Mohammad Rudaki (died ca. 941). Throughout the century that followed, Iranian Sufi poets increasingly wrote in Persian; the most notable of these was Abo'l-Majd Sana'i (died 1131). Sana'i's *Hadīqat al-haqīqat* ("The Walled Garden of Truth") is the first major Sufi poetic treatise in Persian, serving as an inspiration for subsequent Sufi poets including Farid al-din 'Attar, Nezami Ganjavi, and Jalal al-din Rumi. Later Persian writers such as Sa'di and Hafez brought the genre to its fullest stage of development, confirming poetry as one of the central features of Iranian identity. To this day no culture identifies with its poetic tradition more intensely than the Persian, and Sufis are among its most celebrated poets.

### 'ATTAR

Farid al-din 'Attar (died 1221) is best known for his long narrative poem *Mantiq al-tayr* ("The Logic of the Birds"), an allegorical tale in which a group of birds sets off on a quest to find their spiritual master, the mythical Sīmorgh. One by one the seekers fall by the wayside until only thirty are left, only to realize that they themselves are the truth they have been seeking (*sī morgh* in Persian is "thirty birds"):

> Their souls rose free of all they'd been before;
> The past and all its actions were no more.
> Their life came from that close, insistent sun
> And in its vivid rays they shone as one.
> There in the Simorgh's radiant face they saw
> Themselves, the Simorgh of the world—with awe
> They gazed, and dared at last to comprehend
> They were the Simorgh at the journey's end.[8]

In addition to a number of other poetic works, 'Attar is also known for a prose hagiography, the *Tazkirat al-awliyā* ("Biographies of the Saints"), which provides accounts of many important early Sufi figures. 'Attar's moving depiction of the martyrdom of Hallaj made an especially deep impression on generations of later Sufis.[9]

### RUMI

Born in Balkh but spending most of his life in Seljuk Anatolia, Jalal al-din Rumi (1207–1273) is perhaps the best known Persian Sufi poet. Often referred to in Iran as *Mōlavī*, "my master" (or *Mōlanā*, "our master"), his loving devotion and ecstatic mysticism inspired the Turkish order that took his name—the Mevleviyya—whose dancers came to be known in the West as the "whirling dervishes."

**Figure 1.** Hero killing a dragon, Horr (Bāgh-e Šāh) Square, Tehran. Photo by Mitra Mahaseni, used by permission.

**Figure 2.** The lion-king killing the bull Shanzabeh, evoking a Mithraic tauroctony.

Original painting by Manya Saadi-nejad, after a fourteenth-century illustrated manuscript of *Kalila and Dimna*.

**Figure 3.** Postage stamp with image of Anahita/Nanai on a Sasanian-era silver ewer. Photo courtesy of Robert Hunter Stamps and Covers.

**Figure 4.** The Jewish-Iranian queen Esther giving birth to Cyrus the Great. From a foureenth-century illustrated manuscript of the *Ardešīr-nāmeh* (MS 8270, f. 154r). By courtesy of the Library of the Jewish Theological Seminary, New York.

**Figure 5.** 12 metre-long reclining Buddha, 7th century, Ajina-Tepe, Tajikistan (now in National Museum of Antiquities, Dushanbe). Photo by Richard Foltz.

**Figure 6.** Tile painting of hero Rostam battling a demon, Karim Khan citadel, Shiraz. (Note Christian church in upper left corner.) Photo by Richard Foltz.

**Figure 7.** Mani, the Buddha of Light. Cao'an temple, Fujian, China. Photo by Samuel N.C. Lieu, used by permission.

**Figure 8.** Pir-e sabz shrine near Yazd, a major Zoroastrian pilgrimage site. According to legend a grotto miraculously opened here to save Nikbanu, daughter of the last Sasanian king Yazdigerd III as she fled the Arab invaders. Also known as Chak-chak because of water dripping within the grotto, suggesting an association with Anahita. Photo by Richard Foltz.

**Figure 9.** The prophet Zoroaster and the *Ahūna vairya* prayer adorning the entrance to a recently-built apartment tower, Mumbai, India. Photo by Richard Foltz.

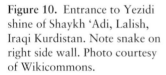

**Figure 10.** Entrance to Yezidi shine of Shaykh 'Adi, Lalish, Iraqi Kurdistan. Note snake on right side wall. Photo courtesy of Wikicommons.

**Figure 11.** Terraced gardens at the Baha'i Universal House of Justice, Haifa, Israel. Photo courtesy of Wikicommons.

**Figure 12.** Wudang group practicing in a public park, Tehran 2010. Photo courtesy of Ali Asghar Koohzadi.

Rumi's monumental work of some twenty-five thousand rhymed couplets, the *Masnavī-ye maʿnavī*, has been called "the Qur'an in Persian," reflecting the extent of its impact on Iranians and neighboring Muslim peoples. The following passage which opens the poem evokes the deep suffering of the mystic Lover, who has been separated from the divine Beloved like a reed ripped out of its bed, and his intense longing to be reunited with Him once again. Anyone who has heard the mournful sound of the reed-flute (*ney*) in Persian music will instantly recognize the appropriateness of the symbol:

> Now listen to this reed-flute's deep lament
> About the heartache being apart has meant:
> "Since from the reed-bed they uprooted me
> My song's expressed each human agony
> A breast which separation's split in two
> Is what I seek, to share this pain with you
> When kept from their true origin, all yearn
> For union on the day they can return."[10]

## SAʿDI

Mosleh al-din Saʿdi (died ca. 1292) is best known as a moralist rather than a mystic; his major works, the *Golestān* ("The Rose Garden") and the *Būstān* ("The Orchard") fall generally into the category of wisdom literature. Such contemporary Iranian scholars as Badiʿ al-zaman Foruzanfar and Zabihollah Safa have downplayed Saʿdi's purported connections with Sufism; Ehsan Yarshater characterizes him foremost as a "humanitarian."[11]

Yet Saʿdi is said to have been initiated into a Sufi order, and his work shows an extensive familiarity with Sufism. Each of his two famous collections devotes a section to mystics and mysticism: the *Būstān* in its third chapter and the *Golestān* in its second. The former is idealistic and theoretical, the latter realistic and down-to-earth.

Like Hafez after him, Saʿdi respects the search for deeper truth, but is extremely hard on religious hypocrites. He devotes a chapter of the *Golestān* to "The Morals of Dervishes," providing a rich collection of anecdotes and pithy sayings to illustrate the difference between outward and genuine piety:

> If an ascetic takes dirhems and dinars,
> Go find another more ascetic than him.
> One whose conduct is good and has a secret with God is an ascetic
> Without the bread of charity or morsels from begging.
> The finger of a beauty and the earlobe of a charmer
> Are lovely without baubles and rings.[12]

## HAFEZ

The much-recited *ghazal*s of Shirazi poet Shams al-din Mohammad Hafez (died 1390) arguably represent the most sophisticated achievement in all of Persian literature. Indeed, his rich, multilayered verses lend themselves to such a wide range of interpretations that the question of whether he was a Sufi or not remains unresolved. Actually, Wheeler Thackston sees this as a "useless" question, noting that by Hafez's time the symbolic language of Persian poetry had been appropriated by Sufis to such an extent that "it was impossible to write a ghazal that did not reverberate with mystical overtones forced on it by the poetic vocabulary itself."[13]

While Hafez's approach is undeniably mystical (*'erfānī*) and his language permeated with Sufi symbols and imagery, his aversion to hypocrisy encompasses the puritanical piety of both clerics and ascetics. To these two types Hafez opposes a third, the *rend*, which Leonard Lewisohn translates as the "Inspired Libertine."[14] Drawing on the earlier *malāmatī* tradition, Hafez's *rend* is an antinomian hero, a nonconformist who disdains the authority of spiritual and political powers alike, living only for the pursuit of love. The following lines, in the English version of contemporary American poet Robert Bly, evoke the *rend*'s indifference to public opinion in his search for the deeper truths love can reveal:

> I'm well-known throughout the whole city
> For being a wild-haired lover; and I'm that man who has
> Never darkened his vision by seeing evil.
>
> Through my enthusiasm for wine, I have thrown the book
> Of my good name into the water; but doing that insures that
> The handwriting in my book of grandiosity will be blurred.
>
> Let's be faithful to what we love; let's accept reproach
> And keep our spirits high, because on our road, being easily
> Hurt by the words of others is a form of infidelity.[15]

Hafez is known and admired across Eurasia; throughout the Persianate world his *Dīvān* is almost as commonly found on bookshelves as the Qur'an itself. And like the Qur'an, it is considered as more than just a physical book, to the extent that it often occupies a place of honour in table arrangements during Nō rūz and at weddings, and is used for fortune-telling (*fāl-gīrī*) at parties. Among non-Muslim Iranians a similar pairing can be found between Hafez's *Dīvān* and holy books such as the Avesta, the Bible, and the Torah. As Lewisohn observes, "For Persian-speakers, his poems remain a sort of trans-sectarian, atemporal sacred text, a hallowed scripture venerated by Muslims, Christians and Jews in Iran, Tajikistan, Afghanistan and all throughout Central Asia, and by

Hindus, Sikhs, and Buddhists in India, not to mention by atheists and secular nationalists everywhere."[16]

## JAMI

'Abd al-Rahman Jami (died 1492) is generally considered the last of the great classical Persian poets. Long employed at the Timurid court in Herat, Jami was a member of the Naqshbandi Sufi order which had close ties to the Timurid family. His poetry is heavily infused with love imagery, as in his retellings of the famous love stories of Yusuf and Zulaykha and Layla and Majnun. On a more philosophical level, Jami's Sufism draws upon that of the Andalusian mystic Ibn 'Arabi (died 1240), in particular the latter's somewhat pantheistic notion of *wahdat al-wujūd* ("unity of being").

The following stanza, from Jami's rendition of the Yusuf and Zulaykha story in his *Haft Awrang* ("Seven Thrones"), expresses a theme long familiar among Sufi poets, namely, that the capacity for earthly love is a prerequisite for loving the Divine:

> Once to his master a disciple cried,
> "To wisdom's pleasant path be thou my guide."
> "Hast thou ne'er loved?" the master answered; "learn
> The ways of love and then to me return."
> Drink deep of earthly love, so that thy lip
> May learn the wine of holier love to sip.[17]

## LIGHT SYMBOLISM IN IRANIAN SUFISM AND ILLUMINATIONIST PHILOSOPHY

Late in his life the theologian Mohammad Ghazali began to explore the metaphysics of light that had been growing popular among Iranian Sufis of his time. His book *Miškāt al-anwār* ("The Niche for Lights") is an extended commentary on the so-called "Light Verse" in the Qur'an (24:35), which reads as follows:

> Allah is the Light of the heavens and the earth
> The parable of His Light is a niche wherein is a lamp
> The lamp is in a glass, the glass as it were a glittering star
> Lit from a blessed olive tree,
> Neither eastern nor western,
> Whose oil almost lights up,
> Though fire should not touch it
> Light upon light
> Allah guides to His Light whomever He wishes
> Allah draws parables for mankind,
> and Allah has knowledge of all things.

While the Qur'anic "niche" image is most likely a borrowing from Christianity (*mishkāt* is a loan-word from Ethiopian), Ghazali's characterization of Light as constituting the Divine Reality itself is very close to that found in Iranian Gnostic traditions, including Manichaeism and Mazdakism:

> It will be unveiled to you, when the degrees of these lights become manifest, that God is the highest and furthest light, and, when their realities become unveiled, that He is the true, real light—He alone, without any partner in that.[18]

Shehab al-din Sohravardi (1153–1191) brought light mysticism to its fullest expression, laying the foundation for a particularly Iranian philosophy he called *ešrāqī* ("illuminationist"). In Sohravardi's vision, the phenomenal world is seen as emanating from a supreme Light of Lights; everything in creation is categorized in terms of its receptivity to light. His concept of worldly existence, in which the divided soul is entrapped in the material body, and his notion of the afterlife, in which the soul ascends to join the absolute Light, both resemble Gnostic notions found in Mandaeism and Manichaeism.

In his Arabic writings Sohravardi relies heavily on the frameworks of peripatetic philosophy in the tradition of Avicenna, but he occasionally draws parallels with ancient Iranian ideas. For example, in the *Kitāb al-mašariʿ wa-l'mutāharāt* ("Book of Paths and Heavens") he equates the rising light of dawn (*nūr al-šāriq*) with the Iranian *xᵛarᵊnah*, the former empowering the mystic in the same way that the latter empowers temporal rulers.[19] In the introduction to his most famous work, *Hikmat al-išrāq* ("The Philosophy of Illumination"), Sohravardi associates the light/dark symbolism upon which he bases his own philosophical system with that of "the Persian sages," including Jamasp, Frašostar, and Bozorgmehr.[20] Sohravardi distinguishes these sages from the Zoroastrian magi, whom he considers "dualist infidels":

> There was a religious community in Persia guided by the truth and doing justice according to it. They were learned sages not resembling the Magians. We have revived their noble wisdom of light in a book entitled *The Philosophy of Illumination*. No one before me did such a thing.[21]

In his Persian-language treatises, meanwhile, Sohravardi's blending of Zoroastrian with Islamic terms and symbols is even more prominent. He refers to the supreme Light both as Bahman (Vohu Manah) and *al-nūr al-aʿzam*, and claims Zoroaster along with a range of legendary Iranian heroes as his philosophical ancestors. In his books *ʿAql-e sorkh*

("The Red Intellect") and *Safīr-e Sīmorgh* ("The Simorgh's Cry"), Sohravardi juxtaposes Islamic with mythological Iranian characters and symbols such as Zal, Rostam, the Simorgh, and Mount Qaf. Sohravardi claims to be a restorer of "ancient Persian wisdom"; in the opinion of John Walbridge, however, he merely exoticizes it, just as the ancient Greeks had done.[22] Even so, it could be argued that Sohravardi's choices demonstrate that for him, as well as for his intended audience, ancient Iranian figures and concepts remained a recognizable part of the available pool of religious symbols.

Illuminationist philosophy re-emerged several centuries later in Shi'ite form under the Safavids with the so-called school of Esfahan, led by Mir Damad (died 1631) and culminating in the theosophy of Molla Sadra of Shiraz (died 1640). *Ešrāqī* thought had a direct connection with its pre-Islamic antecedents through the Zoroastrian high priest Azar Keyvan (ca. 1530–ca. 1612), who taught a number of its Muslim adherents including Molla Sadra's teacher Shaykh Baha'i 'Amili (died 1621).[23] From the mid-twentieth century *Ešrāqī* philosophy became a significant focus of attention among scholars in the West, in particular through the work of scholars such as Henry Corbin, Seyyed Hossein Nasr, and Hossein Ziai.

# 14

# Shi'ism

For eight and a half centuries following the Arab conquest it would seem that most Iranian Muslims at least nominally followed the majority Sunni tradition, and indeed Iranian scholars had a large hand in shaping it. Two of the founding figures of Sunni jurisprudence, Nu'man ibn Thabit Abu Hanifa (699–767) and Muhammad Abu Mansur Maturidi (853–944), were Iranians. The Ash'arite theologian Mohammad Ghazali was Iranian, as was his employer, the prime minister of the ardently pro-Sunni Seljuk Turks, Abu 'Ali Hasan Tusi Nezam al-Molk (1018–1092), a vigorous persecutor of Shi'is who was ultimately murdered by an Isma'ili Shi'ite assassin. Most of the famous Iranian Sufis, from Bayazid Bistami to Jalal al-din Rumi, were Sunni. Only as recently as the sixteenth century did the majority of Iranians accept the so-called "Twelver" form of Shi'ism under pressure from the Safavids, originally a Turkic Sufi order who were former Sunnis.

Shi'ism emerged within the Semitic environment of southern Iraq, and has remained a significant force in much of the Arab world from Lebanon to Bahrain. Because Iran today is known as a Shi'ite country, some observers have been tempted to see in Iranian Shi'ism an element of nationalist assertion vis-à-vis Arabs, but such a connection is not borne out by history. The popularity of Shi'i movements in Iran during the early centuries of Islam most likely has more to do with Iranians' affinity for esoteric religious approaches and resistance to state-sponsored religious authority. It is also noteworthy that prior to the sixteenth century the most prevalent forms of Shi 'ism in Iran were the Isma'ili and Zaydi branches, rather than the Twelver version which dominates today.

## THE ORIGINS OF SHI'ISM

Following the massacre of Muhammad's grandson Husayn and his followers at Karbala in 680 CE Shi'ism became an underground movement, subject to constant persecution by the Umayyad and Abbasid governments (despite the latter dynasty having made use of Shi'ite ideology during their rise to power). Faced with the real danger of extermination Shi'is developed a doctrine of dissimulation (*taqiyya*), through which they could outwardly profess Sunni Islam while secretly adhering to the divinely inspired authority and guidance of the descendants of Muhammad known as the Imams. (Actually, Shi'is consider the Imamate to have existed on earth since the time of Adam, and that the world has never been without an Imam.) Throughout the early centuries of Islam a persistent pattern can be detected whereby people disaffected with the ruling regime would find the martyrdoms of 'Ali and Husayn symbolic of all manner of oppression and injustice faced by God's true believers.

Since Shi'is believed that the divine inspiration and infallible status of the rightful leader of all Muslims was given to only one person at any given time, with the death of each successive Imam there inevitably arose disagreements over who was next in line. An early rift among the Shi'a emerged over the succession of the fourth Imam, Zayn al-'Abidin (died 712); one faction favored his eldest son, Muhammad al-Baqir, while another supported his son Zayd. The latter group, which came to be known as Zaydis, variously controlled parts of Yemen, central Arabia, Morocco, and Andalusia. Zaydi dynasties held parts of northern Iran, especially Gilan, from 864–1126. The Buyid family, who exercised de facto control over the Abbasid Caliphate from the mid-tenth century up to 1055, were from this region, and were originally Zaydis.

Following the death of Ja'far al-Sadiq in 764 CE there was an even greater split among the Shi'a. Some followed the line of his elder son Isma'il who had been the designated heir but predeceased his father, while others believed that authority had passed to his younger son, Musa al-Kazim. The latter faction continued to follow a line up to the Twelfth Imam, Muhammad al-Mahdi, whom they believe went into occultation in 873 CE—he is therefore referred to as "the Hidden Imam"—and will return as a messianic figure at the end of time. This group became known as the "Twelver" (*Ithna 'ashari*) Shi'is. In contrast to other, more revolutionary Shi'ite sects the Twelvers were mostly politically quietist until the rise of the Safavids in the sixteenth century.

Most of the former group—that is, Shi'is who followed the line of Isma'il—trace the descent of living Imams right up to the present. Prince Karim Aga Khan IV, a man known for supporting charitable causes throughout the Muslim world, is revered today by Isma'ilis of the majority Nizari branch as the Imam of the Age. For Isma'ilis, the living Imam is the unique possessor of an esoteric knowledge that enables him to perceive the hidden meanings beneath outward signs, notably the verses of the Qur'an. For this reason their opponents have often referred to them by the derogatory label *bātiniyya*, meaning "esotericists."

The tenth century is sometimes referred to by historians as "the Shi'ite century," since much of the Muslim world at that time had come under the rule of Shi'ite dynasties. From 909–1171 CE northern Africa was ruled by a band of Isma'ili Shi'ites known as the Fatimids, who founded the city of Cairo (*al-Qāhira*, "the Conqueror") and challenged the legitimacy of the Sunni Caliph in Baghdad. The latter post itself became something of a figurehead position as a Shi'ite group from the north of Iran, known as the Buwayhids or Buyids (932–1062 CE), asserted their military control over Baghdad and effectively took over the reins of government. (Having originally followed Zaydi Shi'ism, the Buyids later transferred their loyalties to the Twelver branch, presumably so as not to have to recognize an Imam that was physically present.[1]) Throughout much of this period the Arabian peninsula was also destabilized by the activities of a radical Isma'ili splinter group, the Qarmatians, who had established a power base in Bahrain (both the island itself as well as adjacent territory on the mainland) under the leadership of an Iranian missionary, Abu Sa'id Jannabi, beginning in 899.

During this period some recently Islamicized Turkic tribes from Central Asia—first the Ghaznavids (from 977) and then the Seljuks (from 1038)—were also using their positions as mercenaries in the Caliph's army to vie for power over the Islamic heartlands. The Turks found in the now embattled Sunni Islam an ideology by which they could rally support among the general population, in opposition to both the Fatimid and Buyid ruling classes. The Turks prevailed in Baghdad, driving the Buyids from power, then launched an all-out campaign against the Egyptian Fatimids. The Fatimids aggravated the Seljuk Turks by sending waves of Isma'ili missionaries to proselytize throughout the Seljuk-controlled territories of Mesopotamia and Iran.

## ISMA'ILI SHI'ISM

Under the Fatimids, the Isma'ilis had developed a sophisticated and effective missionary network (*da'wa*), aimed mainly at converting other Muslims. The famous seminary in Cairo, al-Azhar, known today as a major hub of Sunni scholarship, was in fact founded by the Fatimids in around 970 CE as a training center for Isma'ili missionaries. Al-Azhar was transformed into a Sunni institution only during the mid-twelfth century, after the Kurdish warrior Saladin took over Cairo from the Fatimids.

The Isma'ili belief system was drawn from a combination of Islamic sources, Hellenistic philosophy, and Iranian mysticism of light; even some subtle borrowings from Manichaean myth. Its central tenet was the necessity for "authoritative teaching" (*ta'līm*) from an infallible Imam. Especially in its Iranian form Isma'ili thought drew heavily on neo-platonic philosophy, which made it intellectually attractive to many among the elite classes who were major targets for Isma'ili missionaries in Iran.

Salman Farsi, the Iranian companion of the prophet, plays a central symbolic role in Isma'ili esotericism: he is considered to be the human form of the angel Gabriel from whom Muhammad received his revelation, and thus his spiritual initiator. According to Henry Corbin, "The intervention of Salman inaugurates a process that will make esoteric Imamology a paradox in Islam, for Salman will outrank the Prophet himself, and this priority will derive from his quality as *Hujjat*, as Witness and Spiritual Child of the [eternal] Imam."[2]

Iranian Isma'ilis, seen as fifth columnists by the ruling Seljuks, maintained contact with the Fatimids and occasionally traveled to Egypt for education and support. One such person was Naser Khosrow (1002–ca.1077), who wrote his works in Persian and is credited with establishing the Isma'ili communities in Badakhshan (southern Tajikistan) which continue to thrive today. Such luminous figures as the philosophers Avicenna and Naser al-din Tusi, *Shāh-nāmeh* author Abo'l-Qasem Ferdowsi, and the heresiographer Shahrestani, all had Isma'ili connections. In the early eleventh century an Iranian Isma'ili by the name of Hamza ibn 'Ali founded a sect in Cairo which came to be known as the Druze, represented today by communities in Israel, Lebanon and Syria.

The Fatimid state experienced a crisis of succession following the death of its caliph–imam Mustansir in 1094, with some Isma'ilis claiming allegiance to his eldest son Abu Mansur Nizar and others to his younger son Abu'l Qasim Ahmad, known as Musta'li. The Nizari faction in Iran was led by Hasan Sabbah (died 1124), who in 1090 succeeded in taking control of a virtually impregnable castle called Alamut in the Alborz Mountains near Qazvin. It was under Hasan that Persian came to be used as a religious, and not just a vernacular language.[3] For the next century and a half the Nizari Isma'ilis, safely entrenched in a number of mountain strongholds, waged a guerrilla war against the Seljuk state. This struggle was highlighted by spectacular public assassinations of important government figures known for their persecution of Isma'ilis, including the famous vizier Nezam al-Molk.

Indeed, the English word "assassin" derives from fantastic stories about this sect, transmitted to Europe by the Christian Crusaders in Palestine. According to these stories the leader of the Nizari branch in Syria—the "Old Man of the Mountain," as the Franks called him—would command the absolute obedience of his faithful by drugging them with hashish (hence *hašīšiyyūn*—"hashish-takers") in a wonderful garden full of beautiful women and meant to resemble paradise. He would then send the young men out to perform their murderous tasks, promising a permanent return to "paradise" if they succeeded. Compelling as these stories may be, they are without any historical evidence to support them.[4] In the Crusader stories the Syrian Nizaris became confounded with the Iranian branch, and in Marco Polo's colourful narrative the "Old Man of the Mountain" is the ruler of Alamut.

The period of Nizari statehood was punctuated by Imam Hasan II's declaration of the Resurrection (*qiyāma*) in 1164, interpreted as a new antinomian phase in the spiritual existence of the Nizari community, though this was followed some fifty years later by an outward "return" to Sunni practices. Nevertheless, the Nizaris remained formally independent of the Sunni government in Baghdad until 1256, when their stronghold at Alamut was finally penetrated by the Mongol invader Hülegü Khan who massacred much of the population.

After that time Iranian Isma'ilis went largely underground, surviving through the established Shi'ite practice of dissimulation (*taqiyya*).[5] Many apparently identified themselves as Sufis, though without aligning themselves with any particular order; this led to a mixing of Isma'ili and Sufi esoteric traditions. Even the Isma'ili Imams adopted the guise of Sufi *pīr*s. Isma'ili ideas can be detected in a number of Persian Sufi works of the post-Mongol period, raising the question who influenced whom, especially since this convergence has led many Isma'ilis to consider such Sufi figures as Attar, Rumi, and Nasafi as their own.[6]

Having gone underground in Iran, Isma'ilism came to be mostly associated with northwestern India, particularly Gujarat. Isma'ili communities, however, still exist today in northeastern Iran and in the Pamir mountain region of modern Tajikistan where they constitute the bulk of the population. Since the fall of the Soviet Union the Pamiri Isma'ilis have become more visible; many Isma'ili manuscripts have emerged, attracting considerable scholarly attention. The Aga Khan Development Network (AKDN) has become quite active in the region; it is currently building a major new English-language university, the University of Central Asia, with campuses in Tajikistan, Kyrgyzstan and Kazakhstan.

### Other Shi'i Movements

The post-Mongol period saw the emergence of a number of other heterodox movements that made use of Shi'i ideas and symbols. During the middle of the fourteenth century one such group, the Sarbedars ("[Those whose] heads are on the gallows"), even managed to form a small state based in the western Khorasani city of Sabzevar, which lasted from around 1337 until 1381. Another fourteenth-century movement was that of the Horūfīs, who followed a teaching based on the numeric and mystical significance of letters of the alphabet (*horūf*). A Horūfī uprising following the execution of their leader was crushed by Tamerlane, but an offshoot group, the Noqtavīs, survived into the Safavid period. Horūfī ideas can be detected among the Bektaši Sufis of Turkey and the Balkans, and among the Kurdish Yaresan (Ahl-e Haqq) in Iran.

Taken as an ensemble, the constant appearance of so many multifarious sects provides evidence for the notion that Iranian religiosity has historically preferred inspired guidance and esotericism to any kind of imposed formal legalism. It is significant that most of these groups, while outwardly Islamic in character, preserved elements of pre-Islamic Iranian beliefs and symbols. This has led both Muslim heresiographers and some contemporary scholars to assert connections between these various sects over time. For example, the Safavid chronicler Natanzi classifies the Noqtavīs of his period—whom he calls *zindīqs*—as a "satanic" movement in the same category with Manichaeism and Mazdakism.[7] Kathryn Babayan sees the timing of the Noqtavī movement's activity during the reign of Shah Abbas I (reigned 1587–1629) as coinciding with millenarian expectations that the thousand-year "Arab age" was about to be replaced with a return to a neo-Mazdaean "Persian (*'ajamī*) era."[8]

## TWELVER SHI'ISM IN IRAN

The cities of southern Iraq were historically strongholds of Twelver Shi'ism, and remain so to the present. The Iranian Buyid dynasty, which controlled much of the Abbasid Empire from 934–1055, had been nominally Twelver Shi'ite, but as noted above, until the sixteenth century the majority of Iranian Muslims followed other expressions of Islam. Most were outwardly Sunnis, but beneath the surface a wide range of heterodox sects existed throughout the country. Iranians accepted formal Twelver Shi'ism relatively late, under duress, and even then their affinity for the esoteric teachings of dervish shaykhs remained strong.

In the late fourteenth century much of Iran was under the rule of a Turkic dynasty, the Aq Qoyunlu ("White Sheep"—a totemic clan name), based in Tabriz. The northwestern lands had long been contested ground, alternately under the control of Iran and its western neighbor, first the Byzantine Romans and now the Ottoman Turks. The contiguous regions of western Azerbaijan and eastern Anatolia had been home since the eleventh century to various nomadic Turkic tribes (Turkmen)[9] who shunned any form of external authority.

The religiosity of the Turkmen nomads was a hybrid of Islamic and their own pre-Islamic beliefs and practices. One prevalent tendency, however, was a special focus on the person of 'Ali, the martyred cousin and son-in-law of Muhammad. At times their veneration for 'Ali approached deification. Some scholars have been quick to label any such "'Ali-worship" as Shi'ism, but given the clear lack of sophisticated theology among the tribes in question this identification is misleading. A better approach would be to say that such groups as the east Anatolian Turkmen displayed "shi'izing tendencies." The following poem, attributed to the teenage leader of the Safavid Sufi order, Esma'il son of Haydar, exemplifies their unorthodox views about 'Ali:

> He opens the gate of Islam to the world.
> Know him to be God, do not call him human.
> He gives his miracles to the sons of Mary;
> He brings glad tidings to the sons of Adam.
> His mystery was together with God; he brought us into being from non-existence.
> Through him the sanctuary [at Mecca] was ennobled to the station of sainthood, the rank of nobility.
> He was God come down from heaven to earth to show himself to the creatures of the world.
> He intercedes for the universe; he stands to the Prophet as "your flesh is my flesh."[10]

These conceptions are hard to reconcile with any mainstream Islamic tradition, in which no man is believed divine and Muhammad is the final prophet and ideal role model for Muslims.

The Safavid family was named for a thirteenth-century ancestor of Kurdish background, Safi al-din. Based in the town of Ardabil in northwestern Iran, the Safavids had originally been a Sunni order. By the late fifteenth century, however, they and their rustic following— referred to derisively by their Ottoman enemies as *qezelbāš* ("red-heads") after their distinctive headgear—became highly politicized, inspired by millenarian beliefs in religious renewal and a desire to challenge the authority of the Sunni Ottomans, whom they saw as encroaching upon their nomadic freedom. The Safavid leaders abandoned their original Sunni orientation and appealed to the Alid sympathies of Turkmen nomads throughout the region as a way of setting themselves up against the widely resented Ottomans. In 1501, an army under the leadership of the charismatic head of the Safavid family, the precocious fourteen-year-old Esma'il, dislodged the weak Aq Qoyunlu from Tabriz and declared their young guide the new Shah of Iran.

Esma'il's lack of familiarity with any kind of Sunni or Shi'i Islamic orthodoxy is clear from the content of the poems he used to rally his troops. The above poem, which is attributed to him, indicates that the Safavid shaykhs had appropriated the heterodox beliefs of the unlettered

Turkmen they were seeking to mobilize. In the example which follows, young Esma'il shifts the focus of devotion to himself. Esma'il associates himself with all the most powerfully symbolic figures of Shi'ite legend, but hardly stops there:

> My name is Shah Esma'il. I am on God's side: I am the leader of
>   these warriors.
> My mother is Fatima, my father Ali:
> I too am one of the Twelve Imams.
> I took back my father's blood from Yazid [the Umayyad Caliph
>   who ordered his army against the martyr Husayn].
> Know for certain that I am the true coin of Haydar [i.e., 'Ali].
> Ever-living Khezr [prophet of eternal life], Jesus son of Mary,
> I am the Alexander of the people of this age.
> See Yazid, polytheist and accursed one,
> For I am free of the *qibla* of hypocrites.
> In my opinion prophecy is the innermost mystery of sainthood:
> I am a follower of Muhammad Mustafa.
> I have subjugated the world by the sword.
> I am 'Ali Murtada's Qanbar [a faithful slave of 'Ali].
> My ancestor Safi, my father Haydar.
> I am a Ja'far [al-Tayyar, 'Ali's elder brother] of the people of bravery.
> I am a Husaynid, my curse upon Yazid.
> I am Khata'i, I am a servant of the king.[11]

As hinted in the above poem, the Safavids' mostly Turkmen followers believed in a kind of reincarnation, at least for important religious leaders. A popular figure was the charismatic Abbasid commander Abu Muslim, discussed in an earlier chapter, whose exploits were lauded in public recitations of the *Abū Moslem-nāmeh*.[12]

It may certainly be questioned to what extent the views of Esma'il Safavi and his followers resembled any recognized form of Shi'ism. But once in power, the Safavids sought to identify themselves as a Shi'ite state, challenging the legitimacy of the Sunni Ottomans. Among the Iranian population of the time support for Shi'ism was not widespread, however. In fact, due to the shortage of important Shi'ite scholars in Iran, the Safavids had to import them from various parts of the Arab world, including Iraq, Bahrain, and the Jabal 'Amil region of Lebanese Syria. One can only imagine the response of these Arab scholars, trained in the legal tradition of the sixth Shi'ite imam, Ja'far al-Sadiq, and following the teachings of the Twelve Imams, when they were exposed to the bizarre religious beliefs of their new patrons. As foreigners in a new land, however, these Arab jurists were dependent on the support of their Safavid employers.

At first the Shi'ite jurists had to tolerate the heterodox views of the Safavid monarch and his militant tribal following. For a time three groups—the Arab scholars, under the leadership of the Syrian 'Abd al-'Ali al-Karaki (died 1533), the military elite, dominated by the Turkmen *qezelbāš*, and the surviving Persian aristocracy—maintained a tense balance of authority over Iranian society. The scales definitively tipped, however, following the orthodox reawakening of the second Safavid ruler, Tahmasp, in 1532. From this time onward deviant views were more forcefully suppressed, and the Shi'ite jurists were given free rein to impose Shi'ite Ja'fari law throughout the country.

The so-called 'Amili (that is, Lebanese) clergy, whose legal approach relied heavily on the practice of independent reasoning (*ejtehād*), were to have a lasting impact on the development of Shi'i jurisprudence in Iran. Their validation of the rule of the Safavids was a departure from traditional Shi'ite political theory according to which no government could be considered legitimate prior to the return of the absent Imam. This condition had also been held to preclude Shi'is from attending Friday prayers; the 'Amilis overturned this tradition as well, decreeing that participation in the Friday prayer was at least permissible, though whether or not it was obligatory remained a contentious issue.

If these changes were not welcomed by Iran's native Shi'ite clergy, the Sunni majority were even more resistant. Sunni jurists in particular became the targets of government persecution, and Iran's largely Sunni population was compelled to adopt Twelver Shi'ite practices such as cursing (*tabarrā'*) the first three Caliphs—seen as usurpers of 'Ali's position—and commemorating the martyrdom of Husayn during the holy month of Muharram. The process of forced conversion lasted throughout the sixteenth century. In this intolerant atmosphere many Iranians whose talents made them employable elsewhere (particularly scholars and artists) chose to emigrate, especially to India, where Mughal and Deccani patrons typically welcomed them with open arms and generous stipends.

By the end of the seventeenth century Iran had been reshaped into a Twelver Shi'ite nation, and it remains today the only officially Shi'ite state in the Muslim world. Throughout the Safavid period, which lasted until 1722, the Shi'ite clergy exercised a powerful influence over Iranian politics and society. The ultimate character of clerical influence in Iran was determined by an ideological struggle known as the *usūlī-axbārī* conflict which pitted the former, as practitioners of *ejtehād*, against the latter group who were supporters of received tradition. After the fall of the Safavids the *'usūlīs* emerged as the dominant faction, paving the way for the eventual emergence of a jurist-controlled state in the latter quarter of the twentieth century.

### Shi'i Sufi Orders

With the conversion of Iran to Twelver Shi'ism in the sixteenth century two Shi'i Sufi orders became prominent, the Ne'matollahis and the Nurbakhshis. The Ne'matollahi order was founded by Nur al-din Ne'matollah b. 'Abdallah (1330–1431), who was born in Aleppo of Iranian parents but traced his genealogy to the fifth Shi'i Imam, Muhammad Baqir. He relocated to Central Asia, but because of Tamerlane's pro-Sunni policies he later moved to Mahan in south-central Iran, near the city of Kerman. Unlike many Sufis who shunned worldly powers, but like the Sunni Naqshbandis in Central Asia, Nur al-din freely associated with the ruling class. As a result, the Ne'matollahi order has historically been popular among the Iranian upper classes.

The Nurbakhshis were an offshoot of the Kobravi order founded in Central Asia during the late thirteenth century by a saint named Najm al-din Kobra. A member of the Kobravi community in Khorasan, Mohammad ibn 'Abdallah (died 1465), who was called "Nurbakhsh" ("giver of light"), provided this branch with its distinctive Shi'i beliefs. The Ne'matollahi and the Nurbakhshi fraternities experienced their greatest growth under the Qajars in the nineteenth century. Both orders remain active in Iran today, although Sufism has been generally discouraged since the 1979 revolution.

## Shi'a Theosophy

Against the backdrop of the Safavids' political dependence on the Twelver Shi'ite *'ulemā'*, not to mention their own heterodox Sufi origins, competing sources of religious authority were generally suppressed. Adepts of esoteric teachings continued to make use of the age-old practice of *taqiyya*, outwardly subscribing to the official Twelver Shi'ite orthodoxy. Because the Sufi orders were seen by those in power as a particular threat, the very notion of Sufism (*tasavvof*) gradually gave way to that of "gnosis" (*'erfān*). Thus, outwardly reconciling official religion with their own, Iranian esotericism survived by applying approved forms and terminologies onto very old ideas.

It was in this way that the illuminationist philosophy articulated by Sohravardi in the twelfth century was brought into the fold of Twelver Shi'ism. Known as *hekmat-e elāhī*, this reshaping of *ešrāqī* thought was carried out by Mir Damad and his student Molla Sadra during the first half of the seventeenth century in the Safavid capital, Esfahan. During the latter decades of the century, however, *ešrāqī* philosophy was targeted along with Sufism by the powerful cleric Mohammad Baqer Majlesi (1627–1699), whose own orthodox Shi'ite vision drew heavily on claims to having direct access to the twelve Imams.

## Popular Shi'ite Religiosity

As mentioned above, the mostly Turkmen devotees of the Safavid shaykhs who brought the fourteen-year-old Esma'il to power in 1501 were profoundly heterodox in their beliefs, which centered on the quasi-deification of 'Ali. During the early decades of Safavid rule the attitude of state-supported Shi'ite scholars toward folkish rituals and superstitions was ambivalent. Popular religiosity could be both doctrinally suspect and politically dangerous, especially in the case of highly emotional expressions of public piety such as mourning processions during the month of Muharram. At the same time, religious leaders could attempt to channel the religious energy of the masses by setting themselves up as the custodians of popular rituals and the stories associated with them. This approach became pronounced under the later Safavids, as *shaykh al-eslām* Mohammad Baqer Majlesi used his unrivalled religious authority to validate and encourage Iran's popular Shi'ite culture.[13]

Rituals associated with the martyrdom of Imam Husayn during the month of Muharram are the most visible public expressions of Shi'ite piety. Huge numbers of Iranians gather in neighborhood mosques to listen to sobbing recitations (*rawzeh-x$^w$ānī*s) of this tragic event, often breaking into tears themselves out of empathy for the plight of Husayn and his companions. Thousands more participate in mourning processions of chest-beating men, bringing traffic to a halt as they fill the streets. In environments where Shi'ites live side by side with Sunnis, as in South Asia, Muharram processions have sometimes been occasions where inter-communal tensions flare up into violence. (The Shi'ite practice of cursing the first three "illegitimate" caliphs is often a trigger arousing Sunni hostility.) Although in overwhelmingly Shi'ite Iran this kind of tension is less prevalent, there too one sees occasional scuffles when rival processions converge. For example, several nineteenth-century accounts mention that Muharram processions regularly resulted in street clashes between the rival Haydari and Ne'mati Sufi orders (both of which are Shi'ite) in a number of Iranian cities.[14]

As in medieval Christianity and some other religious traditions, Shi'ite mourning rituals sometimes include rhythmic self-flagellations. One common form consists of throwing a chain repeatedly across one's back (*zanjīr-zanī*). Another, less common, has the devotee draw a knife blade across his own skull (*qameh-zanī*).

In Iran, as part of the Muharram commemoration, the events at Karbala have traditionally been re-enacted in a form of popular theatre called *ta'ziyeh*.[15] Largely now confined to villages, the *ta'ziyeh* performances blur the line between actor and audience, and sometimes between fantasy and reality, as on rare occasions when overwrought villagers have actually killed the person playing the role of Shimr, the "evil" general responsible for Husayn's death. Not surprisingly, Shimr's role typically brings a higher fee for the actor.

Another form of popular piety in Iran, which occurs throughout the year, is the making of pilgrimages to the shrines of revered historical figures. Within Iran the most holy of these is the tomb of the eighth Shi'ite Imam, Reza ('Ali b. Musa al-Rida, died 818), in Mashhad. The name of the city itself means "place of the martyr," a reference to the fact that Reza, like all except the last of the twelve Shi'ite Imams, is believed to have died of unnatural causes. (The twelfth Imam is believed to have gone into occultation while still a child, and thus technically to be still alive.) Second in importance is the shrine of Imam Reza's sister Ma'sumeh Fatemeh ("Immaculate Fatima") in the seminary city of Qom.

Iranians flock to these two holy sites from all around the country. On a smaller scale, however, there are countless other shrines dedicated to the various descendants of the Imams, called *emām-zādeh*s, scattered throughout Iran. Important Sufi families have shrines as well. Such places are the frequent destinations of lesser pilgrimages, which may take the form of a weekend outing for a picnic and other kinds of family fun, effortlessly mixing piety and pleasure. As has been previously mentioned, it is likely that many if not most of these shrines were formerly fire temples or other kinds of holy sites, and rituals associated with them may in some cases be continuations of practices that date from pre-Islamic times.

### Iranian Shi'ism Encounters Modernity

From Safavid times the Shi'ite *'ulemā'* engaged in a mutual balancing act with the governing elites, whom they both legitimized and depended upon to maintain their role as religious authorities within Iranian society. And as the *'usūlī-axbārī* conflict illustrates, these very same religious authorities were often involved in jockeying for position among themselves.

Moreover, during the eighteenth century Iran was characterized by socio-political unrest, beginning with the fall of the Safavid dynasty in 1722, and only regaining a modicum of stability with the consolidation of a new dynasty, the Qajars, from 1796 onwards. Qajar power throughout the nineteenth century was largely centered on their capital, Tehran, while much of the rest of the country was for practical purposes under the control of local governors, landlords, and nomadic tribes. The disruptions caused by the millenarian Babi movement of the 1840s are an additional indication of the Qajars' vulnerabilities.

During the second half of the nineteenth century Iran came increasingly to face the many challenges presented by modernity. These challenges came mainly in the form of European ideas brought by Christian diplomats, merchants, missionaries, the sons of wealthy Iranians who had been sent to study abroad, and through the economically-driven interference of European powers in the country's internal affairs.

The Qajar elites were intrigued by the West in some respects—including new technologies such as photography, the telegraph, and eventually cinema—but cautious toward others, such as Enlightenment ideas about individual rights and democratic participation in governance. Unable to finance their taste for Western products and extravagant living, the Qajars resorted to mortgaging Iran's resources for their own short-term gain. In 1872 the Qajar monarch, Naser al-din Shah, went so far as to attempt to sell to a British investor, Baron von Reuter, the unique right to construct a new all-encompassing national infrastructure ranging from transportation and communications to factories and mines.

This concession was ultimately blocked, largely due to protests from Russia, but foreign agents continued to seek ways of controlling Iran's economy. In 1891 the Shah once again tried to sell a concession which would have given a British businessman, Major Talbot, a monopoly on the country's tobacco industry. This gesture was met with a nationwide rebellion in which members of the *'ulemā'* and the merchant classes joined forces to bring about a complete boycott of tobacco products. Once again the Shah was forced to back down, this time by internal rather than external actors, thus demonstrating the hitherto untapped political force of these two groups and revealing the Qajar government's essential weakness.

## THE CONSTITUTIONAL REVOLUTION

Unable to raise sufficient tax revenues to sustain itself, the Qajar government increasingly financed itself through the taking out of loans from European banks and the selling off of smaller concessions to European investors. Popular discontent focused on the Qajars' autocratic style of government, their bankrupting of the nation, and their ceding of Iran's sovereignty to foreign powers; this came to a head in 1905, when riots and strikes began to plague the country. Breaking with the established Twelver Shi'ite position of political quietism several important religious figures, including Mohammad Tabataba'i, Abdollah Behbahani, and later on Fazlollah Nuri, played important roles in leading these popular protests. In the end, on 5 August 1906 a coalition of religious leaders, bazaar merchants, and intellectuals succeeded in pressuring the Qajar ruler Muzaffar al-din Shah to allow for elections to a national "Constituent Assembly," Iran's first-ever elected parliament. The Constitution (*mašrūtiyat*) drawn up by this newly elected body curtailed the Shah's absolute powers for the first time in Iran's history, an event remembered as Iran's Constitutional Revolution.

## REZA SHAH'S MODERNIZATION CAMPAIGN

The aftermath of the Constitutional Revolution, including a military response by Muhammad 'Ali Shah in 1908, which led to a two-year civil war, was complicated by more overt British and Russian intervention and ultimately by the outbreak of World War I. Terminally weakened by these events, the Qajar dynasty was brought to an end in 1921 by an ambitious soldier named Reza Khan (born 1878) who seized power and assumed the title of Shah in 1925. Reza Shah, as he was now known, made a conscious effort to recall Iran's pre-Islamic greatness by calling his new dynasty the Pahlavi.

For the next sixteen years Reza Shah embarked Iran upon a massive modernization campaign, centralizing power in a way the Qajars had never been able to do. He built up the military and an extensive government bureaucracy, enabling him to gain unprecedented control over the lives of his subjects. Following the example of his Turkish neighbor Atatürk, Reza Shah even changed the national dress code, requiring men to wear Western-style suits and hats and women to go unveiled in public. Needless to say the enforcement of such radical changes was not universally welcomed, especially by the more traditionally-minded clergy, but his authority was such that resistance was largely ineffective. It was the British and the Soviets, in fact, who ended his career by forcibly removing him in 1941 amid fear of his Nazi sympathies; they exiled him to South Africa, where he died three years later.

## ANTI-CLERICALISM AMONG THE INTELLIGENTSIA

Reza Shah's modernizing agenda favored those among the traditional clergy, Shariat Sanglaji for example, who showed themselves pliant and willing to preach a reformist version of Islam compatible with the king's goals. At the same time, his nationalist policies encouraged a celebration of Iran's pre-Islamic identity. This included the replacement of some Arabic words and place-names with Persian ones. Many among Iran's intelligentsia were attracted to the national reawakening taking place during the 1930s, which sometimes portrayed Islam as an alien religion that had been imposed through force by a culturally inferior people. Sadeq Hedayat (1903–1951) was among the intellectuals of the time who became deeply attracted to Iran's pre-Islamic civilization and language.

Another well-known intellectual of the period, Ahmad Kasravi (1890–1946), himself trained as a Shi'ite cleric, did not reject Islam as such but rather how it had been interpreted and practiced over the centuries. Kasravi accused his fellow Iranian Muslims of being superstitious, ignorant, and overly attached to the Shi'ite Imams. He was particularly harsh on the Shi'ite clergy, whom he considered "bullies," taking people's money and telling them how to live while themselves remaining disconnected from the world as it really is:

> In any case, they are ignorant people who do not know as much about the world and its affairs as a ten-year-old child. And since their minds are filled with religious jurisprudence,

reported sayings and long, involved fabrications of principles and philosophy, there is no room left for knowledge or information. So much has happened in the world, sciences have appeared and changes have occurred, which they have either not known or understood or have understood but have not paid any attention to. They live in the present, but cannot look at the world except from the perspective of thirteen hundred years ago.[16]

Kasravi's radical views led to his arrest in 1946 on charges of "insulting Islam," and during his trial he was assassinated by members of an extremist group called the "Self-Sacrificers of Islam" (*fedāyān-e eslām*, not to be confused with the later, communist organization *fedāyān-e khalq*). The group's leader, Navvab Safavi, who was responsible for the assassinations of several other figures as well, was himself executed by the government in 1955. The current regime has made Navvab Safavi into a hero; in Tehran an urban expressway and a metro station are named after him.

# 15

# Zoroastrianism After Islam

To this day, the fall of the Sasanian Empire during the 640s is seen by many Iranians as the single greatest disaster to befall their country throughout its long and often glorious history. The fact that this trauma was inflicted by the Arabs, a people the proud Iranians had never taken seriously and whom they viewed as being uncultured in the extreme, adds insult to injury. Arabia was a marginal place of little significance, neither populous nor productive; from an Iranian perspective the region had always lain beyond the fringes of civilization. The epic tenth-century *Shāh-nāmeh*, though compiled by a Muslim for Muslims, paradoxically depicts the Arab conquest as the ultimate and culminating tragedy in the long heroic history of pre-Islamic Iran.

As noted in Chapter 12, the first Arab Muslim rulers were content to live and let live, as long as people acknowledged their authority and paid their taxes. And yet, the attractions of power and success being what they are, over time more and more Iranians chose to adopt the cultural norms and practices of their Arab overlords; this included, of course, the Islamic faith. The Zoroastrian priests, prior holders of religious power in Iran, could not compete once deprived of the state support they had formerly enjoyed.

It may be that in aligning themselves with the Sasanian government the Zoroastrian clergy had lost touch with the interests of the masses—recall that many Iranians were converting to Christianity, Manichaeism, and other religions well before the arrival of the Arabs. It is also the case that under Islamic law the children of mixed marriages—that is, a Muslim man marrying a non-Muslim woman—must be raised as Muslims, and that if one member of a non-Muslim family should convert to Islam, he would inherit the property of all of his non-Muslim relatives. Converts to Islam no longer had to pay the poll-tax (the *jizya*) levied on non-Muslims. Islamic law also governed the transactions of the marketplace, to the general advantage of Muslims.

There is no way of knowing how many Iranian conversions came out of sincere belief in the divine nature of the Qur'an and the noble example of the prophet Muhammad, and how many were merely opportunistic. In any event, within a few short centuries most of Iran's urban population had become Muslim. Conversion was slower in rural areas, but by the thirteenth century it appears that most rural Iranians were Muslims as well.

And yet throughout the Classical Islamic period Zoroastrian literary production flourished as never before, especially during the ninth and tenth centuries. While this may seem ironic at first glance, actually it makes perfect sense when one considers that writing is a kind of defense strategy. The first Zoroastrian books had been written down—albeit often based on much older oral literature—in the face of the threats posed by the worldviews of Manichaeism and Christianity. The threat now was even greater, since Iranians were flocking in droves to the new religion and Zoroastrianism had lost its state support. Of this late literature the most important works are the encyclopaedic nine-volume *Dēnkard* ("Acts of the Faith") and a cosmogonic treatise called the *Bondahešn* ("the Primordial Creation"). At the same time, it is reported that many Zoroastrian books were permanently lost.

## MUSLIM ATTITUDES TOWARD ZOROASTRIANS

Historically speaking Iranian Muslim attitudes toward their Zoroastrian neighbors have ranged from indifference to scorn, most often tending in the latter direction. The Qur'an names Christians, Jews, and Sabeans as "peoples of the book" (*ahl al-kitāb*) entitled to the protection of the Islamic state, and in Iran Zoroastrians acquired this nominal protected status (*dhimmī*) as well.[1] However, at both the popular and official levels the attitudes of Muslim converts and their descendants toward those who held to their Zoroastrian faith were negative and often condescending, sometimes leading to persecution. Moreover, with the emergence of Islamic jurisprudence in the eighth and ninth centuries certain laws detrimental to Zoroastrians were built into the legal code, such as the stipulation (mentioned above) that if a person converted to Islam he would inherit the wealth of his entire family.

Despite the protected status formally accorded Zoroastrians under Islamic law, in practice Muslim administrators and commoners alike often taunted and tormented Zoroastrians, whom they referred to derisively as "fire-worshippers" (*ātash-parastān*) and "infidels" (*gabrān*), in a variety of ways. Muslim officials were known to seize Zoroastrian property on very questionable legal grounds, or violate the sanctity of Zoroastrian sites, such as in 861 when the Caliph Mutawakkil cut down a tree many believed to have been planted by

Zoroaster himself. (The Caliph was assassinated soon after, which Zoroastrians saw as an act of divine retribution.) Muslims would often attack and beat Zoroastrians in the street, or provoke them by torturing dogs—considered semi-sacred animals in Zoroastrianism but spurned as ritually unclean in Islam—a practice that continues in Iranian villages today.[2] Like other religious minorities, Zoroastrians were not allowed to ride horses (a sign of wealth and nobility) they had to ride donkeys instead; and they had to wear distinctive clothing so that they could easily be recognized.[3]

Over the ensuing centuries Zoroastrians were increasingly reduced to a ghettoized, marginalized, and impoverished community, ultimately surviving mainly in the villages surrounding the cities of Yazd and Kerman. On the local level they were often harassed by Muslims, who could generally mistreat them with impunity. Under the Safavids (1501–1722 CE) there were incidences of forced conversion as well, despite the Qur'anic injunction against it.[4] The Afghan invaders of 1719–1724 continued and even exacerbated this trend.[5] European travelers of the period—Pietro della Valle, Jean-Baptiste Tavernier, and Jean Chardin, among others—found Zoroastrian communities to be living in miserable conditions for the most part, increasingly marginalized to rural areas.

## ZOROASTRIANISM IN INDIA

By the ninth century it was clear that Islam had come to Iran to stay. With the majority of the population converted to this new faith, those who clung to the old religion were an embattled minority. Some chose exile, migrating to the more tolerant climate of western India. By the mid-tenth century the community of Zoroastrian refugees in India— where they came to be known as Parsis ("Persians")—was firmly established, mainly in the region of Gujarat where they remain a presence to this day. While the precise details of Zoroastrian migration to India remain unclear, it is likely that it took place in several waves beginning perhaps as early as the eighth century. Unfortunately, the best-known account of Zoroastrian migration to India, the late sixteenth-century *Qesseh-ye Sanjān*, belongs more to the realm of myth than history.[6]

Contacts between Zoroastrians in Iran and India remained intermittent throughout the pre-modern period. From the late fifteenth century up until 1766, Parsi priests engaged in correspondence with their colleagues in Iran—a series of twenty-two letters known as the *Revāyat*s—asking for clarification on a number of points of doctrine and ritual. This would seem to indicate that Iran was still seen as the locus of religious authority by Zoroastrians in India. In light of the fact that Parsis later became known for their staunch opposition to accepting converts, the following exchange from *Revāyat* no. 237 (dated to around 1594) is interesting:

> Q: Can a grave-digger, a corpse-burner and a *darvand* (one of a foreign faith) become *Behdin*s (i.e., be converted to the Mazdayasnian religion)?
>
> A: If they observe the rules of religion steadfastly and (keep) connection with the religion, and if no harm comes on the *Behdin*s (thereby), it is proper and allowable.[7]

During the 1570s the Iranian Zoroastrian priest Azar Keyvan migrated to India, where, with the support of Mughal officials such as Abu'l Fazl 'Allami, he founded a school of philosophy that created a hybrid Mazdaean-Islamic mythical history drawing on Sohravardian *ešrāqī* ideas. Keyvan and his followers produced a set of philosophical texts, some of which they claimed to be "translations" of ancient works. Mohamad Tavakoli-Targhi characterizes this body of texts, which collectively came to be known as the *Dasātīr*, as "the foundational canon of the neo-Mazdean renaissance."[8] To speak of a "neo-Mazdean renaissance" in this context is perhaps a bit of an exaggeration, but it does seem that certain aspects of the emerging self-understanding of Zoroastrians in the modern period can be traced back to Keyvan and his school.

As a result of challenges from British Protestant missionaries, the nineteenth century saw significant changes in how Parsis understood the Zoroastrian religion. Parsi reformists such as Dosabhoy Framjee, B. F. Bilimoria, S. D. Bharucha, and S. A. Kapadia defended their faith according to the categories defined by European Christianity: these included monotheism, rationality, and individual piety. (Martin Haug, James Moulton, and other Western Protestant scholars constructed their understanding of Zoroastrianism along similar lines, though with the aim of demonstrating the superiority of Christianity.) This re-imagining of Zoroastrianism sought to identify an "original" version based on the Gathas, with later texts and practices dismissed as corruptions of Zoroaster's purported message. The resulting interpretations made Zoroastrianism a distinctly modern faith: progressive, ethical, and in line with nineteenth-century Western values.[9]

Throughout the nineteenth century the Parsis were the British imperialists' principal allies in developing Bombay into the commercial capital of the Raj.[10] While the city's skyrocketing population has long since overwhelmed their relatively tiny numbers, the Parsi presence in Bombay (now Mumbai) remains visible. Many important buildings and monuments attest to their legacy (see Figure 9), and the Parsis continue to play an important role in India's economy. The Tata Corporation, for example, one of India's largest companies, is Parsi-owned, and Air India was founded by a Parsi. The husband of the former prime minister, Indira Gandhi (no relation to the Mahatma), was from a well-known Parsi family. Outside India there are long-established Parsi communities in Pakistan, Sri Lanka, Hong Kong and Singapore, and more recent ones in the U.K., North America and Australia.

## APPROPRIATING AND UNIVERSALIZING ZOROASTRIANISM: SOME MODERN EXPRESSIONS

From its very discovery by European scholars in the late eighteenth century Zoroastrianism has attracted a range of Westerners seeking exotic spirituality, and the Victorian passion for the exotic East—most visibly in Edward Fitzgerald's somewhat loose renderings of the quatrains of Omar Khayyam—established once and for all Iran's place in the European spiritual imagination. In British India a Zoroastrian form of theosophy emerged, known as the Ilm-i Khshnoom, later taking an even more eclectic shape in the mid-twentieth century with the teaching of popular guru Meher Baba (1894–1969).

### *Zoroastrian Theosophy: the Ilm-i Khshnoom*

The movement known as Ilm-i Khshnoom, or "science of ecstasy," emerged among the Parsis of British India during the nineteenth century as a Zoroastrian expression of Theosophy. Its earliest exponent, Behramshah Nowroji Shroff (1858–1927),[11] was a native of Surat in Gujarat who claimed to have spent three years in his youth studying esoteric interpretations of the Avesta among a long-hidden Zoroastrian sect, the *sāheb delān* ("Big-Hearted Ones"), a group of 2,002 pious individuals led by seventy-two priests who are said to have been living in caves around Mount Damavand in northern Iran since late Sasanian times. On his return to India, Shroff acquired a following; he founded the Ilm-i Khshnoom Institute in 1910 and in 1923 he established a "*fasli*" agiary (a fire temple using the reformed seasonal calendar) in the Bombay neighborhood now known as Behram Baug. (This temple was formally consecrated only many years later, in 2001.) Shroff's teachings were regularly published in the journals *Frashogard* (ca. 1910–1943), *Parsi Avaz* (1947–1974), *Dini Avaz* (1976– ), *Mazdayasni Connection* (1983– ), and *Parsi Pukar* (1995– ). The Ilm-i Khshnoom teaches vegetarianism, a belief in reincarnation, and occult sciences such as astrology, healing, telepathy, and predicting the future.

Shroff himself is seen today by followers of the Ilm-i Khshnoom as a herald preparing the way for the Rainidar ("one who shows the path," of which there are said to have been ninety-nine so far) of the Aquarian

Age, Shah Bahram Varzavand, whom some believe to be alive today but who has not yet revealed himself. (A quick search on the Internet turns up numerous chat sites eagerly discussing this much-anticipated event.) Over the past quarter-century Shroff's work has been taken up notably by a Parsi woman, Meher Master-Moos, who founded a "Zoroastrian College" in Sanjan, Gujarat in 1986.[12] Enthusiasts from the former Soviet Union, including Tajik President Emamali Rahmon and Prof. Rustom Fuzaylov of Khojand, established relations with the college beginning in 1991, and have become active collaborators in promoting the dream of a worldwide Zoroastrian revival based on Ilm-i Khshnoom principles. Non-resident students from across India, the former USSR, and other countries have pursued higher degrees in a range of subjects, mostly in fields related to development and alternative medicine—though not, as one might expect, Zoroastrianism. It has awarded doctoral degrees to seven Iranians, including former Zoroastrian M.P. Kourosh Niknam. On the other hand, a Latin American graduate has established a "branch campus" in Quito, Ecuador; the College also boasts such "centers" in France, Australia, and Taiwan.

The Zoroastrian College describes itself as "A Spiritual White Light Center," "a Universal Center for Development of Body, Mind, Aura, Halo and Soul":

> Its purpose is to enable souls to evolve spiritually in the quality, purity and speed of White Light. Its main educational purpose is to spread the knowledge of the ANCIENT COSMIC WISDOM. By gaining an awareness and understanding of the DIVINE UNIVERSAL NATURAL LAWS of the Almighty Creator of the Universe, every soul is enabled to exercise its free will correctly. By choosing to obey the Divine Laws, the Will of God, by choosing to help the Almighty in carrying out His Divine Plan of Spiritual Evolution of the Universe, every person can himself/herself evolve spiritually; and attain the ultimate aim of BECOMING ONE WITH THE DIVINE CREATOR. In this manner, PEACE is achieved.[13]

Participation is not limited to Zoroastrians, but open to all:

> It is open to all persons from any country in the world, who genuinely desire to live within this Spiritual Community, and develop their inner consciousness, by practising the daily life disciplines of obedience of the Divine Laws. These are the Cosmic Laws that are administered by the Archangels and Angels—the Amesha Spentas and Yazatas. It is open to any person to reside within this Spiritual Community for some time and then go elsewhere to start another Centre, so that the knowledge of the Cosmic Laws is spread for the Universal Benefit of Humanity, in this 21st Century and the Aquarian Age to come.

The College celebrated its Silver Jubilee with an international conference in Mumbai in January 2011, mostly featuring papers on alternative medicine and spiritual healing. The conference program included letters of congratulation from a large number of religious leaders, politicians and diplomats, and even the Embassy of Iran.

The College's relations with the Islamic Republic are curiously close. Following a protocol signed between the Iranian Embassy's cultural wing and the College in 2009, the College began offering Persian classes and initiated a program for translating books from English into Persian. The person responsible for the Persian language program was appointed by the Consulate of Iran in Mumbai, and the Consul himself awarded a doctoral degree to an Iranian candidate.[14] In April 2010 the Iranian Embassy in New Delhi presented college president Meher Master-Moos with its Dara Shikoh Award honoring contributions to interfaith dialogue.

Even more peculiar, the College website has two photos of a visit by the former Iranian president Mahmud Ahmadinejad's shadowy advisor, Esfandiar Rahim Masha'i, without identifying him by name. Given the College's proclaimed association with the as-yet-unmanifest Shah Bahram Varzavand, it is interesting that Masha'i has been accused by political adversaries such as Abdollah Shahbazi of involvement with followers of Ilm-i Khshnoom, freemasonry, and Kabbala, who are said to be hiding in the mountainous Damavand region east of Tehran.[15]

## Shah Bahram Varjavand

The Zoroastrian renovator Shah Bahram Varjavand is mentioned in a post-Sasanian Pahlavi source, the *Manzūme-ye Bahrām-e Varjāvand*, where it is foretold that he will arrive from India (or Kabul) on a white elephant to free Iran from "ill-wishers and enemies."[16] Tabari's history states that the rebel Qarmatis of Bahrain claimed him as one of their leaders. Carlo Cereti has argued that many of Bahram Varjavand's traits are derived from those of Bahram Gur and Bahram Čubin, and he can also be associated with a son of Yazdigerd III. Since he is absent from the list of saviours provided in Book 5 of the *Dēnkard*, Cereti suggests that he is an invention of early Islamic times.[17]

As mentioned above, Shah Bahram Varjavand is believed by some Zoroastrians to be alive today and biding his time before manifesting himself at the appropriate moment. Dame Master-Moos writes in her 1981 biography of Behramshah Nowroji Shroff:

> The time is now not far when the next great Rainidar of the Zarathushtrian Daena will come and rally the forces of the ancient Zoroastrian people and revive the ancient fires. He will come from the Chaechast var [fortress, or possibly cave], which is located in the hidden mountain regions around the Caspian

Sea . . . And though the population of Parsee Zoroastrians may have dwindled to only about 10–11,000 before his advent, after his advent he will unite all the Zarathushtrian people, expand the borders of Iran and there will be about 10 million Zarathushtrians alive in his time. How this will come about remains to be seen, in the course of nature. But Parsees should not worry unduly about the fall in our population. There is always a fall in Nature before a rise can take place. What is destined to occur in the course of history will occur.[18]

When this happens, "the great rainidar of the Zarathushtrian daena . . . will once again be the monarch of a Zarathushtrian Empire in Iran on this earth,"[19] utilizing the treasures of the Sasanian kings which were said to be hidden in the mountains of Tangestan in southern Iran prior to the Arab conquest.

Like the *var* at Damavand where Shroff allegedly received his spiritual education, the Chaichast fortress (or cave) where the Rainidar is said to be currently living is hidden from the general public by distractive vibrations emitted by its inhabitants. Its entrance is purported to lie beneath the waters of the Caspian. Yet the monastery itself is claimed to be inhabited by no less than one million "first grade souls." Its library is said to contain all twenty-one nasks of the Avesta.[20]

After the Rainidar's appearance, according to Ervad K. N. Dastoor,

. . . there will be one more *kayamat* (*qiyāmat*, uprising) and finally at the end of this *hazara* (millennium) there will be the greatest *kayamat* of all resulting in the great deluge. However, before this, Soshyant or Astavat Ereta will descend on the earth, choose a few souls and take them to the safety of the Aiwithrishva region in the *var* of Jamshed.[21]

### Zoroastrians in Modern Iran

As noted above, by the early nineteenth century the Parsis in India had begun to prosper through their affiliations with the British. Alongside their own improving fortunes came a growing concern among the Parsis about the circumstances of their co-religionists in Iran. A Society for the Amelioration of the Conditions of the Zoroastrians in Persia was founded in Bombay in 1854. The Society sent a Parsi agent by the name of Manekji Limji Hataria to Iran to assess the condition of Zoroastrian communities there, which he found to be abysmal.[22] Manekji, who remained in Iran until his death in 1890, established schools and *anjoman*s (community associations) in Zoroastrian communities and worked for the repeal of the *jizya*, the poll tax levied on Zoroastrians as a non-Muslim community. Through the efforts of the Society and with the help of British pressure on the Iranian government, the tax was repealed in 1882.

Parsis such as Maneckji and others brought with them economic resources, organizational skills, international networks, and reformist ideas, all of which enabled them to dramatically transform Zoroastrian communities in Iran.[23] Parsis continued to support *anjoman*s and the modernization of education, particularly through an organization called the Iran League founded in 1922. The Iran League's aims were stated in its journal, the *Iran League Quarterly*, as follows:

> To renew and continue the connection between the old land of Iran and Hind; to continue and encourage fraternal sentiment towards and interest and enthusiasm in the cause of Iran; to confederate the Zoroastrian population in Iran with a view to increase their number, to ameliorate their condition and to strive for their uplift; to make researches with reference to their religion and ancient Parsi history; to stimulate commercial relations with Iran; to encourage Parsis to visit the old land; as businessmen or as travellers, for change of climate and health; to obtain and spread among Parsis and others, by means of literature, authentic information regarding the state of affairs in Iran; to secure the sympathy of the Imperial Iranian Government and the Iranian subjects toward the cause of the Parsis in relation to Iran.[24]

Inspired by such rhetoric, one well-known Parsi philanthropist, Peshotanji Marker (1871–1965), founded an orphanage and a high school for Zoroastrians in Yazd. The Iran League encouraged and facilitated travel exchanges between Iranian and Indian Zoroastrians. This, combined with the often highly romanticized articles in their journal, did much to help the two communities increase their mutual interest and appreciation. Parsis coming to Iran also brought with them modern understandings of their religion, which sowed the seeds for future reinterpretations among Iranians.

These factors helped to bring about a gradual improvement in the economic conditions of Iranian Zoroastrians. Over the subsequent decades many moved to Tehran, where they saw increased opportunities, and, in the cosmopolitan environment of the capital, they tended to suffer less from daily acts of bigotry on the part of Muslims. After Iran's first parliament was established in 1906 one seat was allocated to a Zoroastrian representative. On the other hand, during the early twentieth century a new surge of Iranian Zoroastrians migrated to India, inspired by the wealth and status of the Parsi community there. This second wave of Zoroastrian migrants to India came to be known as "Iranis," considered a distinct yet related group to the Parsis.

In 1908 Tehran's growing Zoroastrian community established a sacred fire temple, which exists today on a quiet street near the center of the city. From 1925 the modernizing monarch, Reza Shah Pahlavi, promoted a secular nationalist policy (in emulation of his Turkish neighbor Kemal Ataturk) that worked in some ways to the benefit of Iran's Zoroastrians. During his sixteen-year reign pre-Islamic Iranian culture was elevated as being more truly "Persian" than Islam, and in the minds of some Iranians this brought a new respect for Zoroastrianism. This fact was not lost on some Parsi intellectuals in India, who came to champion the Iranian monarch's style of rule over that of the British.[25] Reza Shah took this opportunity to encourage Parsis to migrate to Iran, "the country of your ancestors."[26] Also, intellectuals such as Sadeq Hedayat (1903–1951), Iran's first important novelist, developed a keen interest in the literature of the Sasanian period, and very small numbers of Muslim Iranians even began to "convert back" to Zoroastrianism as being a more authentically Iranian form of religion.

A less visible, but even more significant change for Iran's Zoroastrian community was the dramatic rise in the value of agricultural land, which lifted many rural Zoroastrians from poverty to prosperity virtually overnight. A major result of this newfound wealth was the migration of Zoroastrians to urban centers such as Yazd and Kerman, and increasingly to the capital, Tehran. In the cities Zoroastrians attained higher levels of education and a greater presence in the workforce, while the villages they had left came to be populated by Muslims.

With these dramatic changes in their economic and demographic realities came cultural changes as well. Over the span of a few decades Zoroastrians went from being one of Iran's most economically depressed communities to one of its most advantaged. Their perception and practice of religion changed as well: they became less and less preoccupied with the ritual aspects of their tradition and increasingly focused on its ethical dimension. (South Asian Parsis, meanwhile, have by comparison remained more conservative and ritualistic, especially those who have remained in India.) As Zoroastrians became exposed to modernist ideas, some leading members of the community, such as parliamentary deputy Kay Khosrow Shahrokh (1864–1940), pushed for reforming certain aspects of religious practice. The exposure of corpses, for example, was argued to be a post-Zoroaster innovation, and by the 1960s was abandoned as unhygienic.

Today many Iranian Zoroastrians no longer even wear the *sedreh-koshtī*, the sacred cord and undershirt that since ancient times have defined Zoroastrian identity and been a precondition for participation in religious rituals. Celebrations such as the seasonal *gāhānbārs*[27] have lost much of their formality, with chatter and gossip often drowning out the priest's recitations, and liturgies have been shortened from several hours to thirty or forty minutes. Restrictions on entering holy places have been relaxed: the main fire temple in Yazd is open to tourists, who are able to enter into the presence of a sacred fire that has been burning for at least fifteen hundred years. In Tehran, a priest who showed us around the main fire temple in the city center quipped, "They'd never allow you to do this in India!" (In fact, personal experience tells us that he was right.)

Indeed, Zoroastrianism in Iran has changed so much, especially over the past several decades, that the well-known and oft-cited study of Mary Boyce, *A Persian Stronghold of Zoroastrianism*, which emerged from research she conducted in 1963–1964, seems today to possess a purely historical value.[28] Even the villagers of Sharifabad, whose traditional lifestyle and daily rituals she described in such detail, have now almost entirely left for the cities.[29]

With the Iranian diaspora entering a new phase in the second half of the twentieth century Iranian Zoroastrian communities grew up in places such as London, Toronto, and Los Angeles. The first World Zoroastrian Congress was held in 1960 in Tehran. Subsequent conferences have been held in Iran, India, the United States, and Dubai. There are now Zoroastrian cultural organizations in a number of countries. The World Zoroastrian Organisation in London, the Zarathushtrian Assembly of California, and others are now actively supporting Zoroastrian communities and promoting Zoroastrian teachings both locally and worldwide. A Zoroastrian virtual university, Spenta University, has been set up in Los Angeles and offers on-line programs leading to graduate degrees in the United States, Iran, India, Italy, Switzerland, Brazil, Australia, and Venezuela. In Iran, the Zoroastrians of Shiraz maintain an informational website in both English and Persian. In a sense, Zoroastrianism, one of the world's oldest religions, has only recently become a global one.

# 16

# Two Kurdish Sects: The Yezidis and the Yaresan

The history of religions—like history in general—is usually told from the side of power, which in religious terms means established orthodoxy. However, over-reliance on such narratives obscures the reality of life "on the ground," which in many cases paints a very different picture. Even terms like "minority" and "marginal" can be misleading, since in some cases non-establishment norms can be upheld by most of the population. Recognizing this fact, one may reject using the term "heresy" in the usual pejorative sense, and instead apply it in a more neutral way to perspectives belonging to various non-elite groups.

Orthodox authority is typically urban-centered, and decreases with distance from centers of political power. Thus, villages often show more local distinctiveness than towns, and mountain areas, being difficult to access and control, the greatest resistance of all to central authority. The Kurds, an ancient Iranian-speaking people who have long inhabited the Zagros of western Iran, and other mountainous regions, provide an excellent example of how independent traditions can retain their character through centuries of resistance to external forces.

Since the Kurds' are an Iranian people and given their history of independent-mindedness, it is not surprising to find many survivals of very old Iranian religious beliefs and customs among the various Kurdish peoples of Iran, Iraq, Turkey, Syria, and the Caucasus. Such traces are blended with a range of other influences, primarily Islamic, but their fundamental Iranian character is immediately obvious. A number of Kurdish groups, while clearly drawing from an ancient Iranian cultural pool of beliefs and symbols, have maintained their own traditions parallel to the Iranian mainstream. Two specifically Kurdish types of religious expression stand out: those of the Yezidis (referred to in Iran as *Īzadīs*) and the Yaresan, also known as the Ahl-e Haqq ("People of the [Divine] Truth").

Philip Kreyenbroek has noted the "unexpected and striking similarities" between the legends and imagery of these two groups, which he takes as an indication that "both cults spring from a common, well-defined, non-Islamic tradition." He goes on to suggest that at least some of these shared elements "go back to an ancient faith which was probably dominant among speakers of Western Iranian languages [i.e., proto-Kurdish] before Zoroastrianism became prominent in their areas."[1]

Reza Hamzeh'ee echoes this assessment when he says of the Yaresan that they "have adopted many religious ideas with which they have come into contact, but their basic tenets are an independent development of pre-Islamic ideas."[2] Thomas Bois has highlighted the survival throughout Kurdistan of belief in nature spirits inhabiting trees, rocks, and water sources, recalling the ancient Iranian notion of *mainyu*s. Such natural sites are commonly connected today with shrines to Muslim saints, but as Bois observes, ". . . the cult of saints which has thus often substituted for the cult of the forces of nature has not been able to be extirpated from the hearts of the popular masses despite the severe interdictions of orthodox Islam."[3]

Kurdish scholar Mehrdad Izady has gone even further and proposed an underlying "original" Kurdish religion, which he calls Yazdanism, or according to his translation, the "Cult of Angels,"[4] though his invented religion certainly owes more to contemporary Kurdish national sentiment than to actual religious history. The Kurds are Iranians, and as such have inherited a wide-ranging and ancient cultural pool from which the various Iranian peoples have each assembled their own mix of symbol and ritual.

## THE YEZIDIS

Yezidis today are spread across the Kurdish region, with communities in Iraq, Iran, Syria, and the Caucasus, as well as large numbers of expatriates (mostly from Turkey) living in Germany and other Western countries. Estimates of their total number range wildly, but they probably number over half a million worldwide, with the largest proportion living in northern Iraq, where their most important shrines are located.

Yezidism as a distinct religious community traces its origin back to the twelfth century, when a Lebanese Sufi master from Baghdad by the name of Shaykh 'Adi (died 1162) moved to the Hakkari mountains in northern Iraq, where he acquired a devoted following among the local Kurdish population. Although the sources describe him as an orthodox Muslim, his followers appear to have retained many aspects of their own local, Iranian religion.[5] And while they did at least superficially adopt some Islamic symbols and concepts, adding elements to the existing Iranian pool, by the fourteenth century the Yezidis had come to be considered as a separate, non-Muslim group.

The very name of the sect, whose members refer to themselves in Kurdish as *Êzidî*, is itself problematic. Some consider it to be a corruption of the Persian word *îzadî*, from either *yazata*, "a being worthy of worship," or Yazdan, a name for God, either of which would evoke pre-Islamic origins. Others attribute it to a movement, mentioned even before Shaykh 'Adi's time, of mountain-dwellers, mainly Kurds, who venerated the Umayyad Caliph Yazid, detested by Shi'ites as the figure they hold responsible for the killing of the third Shi'ite Imam, Hussein b. 'Ali. It does not seem possible to answer the question definitively either way; ultimately, since the movement that took shape in the centuries after Shaykh 'Adi appears to have brought together a number of disparate elements, the name "Yezidi" may in fact draw on more than one source.

Like numerous other Sufi groups, the 'Adawiyya, as they were known in Muslim sources, were known for extreme veneration of their leaders and were thus sometimes seen as a political threat. During the leadership of Shaykh Hasan, who was executed in 1254 by the provincial government, which feared his power, Muslim writers noted the prevalence of non-Islamic norms among the 'Adawiyya; this likely referred to surviving pre-Islamic beliefs and practices, in addition to what these writers disparagingly described as "saint-worship." As Kreyenbroek suggests, "there can be little doubt that ideas, practices and attitudes deriving from the culture of the local Kurds gained a degree of acceptance among those members of the 'Adawiyya who resided at Lalish" (the village where their principal shrine is located—see Figure 10).[6]

Indeed, a similar process through which originally foreign Sufi masters established themselves among rural populations by accepting and incorporating elements of local belief and practice can be seen throughout the Islamic world, even up to the present, whether in sub-Saharan Africa, India, or Indonesia. In this respect the 'Adawiyya represent an extreme—though not unique—case, in that their views and practices differed enough from those of mainstream Islam that they eventually came to be considered non-Muslims.

Interestingly, the remarkable spread of Yezidism among the Kurds during the fifteenth century seems to be linked to an increasing openness among the 'Adawi leaders to traditional Kurdish beliefs and practices. The result was persecution by Muslim authorities and the eventual exclusion of the 'Adawiyya from the Islamic community by the *'ulemā'*. In a sense this could be seen as mostly a formal gesture, since in reality a majority of the people concerned may never have been very strongly integrated into the Islamic *umma* in the first place.

Indeed, the Yezidis' strong sense of separate identity, expressed in an origin myth according to which they alone of all peoples are the true descendants of Adam, may well go back to pre-Islamic times and reflect their desire to resist and distinguish themselves from the Zoroastrian elites of the Sasanian period. Noting that the Yezidi and Zoroastrian creation stories seem to be variations on the same original myth, Christine Allison suggests a taxonomy according to which "Yazidism would be, not a form of Zoroastrianism, but a religion possessing an Iranian belief-system akin to it."[7]

In short, the story of Yezidism can be read as an example of the survival of local religious tradition. This is not to say that it is immediately visible as a pre-Islamic Iranian religion. On the contrary, since the time of Shaykh 'Adi and perhaps earlier, Yezidism has acquired such a complex veneer of superimposed terms, symbols, and possibly practices as well, that unraveling its pre-Islamic Iranian elements is challenging to say the least. Moreover, there are many variations among the oral traditions of various Yezidi communities. Until recently reading and writing was forbidden to them, and their texts did not exist in written form. Moreover, the two "sacred books" attributed to the Yezidis, the *Mashafā Reš* and the *Ketēbā Jelwa*, are now considered to be early twentieth-century forgeries made by Westerners. A more authentic expression of Yezidi beliefs can be found in their hymns, called *qawl*s. Nevertheless, with a little digging a number of ancient Iranian traces can be extracted from Yezidi sources.

### Iranian Elements in Yezidism

One of the most important Yezidi rituals is the annual slaying of a bull, which Mehrdad Bahar takes as evidence that the religion is fundamentally Mithraic.[8] Bahar also sees echoes of Mithraism in the fact that Yezidis pray facing the sun. Another ancient element surviving in Yezidism is the myth of the hero who slays the serpent. In a Yezidi story that exists in several versions, Shaykh 'Adi is given the hero's role; in an interesting parallel with a feat attributed to Indra in the Rig Veda, Shaykh 'Adi not only kills the serpent but "releases the waters" which have been sequestered within the rock.[9]

Another fairly transparent Iranian survival is the Yezidi belief in a Divine Heptad, called by them the Seven Mysteries (*haft sirr*), mirroring the Zoroastrian paradigm of Ahura Mazda and the six *Aməša Spəntas*. In the Yezidi version, the identities of these seven holy beings are blurred and somewhat fluid, an ambiguity explained by the notion that in the end they are all expressions of the Divine. This confusion of identities is compounded by the fact that Yezidis believe in reincarnation, which they refer to as "changing the shirt." Thus, when referring to saints or holy beings they may name any number of individual manifestations. The Yezidis pay special reverence, however, to a being they know as Malak Tavus, the Peacock Angel, who is their most prominent divine figure. Four of the other aspects of the divine heptad are associated with the elements: Earth, Air, Fire, and Water, and at times with the Islamic archangels Jibra'il, Mika'il, Israfil, and 'Azra'il. The remaining two are identified with Shaykh 'Adi and one of his successors, Shaykh Hasan.

Like the Zoroastrians, the Yezidis believe that the world will be perfected at the end of time, following a final struggle, after which it will be "smooth like an egg," with neither mountains nor sea. The Yezidis also have numerous taboos against polluting nature, as well as restrictions on interactions with "impure" outsiders. The notion of ritual impurity also applies to women during menstruation. Forbidden foods include not only the usual suspects such as pork, but, rather curiously, such items as lettuce, okra, and cauliflower. For reasons not entirely clear, Yezidis shun the colour blue.

Similar to other Iranian peoples, the Yezidis celebrate four seasonal festivals. Their spring festival is slightly later than the Iranian Nō rūz, however, taking place in early April, and is less important than the Festival of the Assembly (*ježna jema'iyye*) which takes place in late September. The latter celebration likely came to fill the place of Mehragān, the festival of Mithra—which, as has been suggested in a preceding chapter, may have been the most important annual event for Iranians in the pre-Zoroastrian period.

The Festival of the Assembly, held at Lalish in northern Iraq, is meant to mirror the annual gathering together of the Seven Mysteries. All Yezidis are called to participate if they can. The ritual of the bull sacrifice is held on the fifth day, accompanied by music and dancing.

### The Question of "Devil-Worship"

The Yezidis have long been characterized as "devil-worshipers," particularly by their Muslim neighbors. This identification is problematic, and in short, unsupported by the evidence. On the simplest level it should probably be understood as merely a form of anathema commonly used in the polemics of various religious traditions against their ideological competitors. The Zoroastrians may have associated the peacock with Ahriman,[10] which could have played a role in their diatribes against the Yezidis' pre-Islamic predecessors.

In later times, the Yezidis' views on Satan can probably be connected to the teaching of Shaykh 'Adi, who—like many other Sufi masters from Hallaj to 'Adi's own contemporary, Ahmad Ghazali—portrayed the fallen angel Eblis (Satan) as the ultimate lover of God, unwilling to prostrate himself before Adam and prepared to suffer expulsion from

Paradise as the price of his singular devotion. Thus, while they cannot be said to worship Satan, the Yezidis observe a respectful taboo on naming him. In the end, what outsiders perceive as the Yezidis' reverence for evil may in fact stem from their notion that good and evil are equally necessary, one not being possible without the other.

## THE YARESAN

While there are many similarities between the Yezidis and the Yaresan, another, ostensibly Sufi-related group existing among the Kurds of Iran and Iraq, the major difference would seem to be that while the Yezidis are not considered and do not consider themselves to be Muslim, the Yaresan are seen as a heterodox sect within Shi'ite Islam, even though its members do not observe Islamic rituals.[11] They are also egalitarian in their social structure, unlike the Yezidis, who have a firmly established caste system. Reflecting their differences in geographical distribution, the Yaresan speak mainly southern Kurdish (Gurani) as opposed to the Yezidis who mostly speak the northern Kurmanji dialect. The Yaresan are centered in the regions of Luristan and Kermanshah, with some small communities in northeastern Iraq, where they are known as the Kaka'i. Their total population is unknown, but is estimated at anywhere from one to seven million.[12] Traditionally, the Yaresan, like the Yezidis, did not accept converts or intermarriage. More recently, however, the Elahi branch of the Ahl-e Haqq has begun to welcome initiates willing to "entrust [their] head" (*sar sepordan*) to a Yaresan master (*seyyed*).

The hereditary priesthood is divided among eleven "Spiritual Households" (*khāndān*), each of which is led by its own *seyyed*. The initiation ritual itself is seen as a renewal of the primordial contract between God and the "eternal master," named as Jebra'il but considered to have returned in a number of incarnations, most notably one known as Benyamin. This primordial contract, of course, suggests an ancient precedent connected with Mithra.

The Yaresan have historical affinities with a number of extremist Shi'ite movements (*ghulāt*) but began to take on their present form in the late fourteenth/early fifteenth century under the leadership of Sultan Sohak (Eshāq), whose followers believed him to be an incarnation of God. Mehrdad Izady claims that Sultan Sohak can be identified with Aži Dahāka, the demon-king Zahhāk of Iranian mythology. Izady considers the latter to be a historical figure, specifically the last Median king Ršti-vegā, known to the Greeks as Astyages, maternal grandfather of Cyrus the Great. He believes that this "historical" Aži Dahāka—whose name, it will be recalled, gets transformed into the Persian word for "dragon"—became demonized at the beginning of the Achæmenid period by a Zoroastrian priesthood allied with Iran's new Persian ruling class.[13]

The Yaresan resemble other Sufi orders in a number of respects. These include absolute devotion to one's master, performance of mantras (*zekr*), music and dance to induce ecstasy, and the notion of spiritual perfection by stages. What is most distinctive about the Yaresan view is that this process can take many lifetimes, as explained on the group's website:

> It is obvious . . . that such a tremendous task cannot be accomplished in just one lifetime. In His mercy, therefore, God has allotted each soul one thousand lives to achieve the ultimate goal. In His justice, however, this limit is the same for all souls and cannot be extended, although it is possible, and certainly beneficial, to reach the task in less than a thousand lives.[14]

As has been noted in previous chapters, belief in metempsychosis is found in a number of earlier Iranian religious expressions. The recurrence of this and other beliefs has led certain scholars to imagine they represent some kind of unity among a wide range of Iranian sects, overlooking their sometimes dramatic differences. For example, Hamzeh'ee identifies egalitarianism, nativism, millenarianism, and dualism as the central features of the Yaresani religion, remarking that "these were exactly the main features of many Iranian social movements of the past."[15] He includes not just the Kurdish sects under discussion but also others such as the Mazdakites and the Babakites, Isma'ili Shi'ites including the Qarmatians, the Horufis—in short, the full gamut of Iranian heterodox movements. Membrado would remove millenarianism from this list, however, since as she points out, the existing Yaresan texts "are more focused on the fate of the individual soul than on the collective advent of the end of time . . . There exist very few texts on this latter aspect, which doesn't seem to preoccupy the [Yaresan] to a degree that would justify characterizing them as a millenarian movement."[16]

Indeed all these various sects can be shown to have certain shared elements, but to draw from this the conclusion that they all somehow represent expressions of a single "original" Iranian religion would surely be overstating the case. A more cautious approach would admit the widely attested continuity of a broad range of ancient Iranian features, without necessarily attributing to them any kind of meaningful coherence.

## SIMILARITIES BETWEEN THE YEZIDIS AND THE YARESAN

Nevertheless, among all the above-mentioned groups the Yezidis and the Yaresan show the most easily visible common traits. The centrality of the bull sacrifice, which is found in both traditions, has already been mentioned, as has the belief in a divine heptad and in reincarnation (referred to by both groups as "changing the shirt"). Other similarities include the existence of a hereditary priesthood, a three-day fast in mid-winter, and the use of sacred musical instruments to accompany recitations of their holy texts. Both forbid their men to shave their facial hair, possibly a reflection of ancient Iranian notions that dead hair is impure. The two traditions have an institution by which every individual is required to enter into a contract with a "spiritual brother" (or sister) who will testify on their behalf on the Day of Judgment.[17] This notion is also found in the Avesta, and since it involves a contract, recalls Mithraism as well.

The cosmologies of the two sects are remarkably similar, suggesting that they reflect an ancient Iranian origin myth which differs from that found in Zoroastrianism and may predate it. In their shared version, the Creator first makes a pearl which contains all future creation. He then brings forth the divine heptad, with whom he establishes a contract (cf. *miθra*), according to which the principal figure of the heptad is designated as being in charge of the world.

The following excerpts from a Yezidi hymn provide some glimpses of their creation myth:

> O Lord, in the world there was darkness,
> There were neither mice nor snakes.
> You brought it to life for the first time
> Flowers almost burst from it.
>
> . . .
>
> Earth and sky existed
> The world was wide, without foundation;
> There were neither men nor animals.
> You yourself brought order to it.
> In the ocean there was only a pearl
> —It did not progress, it did not progress—
> You quickly gave it a soul,
> You made your own light manifest in it.
>
> . . .
>
> Our Lord, you are merciful
> You brought four elements for us.
>
> . . .
>
> One is Water, one is Light,
> One is Earth, one is Fire.
>
> . . .
>
> Between Adam and the Seven Mysteries there is a strong barrier.
> The Seven Mysteries circled around and came overhead.
> The shape of Adam had remained without movement.
> They said, "O soul, why do you not enter it?"[18]

In the Yaresan version of the creation myth, two of the seven original angels (*haftan*) are transformed into a lion and a bull; the earth is set upon the horns of the bull, the lion stands upon the bull's back, and the heavens upon the back of the lion. The bull, for its part, stands upon the back of a white stone which rests upon the back of a huge fish in the primordial ocean. This cosmological structure, or variations on it, is immediately recognizable to anyone with a basic knowledge of Iranian mythology. Indeed, to this day there is a folkloric notion among Iranians that at the precise instant of the New Year (*tahvīl-e sāl*), the bull tosses the world from one horn to the other and the fish wiggles. In this way popular culture explains the frequency of springtime earthquakes in Iran.

The primordial sacrifice of a bull, which follows upon the process of creation, is another basic feature of the common Iranian mythology. But in contrast to Zoroastrianism, which attributes this act to the evil deity, Ahriman, both the Yezidis and the Yaresan see it as a positive occurrence because it makes possible the generation of subsequent life. Since in the Vedic creation story this primordial sacrifice is also seen as beneficial, Kreyenbroek proposes that the Zoroastrian version must be a later innovation, with Mithra having been the original sacrificer.[19] Mehrdad Bahar (who, as noted above, sees the Kurdish sects as being essentially Mithraic in character) reaches a similar conclusion.[20] The Yaresan refer to their sacrifices as "making green"; that is, ensuring fertility and regeneration.

The Yezidis and the Yaresan each consider themselves to be uniquely privileged within creation. The Yezidis see themselves as being descended from Adam, with the rest of humanity descending, disgustingly, from Eve. The Yaresan consider that they are created from "yellow soil," in contrast to other races, destined for damnation, which are made from black. Interestingly, while the Yaresan today refer to the first human couple as Adam and Eve, formerly they used the Zoroastrian names Mašyā and Mašyānē.[21]

The two groups share a dualistic view of the cosmos which is closer to Zurvanism than Zoroastrianism, in that they see good and evil as coming from the same source. Both consider evil to be a necessary counterpoint to good, and refrain from insulting Satan who is conceptualized as the Peacock Angel, Malak Tāvus.

Recent years have provided an additional, unfortunate parallel between these two Kurdish sects in the form of violent persecutions at the hands of their Muslim neighbors. For the Yaresan in Iran this has come mainly from government agents, while for the Yezidis in Iraq the perpetrators have mostly been Sunni extremists. In Iran many Yaresan have been imprisoned by the authorities on various pretexts, while in Iraq the Yezidis have been the subject of mass murders.

In both countries these persecutions have involved the destruction of holy sites.

Given the theory outlined above, according to which the Yezidis and the Yaresan can be seen as preserving a version of Iranian religion that predates Zoroastrianism and may have been historically hostile to it, it is interesting that for the past several decades a number of Yezidis have sought to identify themselves as Zoroastrian. Contacts have been established with Indian Parsis, and in France and Germany there are associations of "Yezidi-Zoroastrians." Predictably, conservative Parsis have reacted with hostility to these developments.[22]

# Part 5

# THE IMPACT
# OF MODERNITY

# 17

## The Bábí Movement
## and the Bahá'í Faith

The eighteenth century in Iran was a tumultuous period. In 1722 the decadent Safavid regime fell to an army of Sunni Afghans. Authority over the workings of society was tenuously balanced between successive governments—the last Safavids, then the Afshars, then the Zand dynasty of Shiraz, and finally the Qajars from 1785—and various religious leaders and their followings. Most powerful were the Shi'i *'ulemā'*, the legal scholars, who had virtually taken over control of Iranian society by the late Safavid period.

As mentioned in Chapter 14, at this time the *'ulemā'* were loosely divided between those who derived law from a process of reasoning (*ejtehād*—the so-called *usūlī* clergy) and those who relied exclusively on the Qur'an, the hadiths, and the sayings of the Twelve Imams (the *axbārīs*). With the weakening and instability of government, however, came a resurgence of charismatic leadership from among the Sufi brotherhoods, particularly the Ne'matollahis and the Nurbakhshis, whose esoteric teachings held sway over large numbers of the general population. At the same time, many Iranians continued to adhere more or less secretly to heterodox sects, especially in rural areas. One of the most significant of these was the Yaresan (Ahl-e Haqq) in the Kurdish regions.

By the end of the eighteenth century many of the existing trends in Iranian religious thought had been synthesized in the so-called "Shaykhi" (*šayxī*) school of Shaykh Ahmad Ahsa'i (1756–1825), who drew his vision variously from illuminationist philosophy, Akhbari traditionism, and Isma'ili esotericism. The Shaykhi school was similar to Sufism in its focus on charismatic leadership, but differed in its teachings and use of sources. Significant numbers of the clergy became sympathetic to the Shaykhi approach, which privileged the special insight of the movement's leader over Usuli-type legalism. The Usuli class, in response, sought to discredit the Shaykhis (and the Sufis, for that matter) as heretics.

Among its many innovations, the Shaykhi eschatology proposed a radical interpretation of the Islamic notion of resurrection. Ahsa'i taught that after death the body perishes, while the soul goes to a purificatory "interworld" (*barzax*) called Hurqalya,[1] ultimately to be reunited with its original celestial body, cleansed of all earthly tarnish. However, those possessing transcendent insight (that is, dreams and visions) could reach this intermediate zone between heaven and earth while still alive. Transcendence to the intermediary world of Hurqalya would give access to the guidance of the Hidden Imam. Shaykh Ahsa'i himself, naturally, was considered by his followers to possess this ability, and thus to have privileged access to the authoritative teaching of the Hidden Imam.

Considered by his disciples to be "the Perfect Shi'ite"—a notion dating back to the Sixth Imam, Ja'far, and similar in some ways to the "Perfect Man" of the Sufis—Shaykh Ahsa'i was seen as the "gate" (*bāb*) between the earthly sphere and the visionary world of the Imam. As such, Shaykh Ahsa'i could claim a more direct authority in Twelver Shi'ite society than that of the legal scholars, whose connections with the Hidden Imam relied on chains of transmission more than a thousand years old. The fact that a millennium had now passed since the occultation of the Twelfth Imam heightened expectations of his return. Messianic speculations were rife among many Iranian Shi'ite sects of the time, including the followers of Shaykh Ahsa'i. Twelver Shi'ism taught that the return of the Hidden Imam as the *Mahdī* (Messiah) would herald the final victory over the forces of evil, the restoration of true Shi'ism, and ultimately the Resurrection and the Day of Judgment. A fervent longing for this event was central to the Twelver Shi'ite ethos.

While government officials occasionally sought support from charismatic spiritual leaders, on the whole they preferred to ally themselves with the Usuli scholars. As the rationalist Usuli faction was increasingly able to marginalize the traditionist Akhbari jurists, they came to see Sufi and Shaykhi teachers as their main rivals for authority. The attempts by the Usulis to de-legitimize and crush the latter groups escalated throughout the early Qajar period, culminating in the violent, government-supported repression of the recently emerged Babi movement in the 1840s.

## THE BÁBÍ MOVEMENT

The Qajar regime was characterized throughout much of its century-and-a-half of rule by its general lack of authority throughout much of the country and insecurity in the face of numerous domestic and external threats. Arguably the greatest internal disruption in nineteenth-century

Iran was a short-lived but, for the Qajars, highly traumatic challenge known as the Bábí movement from 1844–1852.

The focus of this challenge to the powers that be—that is, the intertwined temporal authority of the Qajar elites and the spiritual authority of the Usuli *'ulemā'*—was a prophetic figure by the name of Seyyed Ali Mohammad, a young merchant of Shiraz, known to his followers as the Báb. As we have seen, the notion of one special person serving as "gate" (*bāb*) to the Hidden Imam had a long history in Twelver Shi'ism, but claims about the status of Seyyed Ali Mohammad did not end there. Eventually he would say he was the promised Mahdi himself, abrogating Islamic law altogether, as a symbol of passage into a new era.

Seyyed Ali Mohammad was born in 1819 into a merchant (*bāzārī*) family, and showed a strong interest in religion from an early age. At twenty he travelled to the holy Shi'ite city of Karbala in Iraq (the site of Imam Husayn's martyrdom in 680), where he made the acquaintance of local Shaykhis and attended a few of the classes held by Shaykh Ahsa'i's successor, Seyyed Kazem of Rasht. Many of the Shaykhis (including Seyyed Kazem himself) were deeply impressed by the piety and insight of the young merchant. After a year or less he returned to Shiraz, but when Seyyed Kazem died in 1844 without designating a successor a number of important Shaykhis eventually came to believe that Seyyed Ali Mohammad, despite his lack of formal legal training, was the new *bāb*, the one person alive with direct access to the Hidden Imam. The timing was significant: by 1844 it had been one thousand lunar years since the disappearance of the Twelfth Imam.

The Báb soon intimated to his disciples that his status was greater than that of his predecessors. His teachings, which he began to write down as sacred books, constituted nothing less than divine revelation. (Orthodox Muslims believed there would be no revelation subsequent to the Qur'an, and that Muhammad had been the "Seal of the Prophets.") The Báb and his followers spread the word throughout Iran and the Shi'ite regions of Iraq that the return of the Twelfth Imam as the promised Mahdi was imminent. They staged an abortive rally in Karbala in 1845 on behalf of the hoped-for Mahdi, and later the same year the Báb was briefly arrested for blasphemy in his hometown of Shiraz. Apparently among his closer disciples the Báb had begun to claim that in fact he himself was the long-awaited one.

In Twelver Shi'ite society such a claim had enormous implications. In the absence of the Hidden Imam, believers were taught to accommodate themselves to the temporal powers that be, and follow the guidance of the *'ulemā'* who were acting as the Imam's vice-regents. With the return of the Imam, both the existing secular and spiritual authorities would become obsolete. It comes as little surprise that as the Báb's following grew, his movement was met with harsh repression from the Usuli clergy who began to issue *fatwa*s (legal opinions) to the effect that the Báb was an apostate and thus eligible for the death penalty. The Qajar government was somewhat slower to perceive the threat, at first seeing the Báb as simply mentally unbalanced.

In the summer of 1848 the authorities acceded to the demands of the *'ulemā'* and the Báb was tried in Tabriz for blasphemy. During the course of this trial the Báb made public his claim that he was the Mahdi. In the wake of the Báb's trial Babi missionaries throughout Iran were increasingly harassed and beaten by the public, egged on by the *'ulemā'*.

Although a large proportion of the Báb's early disciples came from within the Shaykhi movement, many prominent Shaykhis rejected his claims and began to write refutations of his teachings. The Báb responded by branding his leading Shaykhi opponent as the "Tree of Negation" and the "Embodiment of Hell-Fire."[2] Meanwhile, a remarkable Iranian woman by the name of Fatemeh Begum Baraghani (1814–1852), who was also known by the epithets Táhirih ("the Immaculate One") and Qurratul-'Ayn ("Solace of the Eyes"—a title she had received from Seyyed Kazem) had become the leading champion of the Báb's cause in the holy city of Karbala in Iraq. Her fervent support of the Báb polarized that country's Shaykhi community. In 1847 Qurratul-'Ayn was deported by Iraq's Ottoman rulers and returned to Iran where she pursued her activities. Bábí missionaries continued to win converts, largely through tapping into existing networks of Shaykhi clergy and members of the merchant class (the *bāzārī*s) with whom they had close ties.

During the summer of 1848, while the Báb was undergoing his trial and imprisonment in Azerbaijan, a large group of his followers gathered in a village called Badasht in northern Iran to discuss how he might be liberated. Qurratul-'Ayn spoke at the meeting, and shocked the audience by removing her veil. Though some contemporary commentators have seen this as a feminist gesture, more likely it was meant to symbolize the Báb's abrogation of Islamic law. In any case the Badasht event brought together some of the most radical elements from within the Bábí movement, and aroused the concern of the government and the *'ulemā'* alike. Although it is impossible to know how many Iranians were followers of the Báb, it is possible they numbered as much as 100,000—perhaps two and a half percent of the country's settled population.[3] It was no longer possible for the powers that be to take this movement lightly.

In the wake of the Báb's trial and the conference at Badasht, the revolutionary fervor of some Bábís was such that they began a march from Mashhad in eastern Iran, aiming to reach Azerbaijan and free the Báb so that his mission might be fulfilled. They were halted by a mob along the way, however, and after a brief skirmish the Bábís took refuge in a shrine (dedicated to one Shaykh Tabarsi and named after him). They fortified the shrine and holed up for a seven-month siege until they were finally tricked into surrendering and then massacred. The Tabarsi incident established once and for all the conviction in the minds of the Qajar elites that the Bábís were a dangerous insurrectionary movement, not to be tolerated.

Over the next year and a half groups of Bábís engaged in armed struggle against the establishment in several parts of the country, most notably in the towns of Yazd, Zanjan and Nayriz. Finally the government ordered the execution of the Báb, hoping to end the uprisings. In July 1850 the Báb was brought before a firing squad in Tabriz. After the dust cleared from the first volley, the Báb and a condemned companion were seen to have vanished. They turned up after a quick search of the premises— the shots had missed and severed the ropes which held them—and they were then definitively executed. But it would take another two years for the Qajar government to crush the movement once and for all.

After a botched attempt to assassinate the Qajar ruler Naser al-din Shah in 1852, for which the Bábís were blamed and thus subjected to still harsher reprisals, the movement went largely underground. Most of their leaders, including Qurratul-'Ayn, had been killed. Those Bábís who survived adopted the age-old Shi'ite practice of *taqiyya*, dissimulation of one's true beliefs to ensure the survival of the religious community.

### Bábí Beliefs

The teachings of the Báb offered radical reinterpretations of notions drawn from the familiar Iranian and Islamic religious pools. As in mainstream Islam he taught that revelation was progressive, but contrary to the orthodox Islamic position that the Qur'an represented the culmination of all prior revelations, the Báb argued that divine inspiration is ongoing and comes in different guises to meet the needs of different ages. The heart of the Báb's teachings, which he wrote in both Arabic and Persian, was contained in books called the *Qayyúm al-Asmá'* ("The Resurrection of [Holy] Names") and the *Bayán* ("The Exposition"). In all the Báb claimed to have received over a million verses of revelation.

In Bábí thought the concept of Resurrection (*qiyāmat*), which is understood in Zoroastrianism and Islam to be something that will occur after death, was revised to mean something that had begun on earth with the Báb's revelation. Salvation—perceived as inclusion in a "community of light"—would be attained by recognizing the Báb as God's messenger and working to disseminate his message. Redemption was thus an ongoing process undertaken by the individual, rather than a single cosmic future event. The temporal authority of the Twelver

Shi'ite clergy, based as it was on their claim to represent the Hidden Imam until his eventual reappearance, was thereby rendered obsolete.

Though the Báb eventually called for the abrogation of Islamic law, at first he taught his followers to adhere to the *sharī'a*, with some additional practices such as a 19-day fast and special prayers. (He also enjoined them to abstain from smoking, by then an almost universal habit, at least among Iranian men.) After his imprisonment and declaration of Mahdihood, however, the Báb replaced the *sharī'a* with a new set of laws which were contained in the *Bayán*. Ritual prayers were subordinated to individual ones, and the emphasis on ritual purity—which was nothing less than an obsession in legalistic Shi'ism—was superseded by spiritual purity. The obligatory pilgrimage to Mecca was replaced by a pilgrimage to the Báb's home in Shiraz. The traditional Shi'ite notions of martyrdom and holy war were reinterpreted in Bábí terms.

The Báb furthermore called his followers to avoid mixing or intermarrying with non-Bábís, and to shun non-Bábí books and learning. He discouraged polygamy and made divorce more difficult. In business dealings, he allowed the charging of interest (forbidden under the *sharī'a*), and he established a new calendar based on cycles of nineteen. The Báb promulgated a system of occultic protections, requiring his followers to make and carry special talismans. Bábís were to eschew the colour black, not even writing with black ink, as this colour was associated with the Abbasids who had persecuted the Shi'i Imams.

The new world envisioned by the Báb did not come about, and the efforts of his followers to create it ended in bloody tragedy. In light of the Báb's failure to establish a new set of norms in Iranian society, perhaps the greatest legacy of his teaching is his doctrine of expecting "he whom God will make manifest," setting the stage for a subsequent prophet even greater than himself. In the minds of the majority of surviving Bábís, that figure was soon to appear.

## THE EMERGENCE OF THE BAHÁ'Í FAITH

With their leader gone, the disorganized remnants of the Báb's followers began to look for a successor to lead the community. Some twenty-five Bábís came forward to claim leadership of the Babi movement. Among them two half-brothers emerged: Mirza Yahya Nuri (1831–1912), known as Subh-i-Azal ("Morning of Eternity") and Mirza Hossein 'Ali Nuri (1817–92), called Bahá'u'lláh ("Glory of God").

The Nuri brothers were, somewhat atypically among followers of the Báb, from a noble landowning family with ties to the Qajar government. Their social status may have played a role in earning them the respect of their fellow Bábís, and also perhaps helped protect them from government reprisals during the persecutions of 1848–1852.

(At the height of the Bábí disruptions the Qajar prime minister, Amir Kabir, actually offered Mirza Hossein 'Ali a government position in hopes of co-opting his influence.) Though information on the Bábís in the years after the crushing of the movement is scarce, it appears that Mirza Yahya had the largest following among the many contenders for leadership. Indeed it was widely considered that the Báb himself had appointed him as his successor, though some claimed that this was merely a diversionary move to protect the true designate, Mirza Yahya's elder half-brother Mirza Hossein 'Ali.

During this obscure time the movement seems to have split between followers of Subh-i-Azal (that is, Mirza Yahya) and a number of others, including his brother Bahá'u'lláh (Mirza Hossein 'Ali). The government of Iran eventually ordered that Bahá'u'lláh must leave Iran and banished him to Iraq. Subh-i-Azal, mostly keeping a low profile, decided to join Bahá'u'lláh in Iraq two months later. Bahá'u'lláh at this time took on a more public role of teaching and leadership. Tensions arose between the two as Bahá'u'lláh increasingly became the focus of attention for Bábí devotees. By 1866, when Bahá'u'lláh formally advanced the claim that he was the promised one "whom God shall make manifest," his supporters were by far the majority. The smaller Azalí faction remained ideologically close to the original Bábí teachings, whereas Bahá'u'lláh's approach had changed dramatically. In 1868 Subh-i-Azal was banished to Famagusta in Cyprus, where his entourage consisted mainly of his own relatives;[4] a few thousand followers remained in Iran.

Like the Báb, Bahá'u'lláh was incredibly prolific in his writings. It was said that he received as many as one thousand verses of revelation in an hour. A few of his works, such as the *Ode to the Dove* and the *Seven Valleys*, were Sufi-sounding and ecstatic in nature, describing his own religious experiences in heavily symbolic language, while others, like the *Book of Certitude,* are about religious and theological proofs, and *The Hidden Words* is a collection of moral and spiritual teachings.

Perhaps the most significant departure from the Bábí precedent was Bahá'u'lláh's rejection of militancy. His quietistic approach combined with his increasing popularity led some in both the Ottoman and Qajar governments to feel it would be worthwhile to cultivate positive relations with him and his followers. Bahá'u'lláh, however, resisted any politicization of his movement. Even so, his charismatic appeal and growing following brought hostility from the *'ulemā'*, who saw their monopoly on religious authority once again being threatened. In 1863, at the instigation of the Iranian government, Bahá'u'lláh was removed from Baghdad by the Ottomans and transferred to the capital, Istanbul. Surrounded by an adoring entourage of devotees, Bahá'u'lláh offended Ottoman officials by refusing to associate with them, which led to a second exile to Edirne (Adrianople) on the western border of the empire.

The activities of Bahá'u'lláh's followers in Edirne (which likely included attempts to convert local Muslims) and the constant coming and going of pilgrims from Iran did nothing to ease the discomfort of the Ottoman authorities. In 1868 they relocated him once again, this time to the decrepit port of Akka (Akko or Acre) on the Mediterranean coast of Palestine, where he spent the rest of his life. He died in 1892, and his shrine there contains a beautiful garden in the Persian style which is maintained to this day by Bahá'í volunteers from around the world.

### Bahá'u'lláh's Teachings

As in Shaykhi and Bábí teaching, the Bahá'í belief system posits a remote, unknowable God who can be accessed only through the medium of his human manifestations. Bahá'u'lláh was believed by his followers to be merely the most recent in a succession of divine manifestations which included Zoroaster, Abraham, Moses, Jesus, Muhammad, and the Báb, among others. Following a transformative rather than a strictly linear cosmology, Bahá'ís fully expect that other such manifestations will continue to appear in the future. Bahá'u'lláh had a great respect for Christianity and the Bible, which he quoted often in his own writings. Just as he claimed to be the one "whom God will make manifest" to the Bábís, to Christians he implied that he represented the awaited return of Christ, to the Jews he claimed to be the Messiah, and to the Zoroastrians the Saošyant. (His great-grandson, Shoghi Effendi, later claimed that Bahá'u'lláh was an avatar of the Hindu god Krishna.) Not since Mani had a major Iranian spiritual leader done so much to expand the pool of religious ideas and symbols.

The immediate millenarian impulse in Shaykhi and Bábí thought was refocused in the Bahá'í faith to a more distant future, the goal of restoring society through the rule of the Imam being replaced with the notion of a "Most Great Peace." Whereas the former movements had focused on the Shi'ite world of Iran, Bahá'u'lláh's vision encompassed the entire world. All humans, Bahá'u'lláh taught, are of the same essence and substance. The world, in his view, was "but one country, and mankind its citizens." As he put it to the English Iranist E. G. Browne:

> That all nations should become one in faith and all men as brothers; that the bonds of affection and unity between the sons of men should be strengthened; that diversity of religion should cease, and differences of race be annulled—what harm is there in this? . . . Yet so it shall be; these fruitless strifes, these ruinous wars shall pass away, and the "Most Great Peace" shall come . . . Do not you in Europe need this also? Is not this that which Christ foretold? . . . Yet do we see your kings and rulers lavishing their

> treasures more freely on means for the destruction of the human
> race than on that which would conduce to the happiness of
> mankind . . . These strifes and this bloodshed and discord must
> cease, and all men be as one kindred and one family . . . Let not
> a man glory in this, that he loves his country; let him rather glory
> in this, that he loves his kind.[5]

As a step toward fulfilling this universalist vision, Bahá'u'lláh wrote letters to various world leaders (including the Ottoman Sultan, the Shah of Iran, the Tsar of Russia, and the Queen of Great Britain, among others) urging them to meet and set down rules for negotiation among what is called today "the international community." In fact, the details of Bahá'u'lláh's proposal bear a remarkable resemblance to what would come into being in the mid-twentieth century as the United Nations. Interestingly, however, in his writings Bahá'u'lláh does not challenge the institution of monarchy as such; indeed, he idealizes it in the ancient Iranian terms of the king as "Shadow of God on Earth."

Another radical feature of Bahá'í teaching, anticipated perhaps in Bábism, was a reduction in gender inequality that was highly dramatic in the context of patriarchal Iranian society. To some extent this may have been an echo of women's emancipatory movements in Europe, which were reported by Iranian travelers and in the Iranian media which were read by the literate classes. Many aristocratic, and even royal, Iranian women, though often housebound, engaged in written correspondence with Bahá'u'lláh. In his *Most Holy Book* (*Kitáb-i-Aqdas*), Bahá'u'lláh called for the education of girls as well as boys, and urged monogamous marriages. Elsewhere he wrote that "the Servants of God and His handmaidens are regarded as on the same plane,"[6] and "Verily, in the eyes of Bahá women are the same as men. All are God's creation, which He created in his likeness, that is, they are manifestations of his names and attributes."[7] Bahá'u'lláh suggests that future prophets ("manifestations of God," in Bahá'í terms) could be female:

> Know thou moreover that in the Day of Revelation were He to
> pronounce one of the [female believers] to be the manifestation
> of all His excellent titles, unto no one is given the right to utter
> why or wherefore, and should one do so he would be regarded as
> an unbeliever in God and numbered with such as have repudiated
> His truth.[8]

Elsewhere, however, Bahá'u'lláh maintained a degree of gender imbalance. One example is in his treatment of inheritance law. Clearly the reversal of centuries of patriarchy would not occur overnight, but there is a distinct trend in this direction throughout the subsequent development of Bahá'í thought.

Bahá'u'lláh taught that the primary earthly task of all Bahá'ís was to work toward the Most Great Peace, when a majority of the world would have embraced the Bahá'í faith and Bahá'í laws could be implemented. Since this could only be done by actively participating in society, asceticism was shunned. Begging was likewise forbidden, as was giving to beggars. (The needs of poor Bahá'ís would be taken care of through donations to the House of Justice, the central Bahá'í institution.) In a radical departure from the revolutionary politics of the Bábís, Bahá'ís were urged to remain loyal to whatever government they lived under. They were to obey the laws of their society, and associate freely with people of all races and religions. Rather than trying to establish a new religious law by force, Bahá'ís were urged to live exemplary lives that would attract people to the faith.

In terms of religious law, Bahá'u'lláh made significant changes to that promulgated by the Báb. Most notably, he forbade the waging of religious war (*jihād*) that had characterized the Bábí movement, and he eliminated the Bábí (and Shi'i) preoccupation with ritual impurity. He also lifted the Islamic ban on music and the shunning of contact with non-Bábís. At the same time Bahá'u'lláh retained certain aspects of Bábí teaching, such as according holy significance to the number nineteen and prohibiting the Islamic congregational prayer; he also kept the Bábí solar calendar, nineteen months of nineteen days each. Many Bahá'í rituals, like their Bábí equivalents, are adaptations of those inherited from Shi'ism; this is particularly evident in Bahá'í prayers, fasting and pilgrimage.[9]

Bahá'ís should recite a formal prayer either once or three times in a day, and as in Islam the ritual prayer is preceded by an ablution. Bahá'ís pray facing a *qibla*, but this is the Shrine of Bahá'u'lláh near Akko in Israel, not Mecca. As in Islam, the Bahá'í calendar includes a month of daylight fasting, though the month (*Ala*) consists of nineteen days, not thirty. In another parallel, dispensations are made for the elderly, the ill, travellers, or women who are menstruating, pregnant, or nursing. An echo of the Islamic alms tax (*zakāt*) can be seen in the Bahá'í tithe known as *huququ'llah* (God's due"), defined as nineteen percent of one's annual "surplus" income. Similar to the Islamic *hajj*, Bahá'ís are encouraged to make a pilgrimage to their holy sites in and around Haifa, Israel. (Formerly the major pilgrimage sites were the Báb's house in Shiraz and Bahá'u'lláh's in Baghdad, but the latter was taken over by Shi'ite authorities in 1922 and the former was demolished during the Iranian revolution in 1979.)

Bahá'í temples, called Houses of Worship (or *mashriqu'l-adhkar*, "Dawning-place of the Remembrance [of God])," are meant to fulfill social and educational as well as religious functions, similar to the mosque for Muslims.[10] However, to date there are only seven of them in the world, though another, in Santiago, Chile, is currently under construction and many more are planned. (The first Bahá'í House of Worship, in Ashgabat, Turkmenistan, was built in 1908 but seized by the Soviet government twenty years later; it was eventually demolished in 1963 following an earthquake.) Bahá'í temples are nine-sided, with seats facing the Shrine of Bahá'u'lláh, though the architecture of each is intended to reflect local cultural traditions. The Bahá'í House of Worship in New Delhi, India, for example, is in the form of a nine-sided lotus flower.

Bahá'ís recognize nine major holy days on which they are not allowed to work: Naw-Ruz (Nō rūz, the Iranian New Year as marked by the vernal equinox), the first, ninth and twelfth of Ridvan (a twelve-day commemoration of Bahá'u'lláh's declaration of prophethood), the Declaration of the Báb, and the birth and death dates of the Báb and Bahá'u'lláh. Communal gatherings called "nineteen-day feasts" (which are actually only one day) are held on the first of each month of the Bahá'í calendar, usually in a private home.

### The Bahá'í Community in Iran and Beyond

With an established center and charismatic leader (albeit living outside Iran) during the latter part of the nineteenth century, the Bahá'í mission in Iran brought large numbers of converts into the fold. Christian missionaries from Europe, who were becoming active in Iran at the same time, jealously noted the rapid spread of the Bahá'í faith. Some even speculated that it would one day displace Islam as Iran's official religion. To the numbers of Muslim converts were added many from Iran's Jewish and Zoroastrian communities.

Predictably, Bahá'í successes brought a backlash from the country's established Shi'ite clergy and persecutions once again began to rise, most notably in Esfahan. For Jewish and Zoroastrian converts, the question arises why so many individuals chose to leave these persecuted faiths for one that was even more persecuted.[11] Fereydun Vahman has suggested that such conversions were primarily motivated by "the search for modernity and the need to come to terms with the new age."[12]

Bahá'u'lláh's son and eventual successor, 'Abdu'l-Bahá (1844–1921), set up an infrastructure for managing the expanding Bahá'í communities worldwide. This included the establishment of local "spiritual assemblies" and the founding of Bahá'í schools, in Iran as in other nations where Bahá'ís lived. 'Abdu'l-Bahá spelled out his vision of political reform and internationalism in his 1875 work *The Secret of Divine Civilization*, nominally addressed to the Shah of Iran. The tone of this "letter to the king" from an exiled religious figure might strike some readers as presumptuous, yet, remarkably, one of its main features which was 'Abdu'l-Bahá's call to establish a "union of nations," was actually realized during the twentieth century with the founding of the League of Nations and later the U.N.

During the period of 'Abdu'l-Bahá's leadership many Iranian Bahá'ís travelled to other countries as "pioneers," charged with attracting people to the religion more through the example of their lifestyles than through direct proselytization. Often, as in Egypt, Turkey, Russian-held Central Asia, British India, and Burma, they succeeded in converting significant numbers from among expatriate Iranian merchant communities. The most thriving Bahá'í community was that of Ashgabat (in what is now Turkmenistan), which became the site of the first Bahá'í House of Worship.

The Bahá'í Faith was brought to the United States by a Syro-Egyptian convert named Ibrahim George Kheiralla in 1894. Establishing himself in Chicago, by 1900 Kheiralla had won some two thousand American converts. After a rupture between Kheiralla and 'Abdu'l-Bahá in Akka, most American Bahá'ís gave their allegiance to the latter, who himself visited the United States in 1912. American Bahá'ís launched missionary efforts to Europe and the Pacific, and before long the Bahá'í Faith could no longer be considered primarily an Iranian religion.

Bahá'í beliefs and social organization were institutionalized under the leadership of 'Abdu'l-Bahá's Oxford-educated grandson, Shoghi Effendi (1897–1957). The Bahá'í faith today claims upwards of five million adherents of all races and cultural backgrounds, and Bahá'í Houses of Worship have been built on every continent except Antarctica. Having no clergy, Bahá'í communities function on three levels of elected representation: local, national, and through the Universal House of Justice which is located on the slopes of Mount Carmel in Haifa, Israel.

In Iran Bahá'ís maintained their existence as the country's largest non-Muslim community throughout the late Qajar and Pahlavi periods up to the revolution of 1979. Under Shah Mohammad Reza, who was installed on the throne by the British after they exiled his father Reza Shah to South Africa in 1941, Iran's Bahá'ís were tolerated by the government but were often harassed by fanatical Shi'ite elements, especially after the founding of the anti-Bahá'í Imam of the Age Society (*anjoman-e emām-e zamān*, later renamed the Hojjatieh Society) in 1953. Two years later anti- Bahá'í pogroms instigated by members of the *'ulemā'* and carried out with the collusion of the military resulted in the destruction of the dome of the Bahá'í administrative center, Hazirat al-Quds, in Tehran, the firing of many Bahá'ís from their jobs, and the confiscation of Bahá'í properties.[13] Lobbying efforts by the IAS resulted in a law making it illegal to be a Bahá'í, but this was later rescinded.

In fact, the Shah's attitude toward Bahá'ís was ambivalent. While he sometimes sacrificed their interests in an attempt to appease the militant Shi'i clergy whom he feared, he appears to have found their modern outlook and training useful, and during the 1960s and 1970s many Bahá'ís found their way into important positions in industry and academia. The Shah's personal physician, 'Abd al-Karim Ayadi, was a Bahá'í; he also held the rank of general in the army. These factors led Muslims to accuse the Pahlavi government of exercising favoritism toward the Bahá'ís, but more likely Bahá'í successes were due to their emphasis on education, which made them candidates for the kinds of positions that were opening up through the Shah's modernization programs.

While the Bahá'í community in much of the world has increased steadily since the beginning of the twentieth century, in Iran, as in other Muslim countries, their numbers have remained static or declined. Presumably the Islamic ban on apostasy has played some role in this, as well as prejudice stemming from the Bahá'í Faith's origins in an Islamic cultural context. (All Bahá'í activities were banned in Egypt in 1960, and in Iraq in 1970.) With the advent of an Islamic government from 1979 onwards, persecution of Bahá'ís once again became a matter of official policy.

Though reliable figures are currently impossible to obtain, Bahá'ís likely remain Iran's largest unambiguously non-Muslim minority. An educated guess would put their numbers at somewhere around three hundred thousand, but the true figure could well be much more or much less. Since the revolution many Iranian Bahá'ís have emigrated to other countries, especially the United States, and the trend continues. Since 1983 Bahá'ís in Iran have been officially prohibited from assembling, forming administrative bodies, or maintaining contacts with Bahá'ís in other countries, making them vulnerable to prosecution when they do so.

Since the outset of the revolution Bahá'ís have been seen as archetypes of infidelity, suspected of turning Muslims from their faith and of acting as agents for foreign powers. As an unrecognized religious minority they are without legal protection. They have been fired from their jobs and denied access to higher education. Bahá'í assets, including land, holy sites, and cemeteries have been seized by the government. Revolutionary Guards destroyed the house of the Báb in Shiraz in 1979. The following year all nine members of the Bahá'í National Spiritual Assembly of Iran were arrested and presumably executed in secret. A year later eight of their nine successors were executed as well, accused of being spies. During the first five years of the revolution Amnesty International, the United Nations, and other organizations documented over two hundred executions of Bahá'ís in Iran.

As late as 1998 a Bahá'í was executed on the charge of having converted a Muslim, and in 2000 a Bahá'í cemetery in Abadeh was bulldozed. In 2002 the municipality of Tehran granted a small parcel of land to local Bahá'ís to use for burials, but they are not allowed to perform funerals there or to put up individual grave markers. In cases where Bahá'ís are victims of murder or manslaughter, their relatives are not eligible for compensation.

During the presidency of Mohammad Khatami (1997–2005) the drastic strictures on Bahá'ís were relieved somewhat, through indirect means. For example, the elimination in 2000 of the requirement to state one's religious affiliation on marriage forms allowed for the de facto registration of Bahá'í marriages. Two Bahá'ís arrested in 1998 and originally condemned to death were later released from prison. Following the election of Mahmud Ahmadinejad in 2005, however, pressure on Iran's Bahá'ís once again began to increase.

Apart from arrests and executions perhaps the major issue attracting world attention to the plight of Bahá'ís in Iran has been their exclusion from higher education. Since 1979 Bahá'ís have not been allowed to attend or teach at Iran's universities. They have coped with this by forming an underground educational system of their own, the Bahá'í Institute of Higher Education (BIHE), which produces students of sufficient quality that their undergraduate "degrees" have been accepted as a basis for admission to some graduate programs in the West. In 2011 several former BIHE graduates who had returned to teach in Iran after receiving higher degrees in Canada were arrested for "teaching without qualifications."

The position of the present Iranian government towards the Bahá'í Faith strikes many as a prime example of religious intolerance. While the authorities acknowledge the Bahá'ís' existence, they are not described as a religious group at all but rather as an underground political movement bent on selling out the country's sovereignty. Official references to the Bahá'í Faith claim that it is an organization founded by the British in the nineteenth century as part of the latter's colonial project, aimed at the eventual takeover of Iran by foreign interests. In addition, because the shrine of Bahá'u'lláh and the Universal House of Justice happen to be located in what is now the state of Israel (though they predate Israel's existence as a state), Bahá'ís are readily accused of acting as agents of Zionism. Any recognition of the Bábí movement having arisen from within messianic Shi'ism is entirely absent, and the explicit Bahá'í tenet of political non-involvement is ignored. The extreme hostility with which Iran's government regards Bahá'ís today makes it very difficult for anyone living within the country to obtain an accurate understanding of the Bahá'í religion or its history.

On the other hand, while Iran's treatment of Bahá'ís may well seem reprehensible from a human rights point of view, it is not as irrational as it might appear to outsiders insofar as it follows a consistent internal logic. The basic issue is that given its origins within Twelve Shi'ism there is simply no place for the Bahá'í Faith within the framework of Islamic law, which does not admit the category of post-Islamic revelation. As H. E. Chehabi notes, it is "as impossible for a Muslim believer to admit the divine mission of Bahá'u'lláh, as it is for a Jew to recognize Jesus Christ as the Messiah, or for a Christian to concede that Mānī or Muhammad were the recipients of divine revelations that superseded the message of Christ."[14] From the standpoint of the *sharī'a*, Muslim converts to the Bahá'í Faith are apostates, while converts from Iran's other religions are seen as having left a recognized religion for an unrecognized one.

In legal terms, the status of Bahá'ís in an Islamic society is akin to that of the first generations of Christians living under Roman rule, where juridically speaking the latter were held to be merely wayward Jews. Judaism was a recognized category within the Roman legal system, whereas Christianity, at least until Emperor Constantine's edict of 313, was not; this lack of legal status facilitated their persecution. (It may also be noted in passing that the violent suppression of unauthorized religious sects is not unknown in many Western countries today.)

To make matters worse, in the Iranian context the pacifist Bahá'ís are generally conflated with the revolutionary-minded Bábís who preceded them, retaining by association an unwarranted aura of political threat.[15] In short, unless an Islamic figure possessing the status of a Constantine should somehow come along and decree the Bahá'í Faith to be a legitimate religious tradition, the legal status of Bahá'ís in Iran and other Muslim countries is likely to remain precarious.

### The Importance of Iranian Culture for Bahá'ís

The Bahá'í Faith today is truly global, with adherents in over two hundred countries around the world. Of its estimated five million members probably less than ten percent are ethnic Iranians, and in keeping with their universalist ideology Bahá'ís formally consider their religion not to be tied to or to privilege any one ethnicity. Nevertheless, Bahá'ís are mindful of their religion's origins in Iran, which they call "the Cradle of the Cause of God" (*mahd-i-amrulláh*), and they accordingly hold a deep respect for Iranian culture and the Persian language. Formalized Iranian politeness (*ta'rof*) is highly valued.[16] Iran remains a fabled land for many Bahá'ís, and interest in learning Persian is high. The Bahá'í calendar begins with the Iranian New Year, Nō rūz, which they celebrate as a religious holiday. Persian songs and Iranian food are often featured at Bahá'í gatherings.

While English is the official language of the Bahá'í Faith worldwide, at the Bahá'í World Center it shares that status with Persian. Interestingly, however, Persian and Arabic, the languages in which the Bahá'í sacred texts were composed, do not hold the primordial status accorded by Muslims to the Arabic of the Qur'an. In fact, it is from the English translations endorsed by the Universal House of Justice that translations into most other languages are made.[17]

Physical signs of Iranian influence can be found in the domes and Persian inscriptions of Bahá'í temples, and in the architecture and magnificent gardens of the major Bahá'í holy sites in Israel. The most important of these are the Shrine of the Báb in Haifa, the nineteen terraced gardens of which were designed by an Iranian architect (see Figure 11), and the Shrine of Bahá'u'lláh near Akko. Indeed, Israelis refer to the Bahá'í gardens as *"ha-ganim persan,"* or "Persian gardens."[18] And while they do not strictly follow the Iranian *chahār bāgh* style, the heart-soothing beauty of these carefully-maintained grounds perfectly reflects the ancient Iranian notion of the garden as paradise.

# 18

# The Islamic Republic

In 1979 Iranians overthrew their 2,500-year-old tradition of monarchy—the oldest in the world at that time, albeit with occasional interruptions. Iranians themselves were probably more surprised than anyone at this remarkable turn of events. Throughout their long history, they had nearly always been under absolute, autocratic rule of one kind or another, apart from two brief experiments with democracy from 1906–1921 and 1941–1953, during which years a semblance of constitutional rule was operative. The second period, culminating in the election of Mohammad Mosaddeq as prime minister in 1951, even saw the nationalization of Iran's oil industry. This provoked the intervention of the British and American intelligence services, which restored Shah Mohammad Reza Pahlavi to power in 1953 through a now infamous coup.

Once returned to the throne, Shah Mohammad Reza Pahlavi reinvigorated his late father's earlier campaign for the rapid modernization of the country. By the early 1960s Iranian society had been radically transformed through industrialization, urbanization, education and in other domains, but the changes were too radical for some, and the benefits were distributed very unequally. Opposition movements, moreover, were ruthlessly repressed, mainly through the activities of the CIA- and Mossad-trained secret police, the notorious SAVAK.

Nevertheless, dissatisfaction with the Shah's policies was widespread. Many Iranians, traditional as well as modern, identified with the angry sentiments expressed by the writer Jalal Al-e Ahmad (1923–1969) in his 1962 book *Gharbzadegī* ("West-struckness," also rendered as "Westoxication," "Occidentosis," or "Euromania"), which argued that Iran was in the throes of surrendering its identity, values, and dignity to the West. (The term *gharbzadegī* had been coined some time earlier by Ahmad Fardid (1909–1994), a reactionary philosopher who dismissed such principles as democracy, pluralism, and human rights as "Western" obsessions.) Though often criticized as superficial and reductionist, Al-e

Ahmad's nativist critique resonated with many dissatisfied Iranians, setting an anti-Western tone that would retain its force up to the Islamic Revolution and after.

Organized opposition to the Shah's policies was starkly evident by 1963, notably in the seminary city of Qom, where a teacher by the name of Ruhollah Khomeini (1902–1989) was emerging as an outspoken critic of the Shah's modernization program. Following months of confrontations with the Shah's government, Khomeini was finally arrested on 5 June, leading to massive demonstrations in a number of Iranian cities during which nearly four hundred people were killed by government forces. As a result of these events (and perhaps in an effort by his colleagues to protect him) Khomeini was elevated to the supreme scholarly ranks of *Āyatollāh* ("Sign of God") and *Marja'-e taqlīd* ("source of emulation").[1] He was exiled the following year, first to Turkey and then to Iraq, which ironically proved to be a safe haven, from which he could continue to criticize the Shah with impunity. From the Shi'ite shrine city of Najaf he continued to speak out against the Iranian regime, and his speeches were widely circulated in Iran via cassette tapes.

Since Khomeini was able and willing to say what many Iranians felt in their hearts but feared to express, he acquired a kind of populist authority especially among the growing masses of the urban poor, who were mostly displaced peasants seeking menial jobs in the cities. Such people tended to congregate in neighborhood mosques, where Khomeini's tapes were often played. Within his more limited scholarly circle Khomeini also revived a marginal trend in Shi'ite political theory known as *velāyat-e faqīh* ("Government of the Jurist"), which was to succeed in becoming the basis for Iran's government after the 1979 revolution.[2] In the following passage from his lecture "The Form of Islamic Government," given at Najaf in 1970, Khomeini starts with the tacit acknowledgment that in the past the jurist and the ruler were not identical, but swiftly moves to argue that this should change:

> It is an established principle that "the *faqīh* has authority over the ruler." If the ruler adheres to Islam, he must necessarily submit to the *faqīh*, asking him about the laws and ordinances of Islam in order to implement them. This being the case, the true rulers are the *fuqahā* themselves, and rulership ought officially to be theirs, to apply to them, not to those who are obliged to follow the guidance of the *fuqahā* on account of their own ignorance of the law.[3]

Khomeini was not the only major Iranian figure to play a role in mobilizing religious discourse in opposition to the Shah's despotic regime. Beginning in the 1960s Mehdi Bazargan (1907–1995), a French-trained engineer, spoke out against the Shah's marginalizing of traditional Iranian religious values, arguing that Islam and modernization were not incompatible. Bazargan, who founded a party called the Liberation Movement (*Nehzat-e āzādī*) in 1961, would later become the first prime minister of Iran's revolutionary government.

During the 1970s another non-clerical intellectual, Sorbonne-educated 'Ali Shari'ati (1933–1977), won over many Iranians (especially university students) to his personal vision of revolutionary Islamic modernism. Like Al-e Ahmad before him, Shari'ati argued that renewal and change should come from within Iranian culture, particularly Shi'ism, not through the adoption of foreign models.

A similar but somewhat more sophisticated nativism can be seen in the work of philosopher Daryush Shayegan (born 1935), who studied with Henry Corbin (1903–1978) in Paris. Shayegan was deeply influenced by the perennial philosophy which sees ultimate truth being one and re-emerging continuously throughout history in different forms. Like his U.S.-based colleague Hossein Nasr, Shayegan tends to reify "Eastern" and "Western" thought systems, claiming that they represent fundamentally different and, in the end, mutually hostile approaches to reality.

Religious symbolism was also utilized by the *Mojāhedīn-e xalq* ("People's Holy Warriors," or MEK), one of Iran's two major anti-government guerrilla groups leading up to the revolution. The MEK's original founders had been members of Bazargan's Liberation Movement, but were more radical and anti-American. Their particular vision of Islam, first expressed in a tract entitled *The Hossein Movement* (*Nehzat-e hosseinī*), emphasized resistance and martyrdom with the goal of building a classless Islamic society. (A second guerrilla organization, the *Fedā'iyān-e xalq*, or "People's Sacrificers," was more explicitly Marxist, emerging as a revolutionary alternative to the Tudeh party whose leaders they found too accommodationist.) The activist rhetoric of the MEK, alongside the sermons of ideologues such as Khomeini and Shari'ati, were instrumental in giving a religious flavour to the revolutionary impulse that was building in Iran.

Throughout the 1970s broad sections of the Iranian population became increasingly frustrated by the Shah's cronyism and stubborn refusal to allow for the development of democratic institutions. Still, few inside or out of Iran imagined that the monarchy, buttressed as it was by the Shah's U.S.-equipped army, could ever fall to popular pressure. As late as December 1977, U.S. president Jimmy Carter famously referred to Iran as "an island of stability in one of the most troubled regions of the world." Yet a mere twelve months later the Shah, enfeebled by cancer and increasingly unable to react appropriately to growing mass demonstrations, fled the country. Soon after, on 1 February 1979, the nation rallied around the return from exile of Ayatollah Khomeini, who had by then clearly emerged as the revolution's spiritual leader.

In fact during the years leading up to the revolution the range of opposition groups in Iran had run the full political spectrum, from the communist Tudeh party to French-inspired secular intellectuals urging a European-style democracy. None, however, had a leader to rival Khomeini's charismatic appeal, or could mobilize and inspire such a massive following.

Against this backdrop of political contestation Iran was suffering the usual catastrophic corollaries to revolution, including a breakdown in public security, frequent mob rule, looting, and the carrying out of mass executions by ad hoc kangaroo courts. In September 1980 Iran's neighbor, Saddam Hussein of Iraq, fearing the clerics' stated aims to export their revolution to his own Shi'ite majority nation, compounded the chaos by invading the country.

The Iraqis justified their invasion by claiming sovereignty over the contested Shatt al-Arab river that separated the two countries. Saddam was surely also motivated by the hope that a country already in disorder would quickly fall to his better-armed forces. Quite the opposite, however: the emergence of an outside threat galvanized the Iranian people behind their new leadership. In hindsight it seems clear that contrary to the aims of Saddam and the U.S. intelligence services that later supported him, the Iraqi invasion actually strengthened a revolutionary regime that might not otherwise have survived.

Indeed throughout the Iran–Iraq conflict, which lasted until 1988, the Iranian government was able to maintain public support by citing the urgencies of war. Once that distraction was removed, and especially with the loss of a charismatic authority figure on the death of Khomeini in 1989, an economically challenged Iranian populace began to question the regime and hold it accountable for the country's worsening conditions. What began as private murmurs in the late 1980s had erupted by 1997 in a surprising national election, in which more than three-quarters of the vote went to a softly-spoken intellectual reformer, Mohammad Khatami (born 1943). Having previously served as Minister of Islamic Guidance, Khatami had resigned in protest over the government's censorship policies, especially in regard to music. The subsequent parliamentary elections in 2000 swept most of the religious clerics from parliament, replacing them in many cases with people who held Ph.D.s from American or European universities.

The 2001 presidential election that retained Khatami as president was seen by many as confirmation that Iran was changing course. Khatami, himself a member of the clerical class but who cited French and German philosophers as often as he did the Qur'an, repeatedly stated his view that "if religion comes into conflict with freedom, then religion will suffer."

Khatami sees the use of force to impose religion as a sign of intellectual weakness, as he expresses in the following passage:

> If, God forbid, some people want to impose their rigid thinking on Islam and call it God's religion—since they lack the intellectual power to confront the opposite side's thinking on its own terms—they resort to fanaticism. This merely harms Islam, without achieving the aims of the people.[4]

Iranian attitudes by the fourth decade of Islamic revolution appeared to confirm the predictive value of these words. Throughout the Khatami period the reformist program was repeatedly thwarted by the faction of the Supreme Leader, 'Ali Khamene'i. Dissatisfied with the pace of change, Khatami's supporters began to despair of his ability to bring about any kind of genuine reform. Many chose not to vote in the next presidential election in 2005, paving the way for conservative populist Mahmud Ahmadinejad (born 1956) to claim victory.

## RELIGIOUS THOUGHT IN AN ISLAMIC STATE

The elevation of religion from an oppositional force under Shah Mohammad Reza Pahlavi to official ideology under the Islamic Republic placed a new set of burdens upon Iran's religious thinkers. While formerly they could merely criticize, now they were held responsible for the welfare of Iranians. At first the instabilities caused by revolution and war constrained the parameters of religious discussion, and an appropriate governing orthodoxy was urgently sought. But as the theocratic state became established throughout the 1980s, a widening array of perspectives sought expression within the required Islamic framework, pushing the boundaries in many directions.

One major aspect of the evolving religious discussion centered on gender roles, particularly the status of women. Although beginning early in the revolution women were purged from many positions and Islamic covering (*hejāb*) was enforced upon all females over the age of nine, the social conditions of the 1980s could not prevent women from entering or re-entering the public sphere in nearly every field, a process which has been accelerating ever since. With an entire generation of boys and young men involved in the war effort against Iraq, women came to the workforce in ever-increasing numbers and in virtually all professions. The economic and professional empowerment of Iranian women was debated and largely justified through ongoing discussions among religious scholars, particularly the *hawzeh* (religious circle) of the seminaries of Qom.[5]

Another important area of discussion was politics, especially the proper role of an Islamic government. The Islamic Republic, for all its appeal to tradition, was in fact a tremendously radical undertaking. Nothing like an "Islamic" democracy (in the modern sense of "democracy") had ever been tried in the world before, and some wondered if the notion could really even exist. The building of democratic and civil institutions in Iran since the revolution has been an experiment with mixed results.

Can the Islamic Republic of Iran be considered a democracy, especially given that candidates must be vetted by an unelected Council of Guardians of the Constitution (*shorā-ye negahbān-e qānūn-e asāsī*)? Iranians do vote in elections, although many, frustrated by irregularities in the process, are now boycotting them. Personal freedoms remain severely compromised in many ways, and any number of words or deeds can land one in jail. Young Iranians especially are increasingly impatient with the slow pace of reform, as attested in massive street demonstrations by students and others, especially following the disputed 2009 presidential election.

The question of who speaks for Shi'i Islam has acquired a new dimension since the founding of the Islamic Republic. As early as the 1970s the traditional monopoly on religious interpretations of the *'ulemā'* was notably challenged by 'Ali Shari'ati, who despite being considered one of the revolution's inspirational figures is viewed with ambivalence by the present regime.

A later example of an influential religious thinker coming from outside the world of traditional Shi'ite scholarship is Abdolkarim Soroush (born Hossein Dabbagh in 1945), whom American journalist Robin Wright once optimistically dubbed "the Martin Luther of Islam."[6] Soroush, whose formal training was in chemistry, has spent his intellectual career arguing for a dynamic jurisprudence able to answer the challenges of the modern age. In his view, to alter traditional interpretations poses no threat to religion, since religion and interpretations of it are not the same thing:

> The truth is that as long as one has not distinguished between religion and people's understanding of it, one will be incapable of finding an adequate answer to these intriguing questions. Yes, it is true that sacred scriptures are (in the judgment of followers) flawless; however, it is just as true that human beings' understanding of religion is flawed. Religion is sacred and heavenly, but the understanding of religion is human and earthly. That which remains constant is religion; that which undergoes change is religious knowledge and insight.[7]

For a time Soroush's ideas gained him a considerable following among religiously minded intellectuals in Iran, but in recent years he has spent much of his time abroad and his popularity has abated.

In the wake of the reformist stalemate of 2005 and after, the dialogue-based and pluralistic discourse promoted by Khatami, Soroush and others such as Grand Ayatollah Yusef Sane'i (born 1937) was superseded by that of anti-Western neo-conservatives such as Reza Davari-Ardakani (born 1933), a professor of philosophy and President of the Iranian Academy of Sciences, and Ayatollah Mohammad Taqi Mesbah-Yazdi (born 1934), considered by many to be the most conservative of Iran's most prominent clerics. With the election of a new President, Hassan Rowhani in June 2013, many Iranians began to hope for a return to the comparative openness of the Khatami years.

## RELIGIOUS MINORITIES UNDER THE ISLAMIC REPUBLIC

The conditions of Iran's various religious minority communities have varied both according to changing circumstances since the late 1970s and among themselves. The country is about ninety percent Shi'ite Muslim. Sunni Muslims account for perhaps another seven percent, with Bahá'ís, Christians, Jews and Zoroastrians constituting the remainder. Iran's Sunnis are mainly of non-Persian ethnicities, Iran today being only a little over fifty percent native Persian-speaking. Sunnis are mostly found among the Kurds of western Iran, the Baluch of the southeast, the Turkmens in the northeast, and the Arabs in the southwest.

### Muslim Minorities

Sunni Muslims and Sufi orders have complained to international human rights organizations of discrimination by the officially Twelver Shi'ite state and harassment by ordinary citizens. Sunnis have not been allowed to build a mosque in the capital, and frequently perceive insults to Sunni Islam in the government-sponsored media. A number of Iranian Sunni religious leaders have been assassinated. Sufism has been generally discouraged, no doubt due to its occasional heterodox practices and the threat of charismatic leadership; the highly popular Gonabadi order has come under particular pressure.

### Other Religious Minorities

Among the non-Muslim groups, it could probably be said that Armenian Christians, having a centuries-old history of mostly manageable coexistence with Muslim Iranians, have fared the best. By contrast the Bahá'ís, as members of a religion not recognized by Islam, have suffered the most. All Iran's non-Muslim religious communities have seen dwindling numbers, mainly through emigration to the U.S., Europe, and Australia.

The first Assembly of Experts (*Majles-e xebregān*) which drafted the constitution of the Islamic Republic in 1979 included four non-Muslim delegates: one Zoroastrian, one Armenian, one Assyrian, and one Jew. Although in the end their inclusion was perhaps little more than tokenism, Article 13 of the eventual constitution granted each of the recognized minority communities explicit recognition and protection. It reads:

> Zoroastrian, Jewish and Christian Iranians are the only recognized religious minorities who are legally free in the practice of their religious ceremonies, on matters of personal status and education.

Other non-Muslim Iranians, including Bahá'ís and Mandaeans, as well as a tiny community of Iranian Sikhs, were implicitly denied these freedoms and protections. Although the Iranian parliament guarantees five seats for recognized religious minority communities—two for the Armenians, one for the Assyrians and Chaldeans, and one each for the Jews and Zoroastrians—in practice the guarantees provided in Article 13 of the constitution have been violated for all non-Muslim communities at one time or another.

A number of Islamic laws formally discriminate against non-Muslims. One that Iran's religious minorities find particularly egregious is the difference in "blood money" paid to the family of someone who has been unlawfully killed: the sum due to the family of a non-Muslim is half that accorded to that of a Muslim. Thanks to persistent lobbying by non-Muslim parliamentarians this law was finally changed in 2004 through Khamene'i's exercising of his "absolute prerogative of the jurisprudent" (*velāyat-e motlaqe-ye faqīh*).

Non-Muslims were the target of occasional attacks by fanatics in the early years of the revolution. Two Zoroastrian temples were desecrated in 1979, and in 1980 Armenian graveyards were vandalized in several cities. Revolutionary Guards broke into the Armenian cathedral in Tehran, and noticing a scantily clad Jesus in one of the paintings, called for the painter to return and add more clothing. In 1983 the government began appointing unsympathetic Muslim principals and teachers to serve in non-Muslim schools, and reduced the teaching of languages such as Armenian and Assyrian (Aramaic). Non-Muslims were discriminated against in the workplace, notably in the oil industry.

Following the revolution there was increased attention to "protecting" Muslims from the ritually unclean (from the Shi'ite point of view) contact of non-Muslims, even in the context of non-Muslim factory workers touching products that will be consumed by Muslims. Armenian–Iranian political scientist Eliz Sanasarian calls this heightened sensitivity "*nejāsat* (impurity) consciousness."

Since 1999 the U.S. Department of State has designated Iran as a "country of particular concern" under the International Religious Freedom Act.[8] International refugee organizations have tended to be sympathetic to Iranian minorities claiming persecution, but it may be suspected that at least some of these claims are opportunistic. Although Iran's non-Muslims were undeniably subjected to great hardships, especially during the early years of the revolution, it should be acknowledged that Muslim Iranians also suffered from the excesses of revolutionary zealots and eight years of war with Iraq. While non-Muslims in Iran may have been occasionally singled out or denied certain rights and protections, the same is true for minority groups in virtually any society in times of severe social upheaval. Nevertheless, an overall assessment would suggest that in most respects Iran's non-Muslim communities are weaker today than they were prior to 1979.

Iran's Islamic revolution has brought about many paradoxes. Twelver Shi'ite political theory has been dramatically revised, and a historically underdog religious ethos has found itself in a position of temporal authority and accountability. The often hysterical and paranoid voices of religious extremism and intolerance, which had subsided under the presidency of Mohammad Khatami from 1997–2005, re–emerged under his successor Mahmud Ahmadinejad, and the fear that members of religious minorities are acting as spies for foreign governments continued to persist.

At the same time the interest of many Iranians in religions other than Shi'i Islam increased, due at least in part to an ever-growing obsession with an outside world increasingly accessible through travel or the Internet. Part of this may be a reaction against the religious ideology of a regime losing popularity and blamed by many for the continued sense of isolation and deprivation felt by large numbers of Iranians.

Even among the younger generation of seminary students one can see a marked fascination with the study of other religions. This includes the study of not only Christianity and Judaism but also Buddhism, which Muslims have long considered the archetypical "idol-worshiping" religion. (The Bahá'í Faith remains taboo, however.) In recent years a new and very well-funded University of Religions and Sects (*Dānešgāh-e adyān va mazāheb*) has been established in the traditional Shi'ite center of Qom, attracting a number of bright young seminarians from the nearby *hawzeh* who study sacred texts in such languages as Hebrew and Sanskrit.[9] It possesses an impressive and up-to-date collection of library resources, including the latest western scholarship from university presses. The University publishes a scholarly journal devoted to the comparative study of religions, *Haft Asmān* (Seven Heavens), and has helped organize a number of international conferences on interfaith dialogue, human rights, and related subjects.

# Iranian Zoroastrians Today

On the whole it can be said that education, urbanization, and newfound prosperity improved the lot of Iran's Zoroastrians throughout the twentieth century. The 1979 revolution, however, brought renewed problems, especially during the first years. Its spiritual leader, Ayatollah Khomeini, dismissed Zoroastrianism as "an old and inveterate sect," and referred to Zoroastrians as "reactionary fire-worshipers," calling them by the derogatory term *gabr*.[1] Emboldened by this kind of rhetoric, some Muslim families took the opportunity to seize Zoroastrian property, and the nominal respect accorded the community under the Pahlavis quickly dissipated. Muslims were put in charge of Zoroastrian schools, and to cite but one example of what this often entailed, the new principal of Anushirvan School in Tehran consistently ridiculed the religion of her students.[2] On the other hand, Zoroastrians were not necessarily singled out. In fact all non-Muslim minorities suffered during the early years of the revolution, as did indeed the population as a whole, due to widespread social instability which was exacerbated by the eight-year war with Iraq.

On the positive side, Article 64 of the country's new constitution, adopted in 1980, confirmed the right of each of the recognized religious minorities—Zoroastrians, Jews and Christians—to representation in parliament. Their legal rights, as provided under Islamic law, were formally established, although they were not always the same rights extended to Muslims. In fact the first Zoroastrian M.P. under the new government, Rostam Shahzadi, vigorously protested against certain provisions in the constitution, including the ban on religious minorities occupying the highest levels of government and the military.[3] In 1985 he lodged a formal protest against police raids on social events at Zoroastrian community centers, pointing out that joyful celebrations are a basic element of the religion.[4] Shahzadi's tireless activism failed in many respects to alter the course of government policy, but subsequent

Zoroastrian MPs have used their position to at least put the community's complaints on record.

Indeed, the current Zoroastrian deputy, Dr. Esfandiar Ekhtiari, characterizes his role first and foremost as that of "community advocate." "My job is to speak on behalf of any Zoroastrian in Iran, regardless of what his or her situation is," he explained to us.[5] In his capacity as legislator, Ekhtiari seeks to prevent the passing of any laws which could be detrimental to Zoroastrians. At times he also feels the need to remind his colleagues in government of their obligation to protect the rights, or even simply the dignity of his community. In early 2009, for example, he wrote a letter to the Ministry of Islamic Guidance reprimanding them for approving a feature film in which the Zoroastrian *fravahr* appeared emblazoned on the clothing of a criminal, calling it a "disrespectful use of a sacred symbol."[6] In fact, a large part of Ekhtiari's job seems to consist of writing letters. When a Muslim scholar, Parviz Rajabi, criticized Zoroastrianism in the newspaper *E'temād*, Ekhtiari wrote a point-by-point rebuttal that was even longer than Rajabi's original article.[7]

In his capacity as community ombudsman, Ekhtiari keeps open office for people who come and seek his assistance. Among the complaints he most often deals with are discrimination at school or the workplace, and property disputes. One recent case was that of a prospective university student who achieved first place ranking in his entrance exam, theoretically guaranteeing him a place in the incoming class. However, after "additional factors" were taken into consideration, his ranking was lowered to ninth, for a program with only eight places. Ekhtiari wrote letters to the university administration and to the Ministry of Higher Education, asking them to reconsider the student's application.

Another legal case currently pending is that of a Zoroastrian community organization whose land has been illegally occupied by a Muslim; they are seeking to have him evicted, but the courts have so far been unresponsive. Similarly, when the city of Yazd decided to build power lines across lands owned and held sacred by the Zoroastrian community, where their *dakhme*s (towers for exposing corpses) are located, their protests went unheeded.[8] On the other hand, a longstanding claim for the return of land seized from the Zoroastrian Youth Organization after the 1979 revolution was finally resolved in 2010.[9]

Notwithstanding occasional disputes with members of the Muslim majority, Sohrab Firuzfar, the current president of the Yazd Zoroastrian Association, insists that conditions are better now for Zoroastrians in Iran than at any time during the past fourteen centuries. "My father wasn't even allowed to ride a horse," he says, "and now we have full legal rights and a Member of Parliament. Mostly nobody bothers us. Our young people have more freedom than Muslims do, yet unfortunately they still want to emigrate."[10]

In fact, Zoroastrians in Iran enjoy a number of privileges denied to Iran's Muslim majority. At a Yazd community center we saw men and women working out side by side in a mixed gym, clad only in skin-tight exercise attire, a thing normally unheard of in the Islamic Republic. Religious and social occasions are mixed as well, such as *gāhānbār* ceremonies, weddings and *sedreh-pūshī*s ("putting on the [sacred] shirt"—the ceremony by which adolescent Zoroastrians are initiated into the community), or pilgrimages to Pīr-e Sabz and other area shrines. (Zoroastrian religious life, which consists almost entirely of joyful celebrations, contrasts markedly with the mourning ethos of Iran's dominant Shi'a culture. Even at funerals Zoroastrians are not supposed to cry, and when they sometimes do, this behaviour is derided by others as being due to "Muslim influence".) Like Iran's Christians and Jews, Zoroastrians are allowed to produce and consume alcoholic beverages, as long as they don't share them with Muslims (a prohibition they don't always observe). Alcohol is served not just at home but also at community centers as part of celebrations.

Many Zoroastrians in Iran conceded to us that their social freedoms are much greater than for Muslims, a point with particular relevance to the community's youth who enjoy loud dance parties and other social activities. Still, their distinctive rights are not always respected by Muslim authorities, who are either ignorant of the law or choose to disregard it. One of our informants in Yazd told us that he had recently been pulled over while driving through town by a patrol of young Revolutionary Guards, who, finding a bottle of wine in his car, confiscated it and fined him, despite his protests that he had not broken the law. He lodged a formal complaint but it was ignored.

Despite dwindling numbers and occasional outside pressures (or perhaps precisely because of these things), Zoroastrian community life in Iran today is strikingly alive. The sheer number of Zoroastrian organizations of all kinds throughout the country is astonishing, and the list of their activities is endless, from religious festivals to cultural events such as art exhibitions and theatre plays, recreational outings such as picnics and hikes, educational programs such as Avesta classes, scholarly workshops on historical topics, computer classes, and perhaps most visible of all, sports activities. Whether all this is a sign of the vibrancy of the community or a panicked effort to stay alive is open to interpretation.

## RELIGIOUS AUTHORITY: KEEPING
## THE PRIESTHOOD ALIVE

Throughout its long history, the guardians and spokesmen of Zoroastrianism have been the hereditary priestly class, the *mobed*s. As is the case with many religions today, maintaining a sufficient pool of priests-in-training is often a challenge, as the younger generation from priestly families succumb to the attractions of other careers or simply the pressures of earning a living under increasingly difficult economic conditions. In Iran, as in the diaspora, most Zoroastrian priests today must hold down other jobs in order to make ends meet.

Due to the shortage of willing trainees from eligible families, during the 1970s Iran's Mobed Council (*Anjoman-e mobedān*) decided to allow interested candidates from non-priestly lineages to become "assistant" priests (*mobedyārs*). At present there are perhaps sixty priests and assistants in Iran: twenty in Tehran, twenty in Yazd, five in Kerman, three in Shiraz, two in Esfahan, and the remainder in other cities. Of these, one-third are actual priests and the rest are assistants. From 2006–2010 only six new Zoroastrian priests were ordained in Iran.[11] Ceremonies that in the past included the participation of up to eight priests now use only one or two. Moreover, most priests and assistants lack a complete knowledge of the liturgies and the scriptural languages, Avestan and Pahlavi. On the other hand, as of 2010, women began for the first time to be ordained as *mobedyārs*.

As noted above, recent years have seen the simplification of Zoroastrian rituals and a decreasing emphasis on the legalism which characterized the religion from the Sasanian period onwards. For the most part these changes have been accepted and validated by the Mobed Council, as being less burdensome for the laity. As for the latter, whether they participate in community rituals or not, most Iranian Zoroastrians remain strongly attached to the moral message of the Gathas, summarized as practicing "good thoughts, good words, good deeds" which constitute the ethical core of the tradition.

Some among the laity have begun to contest the authority of the hereditary priests, whom they see as upholders of a ritualistic, "more superficial" version of the faith. "Why should we accept what someone says about our religion," one high profile member of the Yazd community complained to us, "just because he was born into a priestly lineage?" Yet most priests we have met are quite forward-looking and liberal in their views. At a *sedreh-pūšī* which we attended in Tehran in July 2010 (a lavish event resembling a large wedding), the officiating priest summarized Zoroastrian teaching before a crowd of some three hundred guests (all Zoroastrians) as consisting of "doing good in the world," and particularly abstaining from any kind of lie or falsehood. "If someone calls the house asking to speak to Dad," he instructed the young initiate, "and Dad doesn't want to talk to him, no saying 'Dad isn't home'!"

Interestingly, recent years have seen a resurgence of *sedreh-pūšīs* in Iran. According to Mobed Firouzgary, before the 1979 revolution very few Zoroastrians youths chose to undergo the ritual, whereas now "they virtually all do."[12] Attendance at the six yearly *gāhānbārs* and other ceremonies (*jašn*s) is another matter; perhaps the "party atmosphere" of *sedreh-pūšīs*—at which the ritual formalities are quickly dispensed with, making way for eating, drinking, and dancing—is more attractive, although since the religion encourages joyfulness and celebration, these elements are generally present at other Zoroastrian ceremonies as well. (The most popular annual festival in Iran, the Persian new year, *Nō rūz*, held at the spring equinox, is celebrated by Iranians of all religious backgrounds, as is the ancient fire-jumping ceremony, *Čahār šanbe sūrī*, which is held the preceding week. Attempts by post-revolutionary governments to suppress these non-Islamic celebrations have been spectacularly unsuccessful. Ironically, Zoroastrian leaders have recently begun denouncing *Čahār šanbe sūrī* as non-Zoroastrian.[13])

## SMALLER FAMILIES, MIXED FAMILIES

Mirroring global trends, one of the most immediately observable effects of the increased prosperity, urbanization, and educational levels of Zoroastrians in Iran has been a dramatic decrease in the female fertility rate, which according to community leaders, now stands at about one percent, well below replacement level. Educated, cosmopolitan women are not only more inclined than their traditional counterparts to devote more time and energy to careers outside the home, they are also more likely to meet and choose life partners from outside the Zoroastrian community.

While in the West it is not unheard of for non-Zoroastrian spouses to join the faith or at least allow their children to have a Zoroastrian upbringing, in Iran (where the non-Zoroastrian spouse is almost sure to be a Muslim) Islamic law ensures that this will not be the case. Thus, at least officially, a Zoroastrian who marries a Muslim is permanently lost to the community, along with his or her eventual children, whether they like it or not. And although some mixed couples do make the choice to maintain a Zoroastrian religious culture within the home, it is not generally possible for them to make this choice public, and the Zoroastrian community cannot formally accept them as members.

Within Iran's Zoroastrian community today the attitude toward out-marriage appears to be mostly one of reluctant resignation. It is viewed with disfavor, but accepted as unavoidable. Families would prefer to see their children marry within the community, but have little power to stop those who choose otherwise. Moreover, with most young women now pursuing careers there is little incentive for Zoroastrian couples to have large numbers of children. The average family now has only one child, which essentially guarantees a halving of the population with every generation, even apart from the issues of out-marriage and emigration. Zoroastrian M.P. Esfandiar Ekhtiari cites his own case as an example: "I tell young couples they should have bigger families," he says with a self-deprecating smile, "but my wife and I have only one child!"[14]

## THE LURE OF EMIGRATION

Beginning in the 1960s but increasingly since the 1979 revolution, large numbers of Iranians of all religious backgrounds have been leaving their country, mainly for the West. For Zoroastrians, as for Iran's other religious minorities, the appeal of emigration includes the additional carrot of special refugee programs (such as the HIAS program in the U.S., through which they can obtain residency within as little as six months),[15] as well as the stick of discrimination and persecution—real or perceived—at home. The result has been a steady drain on Iran's Zoroastrian population, which shows no signs of abating.

Far more than any other issue, Zoroastrians in Iran appear concerned by the threat emigration poses to the survival of their community. The younger generation, in particular, have been leaving in droves, reducing Iran's Zoroastrian population since the 1970s by half. There is a real concern that the culture will be lost. In a recent interview published in a Zoroastrian newsletter the author of a new book on the history of Zoroastrians in Iran, Shiraz University professor Katayun Namiranian calls cultural preservation "our number one duty" in which she hopes every Zoroastrian will play a role:

> We all have a tape recorder or video camera at home; each one of us can sit and record the recollections of our grandparents, and from these recollections we can know when it was that the first automobile entered the town of Yazd, or what happened in such and such a Zoroastrian village that is now emptied of its inhabitants, etc. . . .

But, she notes, "When eighty percent of us are leaving by turns for Austria [a reference to the HIAS program, which transits refugees through Vienna], this seems like a bit of a pipe-dream."[16]

Articles in the Western news media have focused almost exclusively on fears for the survival of Iran's Zoroastrian community. Speaking to the *Middle East Times*, engineer Farhad Dehnavizadeh lamented the loss of the community's youth. "I am very sad that they are leaving," he told reporter Hiedeh Farmani. "Their second generation will have no idea of Iran and Zoroastrian culture."[17] Susan Afshari, cited in the same article, shared his concern. "We are the guardians of traditions and feasts [such as Mehragān]" she said. "If we leave, who is going to keep them going in Iran?"[18] "We are a species on the road to extinction," a pilgrim to the Pīr-e Sabz shrine near Yazd told a reporter from *Agence France Presse*.[19]

Nevertheless, a majority of Zoroastrians we spoke with during our visits to Iran in 2008–2009 and 2010 either planned to emigrate or were encouraging their children to do so. The eventual extinction of the community in Iran was something they saw as sad, but not enough to preclude the opportunity for a "better life" in the West, even though most expressed a strong love for Iran and a faint hope that one day conditions might permit them to return. Most of our informants also agreed that even despite occasional experiences of prejudice and discrimination on the part of the Muslim majority (especially in the realm of professional advancement), in many ways they have an easier life than Muslims and in most cases life in Iran is not unbearable.[20] Moreover, the vast majority of Iranians today suffer from economic and other hardships, and huge numbers of them at least fantasize about emigrating; the difference for Zoroastrians (and other religious minorities) appears to be that in contrast to the case of Muslim Iranians, the emigration process, thanks to HIAS, is almost unbelievably quick and easy. With an open line to Vienna and Los Angeles constantly dangling before their eyes, it is easy to understand why so many Zoroastrians are tempted to give it a try.

The official policy of Zoroastrian associations in Iran is to discourage emigration, but in reality there is little they can do to prevent it. Merely putting up flyers at community centers and holy shrines denouncing emigration as a "betrayal" seems to have little effect. In 2010 *Pārs nāmeh*, the semi-official monthly newsletter of the Iranian Zoroastrian community, ran a two-part interview with three young Zoroastrian men recently returned to Iran after unsatisfactory experiences in the U.S. The repentant interviewees argued that emigrants to the U.S. are likely to wind up as "pizza-sellers" and that their children will learn to disrespect them. They claimed to now realize their opportunities were greater in Iran, and suggested that HIAS is somehow involved with the U.S. government in a scheme to bring cheap labour to the U.S.[21]

Some community leaders speak of the need to offer incentives to keep Zoroastrians in Iran, such as increasing employment opportunities and making it easier for young couples to purchase homes, but few seem convinced that such measures can have any real effect. The difficulties of life in exile—financial, cultural, and emotional—are often brought up in conversation, but the fact is that few of those who leave ever come back.

## CONVERSION: THE SOLUTION WHICH DARE NOT SPEAK ITS NAME

For more than twelve centuries Zoroastrians in India and Iran mostly did not accept converts to the religion, though for different reasons. In Iran, conversion away from Islam was forbidden by Islamic law, as remains the case under the Islamic Republic today. In India the reasons are less clear, but the traditional explanation is that the first Zoroastrian immigrants were prohibited from seeking converts from among the native Indian population. Nevertheless, as noted in a previous chapter, the letters known as *Revāyat*s sent by Parsi priests to their colleagues in Iran from the fifteenth through the eighteenth century include the question of whether conversion is allowable, to which the Iranian priests answered in the affirmative, even stating that it is "meritorious."[22]

Today it is a fact, nervously hushed in Iran even as it is trumpeted in southern California, that considerable numbers of Iranian Muslims disaffected with Islam have sought to identify themselves with their nation's "original," pre-Islamic religious tradition. During the first half of the twentieth century some Iranians—notably the writer Sadeq Hedayat—had expressed this attraction, but the trend has developed mainly as a reaction to the 1979 revolution.

In the Los Angeles region, home to the largest number of Iranian exiles in the world, "re-conversion" has been particularly visible, led by figures such as Ali Akbar Jafarey (himself a former Muslim) who actively solicits converts and promotes Zoroastrianism as a universal religion open to all.[23] Among diaspora Zoroastrians, Iranians have been generally more open to conversion than Parsis, but within Iran itself the subject is taboo for obvious reasons. Nevertheless, it is often claimed by Iranians in exile that the numbers of "*nō zartoštīhā*" ("New Zoroastrians") in Iran are in the millions. If true, this assertion could temper the prevailing pessimistic attitudes about the community's future, but unfortunately there is no way to assess its credibility since a Muslim convert to Zoroastrianism living in Iran would almost certainly never admit to it openly.

Zoroastrian community leaders in Iran are understandably reluctant to discuss the issue. While many are inclined to accept the likelihood that large numbers of self-identified Zoroastrian Iranians exist, they invariably express the strong desire that such individuals stay away from the established, recognized Zoroastrian communities. As one Iranian priest put it to us, "Of course if they want to embrace Zoroastrianism that is good, but they should form their own organizations and keep separate from us, or we will have problems." Others are even less accepting. "I don't like them," a community leader told us. "They aren't real Zoroastrians; they are just making a political statement, and they can cause us a lot of trouble." Although the Zoroastrian grapevine in North America claims the number of "re-verts" in Iran to be as high as three million, given the present political situation in the country it seems pointless even to speculate on the issue. As one of our informants mockingly put it: "Three million? Maybe there are fifteen million, who cares? It has nothing to do with us!"

Thus, there is a substantial gap in how converts are seen by Zoroastrians in and outside Iran. Among exiles, converts represent the main hope for the future, even the possibility that Zoroastrianism could experience a resurgence and regain its historical status as one of the world's great religious traditions. For Zoroastrians in Iran, such an idea is nothing more than a fantasy, and a dangerous one at that.

## REFORM AND REACTION IN INDIA

Far more so than for Iranian Zoroastrians, among the Zoroastrians of India the issues of out-marriage and the acceptance of converts have deeply divided the community. The children of those who marry outside the faith are typically not recognized as Zoroastrians and are denied entry to sacred sites. Iranian visitors to India who wish to enter such sites are required to provide documentary proof of their Zoroastrian lineage, a policy deliberately aimed at excluding the increasing numbers of highly enthusiastic Iranian "new Zoroastrians" who come to India in search of their long-estranged religious cousins.

In recent years many "new Zoroastrians" have come from the former Soviet Union as well, not just Tajiks from Central Asia but also Russians, Zoroastrianism having captured the imaginations of many spiritual seekers of European background following the collapse of Soviet atheism. In 2006, thirty-four "new Zoroastrians" were initiated in a *sedreh-pūšī* ceremony in Tashkent conducted by exiled Iranian mobed Kamran Jamshidi, assisted by two Parsi priests from India, and another twenty in a subsequent ceremony in the Tajik city of Khujand.[24]

Both the Uzbek and Tajik governments have attempted to co-opt Zoroastrian symbols and celebrations as part of their nation-building efforts. Seven stars adorn the center of the Tajik flag, and the government news agency is called Avesta. A book by Tajik president Emomali Rahmon, *The Tajiks in the Mirror of History*, anachronistically claims Zoroaster as a "Tajik" prophet and his religion as one of Tajikistan's principal contributions to world civilization.[25] In 2003, he persuaded UNESCO to declare an "International Year of Zoroaster," with Tajikistan as the host country. Three years later, President Rahmon declared the "Year of Aryan Civilization," again emphasizing the region's pre-Islamic past. During an official trip to India, the Tajik president visited the Zoroastrian College in Sanjan and other Parsi sites in India amid great pomp and fanfare.

As mentioned previously, the Zoroastrian College founded by Meher Master-Moos has since 1991 maintained close ties with Tajiks interested in their ancient ancestors' faith. The College has hosted visits by Tajik scholar Rustom Fuzaylov, a professor at Khojand Technical University and an adept of the nineteenth-century Zoroastrian mystical movement Ilm-i khshnoom, as well as a number of Tajik students. The College has also launched a project with Moscow State University to translate the Avesta into Russian.

According to the College's website:

> The main work and purpose for which Zoroastrian College was founded is to bring about the Spiritual Revival of the Mazdayasnie Zarathushtrian Daene in its original homeland, amongst the people of the countries of Aryana Vaeja, whose ancestors were followers of the faith.[26]

This revival is described in the College's mission statement as spreading "ancient cosmic wisdom" through understanding of "divine universal natural laws." Thus, in marked contrast to traditional Parsi religious centers in India, the College is "open to all persons from any country in the world, who genuinely desire to live within this Spiritual Community, and develop their inner consciousness, by practising the daily life disciplines of obedience of the Divine Laws." Dame Master-Moos herself explained to me that Russians have a particular affinity for Zoroastrianism because "it is their Aryan heritage and the original Airyana Vaeja (*Airyanəm vaējah*) was in their territory."[27]

Such openness does not sit well with conservative Parsis. The young chief priest of the Parsi temple in Bangalore bemoaned to us the fact that so many people now want to convert to Zoroastrianism, going so far as to say "It is our biggest problem. We are often asked to give lectures on our religion at schools and institutes and such," he elaborated, "but afterwards we have to deal with people who find it attractive and want to join."[28] Maintaining the traditional Parsi viewpoint that no one can be considered a Zoroastrian unless born of two Zoroastrian parents, he insisted that converts cannot be accepted. In the case of interested Hindus, he tells them they can hope to be reincarnated as Zoroastrians in a future life. We pointed out that Zoroastrians don't believe in reincarnation, a point he conceded. "So you are giving them false hope?" we asked him. "Well," he replied with a laugh," we have to tell them something!"

We asked him what happens when an Iranian Zoroastrian wishes to enter their temple. "If they are authentic Zarthushtis with documentation and can prove they know the proper prayers, we may let them enter," he replied. But most Iranian visitors to the Bangalore temple are Muslim-born neo-Zoroastrians. "Some of them know more about the religion than even I do," he said, "but nevertheless we cannot consider them Zoroastrians and they may not enter the temple. We allow them to pray outside. One Iranian woman who visited here, Maryam, was so moved by her visit that she cried." Asked if he believed that Zoroaster's teaching represented a universal truth, after some hesitation he affirmed that he did, but insisted that the religion belonged to Parsis and could not accept outsiders. When we asked him what harm would come of allowing converts to join the community, he seemed uncomfortable and could not provide a clear answer, repeating only that "there is no prayer for conversion." He dismissed the main worry shared by many Zoroastrians around the world, that of demographic decline, arguing (against all available statistics) that in India Zoroastrian birth rates are going up. He likewise rejected the official figures which state that fewer than 69,000 Zoroastrians remain in India, asserting that the true number is "at least three or four lakhs" (300,000 to 400,000).

While the greatest resurgence of Zoroastrianism worldwide seems to be coming from southern California, the Bangalore priest singled out Russia as a major source of people wishing to become Zoroastrian. The religion does seem to hold a curious appeal there, and steady numbers of Russians have been visiting India in hopes of learning more about it. A scandal broke out at the Zoroastrian College in Sanjan in February 2010 when a Russian citizen on a tourist visa, forty-eight-year-old Mikhail Chispiakov, was ordained as a Zoroastrian priest by two Parsi priests from Mumbai. When members of the Bombay Parsi Panchayat (BPP) got wind of the event, forty-five of them rushed to Sanjan (three hours away) and stormed the college in protest, creating considerable property damage.[29] The Mumbai High Court granted the college police protection in the wake of the incident, pending an investigation. Meanwhile, the BPP issued the following statement, signed by all six of India's Dasturs (high priests):

> Ms. Meher Master Moos, the priests and the candidate involved have ridiculed, insulted and have made mockery of both the Zoroastrian Religion as well as the religion of the candidate. We, the undersigned High Priests of the Zoroastrian Community, strongly condemn these sacrilegious acts and consider the so-called Barashnum-Navar a farce that has neither religious sanction nor authority.[30]

The unanimous decision of the U.K.-based World Zoroastrian Organization (WZO) in 2010 to allow "any person professing Zoroastrianism" to be a member was officially condemned by no fewer than thirty-five Parsi–Irani anjomans in India, and the Indian chapter of the WZO broke its ties with the U.K. branch. According to BPP trustee Khojeste Mistree, many Central Asians are claiming Zoroastrian identity so as to facilitate immigration to Western countries. "We also have proof of nudists and paedophiles from Latin America professing to be Zoroastrians," he added. Addressing the annual meeting of the Federation of the Parsi Zoroastrian Anjumans of India, Nozer Meherji, vice-president of the WZO's Indian branch, stated that "Just a couple of years ago, a cartel of Mexican drug smugglers, when caught with possession of marijuana, claimed to be Zoroastrians and falsely said the drug was meant to be used in an ancient religious ritual." Meherji also expressed concern that fundamentalist groups could carry out terror acts by pretending to be Zoroastrians.[31]

While today's postmodern society may frown on the kind of communal exclusivism shown by traditional Parsis, it is important to emphasize that from their point of view they are trying to respect a tradition maintained over more than a millennium, under often highly challenging circumstances, and they fear that diluting this tradition would betray the efforts of their ancestors. Firoze Kotwal, one of the world's only six living Zoroastrian high priests (*dasturs*), insists that, in his words, "only we have maintained the authentic tradition of our Iranian forebears. The Iranians themselves have not done it. Do you think it's fun? It has been very difficult!"[32] Along with many conservative Parsis, Kotwal ridicules the recent Iranian innovations of training *mobedyārs*, especially women, as they are considered ritually impure when menstruating and therefore unable to enter sacred sites. At the same time, Dastur Kotwal, unlike some other traditional Parsis, does not shy from admitting that a large part of what conservatives are aiming to preserve is their ethnicity.

Parsis in India are deeply divided over these issues. In private conversation a self-identified "liberal" Parsi, who asked not to be named, took issue with the position that traditionalists are acting out of respect for their ancestors. According to him, "Our prophet told us to teach his message to the entire world. So out of respect for our ancestors we should overturn the directives of our prophet?" He went on to suggest a more cynical explanation for Parsi exclusiveness, the fear that if large numbers of Hindu converts were accepted it would dilute Parsi wealth.[33]

The ideological divide between "reformist" and traditional Parsis in India is growing increasingly bitter, manifesting itself in personal attacks not just in the Parsi press but in the mainstream Indian press as well. In the wake of an election scandal in July 2011, the conservative World Alliance of Parsi Irani Zarthoshtis (whose slogan is "Preserving the Past, Protecting the Future") took out a two-page advertisement in a major Mumbai newspaper, denouncing six of its Parsi opponents, including the Dastur in charge of the Iranshah fire at Udvada (whom they accuse of wanting to desanctify the place by encouraging tourism), and Berjis Desai of the *Mumbai Samachar*, whose opinion columns have advocated the acceptance of converts, cremation of the dead, and the opening up of fire temples to non-Zoroastrians.[34]

## TOWARDS A NEW CENTER OF GRAVITY?

Even as the population of officially recognized Zoroastrians steadily declines in Iran and India, their numbers have been swelling in countries such as the United States, Canada, and Australia, through both immigration and conversion. This simple demographic fact would suggest the possibility, if not the likelihood, that the center of gravity for Iranian Zoroastrian culture may be shifting to the West.[35]

The greater openness to intermarriage and conversion in the Western context, as well as the very real possibility that original Zoroastrian communities in Iran and India may one day disappear, suggest the strong likelihood that in the not-so-distant future the religion's center of gravity may shift to North America.[36] Historically speaking, such geographical shifts have led to significant changes and adaptations in religious traditions, as they absorb new cultural influences and rise to face new challenges. While Christianity has not entirely disappeared from its native Palestine, it has long been seen as a largely Western religion, and its Western forms differ substantially from its Near Eastern expressions, both past and present. Buddhism essentially disappeared from its birthplace on the Indian subcontinent, but thrives elsewhere in Asia and beyond, sometimes in versions that appear radically transformed by local culture. Whether the ancient tradition of Zoroastrianism will follow such a trajectory, or whether it will eventually succumb to the fate of extinct religions such as Manichaeism, will be for future generations to tell.

# Conclusion

## The Ever-Expanding Pool of Iranian Religion

Iranians today, especially the educated urban classes, demonstrate a powerful tendency toward spiritual eclecticism, continuously opening up the available pool of religious ideas and symbols to include an endless array of influences new and not-so-new. While few go so far as to overtly reject their inherited Shiʻite religious background—indeed, to do so would be politically dangerous—huge numbers of Iranian Muslims feel perfectly comfortable supplementing their spiritual lives with a wide range of beliefs and practices, many of them drawn from a variety of contemporary "new age" sources. Indeed, for one familiar with the religious history of Iran and Iranians' age-old affinity for the esoteric teachings of non-establishment *shaykh*s, the "new age" approach to spirituality hardly seems new at all.

In cities throughout Iran today yoga centers abound, often led by "masters" professing traditional Iranian *ʻerfān*; such places are massively frequented. The works of Paulo Coelho are bestsellers in Persian, and self-help manuals by the likes of Wayne Dyer, Louise Hay, and the Dalai Lama are widely read. A Hare-Krishna-affiliated vegetarian restaurant in Tehran, *Govinda*, has managed to survive for a number of years in different locations (most recently the House of Artists), though the group's well-known dancing and chanting rituals are held in private. Many Iranian Muslims see no inconsistency in advocating the Zoroastrian ethic of practicing "Good Thoughts, Good Words, Good Deeds," displayed on the walls of countless Muslim homes along with the *fravahr* and other Zoroastrian symbols. And even within more avowedly Islamic circles, Sufi groups such as the Gonabadis, as well as secretive messianic movements such as the Hojjatiyeh, who are eagerly anticipating the imminent return of the Twelfth Imam, are extremely popular.

Many Iranians today practice various forms of meditation. In 2010 an Iranian master of the Daoist practice of Wudang, Ali Asghar Koohzadi, who also goes by the Daoist name Yu Lixiao, organized a public group meditation in a Tehran park as part of World Meditation Day. In recent years Iranians have taken to Transcendental Meditation (TM) in such a big way that the country's medical establishment has begun to take it seriously as a means of coping with stress, even as a suspicious government tries to slow the movement's spread by denying official operating permits. In 2008 a team of medical researchers in Tehran published an article in a respected international journal which concluded that "Transcendental Meditation may improve mental health [among the] young adult population especially in the areas of somatisation and anxiety, and this effect seems to be independent of age, sex and marital status."[1] In a similar vein, Tehran's Milad Hospital has recently made a concession to overwhelming popular trends, by adding a department for the practice of "Energy Healing" (*enerži darmānī*) and other alternative medicine techniques.

At the same time, the official attitude toward New Age-type movements has been ambivalent, to say the least. During his second term as President, Mahmud Ahmadinejad suggested on several occasions that the government needed to "look into" the activities of organizations practicing non-traditional spirituality, and there have been some arrests. One example is that of Mohammad Ali Taheri, a practitioner of alternative medicine who has accumulated a significant following in Iran and among the Iranian diaspora through his teaching of spiritual healing techniques he calls *farā-darmānī* ("meta-healing") and "psymentology" or "inter-universal mind-psychology." Taheri has been arrested repeatedly, most recently in 2011 when he was charged with "exorcism and cheating people."[2]

Religion continues to be a loaded subject in the Islamic Republic, and the intellectual climate is filled with contradictions and paradoxes so that it is sometimes hard to know which discussions are acceptable and which are not. As long as Twelver Shi'ism remains a cornerstone of state policy this is unlikely to change. Even so, given that spirituality is clearly so deeply entrenched in the Iranian psyche, it seems likely that many Iranians will continue to pursue their curiosity about the world's various faiths in a spirit of objectivity and respect. One wishes them increased opportunities to join with other like-minded souls around the world in contemplating in the broadest possible way the immense role Iranian culture has played in the history of religions.

# Endnotes

## Preface

1. Ehsan Yarshater goes so far as to refer to such barbarian invasions "helpful," since they "injected fresh blood into the veins of the Iranians, providing them with a new source of inner energy" ("Re-emergence of Iranian Identity after Conversion to Islam," in Vesta Sarkhosh Curtis and Sarah Stewart, eds, *The Rise of Islam, The Idea of Iran* vol. 5, London: I. B. Tauris, 2009, pp. 9–10).

2. Jonathan Z. Smith and William Scott Green, *The HarperCollins Dictionary of Religion*, New York: HarperCollins, 1995, p. 893; David Chidester, *Authentic Fakes: Religion and Popular Culture in America*, Berkeley: University of California Press, 2005, p. 1.

3. Ilya Gershevitch's proposal to divide the Avestan corpus into two "religions," "Zarathuštrian" (represented by the Old Avestan texts) and "Zoroastrian" (the Younger Avesta), does not seem to me to really address or resolve the problem (*The Avestan Hymn to Mithra*, Cambridge: Cambridge University Press, 1959, p. 9).

4. Alessandro Bausani, *Religion in Iran: From Zoroaster to Baha'ullah*, tr. J. M. Marchesi, New York: Bibliotheca Persica, 2000, p. 10.

5. This is not to be confused with the Common Pool Theory (CPT) of Garrett Hardin, which refers to the use of natural resources, or the Electron Pool Theory in chemistry and physics.

6. This notion was first coined by the German philosopher Karl Jaspers (1883–1969), and continues to hold a prominent place among religion scholars.

7. Bausani, *Religion in Iran* and Henry Corbin, *Spiritual Body and Celestial Earth: From Mazdean Iran to Shi'ite Iran*, tr. Nancy Pearson, Princeton: Princeton University Press, 1977.

8. Philippe Gignoux, ed., *Recurrent Patterns in Iranian Religions: From Mazdaism to Sufism*, Paris: Association pour l'avancement des études iraniennes, 1992.

9. Patricia Crone, *The Nativist Prophets of Early Islamic Iran: Rural Revolt and Local Zoroastrianism*, Cambridge: Cambridge University Press, 2012, p. vii.

## 1. The Origins of Iranian Religion

1. For a fuller discussion see A. Shapur Shahbazi, "The History of the Idea of Iran," in Vesta Sarkhosh Curtis and Sarah Stewart, eds, *Birth of the Persian Empire, The Idea of Iran vol. 1*, London: I.B. Tauris, 2005, pp. 100–111. For a somewhat different view see Gherardo Gnoli, *The Idea of Iran: An Essay on its Origin*, Leiden: Brill, 1989.
2. Other contemporary Iranian languages include Kurdish, Baluch, Pashtu, Ossetian, Pamiri, and many others.
3. The most detailed study of questions surrounding Iranian origins, written by a Russian archaeologist, is Elena E. Kuz'mina, *The Origin of the Indo-Iranians*, Leiden: Brill: 2007.
4. See for example Michael Witzel, "Evidence for Cultural Exchange in Pre-historic Western Central Asia," *Sino-Platonic Papers* 129 (2003): 1–70.
5. From the verbal stem *dyeu-*, "to shine." (An asterisk * signals a reconstructed word not attested in any written sources.)
6. J. P. Mallory and D. Q. Adams, *The Oxford Introduction to Proto-Indo-European and the Proto-Indo-European World*, Oxford: Oxford University Press, 2006, p. 266.
7. For a full treatment of this phenomenon see Edwin Bryant, *The Quest for the Origins of Vedic Culture: The Indo-Aryan Migration Debate*, New Delhi: Oxford University Press, 2002.
8. Christopher I. Beckwith, *Empires of the Silk Road: A History of Central Eurasia from the Bronze Age to the Present*, Princeton: Princeton University Press, 2009.
9. This explanation, of which archaeologist Marija Gimbutas was an early champion, is known as the "kurgan theory," after the burial mounds (kurgans) found across the south Eurasian steppe region. (See for example Marija Gimbutas, *The Gods and Goddesses of Old Europe*, Berkeley, CA: University of California Press, 1974.) The various arguments are summarized in Mallory and Adams, *The Oxford Introduction to Proto-Indo-European and the Proto-Indo-European World*, pp. 460–463.
10. Remco Bouckaert, et al., "Mapping the Origins and Expansion of the Indo-European Language Family," *Science* 337 (2012): 957–960. Bouckaert's team, which applied a Bayesian phylogeographic analysis developed for mapping virus outbreaks, suggest that the "original" spread of PIE was linked to their development of agriculture 8,000–9,500 years Before Present. In a preface to the same article, Victor Mair points out that the study examines linguistic data exclusively and ignores other areas such as archaeology. Even in the area of linguistics, Bouckaert et al. fail to account for the fact that Hittite and its relatives appear to have been intrusive to Anatolia.
11. See for example the essays in David R. Harris, ed., *The Origins and Spread of Agriculture and Pastoralism in Eurasia*, London: Routledge, 2004.
12. See David Anthony, *The Horse, The Wheel and Language: How Bronze Age Riders from the Eurasian Steppes Shaped the Modern World*, Princeton: Princeton University Press, 2007.
13. Alan K. Outram et al., "The Earliest Horse Harnessing and Milking," *Science*, 6 March, 2009, pp. 1332–1335.

14. The tripartite nature of PIE society has been most fully theorized by the French comparative mythologist Georges Dumézil and his students. (See for example Georges Dumézil, *Les Dieux des indo-européens*, Paris: Presses universitaires de France, 1952.) Others have challenged this approach, however, variously arguing that the paradigm has been applied too rigidly, or that it is not unique to Indo-Europeans.

15. For an exhaustive treatment of the subject see Calvert Watkins, *How to Kill a Dragon: Aspects of Indo-European Poetics*, New York: Oxford University Press, 1995.

16. Watkins, *How to Kill a Dragon*, p. 70.

17. Kuz'mina, *The Origin of the Indo-Iranians*, p. 330. Witzel considers it "quite likely" that the inhabitants of Sintashta spoke proto-Indo-Iranian (Witzel, "Evidence for Cultural Exchange," p. 48).

18. R. S. Sharma, *Looking for the Aryans*, Madras: Orient Longman, 1995, p. 65.

19. Kuz'mina, *The Origin of the Indo-Iranians*, p. 182.

20. It is perhaps equally ironic that the Rig Veda is less relevant for an understanding of Hinduism—which includes much that predates the Aryan arrival in the subcontinent—than modern Hindu scripturalists have tried to argue. While the Rig Veda and other later Vedas do count among the sacred texts memorized by Hindu Brahmin priests for the performance of rituals, their historical role in Hinduism is fairly circumscribed and is in no way analogous to the central and normative role of the Bible or the Qur'an in Judaism, Christianity and Islam, or even the Avesta in Zoroastrianism. The attempts of Hindu nationalists in modern India to endow the Vedas with such a status is very recent, and certainly owes something to imposed Western notions of what constitutes religion.

21. *The Rig Veda*, translated by Wendy Doniger O'Flaherty (New York: Penguin Books, 1981), hymn no. 10.119, pp. 131–132.

22. It is probably significant that the term "shaman" is a word originating from the Eurasian steppes, albeit as a much later appearance in Altaic—that is, non-Indo-European—language.

23. *Karšvar*; the modern Persian word, *kešvar*, means "country."

24. While the "inversion" of these two classes of deities, attributed to Zoroaster, has been central to discussions of the Indo-Iranian split since the nineteenth century, Johanna Narten has gone so far as to question whether speaking of these deities as constituting distinct groups is even appropriate. See her "Zarathustra und die Gottheiten des Alten Iran," *Münchener Studien zur Sprachwissenschaft* 56 (1986): 61–89.

25. The earliest written evidence of Indo-Iranians is found in cuneiform texts from the Mitanni kingdom of northern Mesopotamia. One document, a treaty dating to about 1370 BCE, mentions the Aryan deities Mitra, Varuna, and Indra.

26. *Aitareya Brahmana*, trans. Martin Haug, New York: AMS Press, 1974, 2.6.

## 2. Mithra and Mithraism

1. Or, perhaps, of alliances. For an overview of discussions regarding the etymology and meaning of the term mitra see Hanns-Peter Schmidt, "Mitra Studies: The State of the Central Problem," in Jacques Duchesne-Guillemin, ed., *Études*

*Mithraïques*, Tehran: Bibliothèque Pahlavi, 1978, pp. 345–394. The word seems from ancient times to have implied the notion of "friendly alliance," and thus by extension "peace" (cf. Slavic *mir*), and "love" (cf. NP *mehr*). An additional semantic function, found in Vedic as well as Avestan sources, is that of "mediator" or "arbiter," and by extension "judge."

2. Mehrdad Bahar, *Az ostūreh tā tārīx*, Tehran: Češmeh, 1376 [1997], pp. 297–299.

3. See Paul Thieme, "The 'Aryan' Gods of the Mitanni Treaties," *Journal of the American Oriental Society* 80/4 (1960): 301–317.

4. R. D. Barnett, "A Mithraic Figure from Beirut," in John Hinnells, ed., *Mithraic Studies*, Manchester: Manchester University Press, 1975, pp. 466–469. Barnett observes that while this figure, who is clean-shaven, is often held to be Gilgamesh, the latter is always depicted with a beard.

5. This theme is emphasized in the Avestan Mehr Yašt, especially verses 5 and 8–10.

6. Mary Boyce and Frantz Grenet, *A History of Zoroastrianism*, v. 3, *Zoroastrianism under Macedonian and Roman Rule*, Leiden: Brill, 1991, v. 3, pp. 486–487, n. 629.

7. Jacques Duchesne-Guillemin, "Le dieu de Cyrus," *Acta Iranica* 3 (1974), pp. 11–21.

8. Philippe Swennen, *D'Indra à Tištrya: Portrait et evolution du cheval sacré dans les mythes indo-iraniens anciens*, Paris: Collège de France, 2004, p. 175.

9. Muhammad A. Dandamaev and Vladimir G. Lukonin, *The Culture and Social Institutions of Ancient Iran*, Cambridge: Cambridge University Press, 1989, p. 314.

10. Arrian, *The Campaigns of Alexander*, tr. Aubrey de Sélincourt, New York: Penguin, 1958, 6.29.9–11. (I am grateful to Touraj Daryaee for providing this reference.) The issue of horse sacrifice among the Iranians is treated in detail in Swennen, *D'Indra à Tištrya*.

11. Richard Frye, "Mithra in Iranian History," in *Mithraic Studies*, vol. 1, pp. 62–63.

12. Xenophon, *Cyropaedia*, tr. Walter Miller, Cambridge: Harvard University Press, 1968; v. 7, pp. 5, 53.

13. Frye, "Mithra in Iranian History," in *Mithraic Studies*, p. 64.

14. Parvaneh Pourshariati, *Decline and Fall of the Sasanian Empire: The Sasanian-Parthian Confederacy and the Arab Conquest of Iran*, London: I. B. Tauris, 2008.

15. Strabo, *Geography*, tr. H. L. Jones, London: Heinemann, 1960; 15.13.732.

16. Gershevitch, "Die Sonne das Beste," in Hinnells, *Mithraic Studies*, pp. 69–70.

17. Helmut Humbach, "Mithra in the Kusana Period," in Hinnells, *Mithraic Studies*, p. 136. Humbach points out the Bactrian name of Ahura Mazda, Ooromazdo, has been found on only a single Kushan coin (p. 139).

18. A. D. H. Bivar, "Mithraic Images of Bactria: Are they related to Roman Mithraism?," *Mysteria Mithrae: Atti del seminario su la specificatà storico-religiosa dei misteri di Mithra*, Leiden: Brill, 1979, pp. 741–743.

19. David W. McDowall, "Mithra and the Deities of the Kusana coinage," in Hinnells, *Mithraic Studies*, p. 148.

20. Franz Cumont, "The Dura Mithraeum," in Hinnells, *Mithraic Studies*, pp. 158–159.
21. John R. Hinnells, "Reflections on the Bull-slaying Scene," in *Mithraic Studies*, p. 309.
22. Bruce Lincoln, "Mithra(s) as Sun and Savior," in *Death, War and Sacrifice: Studies in Ideology and Practice*, Chicago: University of Chicago Press, 1991, p. 77.
23. Ibn Nadim, *Fihrist al-'ulum*, tr. B. Dodge, *The Fihrist of al-Nadim: A Tenth Century Survey of Muslim Culture*, New York: Columbia University Press, 1970, v. 2, p. 778.
24. A. D. H. Bivar, "Mithra and Mesopotamia," in Hinnells, *Mithraic Studies*, v. 2, pp. 275–289.
25. Gershevitch, *The Avestan Hymn to Mithra*, 10.8.33–34 and 10.23.93–94 (pp. 88–91 and 118–119).
26. Hinnells, "Reflections on the bull-slaying scene," in *Mithraic Studies*, p. 308.
27. Mary Boyce, "Mihragan Among the Irani Zoroastrians," in Hinnells, *Mithraic Studies*, p. 112.
28. Boyce, "Mihragan Among the Irani Zoroastrians," p. 114.
29. Abu Rayhan Biruni, *Āthār-al-baqiya*, tr. C. Edward Sachau, *The Chronology of Ancient Nations*, London: W. H. Allen, 1879, p. 208.
30. See Philip Kreyenbroek, "Mithra and Ahriman in Iranian Cosmologies," in J. R. Hinnells, ed., *Studies in Mithraism*, Rome: Bretschneider, 1994, pp. 173–182.
31. Bahar, *Az ostūreh tā tārīx*, p. 180.
32. Mohammad Moghaddam, *Jostārī dar bāreye Mehr va Nāhīd*, Tehran: Hirmand, 1388 [2010], pp. 37–39.
33. Hassan Pirouzdjou, *Mithraïsme et emancipation: anthropologie sociale et culturelle des mouvements populaires en Iran: au VIIe, IXe et du XIVe au début du XVIe siècle*, Paris: Harmattan, 1999, p. 10.
34. Pirouzdjou, *Mithraïsme et emancipation*, pp. 216–218.
35. Abolala Soudavar, *The Aura of Kings: Legitimacy and Divine Sanction in Iranian Kingship*, Costa Mesa, CA: Mazda Publishers, 2003, pp. 7–9.
36. Bahar, *Az ostūreh tā tārīx*, pp. 27–41.

## 3. In Search of Zoroaster

1. See especially Jean Kellens and Eric Pirart, *Les textes viels-avestiques*, v.1, pp. 17–20 and Jean Kellens, *Zoroastre et l'Avesta ancien*, Louvain: Peeters, 1991, pp. 59ff.
2. See for example Martin Schwartz, "How Zarathushtra Generated the Gathic Corpus: Inner-textual and Intertextual Composition," *Bulletin of the Asia Institute* 16 (2002): 53–64, and "The Composition of the Gathas and Zarathushtra's Authorship," in Fereydun Vahman and Claus V. Pedersen eds, *Religious Texts in Iranian Languages*, Copenhagen: Royal Danish Academy of Science and Letters, 2007, pp. 45–56.
3. Gherardo Gnoli, *Zoroaster in History*, New York: Bibliotheca Persica, 2000.

4. Adapted from the translation in William W. Malandra, *An Introduction to Ancient Iranian Religion*, Minneapolis: University of Minnesota Press, 1983, pp. 38–39.
5. Ancient Egyptian hieroglyphs depicting kings passing into the next life are accompanied by scales, suggesting an interesting but inconclusive parallel.
6. Zoroastrian eschatology is often considered to be an innovation, as contrasted with other Indo-European religions such as that of Greece and Rome, where there is little attention to the afterlife, or India, where reincarnation makes the question moot. However, some eschatological elements in the Rig Veda suggest an alternative view, that Zoroastrianism actually preserved an ancient Indo-European eschatology (reflected in the myths of Scandinavia) that was lost among other Indo-European peoples. (I owe this observation to Jean Kellens, personal conversation.)
7. This section largely follows the arguments of Jean Kellens, presented in a series of lectures at Concordia University, Montréal, in May 2011.
8. We know this because the form of the Pahlavi Middle Persian alphabet upon which it was based dates from that particular period.
9. At the present time this tiny fragment, found at Dunhuang in China and now in the British Museum, is the only example of Avestan text in Sogdian that has come to light. Mary Boyce believes, on the basis of archaic "peculiarities of diction," that the translation dates back to "Old Sogdian," i.e., contemporaneous with the Achæmenid period, but this seems exaggerated (Boyce, *History of Zoroastrianism*, v. 3, p. 124). Moreover, since Zoroastrians have always recited this prayer in Avestan the translation seems more likely attributable to a Manichaean writer, as Ilya Gershevitch has suggested (appendix to Sims-Williams, "The Sogdian Manuscripts in the British Museum," *Indo-Iranian Journal* 18 (1976): 75–82).
10. Michael Stausberg believes this is a misinterpretation, and that the *Dēnkard* is in fact referring to the totality of the religion, not just the Avesta (personal communication, 15 August 2012).
11. Kellens, Concordia lectures, May 2011.

### 4. Mazda and His Rivals

1. The Elamite version of the Behistun inscription glosses Mazda as "the god of the Aryans (*har-ri-ya*)."
2. The term is commonly translated as "the Mazda-worshiping religion," but "worship" is actually a misleading translation of the Iranian root *yaz-*, which more specifically means "to perform a sacrifice."
3. See D. T. Potts, "Cyrus the Great and the Kingdom of Anshan," in Curtis and Stewart, eds, *Birth of the Persian Empire*, pp. 7–23.
4. P. O. Skjærvø, "The Achæmenids and the Avesta," in Curtis and Stewart, eds, *Birth of the Persian Empire*, pp. 52–84.
5. Josef Wiesehöfer, *Ancient Persia*, London: I. B. Tauris, 1998, p. 100.
6. Wouter F. M. Henkelman, *The Other Gods Who Are: Studies in Elamite-Iranian acculturation based on the Persepolis fortification texts*, Leiden: Nino, 2008, p. 59.

7. Phiroze Vasunia, "The Philosopher's Zarathushtra," in Christopher Tupin, ed., *Persian Responses: Political and Cultural Interaction with(in) the Achæmenid Empire*, Swansea: The Classical Press of Wales, 2007, pp. 237–265.

8. Abu'l-Hasan Ali Mas'udi, *Murūj al-dhahāb (Les Prairies d'or)*, ed. and tr. Barbier de Meynard and Pavet de Courteille, Paris: Société asiatique, 1965, v. 1, p. 289.

9. A. S. Melikian-Chirvani, "The Wine Birds of Iran from Pre-Achaemenid to Islamic Times," *Bulletin of the Asia Institute 9* (1995), p. 41.

10. *Dinkard*, ed. and tr. P. B. and D. P. Sanjana, 19 vols., Bombay, 1928, 413: 2–8.

11. Quoted in R. C. Zaehner, *Zurvan: A Zoroastrian Dilemma*, Oxford: Oxford University Press, 1955, p. 14.

12. Zaehner, *Zurvan*, p. 13.

13. Zaehner, *Zurvan*, p. 16.

14. I have related here but one basic version of the Zurvanite creation myth, of which there exist numerous variations. For example, another version has Zurvan emanate a female partner; it is she who becomes pregnant. Other varying details include the length of Ahriman's reign and the division of history into three periods of three thousand years each.

15. Or, as he somewhat less precisely puts it, "Zervanism was the current form of Zoroastrianism at that time" (Zaehner, *Zurvan*, p. 22).

16. Zaehner, *Zurvan*, p. 21.

17. In fact there are two works bearing this name, which are often confused. The work deemed Zurvanite is referred to by de Blois as "Ulama II". As to why a Zurvanite text appears in so late a version, de Blois surmises that ". . . the author of Ulama II has inserted in his work quotations from a lost Zurvanite treatise from the Sasanian period, a treatise that he found, evidently in a New Persian translation, in some old manuscript." (François de Blois, "The Two Zoroastrian Treatises Called 'Ulama-i Islam'," *The Classical Bulletin* 83/2 (2007), p. 218.)

18. Zaehner, *Zurvan*, p. 410.

19. Abolqasem Ferdowsi, *Shahnameh: the Persian Book of Kings*, tr. Dick Davis, New York: Viking, 2006, p. 376.

20. *Shahnameh*, p. 398.

## 5. Iranian Goddesses

1. Prods Oktor Skjærvø, *The Spirit of Zoroastrianism*, New Haven: Yale University Press, 2011, p. 17.

2. Cf. Digor *urdug*, Iron *u̯rdig* "upright," OInd. *ūrdhva-*, Av. *ərədwa-*; Fridrik Thordarson, "Ossetic," *Encyclopaedia Iranica* online.

3. Emile Benveniste, *The Persian Religion according to the chief Greek texts*, Paris: Librarie Orientaliste, 1929, pp. 27–28, 38–39.

4. Hermann Lommel, "Anahita-Sarasvati," *Asiatica: Friedrich Weller*, Leipzig: Harrassowitz, 1954, pp. 405–413.

5. Žaleh Amuzgar, *Tārīkh-e Īrān-e bāstān*, v. 1, Tehran: Sāzmān-e mota'leh va tadvīn-e kutub-e 'ūlūm-e ensānīye dānešgāhhā, 1380 [2001], p. 69.

6. Panaino, "The Mesopotamian Heritage of Achaemenian Kingship," p. 38.

7. Kellens, "Le problème avec Anāhitā," p. 322.
8. Mary Boyce, "Anāhīd," *Encyclopaedia Iranica* online.
9. Kellens, "Le problème avec Anāhitā," p. 323.
10. See Johannes Hertel, *Die Sonne und Mithra im Awesta, auf grund der awestischen feuerlehre dargestellt*, Leipzig: Haessel, 1927, p. 20, n. 1 and Toshifumi Gotō, "Vasistha und Varuna in RV VI{I} 88 Priesteramt des Vasistha und Suche nach seinem indoiranischen Hintergrund," *Indoarisch, Iranisch une die Indogermanistik*, Wiesbaden: Reichert Verlag, 2000, pp. 160–161.
11. Boyce, *A History of Zoroastrianism*, v. 2, p. 29.
12. Eric Pirart, *Syntaxe des langues indo-iraniennes anciennes*, Barcelona, 1997, pp. 156–159.
13. Kellens, "Le problème avec Anāhitā," p. 325.
14. Herodotus, *The Histories*, Book 4: Melpomene [50].
15. H. S. Nyberg, *Die Religionen des alten Iran*, Leipzig: J. C. Hinrichs, 1938, p. 260.
16. Michael Witzel, "Sur le chemin du ciel," *Bulletin d'études indiennes*, 2 (1984), p. 226.
17. See for example Malandra, *An Introduction to Ancient Iranian Religion*, pp. 118–119, and A. T. Olmstead, *History of the Persian Empire*, Chicago: University of Chicago Press, 1948, pp. 471–472.
18. Panaino, "The Mesopotamian Heritage of Achaemenian Kingship", p. 37.
19. Kellens, "Le problème avec Anāhitā," p. 320.
20. Panaino, "The Mesopotamian Heritage of Achaemenian Kingship," p. 38.
21. See Kuz'mina, *The Origin of the Indo-Iranians*.
22. *Vīdēvdāt*, 1.3.
23. Almut Hintze, "The Cow that Came from the Moon: The Avestan Expression *mah- gaociθra-*," *Bulletin of the Asia Institute* 19 2005 [2009], p. 59.
24. See Prods Oktor Skjærvø, "The Avestan Yasna: Ritual and Myth," in Vahman and Pedersen eds, *Religious Texts in Iranian Languages*, p. 59.
25. B. Schlerath and P. O. Skjærvø, "Aši," *Encyclopedia Iranica* online.
26. Boyce, *History of Zoroastrianism*, v. 1, pp. 65ff.
27. Mary Boyce and Frantz Grenet, *A History of Zoroastrianism*, v. 3, *Zoroastrianism under Macedonian and Roman Rule*, Leiden: Brill, 1991, pp. 486–487, n. 629.
28. B. Schlerath and P. O. Skjærvø, "Aši," *Encyclopedia Iranica* online.
29. Mary Boyce, "Hordād," *Encyclopedia Iranica* online.
30. Johanna Narten, *Die Aməša Spəṇtas im Avesta*, Wiesbaden: Harrassowitz, 1982, p. 72.
31. Guitty Azarpay, "Iranian Divinities in Sogdian Paintings," *Acta Iranica* 4 (1975): 12–21.
32. See Guitty Azarpay, *Sogdian Painting: the Pictorial Epic in Oriental Art*, Berkeley: University of California Press, 1981.
33. Bausani, *Religion in Iran*, p. 30.
34. Khojasteh Kia, *Soxanān sazāvar zanān dar Shāh-nāme-ye pahlavānī*, Tehran: Našr-i Fākhtah, 1371 [1992], p. 212.
35. Manya Saadi-nejad, "Mythological Themes in Iranian Culture and Art: Traditional and Contemporary Perspectives," *Iranian Studies* 42/2 (2009): 231–246.

36. D. Monchi-Zadeh, "Xus-rôv i Kavâtân ut Rêtak," in *Monumentum Georg Morgenstierne*, vol. II. *Acta Iranica* 22, Leiden: Brill, 1982, pp. 47–91.
37. Simin Daneshvar, *Savushun*, Washington, DC: Mage, 1990.
38. Ferdowsi, *Shahnameh*, p. 221.
39. *The Epic of Gilgamesh*, Tablet VI, in Stephanie Dalley, *Myths from Mesopotamia*, Oxford: Oxford University Press, 2008, p. 77.
40. Kia, *Soxanān sazāvar zanān*, p. 144.
41. Prods Oktor Skjærvø, "Eastern Iranian Epic Traditions II: Rostam and Bhīṣma," *Acta Orientalia Academiae Scientiarum Hungaricae* 51 (1998): 159–170.
42. Mary Boyce, "Zariades and Zarer," *Bulletin of the School of Oriental and African Studies* 17/3 (1955): 463–477.

## 6. Judaism

1. Hooshang Ebrami, "Introduction," in Habib Levy, *Comprehensive History of the Jews of Iran: The Outset of the Diaspora*, Costa Mesa, CA: Mazda Publishers, 1999, p. xvi.
2. See Richard Foltz, *Religions of the Silk Road: Premodern Patterns of Globalization*, 2nd ed., New York: Palgrave Macmillan, 2010, especially Chapter 2.
3. Morton Smith, "Iranian Elements in the Bible," in Houman Sarshar, ed., *Jewish Communities of Iran*, New York: Encyclopædia Iranica, 2011, p. 325.
4. Touraj Daryaee, "Indo-European Elements in the Zoroastrian Apocalyptic Tradition," *The Classical Bulletin* 83/2 (2007), pp. 206–207.
5. Mayer I. Gruber, "The Achaemenid Period," in Sarshar, ed., *Jewish Communities of Iran*, p. 12.
6. Esther 9:24–28, *The Tanakh*, Philadelphia: Jewish Publication Society, 1985.
7. James Barr, "The Question of Religious Influence: The Case of Zoroastrianism, Judaism, and Christianity," *Journal of the American Academy of Religion* 53/2 (1985): 201–235.
8. Boyce and Grenet, *History of Zoroastrianism*, v. 3, pp. 376–380.
9. Boyce and Grenet, *History of Zoroastrianism*, v. 3, p. 410.
10. Ebrami, op. cit., p. xv.
11. Jacob Neusner, *History of the Jews in Babylonia*, v. 2, Leiden: Brill, 1966, pp. 75–76.
12. Carol Bakhos and Rahim Shayegan, eds, *The Talmud in its Iranian Context*, Tübingen: Mohr Siebeck, 2010, p. xiii.
13. See Yaakov Elman, "The Other in the Mirror: Iranians and Jews View One Another: Questions of Identity, Conversion, and Exogamy in the Fifth-Century Iranian Empire," *Bulletin of the Asia Institute* 19–20 (2009–10): 15–46.
14. Neusner, *History of the Jews in Babylonia*, v. 5, pp. 11–14.
15. Sascha L. Goluboff, "Are They Jews or Asians? A Cautionary Tale about Mountain Jewish Ethnography," *Slavic Review* 63/1 (2004), p. 114.
16. A Russian-language website, <www.juhuro.com>, covers events pertaining to the worldwide Juhuro community.

17. Levy, *Comprehensive History of the Jews of Iran*, p. 255.
18. According to Netzer, "Shāhīn," as he signed his work—his actual name being unknown—was from Khorasan, not Shiraz. See Amnon Netzer, "Notes and Observations Concerning Shahin's Birthplace," *Irano-Judaica IV*, pp. 187–202.
19. See Vera Basch Moreen, *In Queen Esther's Garden*, pp. 26–31.
20. Bābā'ī b. Lutf, *Kitāb-e Anūsī* ("Book of a Forced Convert"), translated by Moreen in *In Queen Esther's Garden*, p. 281.
21. Levy, *A Comprehensive History of the Jews of Iran*, pp. 170–171.
22. A number of good colour reproductions can be found in Houman Sarshar, ed., *Queen Esther's Children: A Portrait of Iranian Jews*, Philadelphia: Jewish Publication Society, 2002.
23. Jaleh Pirnazar, "The Anusim of Mashhad," in Sarshar, ed., *Queen Esther's Children*, pp. 117–136.
24. See Faryar Nikbakht, "As With Moses in Egypt: Alliance israélite universelle schools in Iran," in Sarshar, ed., *Queen Esther's Children*, pp. 199–212.

## 7. Buddhism

1. See Foltz, *Religions of the Silk Road*, Chapter 3.
2. "Statues in Iran Challenge Theories on Buddhism's Spread," *The Japan Times*, 14 May 2002.
3. Warwick Ball, "How Far Did Buddhism Spread West?," *Al-Rāfidān* 10 (1989): 1–10.
4. The existence of a Persian meaning for this term, "new spring," is most likely coincidental.
5. Boris Stavisky, "'Buddha-Mazda' from Kara-Tepe in Old Termez (Uzbekistan): A Preliminary Communication," *Journal of the International Association of Buddhist Studies* 3/2 (1980): 89–94.
6. Samuel Beal, *Buddhist Records of the Western World*, New Delhi: Oriental Reprints, 1969 [1888], pp. 44–45.
7. Beal, *Buddhist Records*, 45–46.
8. Mas'udi, *Murūj al-dhahāb*, v. 4, p. 79.
9. A. S. Melikian-Chirvani, "L'évocation littéraire du bouddhisme dans l'Iran musulman," *Le monde iranien et l'Islam* 2 (1974), p. 37.
10. Melikian-Chirvani, "*L'évocation littéraire du bouddhisme*," p. 57.
11. Frantz Grenet, "Bāmiyān and the Mehr Yasht," *Bulletin of the Asia Institute* 7 (1993): 87–92.
12. See Gregory Schopen, "Notes on the Cult of the Book in Mahāyāna," *Indo-Iranian Journal* 17/3-4 (1975): 147–181.
13. Ronald E. Emmerick, "Buddhism Among Iranian Peoples," in Ehsan Yarshater, ed., *Cambridge History of Iran*, Cambridge: Cambridge University Press, 1983, v. 3, pp. 955–956.
14. Iwamoto Yutaka, *Jigoku meguri no bungaku*, Tokyo: Kaimei shoten, 1979, pp. 184–199; cited in Stephen F. Teiser, *The Ghost Festival in Medieval China*, Princeton, NJ: Princeton University Press, 1988, p. 24.
15. Rolf A. Stein, *La Civilisation tibetaine*, Paris: Dunod, 1962, pp. 28, 69.

16. Paul du Breuil, "A Study of Some Zoroastrian and Buddhist Eschatological Features," *K. R. Cama Institute International Congress Proceedings*, Bombay: K. R. Cama Institute, 1991, pp. 52–64.
17. Richard Bulliet, "Naw Bahar and the Survival of Iranian Buddhism," *Iran* 14 (1976), pp. 140–145.
18. This section is largely inspired by discussions with my wife, Manya Saadi-nejad, and my Persian translator, Askari Pasha'i.
19. Sohrab Sepehri, in *Šarq-e andūh*, Tehran: Ketābxāne-ye Tahūrī, 1358 [1979], pp. 239–240.
20. Or so she informed the author, at a party in Miami in 2001.

## 8. Christianity

1. Matthew 2:1–12 mentions magi from the east, without specifying their number.
2. Ian Gillman and Hans-Joachim Klimkeit, *Christians in Asia Before 1500*, Ann Arbor: University of Michigan Press, 1999, p. 109.
3. M.-L. Chaumont, *La Christianisation de l'empire iranien: des origines aux grandes persécutions du IVe siècle*, Louvain: Peeters, 1988, pp. v–vi.
4. Chaumont, *La Christianisation de l'empire iranien*, pp. 105–106.
5. Quoted in Gillman and Klimkeit, *Christians in Asia Before 1500*, p. 112.
6. Those who follow this Christology are often referred to as "monophysites" ("single nature"), but they claim that the term "miaphysite" ("compound nature") more precisely reflects their position.
7. This is despite the fact that Nestorius himself did not actually preach diophysitism, whose principal champion was Theodore of Mopsuestia (352–428).
8. The official adoption of Christianity in Armenia has traditionally been dated at 301 CE, but recently scholars have come to posit a date of 314–315 as more likely. See Gillman and Klimkeit, *Christians in Asia Before 1500*, p. 92.
9. Tabari's *History*, cited in Mary Boyce, *Zoroastrians: Their Religious Beliefs and Practices*, London: Routledge and Kegan Paul, 1979, p. 141.
10. Rika Gyselen, *Sasanian Seals and Sealings in the A. Saeedi Collection*, Louvain: Peeters, 2007.
11. See the discussion in Richard E. Payne, "Christianity and Iranian Society in Late Antiquity, ca. 500–700 CE," unpublished Ph.D. dissertation, Princeton University, 2010, pp. 127–128.
12. Alexei Savchenko, "Urgut Revisited," *ARAM: Journal of the Society for Syro-Mesopotamian Studies* 8/1–2 (1996): 333–354.
13. Paul Pelliot, *L'inscription nestorienne de Si-Ngan-Foui*, ed. Antonio Forte, Paris: Collège de France, 1996.
14. Nicholas Sims-Williams, personal communication, 3 July 2012.
15. James R. Russell, "Christianity in Pre-Islamic Persia: Literary Sources," *Encyclopedia Iranica*, v. 5, p. 526.
16. Taken from Aphrahat, "On the Paschal Sacrifice," in *Demonstrations*, tr. Jacob Neusner in *Aphrahat and Judaism: the Christian-Jewish Argument in Fourth-Century Iran*, Leiden: Brill, 1971, pp. 34, 36, 40.

17. *Synodicon Orientale ou Recueil de Synodes Nestoriens*, ed. and tr. Jean-Baptiste Chabot, Paris: Imprimérie nationale, 1902, Canon 25, pp. 417–418; quoted in A.V. Williams, "Zoroastrians and Christians in Sasanian Iran," *Bulletin of the John Rylands Library* 78/3 (1996), p. 42.
18. *Synodicon Orientale*, Canon 14, p. 488; quoted in Williams, "Zoroastrians and Christians in Sasanian Iran," p. 43.
19. *Ausgewählte Akten persischer Märtyrer*, tr. O. Braun, Bibliothek der Kirchenväter, 1915, v. 22, p. 109; quoted in Boyce, *Zorostrians*, p. 140.
20. John C. Reeves, *Heralds of That Good Realm: Syro-Mesopotamian Gnosis and Jewish Traditions*, Leiden: Brill, 1996, pp. 127–128.
21. Baumer, *The Church of the East*, p. 25.
22. Gillman and Klimkeit, *Christians in Asia Before 1500*, p. 137.
23. Quoted in Gillman and Klimkeit, *Christians in Asia Before 1500*, p. 130.
24. J. R. Russell, "Armenia and Iran iii: Armenian Religion," *Encyclopedia Iranica* online.
25. In an interesting precedent, the Sasanian emperor Shapur II transferred much of the Christian and Jewish population of Armenia to Esfahan in 365 CE, an apparent attempt to weaken Armenia's economy and make it more dependent on Iran.
26. Benjamin Weinthal, "Tehran to Execute Christian Pastor for 'Apostasy'," *Jerusalem Post*, 2 October 2011 <www.jpost.com/International/Article. aspx?id=240160>

## 9. Mandaeism

1. Kurt Rudolph, *Gnosis: The Nature and History of Gnosticism*, San Francisco: Harper and Row, 1987, p. 276.
2. Rudolph, *Gnosis*, pp. 282–283.
3. Jason BeDuhn suggests that the Mandaean conception of John the Baptist may have been formed during the early Islamic period, in an effort to be recognized as a "people of the Book" (personal communication, 2 October 2012).
4. Torgny Säve-Soderbergh, *Studies in the Coptic-Manichaean Psalm-Book*, Uppsala: Almqvist and Wiksell, 1949, pp. 137–162.
5. Jorunn Jacobsen Buckley, *The Mandaeans: Ancient Texts and Modern People*, New York: Oxford University Press, 2002, p. 5.
6. On the copyists' tradition see Jorunn Jacobsen Buckley, *The Great Stem of Souls: Reconstructing Mandaean History*, Piscataway, NJ: Gorgias Press, 2005.
7. The *Right Ginza* (GR), quoted in Edmondo Lupieri, *The Mandaeans: The Last Gnostics*, tr. Charles Hindley, Grand Rapids, MI: Eerdmans, 2002, pp. 178–179.
8. The *Right Ginza* (GR), quoted in Lupieri, *The Mandaeans*, p. 180.
9. See the chapter devoted to her in Buckley, *The Mandaeans*, pp. 40–48.
10. The *Left Ginza* (GL), quoted in Lupieri, *The Mandaeans*, p. 195.
11. E. S. Drower, *The Mandaeans of Iraq and Iran: Their Cults, Customs, Magic, Legends, and Folklore*, Leiden: Brill, 1962, p. 104.

12. Drower, *The Mandaeans of Iraq and Iran*, p. xxi.
13. Lupieri, *The Mandaeans*, p. 19.
14. Drower, *The Mandaeans*, pp. 36–37.
15. Drower, *The Mandaeans*, pp. 225–239.
16. Buckley, *The Great Stem of Souls*, p. 2.
17. Majid Fandi Al-Mubaraki and Brian Mubaraki, *Ginza rba*, Sydney: M.F. Al-Mubaraki, 1998.
18. Buckley, *Great Stem of Souls*, p. 17.
19. Buckley, *The Mandaeans*, pp. 49–56.
20. Buckley, *Great Stem of Souls*, p. 161–162.
21. Quoted in Buckley, *The Mandaeans*, p. 140.
22. Drower, *The Mandaeans*, p. 373.
23. Drower, *The Mandaeans*, pp. 369 ff.
24. "Save the Mandaeans of Iraq," Mandaean Associations Union website, 20 April 2009 www.mandeanunion.org

## 10. Manichaeism

1. John C. Reeves, *Prolegomena to a History of Islamicate Manichaeism*, Sheffield: Equinox, 2011, p. 85.
2. The relevant primary texts can be found in Iain Gardner and Samuel N. C. Lieu, *Manichaean Texts from the Roman Empire*, Cambridge and New York: Cambridge University Press, 2004, pp. 46–73.
3. See W. Sundermann, "Mani, India and the Manichaean Religion," *South Asian Studies* 2 (1986): 11–19.
4. See Reeves, *Prolegomena*, p. 40, n.139.
5. Matthew P. Canepa, "The Art and Ritual of Manichaean Magic: Text, Object and Image from the Mediterranean to Central Asia," in Hallie G. Meredith, ed., *Objects in Motion: The Circulation of Religion and Sacred Objects in the Late Antique and Byzantine World*, Oxford: Archaeopress, 2011, p. 75.
6. English translation by D. N. Mackenzie in the *Bulletin of the School of Oriental and African Studies*, 42 (1979): 500–534 and 43 (1980): 288–310. Samuel Lieu suggests that the *Šābūragān* may in fact have been translated into Middle Persian for Mani (personal communication, 8 July 2012).
7. Samuel N. C. Lieu, G. Fox and J. Sheldon, *Greek and Latin Texts on Manichaean Cosmogony*, Corpus Fontium Manichaeorum Series Subsidia 6, Turnhout: Brepols, 2010, pp. 40–41 and 163.
8. Reeves disagrees with this assessment, considering that Mani saw himself first and foremost as a restorer of Christianity (Reeves, *Prolegomena*, p. 130).
9. Translation in Gardner and Lieu, *Manichaean Texts from the Roman Empire*, p. 266.
10. In the first chapter of the *Kephalaia* he attributes much of the corruption of previous religions to the fact that Zoroaster, the Buddha, and Jesus did not write down their revelations themselves but left this task to their followers.

11. Reeves, *Prolegomena*, p. 121, n. 263.
12. Later examples of Manichaean book art have emerged from Central Asia; see for example Zsuzsanna Gulácsi, *Mediaeval Manichaean Book Art: A codicological study of Iranian and Turkic illuminated book fragments from 8th–11th century East Central Asia* (Nag Hammadi and Manichaean Studies, 57), Leiden: Brill, 2005.
13. Quoted in Reeves, *Prolegomena*, p. 122.
14. Qadi Ahmad Qomi, *Calligraphers and Painters: A Treatise by Qadi Ahmad, son of Mir Munshi (circa A.H. 1015/A.D. 1606)*, tr. Vladimir Minorsky, Washington, DC: Smithsonian Institution, 1959, pp. 159, 174, 177–180, 192.
15. Quoted in Reeves, *Prolegomena*, pp. 47–48.
16. This is a clear reference to the Bodhisattva figure in Mahayana Buddhism, who chooses to delay his own passage into nirvana and remain in the world to work for the liberation of all.
17. Text M42, in H.-J. Klimkeit, *Gnosis on the Silk Road*, San Francisco: Harper, 1993, pp. 124–125.
18. See Foltz, *Religions of the Silk Road*, pp. 75–84.
19. See Samuel N. C. Lieu, ed., *Medieval Christian and Manichaean Remains from Quanzhou (Zayton)*, Turnhout: Brepols, 2012, pp. 79–82.
20. Lieu, ed., *Medieval Christian and Manichaean Remains from Quanzhou*, pp. 69–70 and 124.
21. See Luigi Cirillo, "The Mani Logion: 'The Purification that was Spoken About is that which Comes Through Gnosis,'" in Jason David BeDuhn, ed., *New Light on Manichaeism: Papers from the Sixth International Congress on Manichaeism*, Leiden: Brill, 2009, pp. 45–59.
22. M741, in Klimkeit, *Gnosis on the Silk Road*, p. 38.
23. Richard C. C. Fynes, following F. C. Baur, sees this as being more likely due to Jaina than Buddhist influence ("Plant Souls in Jainism and Manichaeism: the Case for Cultural Transmission," *East and West* 46 (1996): 21–44). See also Iain Gardner and Max Deeg, "Indian Influence on Mani Reconsidered: The Case of Jainism," *International Journal of Jaina Studies* 5 (2009): 1–30.
24. Robert A. Kitchen, tr., *The Syriac Book of Steps*, Piscataway, NJ: Gorgias Press, 2009.
25. Baumer, *Church of the East*, p. 118.
26. Jason David BeDuhn, *The Manichaean Body: In Discipline and Ritual*, Baltimore: Johns Hopkins University Press, 2000.
27. Augustinus, *Contra Faustum* V, 10, in Philip Schaff, ed., *Nicene and Post-Nicene Fathers*, Grand Rapids, MI: Eerdmans, 1983, p. 166.
28. See Henry Chadwick, "The Attractions of Mani," in E. Romero-Pose et al., eds, *Pléroma: Salus Carnis. Homenaje a Antonio Orbe*, Santiago de Compostela, 1990, pp. 203–222.
29. TM 389d, in Samuel N. C. Lieu, *Manichaeism in Mesopotamia and the Roman East*, Leiden: Brill, 1999, p. 31.
30. Quoted in Reeves, *Prolegomena*, p. 250.
31. Quoted in Reeves, *Prolegomena*, p. 275.
32 Cyril Glassé, "How We Know the Exact Year the Archegos Left Baghdad," in BeDuhn, ed., *New Light on Manichaeism*, pp. 134–135.

33. Sarah Stroumsa and Gedaliahu G. Stroumsa, "Aspects of Anti-Manichaean Polemics in Late Antiquity and Under Early Islam," *Harvard Theological Review* 81/1 (1988), p. 53.
34. E. G. Browne, among others, has made this argument. See his *Literary History of Persia*, Bethesda: Ibex Publishers, 1997, v. 1, p. 362. Hallaj's biographer, Louis Massignon, disagrees; see *The Passion of al-Hallaj*, tr. Herbert Mason, Princeton: Princeton University Press, 1982, v. 1, pp. 150–151.
35. Larry Clark, "The Conversion of Bügü Khan to Manichaeism," in R. E. Emmerick, W. Sundermann and P. Zieme, eds, *Studia Manichaica – IV*. Internationaler Kongreß zum Manichäismus, Berlin, 14.–18. Juli 1997, Berlin: Akademie Verlag, 2000, pp. 83–123.
36. <http://neomanichaean.wordpress.com>
37. <www.essenes.net/mani/0revival.html>

## 11. Undercurrents of Resistance: Mazdak and His Successors

1. Wilferd Madelung, "Mazdakism and the Khurramiyya," in *Religious Trends in Early Islamic Iran*, Albany, NY: SUNY Press, 1988, pp. 3–4.
2. Nizam al-Mulk, *The Book of Government or Rules for Kings*, tr. Hubert Darke, London: Routledge and Kegan Paul, 1978 [1960], pp. 190–192.
3. Ferdowsi, *Shahnameh*, p. 681.
4. Ferdowsi, *Shahnameh*, pp. 682–683.
5. Muhammad Shahrastani, *Livre des religions et des sectes*, tr. with intro. and notes by D. Gimaret and G. Monnot, 2 vols, Peeters/UNESCO, 1986, v. 1, pp. 663–666.
6. *Dēnkard*, Book 7, 7:24–5, E. L. West translation <www.avesta.org>
7. Ibn Nadim [Abu'l-Faraj Mohamed ibn Ishaq al-Warraq], *Fihrist al-'ulum*, tr. B. Dodge, *The Fihrist of al-Nadim: A Tenth Century Survey of Muslim Culture*, New York: Columbia University Press, 1970, v. 2, p. 817.
8. Patricia Crone, "Kavad's Heresy and Mazdak's Revolt," *Iran* 29 (1991), p. 23.
9. Mehrdad Bahar, "Dīdgāhhā-ye tāzeh dar bāreye Mazdak," in *Jostāri čand dar farhang-e Īrān*, Tehran: Fekr-e rūz, 1374 [1995], pp. 245–278.
10. Similar to the polemics against the Mazdakites and other heterodox groups, such modern sects as the Alevis and Bahá'ís are often accused by their detractors of holding an annual orgy during a ceremony known as the "Extinguishing of Light." See Matti Moosa, *Extremist Shi'ites: The Ghulat Sects*, Syracuse: Syracuse University Press, 1988, pp. 136–138.
11. Shahrastani, *Livre des religions et des sectes*, v. 1, pp. 665–666. Three other associated groups listed by Shahrestani are the *kūdakiyya*, the *māhāniyya*, and the *sapīd-jāmagān*.
12. *Siyāsat-nāmeh*, pp. 206–207.
13. Biruni, *Chronology of Ancient Nations*, p. 194. Crone sees this as a misinterpretation, arguing instead that Muqanna' merely made lawful the women and property of defeated enemies as was common practice throughout history (*Nativist Prophets*, p. 37), but it seems to me that the two interpretations are not mutually exclusive.

14. Abu Bakr Muhammad Narshakhi, *Tārīkh-i Bukhārā*, tr. Richard Frye, Princeton: Markus Weiner, 2007 [1954], p. 74.
15. Shahrastani, *Livre des religions et des sectes*, v. 1, p. 665.
16. *Siyāsat-nāmeh*, p. 236.
17. Mutahhar al-Maqdisi, *Kitāb al-bad' wa'l-ta'rīkh*, Paris: Ernest Leroux, 1899–1919, v. 1, p. 143.
18. Madelung, "Mazdakism and the Khurramiyya," pp. 9–11.
19. Crone, *Nativist Prophets*, p. 445.
20. Joseph Wolff, *Narrative of a Mission to Bokhara*, London, 1848, pp. 297–298.

## 12. Islam

1. Ehsan Yarshater, "The Persian Presence in the Islamic World," in Richard G. Hovanissian and Georges Sabbagh, eds, *The Persian Presence in the Islamic World*, Cambridge: Cambridge University Press, 1998, p. 50.
2. Richard Bulliet, *Conversion to Islam in the Medieval Period: A Study in Quantitative History*, Cambridge MA: Harvard University Press, 1980.
3. Confusingly, the Arabic term *mawlā* (pl. *mawālī*), is applied to both parties in this relationship, client and patron alike.
4. Ibn Ishaq, *Sirāt rasūl Allāh*, tr. Alfred Guillaume, *The Life of Muhammad*, Oxford: Oxford University Press, 1955, p. 683.
5. Quoted in Moojan Momen, *An Introduction to Shi'i Islam: The History and Doctrines of Twelver Shi'ism*, New Haven: Yale University Press, 1987, p. 15.
6. Al-Jahiz, *Al-bayān wa'l-tabyīn*, Beirut, 1948, vol. 3, p. 366, cited in Yarshater, "Re-emergence of Iranian Identity," in Curtis and Stewart, eds, *The Rise of Islam*, p. 8.
7. See C. Edmund Bosworth, "The Persistent Older Heritage in the Medieval Iranian Lands," in Curtis and Stewart, eds, *The Rise of Islam*, pp. 30–43.
8. Quoted in Donald Wilber, *Persian Gardens and Garden Pavilions*, 2nd ed., Washington, DC: Dumbarton Oaks, 1979, pp. 19–20.
9. This magnificent work, commissioned by Shah Esma'il during the early 1520s and completed some two decades later under his son Tahmasp, contains 258 paintings, many by the best masters of the time. In 1959 it was bought by the wealthy American industrialist Arthur Houghton, who had the book dissected and donated or sold its individual paintings up until his death in 1990, after which the remainder was auctioned off piecemeal. The now destroyed masterpiece is sometimes referred to as the "Houghton *Shāh-nāmeh*"; some art historians, who object to naming this masterpiece after the man who destroyed it, prefer to call it the "Tahmasp *Shāh-nāmeh*."
10. Hasan Kashi, *Tārīx-e Muhammadī*, pp. 159–160; quoted in Kathryn Babayan, *Mystics, Monarchs, and Messiahs: Cultural Landscapes of Early Modern Iran*, Cambridge, MA: Harvard University Press, 2002, p. 181. Kashi's authorship of this work is doubtful; Hasan 'Atefi Kashani rather points out that its anonymous author, whose style is markedly different from Kashi's, describes himself as a sixty-year-old who has recent converted to Shi'ism (*Dīvān-e Hasan-e Kāšī*, Tehran: Ketābkhāneh, mūzeh va markaz-e ostād-e

majles-e šūrā'īye eslāmī, 1388 [2009] p. 49). Kashi nevertheless displays a familiarity with the *Shāh-nāmeh* in the *Dīvān* ascribed to him. (I am grateful to Manya Saadi-nejad for providing the latter reference.)

### 13. Persian Sufism

1. Maria E. Subtelny, "Zoroastrian Elements in the Islamic Ascension Narrative: The Case of the Cosmic Cock," in Maria Szuppe, Anna Krasnowolska, and Claus V. Pedersen, eds, *Medieval and Modern Iranian Studies: Proceedings of the 6th European Conference of Iranian Studies (Vienna, 2007)*, Paris: Association pour l'avancement des études iraniennes, 2011, pp. 193–212.

2. Annemarie Schimmel, "Reason and Mystical Experience in Islam," in Farhad Daftary, ed, *Intellectual Traditions in Islam*, London: I.B. Tauris, 2000, p. 142.

3. Ibn Munawwar, *Asrār al-tawhīd fī maqāmāt Shaykh Abū Saʿīd*; quoted in Terry Graham, "Abū Saʿīd ibn Abī'l-Khayr and the School of Khurasan," in Leonard Lewisohn, ed., *Classical Persian Sufism: From its Origins to Rumi*, London: Khaniqahi Nimatullahi Publications, 1993, p. 118.

4. Ibn Munawwar, *Asrār al-tawhīd*; quoted in Hamid Dabashi, "Historical Conditions of Persian Sufism during the Seljuk Period," in Lewisohn, ed., *Classical Persian Sufism*, p. 137.

5. William Montgomery Watt, *The Faith and Practice of al-Ghazali*, London: Allen and Unwin, 1953, p. 14.

6. S. H. Nasr, "The Rise and Development of Persian Sufism," in Lewisohn, ed., *Classical Persian Sufism*, p. 9.

7. Ahmad Ghazzali, *Sawānih: Inspirations from the World of Pure Spirits: The Oldest Persian Sufi Treatise on Love*, tr. Nasrollah Pourjavady, London: Routledge & Kegan Paul, 1986, p. 17.

8. Farid al-din Attar, *The Conference of the Birds*, tr. Dick Davis and Afkham Darbandi, London: Penguin, 1984, p. 219.

9. For an English translation see Farid al-din Attar, *Muslim Saints and Mystics: Episodes from the Tadhkirat al-Auliya'*, tr. A.J. Arberry, London: Penguin, 1966, pp. 264–271.

10. Rumi, *The Masnavi: Book One*, tr. Jawed Mojaddedi, Oxford: Oxford University Press, 2004, pp. 4–5.

11. See the discussion of this question in Homa Katouzian, *Saʿdi: The Poet of Life, Love and Compassion*, Oxford: Oneworld, 2006, pp. 71–74.

12. W. M. Thackston, tr., *The Gulistan of Saʿdi*, Bethesda: IBEX Publishers, 2008, pp. 66–67.

13. W. M. Thackston, *A Millennium of Classical Persian Poetry*, Bethesda: IBEX Publishers, 2000, p. xi.

14. Leonard Lewisohn, "Prolegomenon to the Study of Hāfiz," in *Hafiz and the Religion of Love in Classical Persian Poetry*, London: I. B. Tauris, 2010, esp. pp. 31–43.

15. Robert Bly and Leonard Lewisohn, *The Angels Knocking at the Tavern Door: Thirty Poems of Hafez*, New York: Harper Collins, 2008, p. 21; the original *ghazal* can be found in the Persian edition of Parviz Natel Khanlari,

*Dīvān-e Šams al-dīn Mohammad Hāfez*, Tehran: Entešārāt-e xwarazmī, 1359 [1980], no. 385.

16. Lewisohn, "Prolegomenon," p. 18.
17. Charles F. Horne, ed., *The Sacred Books and Early Literature of the East*, New York: Parke, Austin & Lipscombe, 1917, vol. 8, p. 396.
18. Muhammad Ghazali, *The Niche of Lights*, tr. David Buchman, Provo, UT: Brigham Young University Press, 1988, p. 3.
19. Corbin, *Spiritual Body and Celestial Earth*, pp. 124–125.
20. John Walbridge, *The Wisdom of the Mystic East: Suhrawardi and Platonic Orientalism*, Albany: SUNY Press, 2001, p. 59.
21. *Kalimāt al-tasawwuf* ("Words of Sufism"), p. 117, para. 55; quoted in Walbridge, *The Wisdom of the Mystic East*, p. 60.
22. In Walbridge's view, "There is certainly no warrant whatever for considering Suhrawardi as an exponent of any sort of genuine pre-Islamic wisdom. He shows no evidence of ancient Iran beyond what might be expected of an educated Muslim of his time and place" (Walbridge, *The Wisdom of the Mystic East*, p. 13).
23. Henry Corbin, "Azar Kayvan," *Encyclopædia Iranica* online.

## 14. Shi'ism

1. Momen, *An Introduction to Shi'i Islam*, pp. 75–76.
2. Henry Corbin, *Cyclical Time and Ismaili Gnosis*, London: Kegan Paul, 1983, p. 124.
3. Farhad Daftary, *Ismailis in Medieval Muslim Society*, London: I.B. Tauris, 2005, pp. 131–132.
4. This issue is clarified in Farhad Daftary, *The Assassin Legends*, London: I. B. Tauris, 1994.
5. Shafique Virani, *The Isma'ilis in the Middle Ages*, Oxford: Oxford University Press, 2007, p. 48.
6. Daftary, *Ismailis in Medieval Muslim Society*, pp. 186–187.
7. *Naqāvat al-āsār*, p. 514; cited in Babayan, *Mystics, Monarchs, and Messiahs*, p. 48. Shah Abbas himself put an end to these speculations by first placing the Noqtavī leader Ostad Yusufi Tarkišduz on the throne for three days in August 1593—corresponding to the Arabic lunar year 1001—then having him executed and displayed on a stake for a week (Babayan, *Mystics, Monarchs, and Messiahs*, p. 3).
8. ". . . the rise of a Persian era is expressed in terms of a return to an 'old' age that had passed but that would finally be revived in the form of a final and eternal victory" (Babayan, *Mystics, Monarchs, and Messiahs*, p. 19).
9. The term "Turkmen" etymologically means "Turkic." Its modern usage, however, is more restricted, referring to peoples living in roughly adjacent areas of Turkmenistan, northeastern Iran, and northwestern Afghanistan.
10. Wheeler M. Thackston, "The Poetry of Shah Isma'il I," *Asian Art* (Fall 1988), p. 57.
11. Thackston, "The Poetry of Shah Esma'il I," pp. 56–57.
12. Colin Paul Mitchell, *The Practice of Politics in Safavid Iran: Power, Religion and Rhetoric*, London: I. B. Tauris, 2009, pp. 23, 31.

13. Ali Rahnema sees Majlesi as a spiritual forefather to Ayatollah Mesbah Yazdi (b. 1934), who rose to prominence through his criticisms of Mohammad Khatami's presidency and his support of Mahmud Ahmadinejad (Ali Rahnema, *Superstition as Ideology in Iranian Politics: From Majlesi to Ahmadinejad*, Cambridge: Cambridge University Press, 2011, p. 21). It was also due to Majlesi's efforts that Shi'ite writings began to be widely available in Persian since the earlier generations of Shi'ite scholars, who were mostly of Lebanese origin, wrote in Arabic (Rahnema, *Superstition as Ideology*, p. 190).

14. Ervand Abrahamian, *A History of Modern Iran*, Cambridge: Cambridge University Press, 2008, p. 30.

15. See the essays in Peter J. Chelkowski, ed., *Ta'ziyeh: Ritual and Drama in Iran*, New York: New York University Press, 1979.

16. Ahmad Kasravi, *On Islam and Shi'ism*, tr. M. R. Ghanoonparvar, Costa Mesa, CA: Mazda Publishers, 1990, p. 192.

## 15. Zoroastrianism After Islam

1. For more on this process see Eliz Sanasarian, *Religious Minorities in Iran*, Cambridge: Cambridge University Press, 2000, pp. 20–24.

2. See Richard Foltz, "Zoroastrian Attitudes Towards Animals," *Society and Animals* 18/4 (2010): 367–378.

3. For more on conversion in the early Islamic period see Jamsheed K. Choksy, *Conflict and Cooperation: Zoroastrian Subalterns and Muslim Elites in Medieval Iranian Society*, New York: Columbia University Press, pp. 70–109.

4. For more on the Safavid persecutions see Jamsheed K. Choksy, "Despite Shāhs and Mollās: Minority Sociopolitics in Premodern and Modern Iran," *Journal of Asian Studies* 40/2 (2006), pp. 136–138.

5. Choksy, "Despite Shāhs and Mollās," pp. 139–141.

6. Alan Williams, introducing his critical edition of this late text, remarks that "to read the *QS* with the sole purpose of finding a historically satisfactory chronology of the Zoroastrians down to 1599 is rather like going to see a performance of Hamlet only for the purpose of learning a lesson in Danish history" (*The Zoroastrian Myth of Migration from Iran and Settlement in the India Diaspora: Text, translation and analysis of the 16th century Qesse-ye Sanjan 'The story of Sanjan'*, Leiden: Brill, 2009, p. 19).

7. B. N. Dhabhar, ed., *The Persian Rivayats of Hormazyar Framarz and Others*, Bombay: K. R. Cama Oriental Institute, 1932.

8. Mohamad Tavakoli-Targhi, *Refashioning Iran: Orientalism, Occidentalism and Historiography*, New York: Palgrave Macmillan, 2001, p. 87.

9. For more on this re-imagining process, and the orthodox reaction it generated, see Monica Ringer, *Pious Citizens: Reforming Zoroastrianism in India and Iran*, Syracuse: Syracuse University Press, 2011, especially Chapters 3 and 5.

10. See T. M. Luhrmann, *The Good Parsi: The Fate of a Colonial Elite in a Postcolonial Society*, Cambridge, MA: Harvard University Press, 1996.

11. See John R. Hinnells, "Behramshah Nowroji Shroff," *Encyclopædia Iranica online*, <www.iranica.com/articles/behramshah-naoroji-shroff-1858-1927>

12. Or, in her own words, Shah Bahram Varzavand founded it through her (personal conversation, Mumbai, 22 July 2011).
13. <www.mazorcol.org> (capitalizations in the original).
14. <www.mazorcol.org/index.php/links/16-15-iran>
15. <www.shahbazi.org>
16. Žaleh Amuzgar, *Tārīkh-e Īrān-e bāstān*, v. 1, Tehran: Sāzmān-e motale'eh va tadvīn-e kotob-e 'olūm-e ensānī-ye dāneshgāhhā, 1380 [2001], p. 120.
17. Carlo Cereti, "On the Date of the Zand ī Wahman Yasn," *K. R. Cama Oriental Institute Second International Congress Proceedings*, Bombay: K. R. Cama Institute, 1996, p. 248 and note 29.
18. Meher Master-Moos, *Life of Ustad Saheb Behramshah Nowroji Shroff (including an outline of 14,000 years of Iranian History and Shah Behram Varzavand)*, Bombay: Mazdayasnie Monasterie, 1981, p. xxxviii.
19. Master-Moos, *Life*, p. 37.
20. Cursetji M. Patel, "Raenidar Shah Behram Varzavand," *Jam-e Jamshed* <http://tenets.zoroastrianism.com/raenidar33a.html>
21. K. N. Dastoor, "The Contents of the Vendidad seen through the Eyes of the Ilm-e Khshnoom," *Dini-Avaz* 14/1 (1988), p. 6.
22. See Mary Boyce, "Maneckji Limji Hataria in Iran," in *Golden Jubilee Volume*, Bombay: K. R. Cama Oriental Institute, 1969, pp. 19–31.
23. See Ringer, *Pious Citizens*, Chapter 6.
24. *Iran League Quarterly* (Jan.–Apr. 1938), frontispiece.
25. This dynamic is discussed at length in Dinyar Patel, "The Iran League of Bombay: Paris, Iran, and the Appeal of Iranian Nationalism, 1922–1942," unpublished typescript, 2012.
26. Rustom Masani, "With Dinshah Irani in New Iran," *Dinshah Irani Memorial Volume*, Bombay, 1948, pp. xv–xvi.
27. From *gāh*, "appointed time"; see Mary Boyce, "Gāhānbār", *Encyclopedia Iranica online*, www.iranica.com/articles/gahanbar
28. Mary Boyce, *A Persian Stronghold of Zoroastrianism*, Oxford: Oxford University Press, 1977. Given that this remains the most detailed study of Iranian Zoroastrians to date in a Western language, it was somewhat disappointing to us that no Zoroastrian we have met likes the book, which they claim is full of inaccuracies and misinformation. In particular, they accuse Boyce of overdependence on a single priest who they say was an unreliable source.

    Two other studies exist in English, both anthropological in nature and based on fieldwork done prior to the 1979 revolution: Janet Kestenberg Amighi, *Zoroastrians of Iran: Conversion, Assimilation, or Persistence*, New York: AMS Press, 1990, and Michael Fischer, "Zoroastrian Iran: Between Myth and Practice," unpublished Ph.D. dissertation, University of Chicago, 1973, but being rare and hard to find they are less well known than Boyce's work. A recent book in Persian on the social history of Zoroastrians in Iran by Zoroastrian scholar Katayun Namiranian, who is a professor at Shiraz University, exists in theory but is impossible to find in Iran, even at Tehran's Zoroastrian bookstore.
29. The Zoroastrian Association of Yazd considers that no more than 20 Zoroastrians, all elderly, are left in Sharifabad, the town now having been taken

over by Muslims. On the other hand, there are so many Sharifabadis living in Tehran that they have their own community association.

### 16. Two Kurdish Sects: the Yezidis and the Yaresan

1. Philip G. Kreyenbroek, *Yezidism: its Background, Observances and Textual Traditions*, Lewiston, NY: Edwin Mellen Press, 1995, p. x.
2. M. Reza Hamzeh'ee, *The Yaresan, A Sociological, Historical and Religio-Historical Study of a Kurdish Community*, Berlin: K. Schwartz, 1990, p. 2.
3. Thomas Bois, "Kurdes: Langue et littérature," in *Encyclopaedia Universalis: Connaissance des Kurdes*, Beyrouth: Khayats, 1965, pp. 112–113.
4. Mehrdad R. Izady, *The Kurds: A Concise Handbook*, Washington: Taylor and Francis, 1992, especially Chapter 5. Izady includes the Alevi branch of Shi'ism alongside Yezidism and the Yaresan as the three surviving expressions of this putative original faith.
5. Birgül Açikyildiz, *The Yezidis: the History of a Community, Culture, and Religion*, London: I. B. Tauris, 2010, p. 39.
6. Kreyenbroek, *Yezidism*, p. 33.
7. Christine Allison, "Yazidis," in *Encyclopaedia Iranica* online.
8. Bahar, *Az ostūreh tā tārīx*, p. 302.
9. This parallel is discussed in Kreyenbroek, *Yezidism*, pp. 48–50.
10. Allison, "Yazidis."
11. The French musicologist Jean During, while not denying the existence of an ancient Iranian substrate, emphasizes the Islamic and Sufi aspects of the Yaresan tradition. He sees the movement "rather as an offshoot of a kind of Sufism which adapted itself to Kurdish customs" ("A Critical Survey on Ahl-e Haqq Studies in Europe and Iran," in E. Ozdalga, ed., *Religion, Cultural Identity, and Social Organization among Alevi in Ottoman and Modern Turkey*, Stockholm: Swedish Research Institute in Istanbul, 1998, p. 114). Philip Kreyenbroek has pointed out to me, however, that During's arguments are colored by his association with the Paris-based Elahi sect which is a modernist, Islamizing offshoot of the Ahl-e Haqq (personal communication, 11 July 2012).
12. Mojan Membrado, "Forqân al-Akhbâr de: Hâjj Ne'matollâh Jeyhûnâbâdi (1871–1920), écrit doctrinal Ahl-e Haqq, édition critique, étude et commentaire," unpublished Ph.D. dissertation, Paris: École pratique des hautes études, 2007, p. 11.
13. Izady, *The Kurds*, p. 34. Izady even claims "compelling evidence"—but without providing it—that Aži Dahāka's troops were responsible for the murder of Zoroaster and the overthrow of his patron Vištaspa (p. 139).
14. <www.ahle-haqq.com/other_traditions.html>
15. Hamzeh'ee, *The Yaresan*, p. 3.
16. Membrado, "Forqân al-Akhbâr," p. 74.
17. Kreyenbroek, *Yezidism*, pp. 52–54; Hamzeh'ee, *The Yaresan*, p. 225.
18. Kreyenbroek, *Yezidism*, pp. 183–191.
19. Kreyenbroek, *Yezidism*, pp. 56–59.
20. See note 8.

21. Hamzeh'ee, *The Yaresan*, p. 74.
22. See, for example, Noshir H. Dadrawala, "The Yezidis of Kurdistan: Are They Really Zoroastrians?" <http://tenets.zoroastrianism.com/deen33f.html>

## 17. The Bábí Movement and the Bahá'í Faith

1. Henry Corbin sees Hurqalya, which he defines as the "Earth of visions," as a contemplative goal unifying centuries of Iranian theosophy from pre-Islamic times to the present (*Spiritual Body and Celestial Earth*, p. xii).
2. Peter Smith, *The Babi and Baha'i Religions: From Messianic Shi'ism to a World Religion*, Cambridge: Cambridge University Press, 1984, p. 18.
3. Smith, *The Babi and Baha'i Religions*, p. 48.
4. Margit Warburg, *Citizens of the World: A History and Sociology of the Baha'is from a Globalisation Perspective*, Leiden, Brill, 2006, p. 56.
5. E. G. Browne, *A Traveller's Narrative Written to Illustrate the Episode of the Bab*, Amsterdam: Philo Press, 1975 [1886], v. 2, p. xl.
6. Quoted in Juan R. I. Cole, *Modernity and the Millennium: The Genesis of the Baha'i Faith in the Nineteenth-Century Middle East*, New York: Columbia University Press, 1998, p. 176.
7. Quoted in Cole, *Modernity and the Millennium*, p. 176.
8. Quoted in Cole, *Modernity and the Millennium*, p. 177.
9. See Denis MacEoin, *Rituals in Babism and Baha'ism*, London: British Academic Press, 1994.
10. Warburg, *Citizens of the World*, p. 486.
11. Mehrdad Amanat, "Messianic Expectation and Evolving Identities: The conversion of Iranian Jews to the Baha'i faith," in Dominic Parviz Brookshaw and Seena Fazel, eds, *The Baha'is of Iran: Socio-Historical Studies*, London: Routledge Curzon, 2007, p. 13.
12. Fereydun Vahman, "Conversion of Zoroastrians to the Baha'i faith," in Brookshaw and Fazel, eds, *The Baha'is of Iran*, p. 34.
13. The Shah's tolerance of these anti-Bahá'í activities was likely repayment for the support several leading clerics had given to the CIA coup against Mosaddeq two years earlier.
14. H. E. Chehabi, "Anatomy of Prejudice: Reflections on secular anti-Baha'ism in Iran," in Brookshaw and Fazel, eds, *The Baha'is of Iran*, p. 184.
15. To be fair, the Bahá'ís themselves practice this conflation, whereas sociologists of religion would tend more to see Bábism and the Bahá'í Faith as two distinct religions.
16. Warburg, *Citizens of the World*, pp. 352–353.
17. Warburg, *Citizens of the World*, pp. 26–27.
18. Warburg, *Citizens of the World*, p. 439.

## 18. The Islamic Republic

1. A Shi'ite Muslim is free to choose his "source of emulation," to whom s/he is to accord complete religious authority; religious taxes are also entrusted to one's *Marja'*, meaning that these individuals control enormous wealth.

2. The term traditionally referred to jurists' control of religious foundations. A political application of *velāyat-e faqīh* was advocated during the early nineteenth century by Ahmad Naraghi.

3. Ruhollah Khomeini, *Islam and Revolution*, tr. Hamid Algar, Berkeley: Mizan Press, 1981, p. 60.

4. Mohammad Khatami, "Our Revolution and the Future of Islam," in *Islam, Liberty and Development*, Binghamton, NY: Institute of Global Cultural Studies, 1998, p. 65.

5. See Ziba Mir-Hosseini, *Islam and Gender: The Religious Debate in Contemporary Iran*, Princeton: Princeton University Press, 1999.

6. The Western media being somewhat fickle on this point, this wistful title appears to have since been transferred to the Swiss scholar Tariq Ramadan.

7. Abdolkarim Soroush, "Islamic Revival and Reform: Theological Approaches," in *Reason, Freedom and Democracy in Islam*, tr. Mahmoud Sadri and Ahmad Sadri, Oxford: Oxford University Press, 2000, p. 31.

8. *International Religious Freedom Report: Iran*, Washington, D.C.: Department of State, October 7, 2002.

9. The university's website is: <www.urd.ac.ir>

## 19. Iranian Zoroastrians Today

1. Ruhollah Khomeini, *Majmūe'ī az maktūbāt, soxanrānihā, payāmhā va fatāvi-ye emām Khomeīnī az nime-ye dovvom-e 1341 tā hejrat be Pārīs* (14 Mehr 1357) [*The Collected Writings, Speeches, Messages and Rulings of Imam Khomeini from the second half of 1341 to his Migration to Paris*], Tehran: Čāpxaš, 1360 [1982], p. 277; quoted in Sanasarian, *Religious Minorities in Iran*, p. 30. This is not to say that Khomeini couldn't find something positive to say about Zoroastrians when it suited his purpose. For example, he also said that "Iran is the homeland of all [Iranians], and Divine Unity [*tawhīd*] is the religion of all [Iranians]; we are a united nation, you Zoroastrians have always served this country." Likewise, current head of state Ali Khamene'i has said that "Zoroastrianism came into being in Iran and for our country it is an honour that the world's first prophet was born in Iran." Quoted before Parliament on the occasion of Nō rūz 1389 (New Year 2010) by Zoroastrian M.P. Esfandiar Ekhtiari, *Pārs nāmeh* 10, Farvardīn 1389/April 2010, p. 8. For the term *gabr* see Mansour Shaki, "Gabr" in *Encyclopedia Iranica online*, www.iranica.com/articles/gabr

2. Sanasarian, *Religious Minorities in Iran*, p. 78. For more on treatment of Zoroastrians since the 1979 revolution see Choksy, "Despite Shāhs and Mollās," pp. 161–170.

3. Sanasarian, *Religious Minorities in Iran*, pp. 70–71.

4. Sanasarian, *Religious Minorities in Iran*, p. 91.

5. Personal conversation, Tehran, 13 January 2009.

6. "Eterāz-e Zartoštīān be 'tohīn' be neshān-e fravahr dar film-e īrānī" ["Zoroastrians Complain about 'Insulting' Use of Sacred Symbol in Iranian Film"], *BBC Persian service*, 7 January 2009. The *fravahr*, which is arguably the most well-known ancient Iranian symbol due to its prominence in rock reliefs at Persepolis and elsewhere, consists of a bearded figure rising

out of a winged disc. Long thought to represent Ahura Mazda, it is now believed by most scholars to represent the human spirit, or *fravaši* (Mary Boyce, "Fravaši", in *Encyclopedia Iranica* online, <www.iranica.com/articles/fravasi>, accessed 8 November 2010.

7. "Hamrāhi-ye Zartoštīān dar pāsokh be sokhanān-e nāravā-ye doctor Parvīz-e Rajabī" ["Zoroastrians Unite in Responding to the Unacceptable Words of Doctor Parviz Rajabi"], *Pārs nāmeh* 10, Farvardīn 1389/April 2010, pp. 4–7.

8. Zoroastrians, who hold the earth to be pure and death to be polluting, traditionally exposed their corpses to be cleaned by vultures and "purified" by the sun. This practice was abandoned in Iran for hygienic reasons, but the exposure sites (*dakhmes*) remain sacred for them.

9. *Pārs nāmeh* 15, Shahrīvar 1389/August 2010, p. 3.

10. Personal conversation, Yazd, 30 December 2008.

11. Rostam Vahidi, "Iranian Zarthushti Priesthood," *FEZANA Journal* 24/1 (Spring 2010), p. 55. Mobed Mehraban Firouzgary of Tehran told us that the actual number is probably less than that given in Vahidi's article (private conversation, 26 July 2010). There are currently eleven Iranian Zoroastrian priests and assistants in North America, seven of whom are in California. For purposes of contrast, the directory of the Zoroastrian Society of Ontario in Canada (which has the largest Zoroastrian population in the world after India and Iran) lists fourty priests, all of them Parsis. For a description of the training and ordination of priests in Iran today see Mehraban Firouzgary, "The Iranian Ceremony of Nowe Zooty (Navar) to Become an Iranian Mobed," *FEZANA Journal* 24/1 (Spring 2010): 61–63.

12. Personal conversation, Tehran, 26 July 2010.

13. "Response from Mobed Firouzgary," *Fezana Journal* 24/2 (Summer 2010), pp. 129–130.

14. Personal conversation, Tehran, 13 January 2009.

15. HIAS—the Hebrew Immigrant Aid Society—was originally established to help Jewish refugees but now assists all religious minorities. Under this program Iranian Zoroastrians are first taken to Vienna, under the protection of the Austrian Embassy, before being relocated to the United States.

16. Babak Behziz, "Čerā eftexārātemān-rā be pīš az eslām mahdūd mīkonīm?" ["Why Do We Restrain Our Pride in the Pre-Islamic Period?"], *Pārs nāmeh* 2, Mehr 1387/October 2008, p. 5.

17. Hiedeh Farmani, "Iran's Last Zoroastrians Worried by Youth Exodus," *Middle East Times*, 4 October 2006.

18. Ibid.

19. "Zoroastrians Make Iran Pilgrimage," *BBC News* online, 17 June 2004.

20. A female university student in Tehran told us that "We [Zoroastrians] actually have it pretty good here," but said she was emigrating to Australia, albeit reluctantly, because of her fiancé.

21. Manuchehr Bastani, " Mīz-e gerd-e mohājerāt" ["Emigration Roundtable"], *Pārs nāmeh* 11, Ordībehesht 1389/May 2010, p. 7, and 12, Khordād 1389/June 2010, p. 7.

22. See Chapter 15, note 7.

23. Jafarey is founder of the Zarathushtrian Assembly, based in Southern California <www.zoroastrian.org>
24. Rustam Abdilkamilov, personal communication, 5 July 2012.
25. Emomali Rahmon, *The Tajiks in the Mirror of History*, Dushanbe: Ministry of Culture, 1997.
26. <www.mazorcol.org>
27. Personal conversation, Mumbai, 22 July 2011.
28. Personal conversation, Bangalore, 14 July 2011.
29. Manoj R. Nair and Ram Parmar, "Parsis Storm Zoroastrian College to Stop Conversion of a Russian," *Mumbai Mirror* online (22 February 2010).
30. <www.bombayparsipanchayat.com/readcontent.aspx?contentid=32&categoryid=24>
31. Nauzer K. Bharucha, "Parsis Say No to Conversion," *Times of India* online, 11 October 2010.
32. Personal conversation, Mumbai, 21 July 2011.
33. Personal conversation, Mumbai, 21 July 2011.
34. "WAPIZ pages", *The Free Press Journal* (Mumbai), 22 July 2011, pp. 27–28.
35. This possibility was suggested by John Hinnells in his monumental book *The Zoroastrian Diaspora: Religion and Migration*, Oxford: Oxford University Press, 2005, pp. 485–486.
36. The city of Toronto, where two temples and three community organizations serve a Zoroastrian community of as many as six thousand individuals, now has the largest Zoroastrian population outside India and Iran. See Richard Foltz, "Iranian Zoroastrians in Canada: Balancing Religious and Cultural Identities," *Iranian Studies* 42/4 (2009): 561–577.

### Conclusion: The Ever-Expanding Pool of Iranian Religion

1. Masud Yunesian, Afshin Aslani, Javad Homayoun Vash and Abbas Bagheri Yazdi, "Effects of Transcendental Meditation on mental health: a before-after study," *Clinical Practice and Epidemiology in Mental Health* 4/1 (2008): 1–25.
2. <http://lettertobarackobama.com/letters/dr-mohammad-ali-taheri>

# Bibliography

Abrahamian, Ervand, *A History of Modern Iran*, Cambridge: Cambridge University Press, 2008.

Açikyildiz, Birgül, *The Yezidis: the History of a Community, Culture, and Religion*, London: I. B. Tauris, 2010.

Amighi, Janet Kestenberg, *Zoroastrians of Iran: Conversion, Assimilation, or Persistence*, New York: AMS Press, 1990.

Amuzgar, Žaleh, *Tārīx-e Īrān-e bāstān*, v. 1, Tehran: Sāzmān-e mota'leh va tadvīn-e kutub-e 'ūlūm-e ensānīye dānešgāhhā, 1380 [2001].

Anthony, David, *The Horse, The Wheel and Language: How Bronze Age Riders from the Eurasian Steppes Shaped the Modern World*, Princeton: Princeton University Press, 2007.

Arrian, *The Campaigns of Alexander*, tr. Aubrey de Sélincourt, New York: Penguin, 1958.

Attar, Farid al-din, *Muslim Saints and Mystics: Episodes from the Tadhkirat al-Auliya'*, tr. A. J. Arberry, London: Penguin, 1966.

___, *The Conference of the Birds*, tr. Dick Davis and Afkham Darbandi, London: Penguin, 1984.

Augustinus, *Contra Faustum*, in Philip Schaff, ed., *Nicene and Post-Nicene Fathers*, Grand Rapids, MI: Eerdmans, 1983, v. 4.

Azarpay, Guitty, "Iranian Divinities in Sogdian Paintings," *Acta Iranica* 4 (1975): 12–21.

___, *Sogdian Painting: the Pictorial Epic in Oriental Art*, Berkeley: University of California Press, 1981.

Babayan, Kathryn, Mystics, Monarchs, and Messiahs: Cultural Landscapes of Early Modern Iran, Cambridge, MA: Harvard University Press, 2002.

Bahar, Mehrdad, *Az ostūreh tā tārīx*, Tehran: Češmeh, 1376 [1997].

___, *Jostāri čand dar farhang-e Īrān*, Tehran: Fekr-e rūz, 1374 [1995].

Bakhos, Carol and Rahim Shayegan, eds, *The Talmud in its Iranian Context*, Tübingen: Mohr Siebeck, 2010.

Ball, Warwick, "Two Aspects of Iranian Buddhism," *Bulletin of the Asia Institute* 4 (1976), pp. 103–163.

___, "Some Rock-cut Monuments in Southern Iran," *Iran* 24 (1986): 95–115.

Barr, James, "The Question of Religious Influence: The Case of Zoroastrianism, Judaism, and Christianity, *Journal of the American Academy of Religion* 53/2 (1985): 201–235.

Baumer, Christopher, *The Church of the East: An Illustrated History of Assyrian Christianity*, London: I. B. Tauris, 2006.

Bausani, Alessandro, *Religion in Iran: From Zoroaster to Baha'ullah*, tr. J. M. Marchesi, New York: Bibliotheca Persica, 2000.

Beal, Samuel, tr., *Buddhist Records of the Western World*, New Delhi: Oriental Reprints, 1969 [1888].

Beckwith, Christopher I., *Empires of the Silk Road: A History of Central Eurasia from the Bronze Age to the Present*, Princeton: Princeton University Press, 2009.

BeDuhn, Jason David, *The Manichaean Body: In Discipline and Ritual*, Baltimore: Johns Hopkins University Press, 2000.

BeDuhn, Jason David, ed., *New Light on Manichaeism: Papers from the Sixth International Congress on Manichaeism*, Leiden: Brill, 2009.

Benveniste, Emile, *The Persian Religion according to the chief Greek texts*, Paris: Librarie Orientaliste, 1929.

Bharucha, Nauzer K., "Parsis Say No to Conversion," *Times of India* online, 11 October 2010.

Biruni, Abu Rayhan, *Āthār-al-baqiya*, tr. C. Edward Sachau, *The Chronology of Ancient Nations*, London: W. H. Allen, 1879.

Bivar, A. D. H., *The Personalities of Mithra in Archaeology and Literature*, New York: Bibliotheca Persica, 1998.

Bly, Robert and Leonard Lewisohn, *The Angels Knocking at the Tavern Door: Thirty Poems of Hafez*, New York: Harper Collins, 2008.

Bois, Thomas, *Connaissance des Kurdes*, Beyrouth: Khayats, 1965.

Bouckaert, Remco, et al., "Mapping the Origins and Expansion of the Indo-European Language Family," *Science* 337 (2012): 957–960.

Boyce, Mary, *Zoroastrianism: Its Antiquity and Constant Vigour*, Costa Mesa: Mazda Publishers, 1992.

___, *A History of Zoroastrianism*, v. 2, *Under the Achaemenians*, Leiden: Brill, 1982.

___, *Zoroastrians: Their Religious Beliefs and Practices*, London: Routledge and Kegan Paul, 1979.

___, *A Persian Stronghold of Zoroastrianism*, Oxford: Oxford University Press, 1977.

___, *A History of Zoroastrianism*, v. 1, The Early Period, Leiden: Brill, 1975.

___, "Maneckji Limji Hataria in Iran," in *Golden Jubilee Volume*, Bombay: K.R. Cama Oriental Institute, 1969, pp. 19–31.

___, "Zariades and Zarer," *Bulletin of the School of Oriental and African Studies* 17/3 (1955): 463–477.

Boyce, Mary, and Frantz Grenet, *A History of Zoroastrianism*, v. 3, *Zoroastrianism under Macedonian and Roman Rule*, Leiden: Brill, 1991.

Brookshaw, Dominic Parviz and Seena Fazel, eds, *The Baha'is of Iran: Socio-Historical Studies*, London: Routledge Curzon, 2007.

Browne, E. G., *A Traveller's Narrative Written to Illustrate the Episode of the Bab*, Amsterdam: Philo Press, 1975 [1886].

___, *Literary History of Persia*, 4 vols., Bethesda: Ibex Publishers, 1997.

Bryant, Edwin, *The Quest for the Origins of Vedic Culture: The Indo-Aryan Migration Debate*, New Delhi: Oxford University Press, 2002.

Buck, Christopher, "The Universality of the Church of the East: How Persian was Persian Christianity?" *Journal of the Assyrian Academic Society* 10/1 (1996): 54–95.

Buckley, Jorunn Jacobsen, *The Great Stem of Souls: Reconstructing Mandaean History*, Piscataway, NJ: Gorgias Press, 2005.

___, *The Mandaeans: Ancient Texts and Modern People*, New York: Oxford University Press, 2002.

Bulliet, Richard W., *Islam: The View From the Edge*, New York: Columbia University Press, 1998.

___, *Conversion to Islam in the Medieval Period: A Study in Quantitative History*, Cambridge MA: Harvard University Press, 1980.

___, "Naw Bahar and the Survival of Iranian Buddhism," *Iran* 14 (1976), pp. 140–145.

Canepa, Matthew P., "The Art and Ritual of Manichaean Magic: Text, Object and Image from the Mediterranean to Central Asia," in Hallie G. Meredith, ed., *Objects in Motion: The Circulation of Religion and Sacred Objects in the Late Antique and Byzantine World*, Oxford: Archaeopress, 2011, pp. 73–88.

Chadwick, Henry, "The Attractions of Mani," in E. Romero-Pose et al., eds, *Pléroma: Salus Carnis. Homenaje a Antonio Orbe*, Santiago de Compostela, 1990, pp. 203–222.

Chaumont, M.-L., *La Christianisation de l'empire iranien: des origines aux grandes persécutions du IVe siècle*, Louvain: Peeters, 1988.

Chelkowski, Peter J., ed., *Ta'ziyeh: Ritual and Drama in Iran*, New York: New York University Press, 1979.

Chidester, David, *Authentic Fakes: Religion and Popular Culture in America*, Berkeley: University of California Press, 2005.

Choksy, Jamsheed, *Conflict and Cooperation*, New York: Columbia University Press, 1997.

___, "Despite Shāhs and Mollās: Minority Sociopolitics in Premodern and Modern Iran," *Journal of Asian Studies* 40/2 (2006), pp. 129–184.

Clark, Larry, "The Conversion of Bügü Khan to Manichaeism,' in R. E. Emmerick, W. Sundermann and P. Zieme, eds, *Studia Manichaica - IV. Internationaler Kongreß zum Manichäismus, Berlin, 14.–18. Juli 1997*, Berlin: Akademie Verlag, 2000, pp. 83–123.

Cole, Juan R. I. *Modernity and the Millennium: The Genesis of the Baha'i Faith in the Nineteenth-Century Middle East*, New York: Columbia University Press, 1998.

Corbin, Henri, *Spiritual Body and Celestial Earth: From Mazdean Iran to Shi'ite Iran*, tr. Nancy Pearson, Princeton: Princeton University Press, 1977.

___, *Cyclical Time and Ismaili Gnosis*, London: Kegan Paul, 1983.

Crone, Patricia, *The Nativist Prophets of Early Islamic Iran: Rural Revolt and Local Zoroastrianism*, Cambridge: Cambridge University Press, 2012.

___, "Kavad's Heresy and Mazdak's Revolt," *Iran* 29 (1991): 21–40.

Curtis, Vesta Sarkhosh and Sarah Stewart, eds, *Birth of the Persian Empire, The Idea of Iran* vol. 1, London: I. B. Tauris, 2005.

___, *The Rise of Islam, The Idea of Iran* vol. 5, London: I. B. Tauris, 2009.

Dadrawala, Noshir H., "The Yezidis of Kurdistan: Are They Really Zoroastrians?" <http://tenets.zoroastrianism.com/deen33f.html>

Daftary, Farhad, *The Assassin Legends*, London: I. B. Tauris, 1994.
___, *Ismailis in Medieval Muslim Society*, London: I. B. Tauris, 2005.
Dandamaev, Muhammad A. and Vladimir G. Lukonin, *The Culture and Social Institutions of Ancient Iran*, Cambridge: Cambridge University Press, 1989.
Daneshvar, Simin, *Savushun*, Washington, DC: Mage, 1990.
Daryaee, Touraj, "Indo-European Elements in the Zoroastrian Apocalyptic Tradition," *The Classical Bulletin* 83/2 (2007): 203–213.
Dastoor, K. N., "The Contents of the Vendidad seen through the Eyes of the Ilm-e Khshnoom," *Dini-Avaz* 14/1 (1988), p. 6.
Dhabhar, B. N., ed, *The Persian Rivayats of Hormazyar Framarz and Others*, Bombay: K. R. Cama Oriental Institute, 1932.
de Blois, François, "The Two Zoroastrian Treatises Called 'Ulama-i Islam'," *The Classical Bulletin* 83/2 (2007): 215–225.
du Breuil, Paul, "A Study of Some Zoroastrian and Buddhist Eschatological Features," *K. R. Cama Institute International Congress Proceedings*, Bombay: K. R. Cama Institute, 1991, pp. 52–64.
Duchesne-Guillemin, Jacques, "Le dieu de Cyrus," *Acta Iranica* 3 (1974), pp. 11–21.
___, *La religion de l'Iran ancien*, Paris: Presses universitaires de France, 1962.
Duchesne-Guillemin, Jacques, ed., *Études mithraïques*, Tehran: Bibliothèque Pahlavi, 1978.
During, Jean, "A Critical Survey on Ahl-e Haqq Studies in Europe and Iran," in Tord Olsson, Elisabeth Özdalga, and Catherine Raudvere, eds, *Alevi Identity: Cultural, Religious and Social Perspectives*, Stockholm: Swedish Research Institute in Istanbul, 1998, pp. 105–125.
Drower, E. S., *The Mandaeans of Iraq and Iran: Their Cults, Customs, Magic, Legends, and Folklore*, Leiden: Brill, 1962.
Dumézil, Georges, *Les Dieux des indo-européens*, Paris, 1952.
Elman, Yaakov, "The Other in the Mirror: Iranians and Jews View One Another: Questions of Identity, Conversion, and Exogamy in the Fifth-Century Iranian Empire," *Bulletin of the Asia Institute* 19–20 (2009–10): 15–46.
___, "Middle Persian Culture and Babylonian Sages: Accommodation and Resistance in the Shaping of Rabbinic Legal Tradition," in Charlotte Elisheva Fonrobert and Martin S. Jaffe, eds, *Cambridge Companion to the Talmud and Rabbinic Literature*, Cambridge and New York, 2007, pp. 165–197.
Ferdowsi, Abolqasem, *Shahnameh: the Persian Book of Kings*, tr. Dick Davis, New York: Viking, 2006.
*FEZANA Journal*.
Fischer, Michael, "Zoroastrian Iran: Between Myth and Practice," unpublished Ph.D. dissertation, University of Chicago, 1973.
Flattery, David S. and Martin Schwartz, *Haoma and Harmaline: The Botanical Identity of the Indo-Iranian Sacred Hallucinogen "Soma" and Its Legacy in Religion, Language, and Middle Eastern Folklore*, Berkeley: University of California Press, 1989.
Foltz, Richard, *Religions of the Silk Road: Premodern patterns of globalization*, 2nd ed., New York: Palgrave Macmillan, 2010.
___, "Zoroastrian Attitudes Towards Animals," *Society and Animals* 18/4 (2010): 367–378.

___, "Iranian Zoroastrians in Canada: Balancing Religious and Cultural Identities," *Iranian Studies* 42/4 (2009): 561–577.

Frye, Richard N., *The Heritage of Persia*, London: Weidenfeld and Nicolson, 1963.

___, *The Golden Age of Persia*, London: Weidenfeld and Nicolson, 1975.

Frye, Richard N., ed., *The Cambridge History of Iran*, v. 4, *From the Arab Invasion to the Seljuks*, Cambridge: Cambridge University Press, 1975.

Fynes, Richard C. C., "Plant Souls in Jainism and Manichaeism: the Case for Cultural Transmission," *East and West* 46 (1996): 21–44.

Gardner, Iain and Samuel N. C. Lieu, *Manichaean Texts from the Roman Empire*, Cambridge and New York: Cambridge University Press, 2004.

Gardner, Iain and Max Deeg, "Indian Influence on Mani Reconsidered: The Case of Jainism," *International Journal of Jaina Studies* 5 (2009): 1–30.

Gershevitch, Ilya, *The Avestan Hymn to Mithra*, Cambridge: Cambridge University Press, 1959.

Ghazali, Muhammad, *The Niche of Lights*, tr. David Buchman, Provo, UT: Brigham Young University Press, 1988.

Ghazzali, Ahmad, *Sawānih: Inspirations from the World of Pure Spirits: The Oldest Persian Sufi Treatise on Love*, tr. Nasrollah Pourjavady, London: Routledge & Kegan Paul, 1986.

Gibb, H. A. R., *The Arab Conquests in Central Asia*, London: Royal Asiatic Society, 1923.

Gignoux, Philippe, ed., *Recurrent Patterns in Iranian Religions: From Mazdaism to Sufism*, Paris: Association pour l'avancement des études iraniennes, 1992.

Gillman, Ian and Hans-Joachim Klimkeit, *Christians in Asia Before 1500*, Ann Arbor: University of Michigan Press, 1999.

Gimbutas, Marija, *The Gods and Goddesses of Old Europe*, Berkeley, CA: University of California Press, 1974.

Gnoli, Gherardo, *The Idea of Iran: An Essay on its Origin*, Leiden: Brill, 1989.

___, *Zoroaster in History*, New York: Bibliotheca Persica, 2000.

Goluboff, Sascha L., "Are They Jews or Asians? A Cautionary Tale about Mountain Jewish Ethnography," *Slavic Review* 63/1 (2004), pp. 113–140.

Gotō, Toshifumi, "Vasistha und Varuna in RV VI{I} 88 Priesteramt des Vasistha und Suche nach seinem indoiranischen Hintergrund," *Indoarisch, Iranisch une die Indogermanistik*, Wiesbaden: Reichert Verlag, 2000, pp. 148–161.

Grenet, Frantz, "Bāmiyān and the Mehr Yasht," *Bulletin of the Asia Institute* 7 (1993): 87–92.

Gulácsi, Zsuzsanna, *Mediaeval Manichaean Book Art: A codicological study of Iranian and Turkic illuminated book fragments from 8th–11th century East Central Asia* (Nag Hammadi and Manichaean Studies, 57), Leiden: Brill, 2005.

Gyselen, Rika, *Sasanian Seals and Sealings in the A. Saeedi Collection*, Louvain: Peeters, 2007.

Hamzeh'ee, M. Reza, *The Yâresan, A Sociological, Historical and Religio-Historical Study of a Kurdish Community*, Berlin: K. Schwartz, 1990.

Harris, David R., ed., *The Origins and Spread of Agriculture and Pastoralism in Eurasia*, London: Routledge, 2004.

Henkelman, Wouter F. M., *The Other Gods Who Are: Studies in Elamite-Iranian acculturation based on the Persepolis fortification texts*, Leiden: Nino, 2008.

Herodotus, *The Histories*, tr. Aubrey de Sélincourt, rev. A. R. Burn, New York: Penguin, 1972.

Hertel, Johannes, *Die Sonne und Mithra im Awesta, auf grund der awestischen feuerlehre dargestellt*, Leipzig: Haessel, 1927.

Hinnells, John, *The Zoroastrian Diaspora: Religion and Migration*, New York: Oxford University Press, 2005.

Hinnells, John, ed., *Mithraic Studies*, 2 vols, Manchester: Manchester University Press, 1975.

Hintze, Almut, "The Cow that Came from the Moon: The Avestan Expression *mah- gaociθra-*," *Bulletin of the Asia Institute* 19 2005 [2009]: 57–66.

Hodgson, Marshall, *The Venture of Islam*, 3 vols, Chicago: University of Chicago Press, 1974.

Horne, Charles F., ed., *The Sacred Books and Early Literature of the East, v. 8: Medieval Persia*, New York: Parke, Austin & Lipscombe, 1917.

Hovanissian, Richard G. and Georges Sabbagh, eds, *The Persian Presence in the Islamic World*, Cambridge: Cambridge University Press, 1998.

Ibn Ishaq, *Sirāt rasūl Allāh*, tr. Alfred Guillaume, *The Life of Muhammad*, Oxford: Oxford University Press, 1955.

Ibn Nadim [Abu'l-Faraj Mohamed ibn Ishaq al-Warraq], *Fihrist al-'ulum*, tr. B. Dodge, *The Fihrist of al-Nadim: A Tenth Century Survey of Muslim Culture*, 2 vols, New York: Columbia University Press, 1970.

Izady, Mehrdad R., *The Kurds: A Concise Handbook*, Washington: Taylor and Francis, 1992.

Joseph, John, *The Modern Assyrians of the Middle East: Encounters with Western Christian Missions, Archaeologists, and Colonial Powers*, Leiden: Brill, 2000.

Kasravi, Ahmad, *On Islam and Shi'ism*, tr. M. R. Ghanoonparvar, Costa Mesa, CA: Mazda Publishers, 1990.

Katouzian, Homa, *Sa'di: The Poet of Life, Love and Compassion*, Oxford: Oneworld, 2006.

Kellens, Jean, *La Quatrième Naissance de Zarathushtra*, Paris: Seuil, 2006.

___, "Le problème avec Anāhitā," *Orientalia Suecana* 51/52 (2002–3): 317–326.

Kellens, Jean and Eric Pirart, *Les textes viel-avestiques*, 3 vols., Wiesbaden: Reichert, 1988–1991.

Kestenberg Amighi, Janet, *Zoroastrians of Iran: Conversion, Assimilation, or Persistence*, New York: AMS Press, 1990.

Khanbaghi, Aptin, *The Fire, the Star and the Cross: Minority Religions in Medieval and Early Modern Iran*, London: I. B. Tauris, 2006.

Khatami, Mohammad, *Islam, Liberty and Development*, Binghamton, NY: Institute of Global Cultural Studies, 1998.

Khomeini, Ruhollah, *Islam and Revolution*, tr. Hamid Algar, Berkeley: Mizan Press, 1981.

Kia, Khojasteh, *Soxanān sazāvar zanān dar Shāh-nāmeye pahlavānī*, Tehran: Našr-e Fāxteh, 1371 [1992].

Kitchen, Robert A., tr., *The Syriac Book of Steps*, Piscataway, NJ: Gorgias Press, 2009.

Klimkeit, Hans-Joachim, *Gnosis on the Silk Road*, San Francisco: Harper, 1993.

Koshelenko, G., "The Beginnings of Buddhism in Margiana," *Acta Antiqua Academiae Scientarum Hungaricae* 14 (1966): 175–183.

Kreyenbroek, Philip G., *Yezidism: its Background, Observances and Textual Traditions*, Lewiston, NY: Edwin Mellen Press, 1995.

___, "Mithra and Ahriman in Iranian Cosmologies," in J. R. Hinnells, ed., *Studies in Mithraism*, Rome: Bretschneider, 1994, pp. 173–182.

Kuhrt, Amélie, "The Problem of Achaemenid 'Religious Policy'," in Brigitte Groneberg, Hermann Spieckermann and Frauke Weierhauser, eds, *Die Welt der Götterbilder*, Berlin: De Gruyter, 2007, pp. 117–144.

Kuz'mina, Elena E., *The Origin of the Indo-Iranians*, Leiden: Brill, 2007.

Lewisohn, Leonard, ed., *Classical Persian Sufism: From its Origins to Rumi*, London: Khaniqahi Nimatullahi Publications, 1993.

___, *Hafiz and the Religion of Love in Classical Persian Poetry*, London: I. B. Tauris, 2010.

Levy, Habib, *Comprehensive History of the Jews of Iran: The Outset of the Diaspora*, Costa Mesa, CA: Mazda Publishers, 1999.

Lieu, Samuel N. C., *Manichaeism in Central Asia and China*, Leiden: Brill, 1998.

___, *Manichaeism in Mesopotamia and the Roman East*, Leiden: Brill, 1994.

___, *Manichaeism in the Later Roman Empire and Medieval China*, Tübingen: Mohr, 1992 [1985].

Lieu, Samuel N. C., ed., *Medieval Christian and Manichaean Remains from Quanzhou (Zayton)*, Turnhout: Brepols, 2012.

Lieu, Samuel N.C., G. Fox and J. Sheldon, *Greek and Latin Texts on Manichaean Cosmogony*, Corpus Fontium Manichaeorum Series Subsidia 6, Turnhout: Brepols, 2010.

Lincoln, Bruce, "Mithra(s) as Sun and Savior," in *Death, War and Sacrifice: Studies in Ideology and Practice*, Chicago: University of Chicago Press, 1991, pp. 76–95.

Litvinsky, B. A., "Central Asia" in *Encyclopaedia of Buddhism*, ed. G. P. Malalasekera, Columbo, 1979, v. 4, fasc. 1, pp. 21–52.

Lommel, Hermann, "Anahita-Sarasvati," *Asiatica: Friedrich Weller*, Leipzig: Harrassowitz, 1954, pp. 405–413.

Luhrmann, T. M., *The Good Parsi: The Fate of a Colonial Elite in a Postcolonial Society*, Cambridge, MA: Harvard University Press, 1996.

Lupieri, Edmondo, *The Mandaeans: The Last Gnostics*, tr. Charles Hindley, Grand Rapids, MI: Eerdmans, 2002.

MacEoin, Denis, *Rituals in Babism and Baha'ism*, London: British Academic Press, 1994.

Mackenzie, D. N., "Šābūragān I," *Bulletin of the School of Oriental and African Studies*, 42 (1979): 500–534, and "Šābūragān II," *Bulletin of the School of Oriental and African Studies*, 43 (1980): 288–310.

Madelung, Wilferd, *Religious Trends in Early Islamic Iran*, Albany, NY: SUNY Press, 1988.

Malandra, William, *An Introduction to Ancient Iranian Religion*, Minneapolis: University of Minnesota Press, 1983.

Mallory, J. P. and D. Q. Adams, *The Oxford Introduction to Proto-Indo-European and the Proto-Indo-European World*, Oxford: Oxford University Press, 2006.

Maqdisi, Mutahhar, *Kitāb al-bad' wa'l-ta'rīkh*, 6 vols, Paris: Ernest Leroux, 1899–1919.

Masani, Rustom, "With Dinshah Irani in New Iran," *Dinshah Irani Memorial Volume*, Bombay, 1948.

Massignon, Louis, *The Passion of al-Hallaj*, tr. Herbert Mason, 4 vols, Princeton: Princeton University Press, 1982.

Master-Moos, Meher, *Life of Ustad Saheb Behramshah Nowroji Shroff (including an outline of 14,000 years of Iranian History and Shah Behram Varzavand)*, Bombay: Mazdayasnie Monasterie, 1981.

Mas'udi, Abu'l-Hasan Ali, *Murūj al-dhahāb*, *(Les Prairies d'or)*, ed. and tr. Barbier de Meynard and Pavet de Courteille, Paris: Société asiatique, 1965.

Mazzaoui, Michel, *The Origins of the Safawids: Shi'ism, Sufism, and the Ghulat*, Wiesbaden: F. Steiner, 1972.

Melikian-Chirvani, A.S., "L'évocation littéraire du bouddhisme dans l'Iran musulman," *Le monde iranien et l'Islam* 2 (1974): pp. 1–72.

___, "Recherches sur l'architecture de l'Iran bouddhique I: Essai sur les origines et le symbolisme du stoupa iranien," *Le monde iranien et l'Islam* 4 (1975): pp. 1–61.

Membrado, Mojan, "Forqân al-Akhbâr de: Hâjj Ne'matollâh Jeyhûnâbâdi (1871–1920), écrit doctrinal Ahl-e Haqq, édition critique, étude et commentaire," unpublished Ph.D. dissertation, Paris: École pratique des hautes etudes, 2007.

Mir-Hosseini, Ziba, *Islam and Gender: The Religious Debate in Contemporary Iran*, Princeton: Princeton University Press, 1999.

Mirecki, Paul and Jason BeDuhn, eds, *Emerging From Darkness: Studies in the Recovery of Manichaean Sources*, Leiden: Brill, 1997.

___, *The Light and the Darkness: Studies in Manichaeism and its World*, Leiden: Brill, 2001.

Mitchell, Colin P., *The Practice of Politics in Safavid Iran: Power, Religion and Rhetoric*, London: I. B. Tauris, 2009.

Moghaddam, Mohammad, *Jostārī dar bareye Mehr va Nāhīd*, Tehran: Hirmand, 1388 [2010].

Momen, Moojan, *An Introduction to Shi'i Islam: The History and Doctrines of Twelver Shi'ism*, New Haven: Yale University Press, 1987.

Monchi-Zadeh, D., "Xus-rôv i Kavâtân ut Rêtak," in *Monumentum Georg Morgenstierne*, vol. II. *Acta Iranica* 22, Leiden: Brill, 1982, pp. 47–91.

Moosa, Matti, *Extremist Shi'ites: The Ghulat Sects*, Syracuse: Syracuse University Press, 1988.

Moreen, Vera Basch, tr., *In Queen Esther's Garden: An Anthology of Judeo-Persian Literature*, New Haven, CT: Yale University Press, 2000.

al-Mubaraki, Majid Fandi and Brian Mubaraki, *Ginza rba*, Sydney: M. F. Al-Mubaraki, 1998.

Narshakhi, Abu Bakr Muhammad, *Tārīx-i Bukhārā*, tr. Richard Frye, Princeton: Markus Weiner, 2007 [1954].

Narten, Johanna, "Zarathustra und die Gottheiten des Alten Iran," *Münchener Studien zur Sprachwissenschaft* 56 (1986): 61–89.

___, *Die Aməša Spəntas im Avesta*, Wiesbaden: Harrassowitz, 1982.

Neusner, Jacob, *History of the Jews in Babylonia*, 5 vols., Leiden: Brill, 1965–1970.

___, *Aphrahat and Judaism: the Christian-Jewish Argument in Fourth-Century Iran*, Leiden: Brill, 1971.

Nizam al-Mulk, *The Book of Government or Rules for Kings*, tr. Hubert Darke, London: Routledge and Kegan Paul, 1978 [1960].

Nyberg, H.S., *Die Religionen des alten Iran*, Leipzig: JC Hinrichs, 1938.

Olmstead, A. T., *History of the Persian Empire*, Chicago: University of Chicago Press, 1948.

Panaino, Antonio, "The Mesopotamian Heritage of Achaemenian Kingship," in S. Aro and R. M. Whiting, eds, *The Heirs of Assyria*, Helsinki: The Neo-Assyrian Text Corpus Project, pp. 35–49.

*Pārs nāmeh.*

Patel, Dinyar, "The Iran League of Bombay: Paris, Iran, and the Appeal of Iranian Nationalism, 1922–1942," unpublished typescript, 2012.

Payne, Richard E., "Christianity and Iranian Society in Late Antiquity, ca. 500–700 CE," unpublished Ph.D. dissertation, Princeton University, 2010.

Pelliot, Paul, *L'inscription nestorienne de Si-Ngan-Foui*, ed. Antonio Forte, Paris: College de France, 1996.

Pirart, Eric, *Syntaxe des langues indo-iraniennes anciennes*, Barcelona: Ausa, 1997.

Pirouzdjou, Hassan, *Mithraïsme et emancipation: anthropologie sociale et culturelle des mouvements populaires en Iran: au VIIIe, IXe et du XIVe au début du XVIe siècle*, Paris: Harmattan, 1999.

Pourshariati, Parvaneh, *Decline and Fall of the Sasanian Empire: The Sasanian-Parthian Confederacy and the Arab Conquest of Iran*, London: I. B. Tauris, 2008.

Qomi, Qadi Ahmad, *Calligraphers and Painters: A Treatise by Qadi Ahmad, son of Mir Munshi (circa A.H. 1015/A.D. 1606)*, tr. Vladimir Minorsky, Washington, DC: Smithsonian Institution, 1959.

Rahmon, Emomali, *The Tajiks in the Mirror of History*, Dushanbe: Ministry of Culture, 1997.

Rahnema, Ali, *Superstition as Ideology in Iranian Politics: From Majlesi to Ahmadinejad*, Cambridge: Cambridge University Press, 2011.

Reeves, John C. *Prolegomena to a History of Islamicate Manichaeism*, Sheffield: Equinox, 2011.

___, *Heralds of That Good Realm: Syro-Mesopotamian Gnosis and Jewish Traditions*, Leiden: Brill, 1996.

Ringer, Monica, *Pious Citizens: Reforming Zoroastrianism in India and Iran*, Syracuse: Syracuse University Press, 2011.

Rudolph, Kurt, *Gnosis: The Nature and History of Gnosticism*, San Francisco: Harper and Row, 1987.

Rumi, *The Masnavi: Book One*, tr. Jawed Mojaddedi, Oxford: Oxford University Press, 2004.

Saadi-nejad, Manya, "Mythological Themes in Iranian Culture and Art: Traditional and Contemporary Perspectives," *Iranian Studies* 42/2 (2009): 231–246.

Sanasarian, Eliz, *Religious Minorities in Iran*, Cambridge: Cambridge University Press, 2000.

Sarshar, Houman, ed., *Jewish Communities of Iran*, New York: Encyclopædia Iranica, 2011.

\_\_\_, *Esther's Children: The Jews of Iran: Their Story, Their History, Their Lives*, Philadelphia: Jewish Publication Society, 2002.

Savchenko, Alexei, "Urgut Revisited," *ARAM: Journal of the Society for Syro-Mesopotamian Studies* 8/1–2 (1996): 333–354.

Säve-Soderbergh, Torgny, *Studies in the Coptic-Manichaean Psalm-Book*, Uppsala: Almqvist and Wiksell, 1949.

Schopen, Gregory, "Notes on the Cult of the Book in Mahāyāna," *Indo-Iranian Journal* 17/3–4 (1975): 147–181.

Schimmel, Annemarie, "Reason and Mystical Experience in Islam," in Farhad Daftary, ed., *Intellectual Traditions in Islam*, London: I. B. Tauris, 2000, pp. 130–145.

Schwartz, Martin, "How Zarathushtra Generated the Gathic Corpus: Inner-textual and Intertextual Composition," *Bulletin of the Asia Institute* 16 (2002): 53–64.

Scott, David Alan, "The Iranian Face of Buddhism," *East and West* 40 (1990), pp. 43–77.

Sepehri, Sohrab, *Šarq-e andūh*, Tehran: Ketābxāne-ye Tahūrī, 1358 [1979].

Shahrastani, Muhammad, *Livre des religions et des sectes*, tr. D. Gimaret and G. Monnot, 2 vols, Peeters/UNESCO, 1986.

Shaked, Shaul and Amnon Metzer, eds, *Irano-Judaica*, 6 vols to date, Jerusalem: Ben-Zvi Institute, 1982–2008.

Sharma, R. S., *Looking for the Aryans*, Madras: Orient Longman, 1995.

Shizuka, Sasaki, "A Study on the Origin of Mahayana Buddhism," *The Eastern Buddhist* 30/1 (1997), pp. 79–113.

Skjærvø, Prods Oktor, *The Spirit of Zoroastrianism*, New Haven: Yale University Press, 2011.

\_\_\_, "Eastern Iranian Epic Traditions II: Rostam and Bhīṣma," *Acta Orientalia Academiae Scientiarum Hungaricae* 51 (1998): 159–170.

Smith, Jonathan Z. and William Scott Green, *The HarperCollins Dictionary of Religion*, New York: HarperCollins, 1995.

Smith, Peter, *The Babi and Baha'i Religions: From Messianic Shi'ism to a World Religion*, Cambridge: Cambridge University Press, 1984.

Sohravardi, Shehab al-din, *The Book of Radiance*, tr. Hossein Ziai, Costa Mesa, CA: Mazda Publishers, 1998.

\_\_\_, *Philosophical Allegories and Mystical Treatises*, tr. W. M. Thackston, Costa Mesa, CA: Mazda Publishers, 1998.

Soroush, Abdolkarim, "Islamic Revival and Reform: Theological Approaches," in *Reason, Freedom and Democracy in Islam*, tr. Mahmoud Sadri and Ahmad Sadri, Oxford: Oxford University Press, 2000.

Soudavar, Abolala, *The Aura of Kings: Legitimacy and Divine Sanction in Iranian Kingship*, Costa Mesa, CA: Mazda Publishers, 2003.

Stavisky, Boris, "Kara Tepe in Old Termez: A Buddhist Religious Centre of the Kushan Period on the Bank of the Oxus," in J. Harmatta, ed., *From Hecataeus to Al-Huwarizmi: Bactrian, Pahlavi, Sogdian, Persian, Sanskrit, Syriac, Arabic, Chinese, Greek and Latin Sources for the History of Pre-Islamic Central Asia*, Budapest: Academiai Kiado, 1984, pp. 95–135.

\_\_\_, "'Buddha-Mazda' from Kara-Tepe in Old Termez (Uzbekistan): A Preliminary Communication," *Journal of the International Association of Buddhist Studies* 3/2 (1980): 89–94.

Stein, Rolf A., *La Civilisation tibetaine*, Paris: Dunod, 1962.

Strabo, *Geography*, tr. H. L. Jones, London: Heinemann, 1960.

Stroumsa, Sarah and Gedaliahu G. Stroumsa, "Aspects of Anti-Manichaean Polemics in Late Antiquity and Under Early Islam," *Harvard Theological Review* 81/1 (1988): 37–58.

Subtelny, Maria E., "Zoroastrian Elements in the Islamic Ascension Narrative : The Case of the Cosmic Cock," in Maria Szuppe, Anna Krasnowolska, and Claus V. Pedersen, eds, *Medieval and Modern Iranian Studies: Proceedings of the 6th European Conference of Iranian Studies (Vienna, 2007)*, Paris: Association pour l'avancement des études iraniennes, 2011, pp. 193–212.

Sundermann, W., "Mani, India and the Manichaean Religion," *South Asian Studies* 2 (1986): 11–19.

Swennen, Philippe, *D'Indra à Tištrya: Portrait et evolution du cheval sacré dans les mythes indo-iraniens anciens*, Paris: Collège de France, 2004.

Tavakoli-Targhi, Mohamad, *Refashioning Iran: Orientalism, Occidentalism and Historiography*, New York: Palgrave Macmillan, 2001.

Teiser, Stephen F., *The Ghost Festival in Medieval China*, Princeton, NJ: Princeton University Press, 1988.

Thackston, Wheeler M., *The Gulistan of Sa'di*, Bethesda: IBEX Publishers, 2008.

___, *A Millennium of Classical Persian Poetry*, Bethesda: IBEX Publishers, 2000.

___, "The Poetry of Shah Isma'il I," *Asian Art* (Fall 1988), pp. 37–63.

Thieme, Paul, "The 'Aryan' Gods of the Mitanni Treaties," *Journal of the American Oriental Society* 80/4 (1960): 301–317.

Vahman, Fereydun and Claus V. Pedersen, eds, *Religious Texts in Iranian Languages*, Copenhagen: Royal Danish Academy of Science and Letters, 2007.

Vasunia, Phiroze, "The Philosopher's Zarathushtra," in Christopher Tupin, ed., *Persian Responses: Political and Cultural Interaction with(in) the Achaemenid Empire*, Swansea: The Classical Press of Wales, 2007, pp. 237–265.

Virani, Shafique, *The Isma'ilis in the Middle Ages*, Oxford: Oxford University Press, 2007.

Walbridge, John, *The Wisdom of the Mystic East: Suhrawardi and Platonic Orientalism*, Albany: SUNY Press, 2001.

Warburg, Margit, *Citizens of the World: A History and Sociology of the Baha'is from a Globalisation Perspective*, Leiden, Brill, 2006.

Waterfield, Robin E., *Christians in Persia*, London: George Allen & Unwin, 1973.

Watkins, Calvert, *How to Kill a Dragon: Aspects of Indo-European Poetics*, Oxford: Oxford University Press, 1995.

Watt, William Montgomery, *The Faith and Practice of al-Ghazali*, London: Allen and Unwin, 1953.

Wiesehöfer, Josef, *Ancient Persia*, London: I. B. Tauris, 1998.

Wilber, Donald, *Persian Gardens and Garden Pavilions*, 2nd ed., Washington, DC: Dumbarton Oaks, 1979.

Williams, Alan V., *The Zoroastrian Myth of Migration from Iran and Settlement in the India Diaspora: Text, translation and analysis of the 16th century Qesse-ye Sanjan 'The story of Sanjan'*, Leiden: Brill, 2009.

___, "Zoroastrians and Christians in Sasanian Iran," *Bulletin of the John Rylands Library* 78/3 (1996): 37–53.

Witzel, Michael, "Sur le chemin du ciel," *Bulletin d'études indiennes*, 2 (1984): 213–279.

___, "Autochthonous Aryans? The Evidence from Old Indian and Iranian Texts," *Electronic Journal of Vedic Studies*, 7/3 (2001).

___, "Evidence for Cultural Exchange in Prehistoric Western Central Asia," *Sino-Platonic Papers* 129 (2003): 1–70.

Wolff, Joseph, *Narrative of a Mission to Bokhara*, London: Blackwood and Sons, 1848.

Xenophon, *Cyropaedia*, tr. Walter Miller, Cambridge: Harvard University Press, 1968.

Yarshater, Ehsan, ed., *The Cambridge History of Iran*, v. 3, *The Seleucid, Parthian, and Sasanian Periods*, Cambridge: Cambridge University Press, 1983.

___, *Encyclopædia Iranica*, London: Routledge and Kegan Paul, 1982–1989 and New York: Bibliotheca Persica, 1992–present; online edition <www.iranica.com>

Yunesian, Masud, Afshin Aslani, Javad Homayoun Vash and Abbas Bagheri Yazdi, "Effects of Transcendental Meditation on mental health: a before-after study," *Clinical Practice and Epidemiology in Mental Health* 4/1 (2008): 1–25.

Zaehner, R. C., *Zurvan: A Zoroastrian Dilemma*, Oxford: Oxford University Press, 1955.

# Index